PHILIP WEBSTER was Political Editor of *The Times* from 1993 to 2010 having previously been Chief Political Correspondent. Later, as Assistant Editor (Politics), he was in charge of *The Times* Red Box political website and was the first editor of the ground-breaking Red Box daily briefing email. He became a Lobby correspondent in 1981 after working as a reporter and subeditor on the paper for the previous eight years. He began his career on the *Eastern Daily Press* in Norwich. He is a lifelong and passionate supporter of Norwich City FC.

Praise for Philip Webster:

'Thoughtful and accurate as ever'   EDWINA CURRIE

'Webster is simply the best – a journalist with a sensational range of stories'   ANDREW MARR

'Philip Webster is a journalist of real intelligence and integrity with an ability to get on with all sides of the political spectrum'
ALASTAIR CAMPBELL

'One of the greatest political journalists of my lifetime'
FRASER NELSON, editor of the *Spectator*

'A brilliant journalist'   TONY BLAIR

'This book is not, nor does it try to be, a complete political history of the period. All the better for it. This is history vignette by vignette. Regardless of how politics changed over four decades, Webster's essential activity remained the same – finding out things. He did that with distinction, through seven prime ministers, not to mention nine editors of *The Times*'   *The Times*

Inside Story

Politics, Intrigue and Treachery
from Thatcher to Brexit

Philip Webster

WILLIAM
COLLINS

William Collins
An imprint of HarperCollins*Publishers*
1 London Bridge Street
London SE1 9GF

www.WilliamCollinsBooks.com

First published in Great Britain by William Collins in 2016
This William Collins paperback edition published in 2017

1

A catalogue record for this book is
available from the British Library

ISBN 978-0-00-820136-4

Printed and bound in Great Britain by
CPI Group (UK) Ltd, Croydon, CR0 4YY

This book is produced from independently certified FSC paper
to ensure responsible forest management

For more information visit: www.harpercollins.co.uk/green

To my late sister, Kay, for encouraging me to become a journalist, and to Sally, for encouraging me to write this book.

Contents

Introduction

Life is full of chances. A chance visit to *The Times*'s office at Westminster on a Tuesday in July 1972 led me to an adventure lasting more than four decades which finally ended in January 2016, after my 15,932nd day as an employee of the world's greatest newspaper. I am lucky to have been part of a small chunk of its 230-year history.

In those days *The Times* had far more reporters in Parliament than any other paper and gave far more column inches to coverage of parliamentary affairs. Unlike many other papers, it had its own office, known as The Times Room. I walked into The Times Room on that July afternoon during a tour round the House of Commons. I was a subeditor on the *Eastern Evening News* in Norfolk, and Tuesdays happened to be my day off. I had been to the office of the Commons Official Report, known as *Hansard*, next door and the editor kindly took me to meet the head of *The Times*'s parliamentary staff, Alan Wood. It being a Tuesday, Prime Minister's Questions were about to happen. In those days it was two fifteen-minute sessions on Tuesday and Thursday. Alan gave me a notebook and took me into the gallery, asking me to have a go at recording the exchanges between Edward Heath and Harold Wilson. I had good shorthand, which Alan could see, but my efforts at reading it back were patchy to say the least. In any case there were no jobs going.

Four months later I received a handwritten letter from Alan telling me a vacancy had arisen and asking if I would be interested. I went down to the Commons again in mid-January. It was again on a Tuesday and my left arm was in a sling after a football injury that Saturday. The cynics in the office smiled to themselves, thinking I had come up with the ultimate alibi for a failed test in the gallery. Fortunately, I'm right-handed.

Alan Wood put me through the same process and, this time, knowing what to expect, I made a good fist of it. He asked me to head down to Printing House Square at Blackfriars, then the home of *The Times*, where I was interviewed by John Grant, the managing editor. He was at the time president of the National Council for the Training of Journalists (NCTJ) and it helped a lot that I had been on one of the NCTJ's pioneering full-year courses, and had secured the NCTJ diploma at the end of my training period. He offered me a job and I bit his hand off. It was the biggest decision of my life but it was not at all difficult.

Forty-three years later I have written this account of my career covering politics for *The Times*. It does not pretend to be a political history of the period. Enough biographies and autobiographies have been written to do that job many times over. But I have found myself at the centre of most of the big stories of the last thirty-five years – the fall of Labour in 1979, the rise and fall of Margaret Thatcher, the emergence and fall of John Major, the rise and fall of Tony Blair and his wars with Gordon Brown, the aftermath of 9/11, the war in Iraq, the fall of Brown, the rise and rise of David Cameron, and the shock election of Jeremy Corbyn. This is my take on some of the big things that happened, and how I covered and unearthed them.

Being a political correspondent of *The Times*, including eighteen years as its political editor, has given me a ringside seat at the most dramatic political events of the last quarter of the twentieth century and the early years of the twenty-first. Although my predecessors have probably felt the same – and despite having no illusions myself – this to me has seemed like a golden era of political journalism and I am lucky to have been part of it. During all those years I was a member of the Westminster Lobby, whose merits or otherwise I deal with later.

It was a position that gave me ready access to politicians of all parties and I got to know them well, including four prime ministers, any number of Cabinet ministers and countless back-benchers, as well as the hundreds of officials and advisers who support the ministers and their shadow ministers in their jobs.

It was a role that gave me the opportunity to travel the world – a rough calculation puts my total air miles in the service of *The Times* at

THE TIMES

Times Newspapers Limited, Printing House Square, London, EC4P 4DE

Telephone: 01-236 2000 ~~Telex 88521~~

Ext 412

The Times Room,
Press Gallery,
House of Commons.
Westminster, SW 1

Dear Mr Webster,

Some months ago when you visited the
Press Gallery, you expressed interest in a
job as a parliamentary reporter if and
when the opportunity occurred. We now have
a vacancy and if you are still interested
I would be grateful if you could telephone
me as soon as possible, preferably at about
7pm, any evening this week except Friday.

I look forward to hearing from you.

Yours sincerely,

Alan H Wood.

Head of Parliamentary
Staff

Mr Philip Webster,
East Home,
Rockland St Mary,
Norwich,
Norfolk.

close to the million mark – as well as a seat in the Commons Press
Gallery at every significant event. I was there the night Michael
Heseltine brandished the mace, the night the Callaghan government

fell, the day Sir Geoffrey Howe brought down Margaret Thatcher, the days she and Tony Blair said farewell, the night MPs voted for war in Iraq, and for every Budget and autumn statement for forty years.

Occasionally it was a role that landed me in the most unexpected, even dangerous, scrapes. But most of it was fun, and if the reader does not get the impression after reading this that I had a very good time I have failed in my task.

It was also a position of huge responsibility, something of which I was well aware and about which I sometimes worried. The political press clearly has an important role in holding politicians to account. But what we write shapes events and makes or breaks careers, including those of party leaders. A few reporters have gone on to work for political parties but the vast majority are not players. Most political correspondents have no allegiance to a party. I never have or will but I have good friends in all the parties. The reader may find this strange, but in the tens of thousands of conversations I had with politicians while I was a senior political correspondent, not one asked me how I voted. I imagine they felt that as an impartial reporter I would have been insulted by the question, but I would have had an answer: I did not vote during those years.

Political correspondents are without doubt an integral part of the political process. It places a severe duty on us to get our stories right, ensuring they are fair, accurate and impartial – the mantra that is drummed into us from our first day in journalism school. When I appeared before the Leveson Inquiry into press standards in 2012, one point I tried to make very firmly was the importance of separating fact and comment in newspaper coverage, a line that has occasionally been blurred in recent years.

What I have tried to do here, having written about all these events as they happened, is to offer a fresh insight on them and reveal, as far as I can without compromising living sources, how stories I wrote at the time came into my hands and influenced events as they unfolded. Sometimes the stories originated from me learning from one source or another that something was brewing, and then nagging the people in a position to know until I was able to write. Sometimes, particularly when the parties started pre-briefing announcements rather than waiting for them to be put to MPs in the Commons – a practice that has infuriated successive speakers – they have come to me without a struggle. There was a time in the early years of New Labour, in government and opposition, when I would be surprised if there was NOT a phone call from Alastair Campbell or his Conservative counterpart when I came off the golf course on a Sunday lunchtime, on what until then had been a day off. On those occasions I would often spend the next few hours in my car, making calls to the office and contacts.

It could be a risky business. In the pages that follow I tell of many occasions when I pushed a story to the limits and spent worrying hours wondering if I would be embarrassed when it appeared.

Britain had eight prime ministers during my years as a reporter at *The Times*. I worked under nine editors, starting with William Rees-Mogg and finishing under John Witherow. Labour was on its way to power, or in power, for most of my eighteen years as political editor and for obvious reasons those years are covered comprehensively in what follows. I was fortunate that in my time as a junior Lobby man I was assigned the Labour beat when it was in opposition, meaning that I got to know well the men and women, and their aides, who were to become the leading figures in the party as Blair pushed for power, and he and Gordon Brown held sway for thirteen years.

I left Westminster in 2010 and after a four-year period as editor of *The Times* digital editions, I grabbed John's offer to become assistant editor (politics) of *The Times* and to be the first editor of the 'Red Box' daily political bulletin and website. It meant I was back reporting on politics in time for the 2014 Scottish referendum and the 2015 general election. I had never been far away, though, and had continued to write about politics in the interim period, so this was another chance in a life of chances that I was not going to pass up.

As I've looked through mounds of my cuttings while writing this book, I've been struck by just how much I did. I only kept sparse notes of key conversations and cuttings of which I was particularly proud. I have a strong – my friends say nerdish – memory for the minutiae of the major political events in which I was involved, but in my trawl of the files I have come across stories under my byline and trips to the other side of the world which had temporarily gone from the memory.

Political journalism has changed in my years, as I explain later. Television has taken over from the House of Commons as the cockpit of political debate. Power has shifted from Westminster to the television studios, to Europe and to Scotland. But my successors need have no fear. There will always be a need for journalists to work and watch closely as politicians exercise their power.

My story is of one journalist who stuck with the same paper, the one he had always dreamt of working on, and resisted the occasional blandishments of rival editors who told him his career would progress faster if he moved over to them.

This book is about the story behind the stories that ran across the front pages of *The Times* for four and more decades. There were serious, tragic, sad, dramatic and traumatic moments behind those stories. But chasing them and writing them was a great joy and privilege.

I start with the momentous events of 23 June 2016 that changed all our lives, finished off another prime minister, split the country in two and left British politics in utter turmoil.

A Nervous Breakdown as Britain Votes 'Out'

A much-diminished David Cameron said an emotional farewell to the twenty-seven other heads of European governments in Brussels on 28 June 2016. It was a sombre occasion for the man who will go down in history as the leader who took Britain out of the European Union, and possibly broke up the United Kingdom. Five days earlier a chastened Cameron, along with George Osborne, his chancellor, watched their dreams turn to dust as Britain voted against their wishes, and the odds, to say goodbye to Brussels.

As the leader who gambled on a referendum that the country was not demanding at the time he announced it, Cameron knew that it was his fault. Within three hours of the final result he stood on the steps of 10 Downing Street and resigned. He was gone three weeks later. Osborne's chances of succeeding Cameron, already slim because he was felt to have overstated his economic warnings during the referendum campaign, disappeared. He was not a candidate in the leadership election that followed. And his humiliation was not complete.

On the day of the vote, Cameron and his aides, and Osborne, had discussed what would happen if they lost, although at that time they were expecting to win. The chancellor, I was told, said there was a case for Cameron staying on to bring stability, as well as one for him going. Cameron was adamant that he must depart in those circumstances and his aides did not try to dissuade him. He went to bed for a few hours after the result became known; his mind was made up. Twenty days later – after a vicious but truncated leadership election – he was succeeded by Theresa May, who became Britain's second woman prime minister at the age of fifty-nine.

Within hours she had stamped her authority with a ruthless reshuffle that saw few ministers stay in their jobs, and many of Cameron's closest allies purged. Osborne was sacked, as was Michael Gove, the justice secretary. The 'chumocracy', the name given by detractors to the tight group of friends around Cameron which was reputed to take most government decisions, was brutally slain.

Britain woke up on 24 June, the morning after the referendum, a divided nation. We were a country split between young and old, better off and poor, north and south. The young, rich and parts of the south, particularly London, had voted 'In'. The old, the angry and disadvantaged, and the north, had voted 'Out'.

The kingdom was divided, with Scotland and Northern Ireland voting to stay in the EU, England and Wales opting for out. Nicola Sturgeon, leader of the Scottish National Party, said a second referendum on independence was highly likely. Scotland could leave the UK within years, and Brexit, as our departure will forever be known, will be to blame.

Apart from the leader of the United Kingdom Independence Party (UKIP), the irrepressible Nigel Farage – whose referendum and victory it was – few of the leaders of the 'Leave' campaign offered outward signs of jubilation. They had not expected to win, and secretly many had probably hoped they would not. Many who had voted to leave wondered what they had done. Some recanted on the airwaves within hours. It was too late. Out was out.

In the days that followed, British politics descended into a form of insanity. The two men who had led the campaign to leave, Boris Johnson (the former London mayor) and Michael Gove, killed each other's chances of leading their party – the latter accused of committing an act of treachery without parallel in modern political history; Jeremy Corbyn, the Labour leader, was pushed to the brink of resigning from his party; Farage stood down in triumph, his job done; and for a few days it looked as if the country was running without a government or opposition.

Andrea Leadsom, the energy minister who became the main Brexit candidate as Johnson and Gove fell away, was chosen by MPs to go into a run-off with Theresa May. But then she stunned an already shell-shocked Westminster by suddenly withdrawing only an hour after May formally launched her campaign, leaving the home secretary the victor without the need for an election by party members. After starting her own campaign, Leadsom had suffered a torrid weekend, fiercely criticized by the Conservative press and MPs after claims that she had exaggerated her CV, questions over her tax return, and an interview with *The Times* in which she appeared to suggest that as a mother she had an advantage over the childless May.

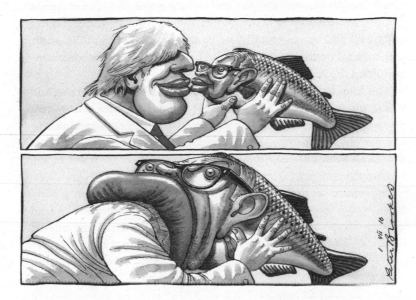

The rest of Europe, and much of the world, looked on in horror and amazement. The Dutch prime minister, Mark Rutte, not known for hyperbole, suggested: 'England has collapsed politically, monetarily, constitutionally and economically.'

The bloodletting was by no means over, and the twists and turns in this fast-moving epic continued. First May called in Osborne and told him she needed a new chancellor after using her leadership campaign to distance herself from his economic stance. As the principal architect of 'Project Fear', the name given to the torrent of gruesome economic warnings that emanated from the Treasury during the campaign, and which was felt to have backfired, he harboured little hope of surviving.

Then she revived Johnson's tottering career by making him foreign secretary. She had texted him expressing sympathy on the morning when he had been suddenly deserted by Gove. Boris claimed to be 'humbled' and his elevation surprised him and most of the political world, which had started to write him off.

The next morning May called in Gove, with whom she had sharply clashed in government, and sacked him as well in what friends called an 'impeccably polite' exchange. So Boris was in the Cabinet for the first time and Gove, who had struck him down just days earlier, was out.

Nicky Morgan, the education secretary who had made the mistake of backing Gove, was shown the door as well. The speed of events was startling and May, having watched a fortnight of political assassinations, proved to be a brutal axe-woman when her time came. In just forty-eight hours the old guard had retired from the fray, with Cameron and Osborne spotted having coffee in a Notting Hill cafe, and the new regime was in place.

Until 2016, Harold Macmillan's 'Night of the Long Knives' in 1962, when the then prime minister ejected seven ministers from his Cabinet, was deemed the most ferocious exercise in prime ministerial power in history. No longer. May culled Cameron's team and sent nine of them to the back-benches. Cabinet executions are normally done by telephone. But May looked them in the eye as she did it. Her aides said it was a matter of courtesy, but some of the victims wished they had not been put through the ordeal. She even gave Gove a lecture in loyalty as she despatched him. May had shown herself to be fearless and not a leader to be messed with. But her Commons majority is tiny and one day she may regret making so many enemies in one fell swoop.

The nervous breakdown that gripped Westminster overshadowed the gravity of the decision that Britain had taken and the mess that the departed leaders had left for others to clear up. Yes, Britain now had a new prime minister. But this was of much less significance than what else had happened. After forty-three years, the United Kingdom was cut adrift from the organization with which it had always lived uneasily but which, until the referendum dawned, people had seemed prepared to accept.

Now we were on the outside, and the nation was in shock, most not having expected the outcome even if they voted for it. The pound slumped to its lowest level in a generation, firms voiced doubts about investing here, young people marched on Parliament complaining that their futures had been compromised by what they called the lies of the 'Leave' campaign, and Osborne was forced to drop his plan to take the economy into surplus by 2020. At the same time, there was a disturbing rise in racially motivated attacks, with Polish and other migrants saying they no longer felt welcome.

Europe had killed another prime minister. But far more important than that, the vote had left Britain with a deeply uncertain future, facing at least two years of negotiations about its relationship with the body it had abandoned.

In truth it will be years before the full impact of cutting formal links with our biggest market can be assessed, but the Treasury is fully expecting a bleak 2017, and the outlook for future years is not much better. A friend said of Osborne: 'George fears that an awful lot of hard work by the country and us has gone up in smoke.'

This is a chronicle of events in a nutshell. The details, however, bear much closer examination.

I have known Boris Johnson and Michael Gove for years. I remember little of Boris's brief spell on *The Times* as a young reporter, but got to know him pretty well on my regular trips to European summits when he was the Brussels chief for *The Daily Telegraph*. I knew Michael well from his time as comment editor and news editor at *The Times*, when we would have several conversations every day about the political stories of the moment.

I got on very well with both of them but neither I nor anyone who worked with them could have dreamt that one day they would have the destiny of the nation in their hands. Boris made us laugh and was wonderfully indecisive, as I describe in a later chapter. Govey, as many in the office called him, was bookish, polite, deeply knowledgeable about politics, humorous. We knew that Gove, a Conservative, was looking for a parliamentary seat. But political leaders? It never occurred to us.

Yet here they were, on the morning of 24 June, squinting into the cameras, speaking in hushed, statesmanlike tones about the seriousness of the decision that had been taken. They together had been the public face – along with Farage – of the 'Leave' campaign. And here on the dawn of victory it was obvious they had no idea what would happen next. That ignorance was shared by most of the rest of the Government.

As the markets tumbled, and as recriminations broke out between the rival campaigns, government came to a stop and it was clear that there had been little planning for a Brexit outcome.

As the Government floundered, Her Majesty's Opposition fell apart. The campaign to stay in the EU, dubbed 'Remain', lost because millions of traditional Labour supporters in its heartlands voted to leave, rebelling at last at what they saw as a southern elite telling them what was good for them and failing to heed their worries about excessive immigration. Many saw themselves as the victims of what the southerners called globalization and what they saw as foreigners taking their jobs.

Labour was distraught because as a party it was strongly in favour of staying in. But Jeremy Corbyn had a long history of animosity towards the EU and was felt at best not to have pulled his weight during the campaign and at worst to have allowed his hard-left aides to undermine it. His shadow Cabinet and front-bench walked out on him, a motion of no confidence was easily passed against him, and senior figures dithered over challenging him. He refused to step down and vowed to fight on. Angela Eagle, shadow business secretary and shadow first secretary, who had excelled during the previous year when standing in for Corbyn at PM's Questions, announced she was running but then pulled out, leaving Owen Smith, former shadow work and pensions secretary and an MP for only six years, to take on Corbyn. A leadership contest – for the second summer in succession – was under way as this book went to the printers.

Within a week of the referendum the Tory party was in complete chaos. Johnson was briefly and magically transformed from the assassin of the Prime Minister into the unity candidate best able to uphold the values of liberal Conservatism. Gove promised to be his campaign manager for what looked likely to be a relatively straightforward victory. We should have known, however, that nothing is simple in the Tory party.

Gove, his campaign team, and his wife, the journalist Sarah Vine, began – according to their side of the story – to have doubts about Johnson's ability to be prime minister, leading Gove, just a week after the vote, to withdraw support from Johnson, announce he was standing himself and decry the leadership qualities of his friend and colleague.

The betrayal stunned Johnson, who swiftly pulled out, leaving May, the home secretary, the clear favourite, and his team went to war on Gove. One suggested there was a 'deep pit reserved in hell' for Gove, Johnson's sister Rachel accused Gove of being a political psychopath, and Ben Wallace, another Johnson campaign aide, said Gove could not be trusted to be prime minister because he has 'an emotional need to gossip, particularly when drink is taken, as it all too often seemed to be'. The governing party was in turmoil.

How did the two men who had done more than any, apart from Farage, to bring Brexit about fall out so spectacularly and so quickly?

Friends told me that Johnson had asked Gove to be his campaign manager on the Friday after the vote. Gove asked for twenty-four hours to think it over and was approached by several colleagues to run. He pointed out that he had always said he did not want to be prime minister and felt that Boris was the man.

Gove's friends said that, although he had known Boris for twenty years, he had never worked closely with him. Johnson had risen to the occasion during the campaign and Gove assumed he was ready for the top job. But that confidence was to be swiftly shattered. According to friends, he found that Johnson had only a ramshackle leadership campaign operation in place and did not appear to be taking seriously the coming moment when he switched from the populist ex-mayor liked by the voters to the serious job of prime minister. Little work had been done on setting out a programme or vision for leadership.

For three days Gove campaigned for Johnson, growing more and more concerned that he seemed unfocused on the task in hand. For Boris, it was vital to have Andrea Leadsom, who had won plaudits for her role during the referendum campaign, on board. I have learnt that on the morning of Wednesday, 29 June, an astonishing meeting took place in a Commons office. Three of the leaders of the Brexit cause met privately to discuss what jobs would be allocated if Johnson won.

They were Johnson, Gove and Leadsom. The latter, at the time an energy minister, asked to be chancellor in return for supporting Johnson. Gove pointed out there were two top jobs, the other being deputy prime minister, who would also have the job of running the negotiations with the EU on Brexit. Leadsom said she assumed Gove would do the latter job but Johnson said he wanted Gove to be chancellor. Finally it was agreed that Leadsom would have one of the top jobs and that Johnson would make this clear in a letter, and send out a tweet saying that Leadsom was on board with his campaign.

As has been revealed since, the letter did not reach Leadsom by the time she had stipulated and the tweet did not materialize. As a result she prepared to announce that she would stand, having already built up a serious level of support among MPs. That Wednesday, Johnson was also supposed to be writing his launch speech for the next day, but by midnight he had scarcely done any of it. The Leadsom fiasco and the failure to prepare were two last straws.

Gove and other figures like Nick Boles, the skills minister, were dismayed, and Gove finally decided that Johnson did not have the qualities to be prime minister. He told allies: 'I could not in those circumstances bring myself to recommend to my friends and fellow MPs that Boris was suitable to be PM. When Gordon Brown was about to become prime minister a lot of senior people believed he would not be up to it but stayed silent. I could not do that. I had to be honest about what I saw as Boris's failings.'

Gove then announced he would stand, and within minutes Johnson, appearing at what would have been his launch, pulled out, stunning his supporters in the audience who had not been forewarned.

Gove was surprised. He had expected Johnson to stay in the race and to tell him (Gove) that he would show him that he was good enough, friends said. May, who had a long-running dispute with Johnson when he was mayor when she opposed the use of water cannon on the streets of the capital, had barely launched her campaign when she learnt her long-time foe was out of the race.

As the carnage continued, Johnson backed Leadsom, stressing her trustworthiness in what was clearly a rebuke to Gove. Johnson's team claimed that Gove had planned his desertion all along and that he had used their man to get the Brexit result and then stabbed him in the back and front, while running over him at the same time. That is denied by Gove's team, who point to his constant disavowals of interest in the job.

After the first round of voting May was ahead, with Leadsom second and Gove third, his standing obviously harmed by his treatment of Johnson and Johnson's decision to fall in behind Leadsom. Then came another twist. Boles quietly approached figures in the May campaign and asked if they could 'lend' Gove some votes so that he could finish second in the next ballot and keep Leadsom out of the final two-way run-off which would be decided by some 150,000 party members and not the MPs.

May would hear none of it and one of her team, I understand, told Boles that she was 'going for gold' and believed that the higher the number of MPs backing her, the greater her chance of defeating Leadsom or Gove, whoever came second. So Boles embarked on an extraordinary freelance operation which probably cost Gove any chance of making the final two.

Boles sent an e-mail to ten friends in the May camp suggesting there was a risk that if Leadsom's name went through, members might back her because she shared their attitudes to modern life. He added that Gove would not mind taking a 'good thrashing' for May in the party's interest.

By now the political world was immune to shocks in this astonishing saga but the Boles e-mail – which was leaked by a disaffected recipient and swiftly made public by Sam Coates of *The Times* – took a prize for infamy. Gove, having stopped Boris, was now it seemed prepared to go to any lengths to kill Leadsom's hopes. This was unfair because Boles did not tell Gove about his manoeuvre. But the damage was done – and fatally.

I reproduce the e-mail in full. It said:

> I would be really grateful if you would treat this in strict confidence. You are my friend. I respect the fact that you want Theresa May to be PM. It is overwhelmingly likely that she will be. And if she does I will sleep easily at night.
>
> But I am seriously frightened about the risk of allowing Andrea Leadsom onto the membership ballot. What if Theresa stumbles? Are we really confident that the membership won't vote for a fresh face who shares their attitudes about much of modern life? Like they did with IDS.
>
> I am not asking you to respond unless you positively want to have a chat. But I hope that you will reflect on this carefully. Michael doesn't mind spending 2 months taking a good thrashing from Theresa if that's what it takes but in the party's interest and the national interest surely we must work together to stop AL? x

Gove had stabbed Johnson, Boris had stabbed Gove, Gove's friends had tried to stab Andrea. There were times during this period when an hour seemed a long time in politics.

Leadsom finished second in the next ballot and Gove was eliminated. Members were left with a choice between May's substantial experience, including six years as home secretary, and her cautious but modern conservatism – it was she who first told the party to throw off its 'nasty' image – and Leadsom's appeal to the party's traditional core values: self-reliance, dislike of regulation, suspicion of social change such as same-sex marriage, and deep Euroscepticism.

The run-off began no less controversially than the early legs of the contest. Leadsom received a barrage of attacks after her 'motherhood' remarks to *The Times* on 9 July 2016. She was criticized by MPs for her lack of experience and naivety. Then on Monday, 11 July, just as May was officially launching her campaign in Birmingham and Cameron was speaking at the Farnborough air show, word emerged that Leadsom had had enough.

Surrounded by her supporters, she came out of her house and said she had decided to withdraw. Although she had won the backing of eighty-four MPs, she said that this was less than twenty-five per cent of the total, which was not enough to lead a strong and stable govern-

RED CARPET TREATMENT...   10

ment if she won the ballot of members. She departed saying it was in the best interests of the country and party that she was no longer a candidate. She made no mention of her notorious interview but she had already apologized to May over it and her friends later spoke of the 'brutal' way she had been treated. They added that the contest had come too soon for her and that she had never expected to run.

So eighteen days after Cameron said he was leaving the stage, the three most prominent leaders of the Brexit campaign had been vanquished, their ambitions at best put on hold and at worst killed. They had handed the keys of Number 10 to a minister who had campaigned to stay in the EU.

Now May's main task was to handle the consequences of that fateful vote. 'Brexit means Brexit and we are going to make a success of it,' she said at her launch. Quite what Brexit really means will only become clear in the years ahead, but on one thing May was clear: 'There will be no attempt to remain in the EU.'

May, though, made plain that she is determined to get the best possible deal for Britain from the negotiations that will set the terms of departure.

She put the astute and pragmatic David Davis, a former Europe minister, in charge of a new department that will implement Brexit. Though he and Johnson backed the 'Leave' effort, neither are ideologically 'anti-Europe' and May is clearly hoping they can secure an outcome that will maintain some kind of access from outside to the single market while securing concessions on freedom of movement. It may take years.

I covered the removal of Margaret Thatcher as prime minister, as I describe later in this book. Whatever you felt about her, Thatcher's downfall was a personal tragedy, a Shakespearean drama as the MPs and ministers she had helped to three election victories turned on her because they felt she could not win a fourth. June 2016 was a personal tragedy for Cameron. Whether the nation will regret or embrace the outcome in the long term is impossible to tell. But the aftermath at the top of the Conservative Party seemed at times more like farce than tragedy.

How could it have come to this? How could David Cameron, the man who told his party to stop banging on about Europe, have somehow contrived to take his country out of it? How was it that the PM who earned a reputation as a lucky general ran out of luck when it mattered most?

The story begins with his party's recent history. Cameron became party leader after he wowed the party faithful in 2005. But his MPs were never as certain about him as his activists were. They were unsure about his efforts to modernize the Tories but went along with him in the expectation that he would see off Gordon Brown easily in 2010 and return them to power. He became prime minister, yes, but only in a coalition with the Liberal Democrats, and his half-victory left many MPs disappointed with him.

23 January 2013 was the day that sealed the fate of Cameron, many in his government and the country. He announced there would be an 'in-out' referendum by the end of 2017 at the latest. In October 2011 some eighty-one Tory MPs had demanded a referendum in a Commons vote, showing him the scale of the internal problem he faced. UKIP was on the march, winning the European elections in 2014 while two Tory MPs were to defect and win by-elections under the UKIP banner.

Cameron had agonized discussions with his Cabinet, in private one-on-one conversations and together. I can confirm that both George Osborne and Michael Gove urged him not to do it, Osborne because he feared the country might vote to leave, and Gove because, as a devout sceptic, he could see himself ending up fighting his friend and prime minister.

In an e-mail to Cameron, Gove warned that if he granted a referendum it would not bring peace to the party and that he would continue to be 'harried', and that it was dangerous to commit to a plebiscite before it was known what reforms Europe would offer up. Gove, at this stage, did not explicitly say to Cameron that he would campaign against him, but the PM could have been in no doubt about his deep concerns.

As the negotiations with Brussels reached their climax in the winter of 2015, Cameron several times asked Gove's friends – including Osborne, Ed Vaizey (culture minister) and Nick Boles – whether Gove would be 'all right' when the time came. But it was clear from a number of newspaper stories since the party conference in October that Gove was likely to be in the opposite camp and that he was 'conflicted' about opposing his friend the prime minister.

As Cameron prepared to announce the referendum date on Saturday, 20 February, Ed Llewellyn (his chief of staff) approached Gove and told him Downing Street needed to know that he would be on side in view of the extensive media coverage the coming weekend. Gove told him that he could not be and would campaign in line with his long-stated beliefs. It was a big blow to Cameron.

Cameron himself confirmed the news publicly: 'Michael is one of my oldest and closest friends but he has wanted to get Britain to pull out of the EU for about thirty years,' he said. 'So of course I am disappointed that we are not going to be on the same side as we have this vital argument about our country's future. I am disappointed but I am not surprised.'

Gove said:

It pains me to have to disagree with the Prime Minister on any issue. My instinct is to support him through good times and bad.

But I cannot duck the choice which the Prime Minister has given every one of us. In a few months' time we will all have the opportunity to decide whether Britain should stay in the European Union or leave. I believe our country would be freer, fairer and better off outside the EU. And if, at this moment of decision, I didn't say what I believe I would not be true to my convictions or my country.

Johnson and Gove had dined together and agreed that a late initiative by Oliver Letwin, the Cabinet Office minister and Cameron's close adviser, to change the Act authorizing the UK's accession to the EU to bolster the UK's parliamentary sovereignty was not sufficient to assuage their doubts, but Gove was as much in the dark as Cameron about what Johnson would decide. He only learnt that he was to be in the Brexit camp on the Saturday afternoon before Johnson made his announcement on Sunday, 21 February.

After winning what most considered an underwhelming renegotiation package, Cameron had bitten the bullet and announced 23 June as the day of decision. He had gone for the fastest-possible timetable, rejecting the advice of his strategist, Lynton Crosby, who warned that it could turn into a protest vote.

Cameron had hoped to persuade Johnson to come on side, and at a forty-minute meeting in Number 10 the previous week, he offered him various posts in the coming reshuffle. The former mayor was undecided until the very last minute. When he did declare, Cameron and others accused him of doing so for opportunistic reasons of self-advancement. There can be little doubt that he did it because he saw it as a way eventually of taking Cameron's job.

I learn there were few tears in Downing Street when Gove plunged the knife into Johnson, although Cameron believed that Gove's behaviour would win sympathy in the party for Johnson. Gove earned the displeasure of Cameron and close friends for campaigning with vigour for Brexit. They had hoped and believed he would play a low-key role. Gove's position was known but Cameron had not expected his erstwhile friend – the atmosphere between them now as I write this is glacial, according to an insider – to campaign so strongly and, he felt, personally against him.

As was widely reported, Cameron's wife, Samantha, had a stand-up row with Gove's wife, Sarah Vine, at a friend's party, accusing Gove of betrayal and abandoning her husband's premiership. Other friendships and family relationships across the country were similarly strained as the campaign developed into mud-slinging and bitterness. Gove told me after he had pulled out of the contest:

> I did not relish being on the opposite side to David but it became clear to me during the course of the campaign that if it was going to be conducted in a professional way, I had to speak up for my beliefs. Having made the decision, I had to argue in the way I did. But I tried to make the case without personal attacks and on the basis of principle.

The warnings from Osborne and Gove were acutely prophetic but back in 2013, Cameron, the gambler, had had enough of the Tory Right, he was worried about UKIP and he thought that when the time came he could negotiate a good deal out of Brussels and win. Cameron's aides and supporters believed that he had no choice and that the time to settle the issue had come. One told me after 23 June: 'There really was little alternative. The political pressure was unstoppable.'

But it has to be said that Cameron called the referendum for party political reasons and not for the national interest. There was no clamour for it in the country and the decision was to blow up in his face and put the country on a deeply uncertain path.

I believe the referendum was a mistake. Cameron could not be sure of winning, and he lost. Thatcher once said that referendums 'sacrificed parliamentary sovereignty to political expediency' and most leaders hate them because voters do not necessarily use them to decide the issue in question but to make a protest. In this referendum, 'Leave' voters did so for all kinds of reasons. 'Remain' voters just voted to remain.

By the time he capitulated to the Right, Cameron had often been called the 'essay-crisis' PM, the leader who only turned his attention to problems at the last moment and then rushed through an answer to them. The referendum pledge helped him see off his own right wing and the threat of UKIP, and may well have helped him win outright in 2015. But the country was landed with a critical decision on its future and millions felt ill-equipped to make it.

Cameron's second-biggest error was overconfidence. As recently as December 2015 he told his European colleagues that he was a winner and they should not worry too much. His serendipity may have led to him accepting a deal from Brussels that was not good enough, and once the campaign was under way he did not use all the weapons available to him, as I will explain.

In March 2016, Cameron's campaign was abruptly thrown off course by an event that he should have anticipated but did not. Two days after the 2016 Budget, Iain Duncan Smith, the work and pensions secretary, resigned. The immediate issue was cuts to disability benefits. The reason was George Osborne.

Osborne and the man in charge of the biggest government budget did not get on. IDS had row after row with the chancellor over his repeated attempts to cut benefits for working people as his main weapon to tackle the deficit. I understand the resignation had been brewing since January 2014, when Osborne announced he would make a further £12 billion of cuts in welfare in the next parliament. He had not discussed the plan with IDS. 'It was a bounce,' he has since told friends.

We know that Osborne did not have a high opinion of his colleague. As Matthew D'Ancona told us in his book *In It Together*: "'He opposes every cut," Osborne complained to one friend.' Nor was he confident that IDS had the IQ. 'You see Iain giving presentations,' he confided in allies, 'and realize he's just not clever enough.' IDS, I learnt, has no higher opinion of the ex-chancellor. A friend said: 'Iain regards George as arrogant. He is not collegiate. He lands the government in one shambles after another by his refusal to consult. He fancies himself as the master strategist. His record does not justify such pride.' Another friend said: 'Iain does not like George or his cronies. He encroaches on everyone's pitch. He is mad for a headline – so in the 2016 Budget we got his great announcement that all schools would have to become academies. Then six weeks later poor old Nicky Morgan [former education secretary] had to retreat. It is one omnishambles after another.'

That was a reference to Osborne's 2012 Budget when what seemed like a decent package on the day collapsed quickly with retreat after retreat on matters such as taxes on Cornish pasties and caravans. It became known as the 'Omnishambles Budget'.

But when, on the early evening of 18 March 2016, Downing Street received a letter from IDS resigning over the disability cuts, a shocked Cameron realized this was deadly dangerous to him. He called IDS, asking him to hold off until they had spoken face to face. Soon government sources were briefing that the £1.3 billion cuts were being 'reviewed'.

But IDS had had enough, and in a second telephone call told Cameron his mind was made up. During furious exchanges, Cameron was reported to have called IDS a 'shit', something that neither side has seen fit to deny. Duncan Smith's friends maintain he had been surprised by Osborne's decision to put the cuts in the Budget so that they could be counted as billions of savings in the deficit battle, but that the last straw was to put them in the same package as tax cuts for the better off. 'It went against Iain's whole social justice message, and he had to go,' an insider said.

IDS had been in constant rows with Osborne over the previous six months about the chancellor's plan to cut tax credits for three million people, eventually defeated by the Lords and dropped, and the IDS plan to merge several benefits into a universal credit. One friend said: 'Iain regrets not going earlier. He thought about resigning before Christmas 2015 and wishes he had. He tried to defend the Budget but lost heart and realized he could not in all honesty do so.'

IDS, for decades an opponent of the European Union, has insisted since that his resignation had nothing to do with Europe, and he stayed out of the campaign for a few weeks to show that. But his enemies maintained that the whole exercise was designed to damage Cameron and Osborne at a time when they could least afford it. Some claimed that IDS had planned to quit the Government dramatically during the Budget debate, something his friends have denied.

I can confirm, however, that he was one of several ministers who called on Cameron privately earlier in the year to allow ministers freedom to speak out during the referendum campaign. IDS told him that if he did not grant the concession, ministers would resign and that would be far more damaging to the Government. I understand that the key figure in persuading the PM to give way – much to the unease of key pro-Europeans like Michael Heseltine – was Chris Grayling, leader of the House of Commons.

By the end of 2015, Grayling had concluded that the deal the Prime Minister had been negotiating with Europe would not be good enough to change his view that Britain would be better off out. He decided that he would campaign to leave but delayed until the New Year before telling Cameron. After the regular 8.30 a.m. meeting of ministers, aides and Commons business managers on Monday, 5 January, Grayling stayed on for a private chat with the PM. He told him that he intended to campaign for an 'Out' vote and offered to resign. On the same day, Theresa Villiers, the Northern Ireland secretary, had a similar conversation.

Cameron had been moving towards allowing ministerial freedom as Harold Wilson had for Labour ministers in the 1975 referendum but he had not intended to announce it at this stage. While Grayling's remarks were an offer to resign, Cameron would have seen them as a threat, and concluded that ministerial resignations would be more damaging than allowing them latitude. He may have concluded that keeping them inside the tent would avoid the more abrasive campaigning that would be inevitable if they were speaking from outside the Cabinet. He got that wrong. He was to be shocked by the interventions of Outers such as Gove, Johnson, Leadsom and others.

So why in the end did Cameron lose a campaign that he believed from 2013 that he would win and win well?

As they gathered on the morning before referendum day there was cautious confidence – much more than there had been for some time – among the leaders of 'Britain Stronger In Europe', the official all-party campaign to remain in the EU.

Andrew Cooper (Lord Cooper of Windrush), the founder of the polling company Populus and director of strategy for David Cameron between 2011 and 2013, had for a few days been bringing better news to the gathering of Downing Street aides (including Craig Oliver, the communications chief) and Labour and Lib Dem strategists. Less than twenty-four hours before the polls opened the PM was told that he would win by several points.

But the late confidence was misplaced because Downing Street and other campaigners had underestimated the impact of immigration on the campaign and overestimated the impact of the economy. The Tories had won the 2015 election on the back of economic competence and thought they could do it again. There appears to have been a basic mistake in the so-called 'playbook' on which the campaign was based.

The previous summer, on the basis of a survey involving thousands of respondents, Populus presented the board of 'Stronger In' with a finding that suggested that the economy was massively more important than immigration to most voters. The conclusion was not challenged and treated as a *fait accompli*, according to campaign sources. It meant that from the moment Cameron fired the starting gun, warnings about the impact of a Brexit on the economy flowed from the mouths of Chancellor, Prime Minister, Bank of England Governor and any half-respectable think-tank or international body, with the President of the United States pitching in to suggest that Britain would drop to the back of the queue in the negotiation of post-Brexit trade deals. Little had been prepared on immigration.

The sheer ferocity of the warnings from George Osborne – he threatened an emergency Budget in the final days of the campaign – appears in the end to have been counter-productive, with ordinary voters accusing ministers of going over the top and not believing what they were told in any case.

The survey finding may also have resulted in Cameron asking for and winning less from Brussels in his winter negotiations to tackle fears over immigration than his party or the country expected. Earlier suggestions that he would get changes to the EU's freedom of mo__ment rules did not materialize, and Cameron came back only with a__ agreement that migrants would have to stay in the UK for four years before being entitled to benefits. Whether Cameron would have insisted on more if he had been told that immigration was a much bigger priority for voters than he expected, we will never know.

Some within Number 10 felt Osborne was given too much prominence in the campaign and that his apocalyptic warnings came so often that they were not believed. In *Cameron at 10: The Verdict*, Anthony Seldon and Peter Snowdon said there was frustration among Cameron's aides about the Chancellor's conduct. 'He had to be restrained several times,' they say. They warned him that his reputation was often a hindrance. 'This wasn't a general election and it required diplomacy and subtlety.'

Others claimed Osborne and Cameron had to do more than they intended because Corbyn did not do enough big events on behalf of the joint campaign. Less than three weeks before the vote there was deep concern in the Cannon Street, London, headquarters of 'Stronger In' when Cooper reported that 'Remain' was behind for the first time and that immigration was drowning out the message on the economy.

Despite independent authorities – from the Bank of England to the International Monetary Fund – warning of the dangers of Brexit, the country seemed increasingly immune, apparently believing these organizations were doing the work of the ruling elite against whom they were about to rebel. Nothing infuriated Cameron more than Gove's television claim on 3 June that 'people in this country have had enough of experts'. 'It was utterly irresponsible. Dave and Samantha had already had it with Michael by then. But this was the last straw,' a friend said.

Then Gove and Johnson, trying to give the appearance of being an alternative government, announced a series of policies including an Australian-style immigration points system. A 'Stronger In' campaign source told me: 'It cut straight through to voters. Their call for an immigration points system hit the spot. It was simple.' Claims that Turkey would join the EU also gained huge traction despite constant denials from the Government.

However, the basic mistake in planning meant that the 'Remain' campaign felt unable to respond on immigration as the battle reached its final days. A source told me: 'This was the crime. We had nothing to say. Campaigns have to be fluid and adapt and this one had nothing on immigration and the country clearly felt like "they" were not listening.'

So worried were they that ministers, pressed by the campaign team, considered returning to Brussels for more concessions. Cameron spoke to Angela Merkel, the German chancellor, to take her views on whether there could, even at this stage, be a belated offer on freedom of movement. She was not optimistic and the idea was soon shelved in any case because of fears that such a late move would look panicky and would mean that the 'Inners' would be fighting on the 'Leave' camp's turf.

Then came a horrifying turn of events when Jo Cox, a popular Labour MP, was shot and stabbed in her constituency by a man who was heard to shout 'Britain first' as he attacked and killed her. It was a tragedy that shocked the nation and the world. The referendum campaigns were suspended and Parliament was recalled to pay tribute to her. The mood of the campaign became calmer and less divisive.

It appeared that the killing might benefit the 'Remain' campaign because of the circumstances surrounding it and the late MP's support for Europe. The polls switched from 'Leave' to 'Remain' in the final days. Populus, both in its private findings for the 'Remain' camp and in its public surveys, produced the most optimistic findings. The misplaced confidence in Number 10 as the referendum approached also meant that the campaign did not use two pieces of ammunition that insiders believe could have had a vital impact during the final days.

I have seen a poster, created by the international advertising agency Saatchi & Saatchi, of a smiling Nigel Farage lying comfortably in bed with the message 'Don't wake up having done something you regret.' It could, in the eyes of key strategists working for the campaign, have been as devastatingly effective as the poster depicting Ed Miliband in the pocket of Alex Salmond, the former Scottish National Party leader, during the 2015 election campaign.

But it was not used because the Downing Street team in the form of Craig Oliver said it was 'too personal'. Their conclusion was not challenged at the time by the other parties but senior figures have since told me of their huge regret it was not used. A Number 10 insider told

DON'T WAKE UP HAVING DONE SOMETHING YOU **REGRET**

VOTE **REMAIN** ON JUNE 23ᴿᴰ   **BRITAIN STRONGER IN EUROPE**

me that it was pulled because it seemed wrong to use such a toxic picture so close to the death of Jo Cox. Similarly, an idea to create a nationwide poster with a photo of Boris Johnson in a woolly hat knocking on the door of Number 10 – taken when he negotiated with Cameron before his decision on where to stand in the referendum – and a message advising voters 'be careful what you wish for' never saw the light of day. It was considered to be unnecessary, potentially counter-productive and, again, 'too personal'. Throughout, Cameron had given orders to avoid personal attacks on Johnson.

Strategists also regret that polls showing 'Remain' with a comfortable lead were published during the day of voting. It may well have contributed to the growing national feeling that the 'In' camp was heading for certain victory and may have encouraged the wave of protest votes against 'the Establishment'. For days afterwards the airwaves were full of people admitting they had voted 'Leave' in the expectation of losing, explaining that they wanted to give a kick to the Brussels machine.

They were not the only ones. Johnson admitted when he declared for 'Leave' that he did not expect to win, and sources close to the 'Leave' campaign have told me that Johnson privately was never confident. The strong view at Westminster and elsewhere was that Johnson had signed up to 'Leave' to boost his own standing with the Conservative parliamentary party and, crucially, with the members who would pick the next leader. One former minister told me: 'Of course Boris did not expect to win and he did not want to win. A narrow victory for Cameron would have suited him better than a Brexit for which he and no one else had prepared.'

At 10 p.m. as voting closed, 'Remain' thought it had won and started briefing why. Farage conceded prematurely; Michael Gove went to bed believing he had lost. Then came the result from Sunderland which showed that the 'Leave' vote was far higher than expected in that Labour area. It was not a rogue outcome and was matched as further results came in. Farage withdrew his concession. In Number 10, Cameron knew that his gamble had failed and prepared his resignation speech.

The essay-crisis PM got through until 2016 but then the Great Examiner, the British people, caught up with him. Now Theresa May is picking up the pieces.

Cameron got it wrong. It will be years, perhaps a decade, before Britain knows for sure whether it has benefited or suffered from his mistake.

John and Edwina:
The Liverpool Novel

At around 9 p.m. on the evening of 27 September 2002, Robert Thomson, editor of *The Times*, stunned his colleagues by doing an impromptu jig around the office. Thomson suffered from a notoriously bad back and his manoeuvres might normally have caused him some pain. But the editor was too excited to feel any discomfort. He had just received from me a statement from John Major, the former prime minister, confirming that he had an affair with Edwina Currie.

It was the trigger that meant a specially prepared, secret edition of the paper – replacing a phoney earlier one that had been sent out to fool rivals – could be published and a story that was to shake the political and non-political worlds would arrive at the breakfast tables. I have been told by many people over the years that it was one of those jaw-dropping stories that made them remember where they were when they first heard it. Major was seen as the ultimate grey man, while Currie had been one of the country's most flamboyant political figures with a gift for publicity matched only by Margaret Thatcher.

It was the culmination of an extraordinary cloak-and-dagger operation that depended on the few people who knew about the contents of Currie's diaries maintaining complete and utter confidentiality about them. It was a scheme that could have gone wrong at any point. It would be an astonishing scoop for the publishers Little, Brown and for the paper, which had paid to serialize it, but it was no good to either if the story leaked and it ran across the front pages of other papers as well.

I had been assigned the task of reading the diaries, satisfying myself that the story was true and plausible, and then assuring everyone else in the loop that it was. Further, my job would be to write it up as the main front-page story, known in the industry as the 'splash', and most important of all to contact John Major on the day, breaking the news to him that a secret he had lived with for much of his life was out, and getting a reaction from him if that was at all possible. That was all!

Robert Thomson was adamant that the story would not be published unless Major had been told. Normal journalistic courtesy and propriety demanded it. Whether he would confirm it, we had no way of knowing. If he denied it, we were in trouble. But getting to him was paramount. And on the night of 27 September 2002, I nearly failed in one of the most critical missions an editor has ever asked me to undertake.

The story of how it almost went horribly wrong has never been told – until now.

Robert had called me down to the office two weeks beforehand. He had been editor for six months, having joined *The Times* from the *Financial Times*. We had immediately struck up a good relationship, with me organizing a series of lunches and dinners at which he got to know leading politicians. He asked me what I knew about Edwina Currie and John Major and whether it was possible they had ever had a relationship. I was agog. He knew that, if true, it was an extraordinary story. But having spent most of his working life away from British politics, he was testing whether I saw it in the same light. My reaction told him. He asked me to read the diaries – but without telling a soul.

A manuscript arrived at my home by special delivery and I spent the next few nights racing through it, growing more and more stunned. I knew Major pretty well, and in the years before he soared to very high office he was someone with whom I often discussed the issues of the day. At this stage I was reading only the early entries in the diaries and Currie was writing intimately about her relationship with a man she called 'B'. She called him B for no other reason than he was the second man in her life.

A typical entry was this: 'Spoke to B this evening – I'm so glad he was in. Oddly enough I need the diary more now that he's so busy. I wonder if it will start to fade. It's so hard when I don't see him. Still, I've thought that every year and we are still at it.' The affair had started in 1984 and this was September 1987.

Another entry read: 'I saw B again on Friday. I was in the area where he lives and his wife offered their home for a rest, which I appreciated. It's nice, a bit plain and unimaginative. To my horror, the magic started to work again and in a very big way. When we parted he held my hand a long time and squeezed it, even though other people were there.'

Or this one: 'Then B came along, and he was so bloody nice and attractive, and so quiet in public that it was a challenge to unearth the real person and to seduce him – easy! And it was unexpectedly spectacularly good for such a long time.' This was not my normal terrain but I was riveted.

There were enough clues for me to realize quite quickly that B was indeed John Major. When I raced on to much later entries, after the affair ended in 1988 when B had become 'John', it was confirmed in my mind that, unless Currie had been victim to a lengthy fantasy, one of the most unlikely of political couplings had happened. I had to smile. Major was a Conservative whip when the affair started. The whips make it their business to know the private business of every one of their MPs, allegedly keeping notes in a black book. Here was one ex-whip who had kept a massive secret from his colleagues; even more surprising was that the affair was with one of the more colourful and controversial of their charges.

Brian MacArthur, our associate editor who was in charge of the whole operation and whose extensive publishing-world contacts helped us to get a first sighting of the diaries, had also read the extracts. I told Robert that it was clear it was Major. He asked me point-blank: 'Do you believe it?' I replied that I had to believe it, although if I had not seen the evidence I would not have done.

Next came a trip to the publishers Little, Brown on Waterloo Bridge, where MacArthur, George Brock (managing editor), myself, Ursula Mackenzie (the publisher), Alan Samson (the book's editor), and our publicity chief, Mary Fulton, discussed issues such as where Currie would be over the crucial weekend after next and how I would approach Major. Our lawyer, Pat Burge, had warned from the outset that there might be two grounds for action of which we had to be aware – defamation if the story was wrong and breach of privacy. At that meeting the greatest worry was that Major might attempt to take out a privacy injunction when he learnt of what we intended to run.

The general view was that I should leave the call to Major as late as I dared, to minimize that risk. But I stressed again the editor's bottom-line demand: Major MUST be contacted.

Roy Greenslade, of *The Guardian*, wrote later that it was at a meeting in Wapping on 20 August that MacArthur and Thomson had first been told of the explosive, alleged contents of the diaries after signing confidentiality agreements. Both had agreed it was a great story, but asked if it could possibly be true. They were assured that it was. The publishers had come to *The Times* first because it was there that Currie hoped the book would be serialized.

As Friday, 27 September approached there was still in my mind, and in those of the handful who knew, that nagging doubt about what would happen when I got to Major with the news. Would he deny it, would he apply for an injunction, would he put out a press release telling the world in general and scuppering our exclusive? Knowing him, the latter was unlikely, but I was unsure on the other points.

No one in my office at Westminster was aware of what I had been doing. I went into the office very early that Friday morning and got the splash story written before anyone else appeared. I had during the week collected every possible number for Major – two office numbers in London, a Huntingdon constituency number, and several numbers for former close aides and friends. He was no longer in the Commons and my contact with him had been limited since the 1997 election defeat.

Peter Riddell – our chief political commentator – arrived back from the Lib Dem conference in the late morning. Peter was always my most trusted adviser and I confided in him about what we had got and showed him some of the relevant entries in the manuscript. If I was ever in danger of going over the top with a story, I could rely on Peter to pull me back from the brink, but this morning he said something I just did not want to hear. He wondered whether it was all an Edwina fantasy, the very doubt that had entered the head of Robert Thomson, me and others when we first learnt about it. At this stage I had not explained to Peter quite how much was at stake – the cost of the memoirs, the phoney first edition, the rest.

But I assured him I was satisfied and tried not to let any further doubts enter my head. The day went slowly by. At about 4 p.m. I was itching to call Major's office number, but it was still too early. I would have some explaining to do if I called prematurely and an injunction swiftly followed.

At *The Times* the secret had been kept for thirty-eight days despite the number of people knowing about it gradually increasing, as the marketing director, picture editor, Ginny Dougary (who was to interview Currie in advance), and the night and design editors who were to work on the Currie edition, were all told. In the office the codename for the book among those who were in on it was 'the Liverpool Novel', after Currie's birthplace.

Six p.m. arrived. OK. A deep breath. I had often in recent days framed in my mind how I would tell Major what we were about to publish. I rang the first number I had for the London office, which I had found in the past was always manned. No reply. I rang the second number. No reply. And no answerphone message on either. I had a mobile number for Arabella Warburton, Major's chief of staff, too. No luck. It did not work.

This was worrying. I rang Huntingdon. Again no reply. Things were now serious. Not quite panic yet. But serious. I then, almost at random, started calling other people who might know where he was. I rang an ex-colleague, Sheila Gunn, who had gone on to work as a press adviser to Major. She did not know where he was and was very curious. I rang Jonathan (now Lord) Hill, his former political secretary. No joy. At Peter's suggestion I rang Tristan Garel-Jones, a former minister and great friend of Major, on his number in Spain. No reply. In between all these calls I kept trying the London office numbers.

At head office everyone was busy preparing what they thought would be the paper's main edition. Only the chosen few realized it was due to be just the first edition, so that rivals would not see the big one when it dropped in most newsrooms at around 10.30 p.m. It was agreed to put a story about Jeffrey Archer across the top of the front page. Full-page ads for the electrical firm Currys were put on pages four and five. Robert Thomson liked a joke. The staff were unaware that in another part of the building, a handful of their colleagues were preparing the real edition.

I told no one at the office at this stage that I was becoming desperate and that the whole thing was in danger of collapsing.

By now my deputy, Tom Baldwin, had arrived and I kept him in the dark, too – for the time being at least. But he could tell that his normally unflappable boss was anything but, and offered to help. Nobody could help, though; I needed someone, anyone, to answer one of these phones. I rang Huntingdon for the umpteenth time. London yet again. I tried Arabella's number once more.

It was well after 7 p.m. when I tried the London office one last time, thinking that I was soon going to have to tell Robert that I could not find Major. Someone answered, apparently a secretary. I asked if Mr Major was there. No. I asked if Arabella was there. No. Aagh! I then told her that it was a matter of absolute life and death that I get hold of one of them. Was there anything she could do to help? She said she would try and I gave my Commons number. I repeated that it was of the utmost urgency and that they would be grateful to her if she could put them in touch with me. If I sounded desperate, I was.

No more than five minutes later, the phone rang. It was Arabella. I did not know how this conversation was going to go, but never had I been more relieved to receive a call. It sounded like a long-distance call and she told me she was in Chicago, where Major was about to make a speech. Yes, Chicago! I said that I must speak to him about something that *The Times* was about to run. I had to speak to him personally. She said: 'You know, Phil, that you can tell me so that I can tell John.' I said that on this one occasion it was difficult and that I really had to speak to him. Arabella could tell that I was serious and she must have wondered what on earth it was all about, given my insistence. She said that she would talk to Major. But I said: 'Please don't ring off – I don't want to lose you at this stage.' Arabella, who had always been the most straightforward person to deal with, was magnificent. She came back on the phone very quickly and said that whatever it was, however personal, I could tell her and that Major was happy that I should.

Tom Baldwin had been listening, and asked if he could get me a drink. I gave him the thumbs up and he raced off. I now had to tell Arabella what we were about to run. In my own mind I suppose I assumed that Major may have by now guessed what was coming. I did not know if he had picked up from somewhere that the Currie diaries were imminent. In any case I supposed this was something he had known might be revealed at any stage in the last thirteen years.

I told Arabella the essentials of the *Times* splash – that we were serializing Currie's diaries and that she had disclosed that she and John

Major had had a four-year affair. Arabella was clearly shocked but she was utterly professional. Her calm in the face of what I told her made me feel that there was unlikely to be a denial or any attempt to stop the story. The reaction was more one of sad resignation. I told her that if it was possible to have some response from her boss – and quick – I would be massively grateful. By now my anxiety had given way to huge relief. I had fulfilled Robert's command.

And I now told him that the contact had been made, and that I was hopeful of getting some kind of comment from Major. It was by then close to 8.40 p.m. Arabella asked if I could give her twenty minutes and I said of course, but please come back to me even if there is nothing other than a 'no comment'.

Tom Baldwin returned with beers and pizza. The Press Gallery bar was closed, it being a Friday. He had been up to Victoria Street. I was starving and thirsty. Again I told Robert that we were nearly there. Maybe twenty-five minutes later my phone rang again and I knew it would be Arabella. As I said hello, I quietly dialled Robert's direct line in the office and heard him pick it up. She did indeed have a statement. And as she read it I repeated it out loud so that Robert could hear. It was 9.12 p.m. The statement read: 'Norma has known of this matter for many years and has long forgiven me. It is the one event in my life of which I am most ashamed and I have long feared it would be made public. Neither Norma nor I has any further comment.'

Major has stayed true to that statement ever since. His first thought when he learnt of what we were running was for his family, and he obviously wanted to tell them what was appearing. But he has never since that day said another word on the subject.

I thanked Arabella. She in turn thanked me for giving Major advance knowledge and a chance to respond. It was a stunning result for the paper. Not only was the story confirmed by the main subject, he had also given a very good quote talking about his shame at what had happened. Even at that stage Tom and I surmised that Currie – hidden away in France – would not take too kindly to Major's response. It gave us a follow-up for Monday morning.

My office sources tell me that it was at this stage that the editor of *The Times* gave out a whoop of delight and did his jig. I swiftly e-mailed Major's words to the night editor, Liz Gerard.

Burge, Pat

Edwina
Currie

From:	Gerard, Liz
Sent:	27 September 2002 21:20
To:	Burge, Pat
Subject:	FW:

-----Original Message-----

From:	Webster, Philip
Sent:	27 September 2002 21:14
To:	Gerard, Liz
Subject:	

Mr Major said: "Norma has known of this matter for many years and has long forgiven me. It is the one event in my life of which I am m ost ashamed and I have long feared it would be made public. Neither Norma nor I has nay furhter comment."

The main paper of the night was then prepared at lightning speed.

As Brian MacArthur wrote later: 'We had our scoop. Our rivals had the spoof. The new front page and pages four and five – carrying the Dougary interview – were ready to go immediately and were being printed by 9.36 p.m. Out of 655,000 copies printed from London, only 18,000 were the spoof edition. Luck plays as big a part in news-papers as in other areas of life and none of the nightmare scenarios we had considered occurred on the night.'

I didn't tell them even then that for ninety minutes or so I had gone through a real nightmare. But I've mentioned since to George Brock, among others, that it nearly didn't go all right on the night. George replied: 'OK, there was the odd ripple of alarm. We knew you'd manage and you did.'

When the edition was done, a glass or two of champagne was drunk at the office – well deserved given the brilliance of the operation marshalled by Thomson, his deputy, Ben Preston, and the rest of the team. Tom and I had our beer.

I went home shattered but the tension of the night made sleep impossible. I was up early and in my car driving north to the Labour conference in Blackpool (via a Norwich match against Preston at Deepdale) when Robert Thomson was introduced on the *Today* programme by John Humphrys and interviewed about one of the great scoops of recent years. Piers Morgan, then editor of the *Daily Mirror*, who was woken after 2 a.m. when our Currie edition landed in his office, wrote that it rated as a story alongside 'Elvis Dead' and 'Man on the Moon'.

A Day in the Desert as John Major Sues

My job was full of coincidences. Nine years earlier, I had been with John Major when he announced he was suing two magazines for libel for alleging – falsely – that he had an affair with Clare Latimer, a Downing Street caterer.

Stopping off in Oman – where he went off to the desert to see the sultan, on his way between Mumbai, India, and Riyadh, Saudi Arabia – Downing Street officials announced that he was taking legal action against the *New Statesman & Society* and *Scallywag* over the allegations about his private life. Clare Latimer also took action.

News that the *New Statesman* had repeated rumours that had appeared in the satirical magazine the previous month reached Major and his team very late the previous night in Bombay. It meant little sleep for him or the travelling press, who raced around for most of the early hours looking for comments, and in the paper of 29 January, I chronicled the events in Major's extraordinary thirty-hour day.

All of us were up at around 5 a.m. on the Thursday, after at the most three hours of sleep. The decision to sue was taken on the plane to Muscat and announced by Gus O'Donnell, the PM's press secretary, on arrival. Returning from the overpowering heat of the desert, Major staged a press conference and took the inevitable questions from UK reporters who were not too interested in the news of orders received from the Omani Government.

At 6 p.m. that night we put down in Riyadh, where Major had six hours of talks with King Fahd and other ministers. At midnight we were told that British Aerospace was to supply forty-eight Tornado aircraft to Saudi Arabia in what was Britain's second-biggest defence contract. Both the libel and Tornado stories were spread across the front page of *The Times*. In the early hours of Friday we then got on the plane for Heathrow. A long day in our lives.

Fast-forward nine years and an angry and relieved Clare Latimer voiced her satisfaction that the 'shabby truth' had come out at last. She spoke of her pleasure that the real 'other woman' in Major's life had identified herself, sparing herself the fate, as *The Times* reported, of becoming a footnote in the history of Conservative sleaze in the 1990s. 'The world will now hopefully believe I did not hop into bed with John Major,' she said.

There were other spin-offs from our sensational revelation that Saturday. As Tom Baldwin and I had predicted, Currie was not best pleased. From her hideaway she spoke of the hurt she felt at his describing his shame over the affair. 'He was not very ashamed of it at the time I can tell you. I think I'm slightly indignant about that remark.'

And for the Kremlinologists of Westminster – those of us who enjoyed analysing every word and gesture from politicians to divine their motives and feelings – it threw some light on Major's decisions not to bring back Currie to the Government from which she had resigned as health minister in 1988 over remarks about salmonella in eggs.

In her diaries she claimed Major had told her shortly before he became prime minister in 1990 that she might become housing minister in the reshuffle that followed his win. But no offer came.

Then, after Major's victory in 1992, we watched on reshuffle day as Currie marched happily up Downing Street. We expected her to get a Cabinet job but Major offered her the post of prisons minister under Kenneth Clarke, the home secretary. But their relations were not good when Clarke was her boss at health and she refused, and walked down Downing Street, this time less happily.

In 1991 she had written in the diaries: 'He did not keep his promise to me … that hurt so terribly. I think I'd like the man to know exactly what he did last winter and how I felt, preferably not when the knowledge can do any damage, but he won't always be prime minister and it won't always matter.'

It was, indeed, a prophetic entry, and it was another eleven years before she did the deed.

1970s: Scary Days in the Commons Gallery

It was 1973 and the call came from the editor, William Rees-Mogg, in mid-afternoon. William, the first of my nine editors at *The Times*, wanted a team of reporters to stay on into the night to cover verbatim President Nixon's address to the American nation. The Watergate Scandal was in full swing and this was Nixon's attempt to give to the American people his side of the story that was eventually to finish him.

It was a terrifying request. The plan was that the fastest shorthand writers on *The Times* parliamentary staff would, in relays, take down every word of the president's broadcast, dictate immediately to a team of copy-takers, and a special edition of the paper would be printed in the early hours, proving yet again that *The Times* was the paper of record. I'm not sure anyone on the team possessed a tape-recorder and they would have been of no use anyway. The aim was to have the paper out within minutes of the president finishing and that allowed no time for listening to recordings.

I had only been on the paper for a few weeks, but I had arrived armed with fast shorthand, a prerequisite to being a Press Gallery reporter for *The Times*, or any other paper that claimed to be reporting the proceedings of Parliament. I had managed to get up to 140 words a minute on one of the pioneering full-year journalism courses at Harlow in Essex, followed by night school once I started working full-time at the *Eastern Daily Press* (based in Norwich), which had sponsored my course at Harlow.

So I was swiftly told by the head of the parliamentary team, Alan Wood, that I had been chosen for this 'honour', as he put it. The editor had commanded and we would deliver. We strengthened our team with a reporter, Ian Church, who had moved from *The Times* to *Hansard*, the official report of Parliament.

However strong your shorthand, covering the president of the United States delivering an address full of names that might have been familiar to scholars of Watergate but which were not easy to comprehend in the early hours of the morning after a full day's work, was a scary task. Nixon began talking at around 2 a.m. our time. We reported him in five-minute 'takes' each, dictating immediately to a copy-taker the second our stint ended, then making ourselves ready for another five-minute spell twenty minutes later.

It was nightmarish but somehow we got out something that passed for a verbatim report. The special edition of the paper published at around 4 a.m. and we got our 'hero-grams' from the editor the next day. The colleague who drove me home, a lovely man called Bernard Withers, was convinced that we – or at least he – would be sacked the next day for missing out some words. I'm sure we did miss some but no one complained.

Young reporters today would probably find that story bewildering. If it happened now, there would be a way of taping the words and transmitting them automatically. But the one piece of advice I have always given to young people starting in the business is to learn shorthand, because there is no substitute for it. Throughout my career I have used shorthand when interviewing leading figures – it takes much less time to write up an interview if you don't have to spend your time replaying tapes – and to take down words from politicians on television and radio.

The reporting of Parliament has changed so much since I started. When I joined *The Times* in February 1973, I was one of a team of twelve whose role was to report the proceedings in both Houses of Parliament. That was three times the size of the Lobby team. Now papers have sketch-writers to chronicle parliamentary events, but no reporters dedicated solely to covering the debates of MPs and peers.

There were eight or nine reporters, a couple of editors and an office chief on the team. Two were allocated to the Lords for a week in every month. Two stayed on late each night until the House rose; they were called 'the victims'. For a few years we covered the European Parliament, one of us going each month for a week in Strasbourg or Luxembourg. I had decent French, so was fortunate to be a regular.

One of the Nixon team was Gordon Wellman, a great man whose son John also worked for *The Times*. From my first day in the Commons, Gordon was my so-called 'victim partner', which meant that we worked together on the late shift and did the monthly Lords stint together. He was a hilarious colleague who delighted in regaling us with some of the greatest intros of all time. His favourite was one by the *Guardian* writer Norman Shrapnel, who once began a sketch with the words: 'In scenes reminiscent of Colonel Nasser's funeral ...'

He had been reporting in the gallery since the Second World War. His shorthand did not match mine, but he never missed a thing. If he knew he had failed to get correctly the words of an important intervention he would slip next door to *Hansard* and check them out when he left the gallery. Most of us were scared to do that.

Gordon had an instinct that told him precisely when something significant was about to be said. He taught me the importance of listening and understanding remarks as they were being said. The best shorthand note in the world would not help if you had not really listened to what was being uttered. I learnt much from him.

The task of the team was to fill at least a full page every day, eight columns of pretty small print, with coverage of Question Time and the main debates. It was essential reading for MPs, who would let you know if they felt they had deserved to be covered and somehow were not. Tapes were not allowed in the Press Gallery until much later on, so you really had to be able to cover speeches verbatim to avoid questions being asked about your abilities. My own first front-page story in *The Times* was a report of the maiden speech in the Lords of the Prince of Wales – another frightening experience because he spoke at length, head down looking at his notes, and very fast.

It was a tough school in The Times Room, as it was known throughout the Palace of Westminster. Reporters whose shorthand notes sometimes failed under the pressure were told in no uncertain terms that they needed to up their game. I got in because the reporter I replaced was not fast enough with his notes; he went on to a highly successful career elsewhere.

Accuracy and clean copy were absolute musts. Grammarians today are divided on the split infinitive. There was no such doubt in the mind of our beloved leader, Alan Wood. If we committed the crime of writing, for example, 'The minister promised to quickly follow up the MP's complaint', or failed to correct the MP who had committed this abuse of the language, the cry of 'Split infinitive!' would disturb the comparative silence in which we worked.

These were pre-computer days and we used typewriters for writing our stories. For a handful of us the job also involved travelling down to the office each night and overseeing our page or pages as they were prepared by the compositors, and then taking a page proof back to the office for later-edition changes. In another room upstairs in the Commons, we had an operator who would type our copy into a tickertape transmitting machine. It would come out as code in an inch-wide paper tape with holes punched in it. This would then be fed back into the machine and transmitted to head office in 'takes', where it would be set in type.

In those days *The Times* was regarded as providing a sort of mini-*Hansard*. When *Hansard* was overstretched with its coverage of every word that was spoken in Parliament – including in the plethora of standing committees – it was not averse to asking if we could step into the breach in our spare time and earn a little extra cash. I once did a full day for *The Times*, then took over for *Hansard* at 10 p.m. and worked through the night, and then had a couple of hours' sleep before covering a morning standing committee. Crazy times.

By the 1980s, however, the way newspapers covered Parliament and politics was fast changing. Apart from the big set pieces, there was much less interest in events inside the chamber than in what was going on outside in the lobbies. The three comfortable Thatcher election victories also meant that Parliament appeared to matter less, with few critical late-night votes. None of us who were there would forget Michael Heseltine seizing the mace in 1976 and brandishing it at Labour left-wingers singing 'The Red Flag' after winning a vote to nationalize the aircraft and shipbuilding industries.

But in later years the rules were changed and reporters were allowed to take tape-recorders into the gallery. Ministers and MPs started handing out their speeches in advance, to be checked against delivery, and governments aimed their big announcements at the early evening news rather than saving them for the winding-up speech in the Commons.

Soon the parliamentary teams of all papers that had them were being swiftly reduced, much to the chagrin of MPs with an increasing sense of grievance that they were not appreciated. As the age of spin took over, journalists and their papers took more note of what was going to be said tomorrow rather than what had just been said today.

In those days, The Times Room at the Commons was right next door to *Hansard*, just a few yards from the Commons gallery, but our premises were later colonized by *Hansard* and we had to move upstairs to a room that had previously been the television lounge. *The Times* still inhabits that room.

In those early days we would often run into MPs right outside our door as they went into the *Hansard* office to run the rule over their words and hand across to them papers or books from which they had quoted in their speeches.

As reporters we had MPs whom we liked to report, and those we feared. Harold Wilson was fluent but impossibly fast at times. Enoch Powell was slow but spoke in lengthy, well-constructed sentences, which had to be transcribed in full for them to make sense. Miss a subclause and you were in serious trouble, reporting the opposite of what he meant. He spoke without notes. Michael Foot was always a good turn, funny, and with plenty of pauses for effect to give the writing arm a rest.

There were back-benchers like the Scottish MP John Mackintosh, who died tragically young at forty-eight, and Brian Walden, who went on to become a frontline broadcaster, who could make wonderfully fluent speeches without looking at a note.

The chamber would quickly fill when the names Powell or Foot went up on the annunciators telling MPs and the Press Gallery who had just risen to speak. There are no modern-day equivalents.

Return of *The Thunderer*

The Times defied gravity in the period 1978–9. What other paper in the world could cease publishing for a year – the year of all years when Margaret Thatcher became Britain's first woman prime minister – and come back stronger? Perhaps only *The Thunderer* (the nickname for *The Times* dating from the nineteenth century) could have done it.

The Times, *The Sunday Times* and the supplements were taken off the streets during a fierce industrial dispute between management and printers, leaving readers to pine for their return and take other papers while they waited. Their loyalty was tested to the full. Month after month, they waited. And in the end they were rewarded for their patience.

To understand how this all happened the reader needs to be reminded of the circumstances of the time. The disappearance of *The Times* from the news stands took place during a time of extraordinary industrial disharmony.

James Callaghan, who became prime minister after a Labour leadership election when Harold Wilson suddenly stood down in March 1976, had a miserable period in charge. Wilson had led Labour to a three-seat majority in October 1974 but by March 1977 that advantage had gone because of by-election defeats. Faced with a motion of no confidence that would have brought him down, Callaghan negotiated a deal – the Lib–Lab Pact – with David Steel, leader of the Liberals. Steel's party would keep the Government in power in return for concessions on policy.

It was an unhappy time and the pact was torn up in September 1978. At that time it looked certain that Callaghan would call a general election but he confounded us all. Appearing at the Trades Union Congress (TUC) conference where he was expected to name the day, Callaghan dashed expectations. 'There was I waiting at the church,' he sang. He wrongly attributed the song to Marie Lloyd; it was by music-hall star Vesta Victoria. Whatever, the message was clear and a surprise: no election.

He must have regretted that decision more than any other. As the *Times* dispute reached a climax, Britain was entering what became known as the Winter of Discontent. Shakespeare's opening line from *Richard III* was used to describe the period of widespread public strikes by unions opposing the five per cent pay cap set by the Government in a departure from its voluntary social contract with the unions.

Strikes by gravediggers, refuse collectors and health workers led to delays in funerals, rubbish piling up in the streets and hospitals doing emergency operations only. It gave the impression of a Britain in chaos and made Thatcher's election in May 1979 a foregone conclusion. It also rendered her subsequent assault on union power far easier to push through. Snow and freezing conditions in the coldest winter since 1962 did nothing to help matters. The country has seen nothing like it since.

I was then on the parliamentary staff of *The Times*, and Callaghan's TUC speech was one of my last jobs before the paper's closure. The industrial climate in the country was worsening and at *The Times* it was becoming critical. The unions were militant and the print unions more militant than most. They had tremendous power: stopping a paper to show your muscle was a simple business. If the printers walked out, no one else could do their job. Managements felt impotent.

In April 1978, Marmaduke Hussey, then chief executive of Times Newspapers, had told the unions he was prepared to close the papers if he did not get an agreement to install computer typesetting. This was a forerunner of the war of Wapping, which was to end so differently. The date for closure if talks failed was set for 30 November. Nothing came from the talks in the end and the papers were duly shut down on 1 December. They were subject to what we knew was an uncertain future, even though Lord Thomson of Fleet, the proprietor, insisted there was no question of selling the papers or permanently closing them.

It was a deeply unsettling experience and took some getting used to. In his final article before the paper went to sleep, Paul Routledge, our labour editor (so important were the unions in those days that

most of the broadsheets had two, three or even four labour correspondents to cover their dealings), quoted management sources as
expecting a suspension of two to three months.

That would get us through Christmas. Those of us working at
Westminster had the Commons to entertain us. We retained our passes
and went along whenever anything interesting was happening. There
was plenty at this time as Callaghan's decision began to look less and
less clever. But it was strange being unable to report.

As the New Year dawned it was obvious that we would not be
going to work any time soon. Our National Union of Journalists
(NUJ) meetings were things to look forward to, giving us the chance
to meet up and tell each other how we were spending our time. I
raced through a long-planned book on the recent history of my
beloved Norwich City FC, as seen through the eyes of Kevin Keelan
(a goalkeeper who still holds the appearance record for the club, and
who by then – late in his career – was playing for Norwich in the
winter and the New England Teamen in Boston in the off-season).

I worked for various magazines. I even followed a colleague who
was making good money working for a major car-rental company
delivering cars – at speed – from one depot to another. It was when I
was working with eight others to deliver brand-new Volvos from a
Buckinghamshire factory to Heathrow Airport and my machine broke
down just a few miles from the factory – prompting cries of anguish
from drivers for whom this was the main source of revenue – that I
decided it was not for me.

I worked for a few exciting weeks as a subeditor on *The Guardian*,
handling political stories written by the likes of Ian Aitken, Julia
Langdon and Michael White, and taking orders from a long-haired
genius chief sub called Roger Alton. He was to resurface in my life
later, on the ski slopes and the cricket pitch and at *The Times* after
spells as editor of *The Observer* and *The Independent*.

They were strange days indeed because great stories were happening and we had nowhere to write them. The consolation was a year
on full pay while at the same time being encouraged to write for
other organs to keep our hands in.

The whole parliamentary team – all of us – went to a pub near the
Commons on the night of 28 March and then went to watch the last
rites of Old Labour in government. Thatcher, as Opposition leader,

had tabled a motion of no confidence in the Government and won it by one vote, 311 to 310, amid scenes of pandemonium as the Tories cheered and Labour sang 'The Red Flag'. Labour would not return to power for eighteen years: a political lifetime.

Worst of all for us political writers was to miss the historic election night on 9 May 1979, when Thatcher swept to power and promised to bring harmony where there was discord. I and many other reporters could not bear to be at home and spent our evening trailing round party headquarters pretending we were working.

Meanwhile, NUJ meetings rolled irrelevantly on amid deadlock between management and the unions that mattered. It was a dispute that the management was not going to win, and by the autumn of 1979, all sides were looking for a way out.

In his obituary of Duke Hussey in 2007, William Rees-Mogg, editor of *The Times* for fourteen years, admitted that the papers had reopened on 13 November 1979 (nearly a year after closing) on what he called unsatisfactory terms. This led first to Hussey being replaced as chief executive and eventually to the sale of Times Newspapers by the Thomson family. Rees-Mogg wrote: 'If his struggle at *The Times* proved a failure – and it was a policy I supported from beginning to end – it had much more positive long-term consequences. It led to the next struggle against the militant chapels when Times Newspapers moved to Wapping, and that battle was won under Rupert Murdoch.'

When the paper came back, the BBC reported the dispute was estimated to have cost the Thomson organization £30m. Thatcher welcomed the reappearance of *The Times* 'with enthusiasm'. She said: 'The absence of *The Times* has been tragic and overlong.' Although we had found interesting ways of spending our time, the journalists agreed with every word of that.

Some 200,000 more copies of *The Times* were published on the day it came back than on its last print run, while readers announced births and deaths spanning the period of its absence. *The Times* also published three special obituary supplements to cover the period. It was an event that showed again the loyalty of *Times* readers and it paved the way for Murdoch's eventual victory, which led to other newspapers adopting new technology and moving to cheaper premises in east London.

The Thunderer had risen again and within days it was business as normal.

The Iron Lady: Early Lobby Years

I had been in the Lobby for only a few months when, on 2 April 1982, Argentine forces invaded the Falkland Islands.

I was doing Friday duty on my own when the news came through, and we were told that the Commons would meet next day – it remains the only Saturday sitting in my career – to debate what seemed like a national humiliation and the Government's likely response to it.

It was to be the turning point of Margaret Thatcher's career as she ignored the voices of caution and sent a task force to reclaim the islands, anchoring in the public mind the idea of an uncompromising leader who would always stand up for Britain's interests. But on that Friday night she could not have expected this. The Government had been caught napping and its apparent lack of commitment to the islands during years of negotiations about their future had convinced Galtieri's junta, under pressure at home, that it could get away with it. UK defence cuts in the 1981 recession Budget had also sent the wrong kind of signal to Argentina.

In my Saturday morning front-page story, I said that in a political and military crisis without parallel since the Suez operation of 1956, Thatcher would face a hostile Commons demanding to know why British interests had not been protected. I said there was a sense of humiliation among Tory MPs that a government that had come to power promising to strengthen the nation's defences had not been able to prevent the invasion of one of our few remaining overseas territories.

Within the Government there was a feeling of panic. On that Friday, as the news started to reach Whitehall that the invasion had indeed started, ministers and officials blustered, waiting for the Commons to rise for the day to avoid being called to explain something they did not yet understand.

Only months earlier Thatcher had looked beaten and battered as the 'wets', the name she and her allies gave to the liberal-minded patrician Tories who opposed her, openly conspired against her. It is often forgotten that Thatcher's early years in office after defeating James Callaghan in the 1979 general election were far from easy.

She became leader in February 1975, after surprisingly challenging Edward Heath, who had lost two general elections to Harold Wilson in 1974. He had called the election to reassert his authority but the gamble misfired badly when Thatcher, superbly assisted by her campaign manager, Airey Neave, capitalized on the discontent of Tory back-benchers and defeated him on the first ballot. She was just short of the required fifty per cent of the votes but got there easily after Heath withdrew and she beat Willie Whitelaw, Geoffrey Howe and others on the second ballot.

Many of the Tory establishment – Whitelaw, Lord Carrington, James Prior, most on the liberal wing of the party – supported Heath. Some of them, including Heath, never forgave her and were to give her a rough time when she took over. They did not like the hard-line economic thinking of Thatcher and her mentor, Sir Keith Joseph. There was something about the rich and patrician that rubbed the Prime Minister up the wrong way. Her biggest assault on the 'wets' came in September 1981, when she finally acted to give herself a Cabinet that was more in tune with her tough monetarist stance and with that of her chancellor, Sir Geoffrey Howe, who was very much in her good books in those days.

On 12 September 1981, I wrote in *The Times* that the 'wets' in the Cabinet feared that her move against them would be more extensive than expected.

I knew Sir Ian Gilmour well from my spell as a young reporter in Norfolk when he was an MP there. He kindly always used to invite me to his annual summer party in Isleworth on the Thames – not far from my home across the A4 in Osterley – which was always full of like-minded MPs and figures from other parties to whom he felt closer than some in his own. At around 10.30 on the Monday morning following publication of my article, I picked up a ringing phone in The Times Room in the Commons. It was Gilmour who, calling from the phone box at the end of Whitehall after he left Downing Street, had rung to tell us that 'She' had just sacked him.

Gilmour knew several of us in the office quite well and I passed him across to Julian Haviland, the political editor. Gilmour knew in advance that his fate was sealed and read out his prepared remarks, stating that while it did no harm to throw the occasional man over-

St Margaret of Assisi 1983

board 'it does not do much good if you are steering full-speed ahead for the rocks'. Other casualties that day were Mark Carlisle (from education), Lord (Christopher) Soames (leader of the Lords) and Lord Thorneycroft (party chairman). Just as important, Jim Prior, who had not gone as far as Thatcher wanted on trade union reform, was sidelined to the Northern Ireland Office.

Thatcher told in her memoirs that Gilmour had been huffy, and had gone out and denounced government policy, giving a 'flawless imitation of a man who had resigned on principle'. Soames was equally angry but in a grander way. 'I got the distinct impression that he felt he was being dismissed by his housemaid,' recalled Thatcher. She had acted after a Cabinet meeting in July when the 'wets', backed by some ministers who would normally have supported her, opposed her plans to make a further £5 billion cut to public spending.

In a recent book, Conservative MP Kwasi Kwarteng argued that the reshuffle marked the end of a six-month period that defined Thatcher, helping her to two more election victories and delaying for nine years the moment when, in Gilmour's words, she finally hit the rocks. The period had begun with the Howe budget of March 1981 that slashed spending and raised taxes in the quest of sound finances. Thatcher then had to cope with the IRA hunger strikes, the Brixton and Toxteth riots, and the formation of the Social Democratic Party (SDP) by the Gang of Four – Roy Jenkins, Shirley Williams, David Owen and William Rodgers – who quit the Labour Party in protest at its leftward shift.

But the reshuffle did not stop the dissent, which again erupted at the October conference. Thatcher looked far from the dominating figure she was to become and few believed she could take the Tories on to more victories. The economy was still in trouble and the SDP was riding high. The Falklands changed all that. Both Houses of Parliament met that Saturday with a sense of national shame hanging over the Government. Lord Carrington resigned shortly afterwards as foreign secretary, and two of his ministers went as well. They were not pushed but went as a matter of honour, recognizing the Foreign Office's failure to anticipate events.

Thatcher told MPs that the islands would be recaptured but there was no contingency plan in play. Some on her own side advised against going to war. But Thatcher overruled the worried voices and ordered the task force to sail on 5 April. The aircraft carriers *Hermes* and *Invincible* were in a fleet that eventually contained thirty-eight warships and 11,000 soldiers and marines.

Thatcher was to turn humiliation for Britain to national and personal glory, winning her the Iron Lady sobriquet, one that would stick throughout her leadership. Securing a landslide victory over Michael Foot's Labour in 1983, she used her popularity to press on with her revolution, but first she had some more personnel business to do. Thatcher had made Francis Pym her foreign secretary after Lord Carrington resigned in the wake of the Falklands invasion by Argentina in April 1982. But she soon regretted promoting a man who, as defence secretary, had opposed cuts sought by the Treasury. When she made him Commons leader, he had become more and more associated with those backing an alternative economic strategy.

Now at the Foreign Office during the war, he allied himself with those in the USA and Peru who favoured some kind of compromise. It confirmed Thatcher's view of the Foreign Office and Pym, and when he spoke of the dangers of landslide governments during the election campaign it was a nail in the coffin. She was furious and had had enough of him. Her ruthless reshuffle put a stop to Pym's career but she was not satisfied. When it came to making changes again in 1983, she still wanted to beef up her team with more who shared her view of life. 'There was a revolution still to be made, but too few revolutionaries,' she was later to write.

So Willie Whitelaw went to the Lords and was succeeded as home secretary by Leon Brittan, Nigel Lawson came in as chancellor, Cecil Parkinson for a brief time ran the Department of Trade and Industry (DTI) before resigning (see next chapter), and crucially John Wakeham – who was to become a vital figure in the latter years – became her chief whip. After Parkinson went, Norman Tebbit was promoted to the DTI and Nick Ridley, of whom she was greatly fond and compared to her mentor, Keith Joseph, also came into the Cabinet.

The 'wets' were vanquished and the revolution proceeded. The Iron Lady had set herself free.

How I Upset the Commons
by Doing My Job

The Falklands was a brilliant story to cover. But it was its aftermath
that got me into trouble with the Commons authorities. It was Sunday,
17 April 1983. I was the Sunday duty man and had a splash of splashes
to tell the news desk about. In my hands was a copy of an explosive
draft report on the aftermath of the Falklands war.

For six months the Commons Foreign Affairs Select Committee
had been deliberating on the future of the islands in the wake of the
war and had come to the conclusion that Margaret Thatcher's so-called
Fortress Falklands policy – retaining enough British forces on the
island to deter future aggression from Argentina – was untenable over
the long term. Furthermore, the committee (which had a Conservative
majority) was proposing that the Government should not turn its back
on future talks with Argentina to achieve a negotiated settlement.
Reporters were then – as now – often briefed on what was likely to
appear in select committee reports. Provided we kept it reasonably
vague, without specifically mentioning anything directly from the
reports themselves, we could probably get away with publishing without attracting the ire of the Commons authorities (who regarded leaks
with dread and threatened punitive action against anyone responsible
for them, particularly if they were MPs). This was different. In my
hands I had an actual copy of the report given to me by an extremely
good source. The protection I guaranteed him then still applies.

A very excited Charles Douglas-Home, editor of *The Times* from
1982 until his death in 1985, came over to me to discuss the story. We
got on well. On the day Harold Evans appointed me to the Lobby in
1981, Charlie, then foreign editor, had offered me a posting in

Washington – unaware of the other approach. I chose the Lobby and everyone understood. He was my third *Times* editor. I told him there were two choices. I could write up the story in a Lobby-style way, with a lot of 'it is understood' and 'it is believed to say' hiding the fact that I was in possession of the report, or I could write the story as hard as possible, effectively flaunting the fact that I had got hold of this precious document whose publication would create an almighty stir. I reminded Charlie – who was a reporter's editor and loved the break-ing of exclusive news stories – that if we went ahead with the latter choice, both he and I could be called to the Bar of the Commons for breaching parliamentary privilege. His eyes lit up. I had the sense that this was a prospect that did not alarm him in any way. In fact, I suspect he would have enjoyed appearing before MPs to defend his newspa-per's right to publish and be damned.

'OK, let's go for full-on publication. We will splash on it, and you and I will take the consequences,' said Charlie. It was one of the reasons why we all loved him. He had unbelievable enthusiasm and energy, and his tragic early death just a few years later was a massive loss for *The Times* and journalism. Charlie passed by the news desk and told them: 'Phil's doing the splash and it will be a strong one.'

Even though it was early in my Lobby career, I was not in the habit of holding back, and the desk visibly relaxed, knowing that it had a splash for the night. I set about writing it up. I threw in a couple of 'apparently's to raise a little doubt in the mind of angry MPs when they read it the next morning, but in all honesty I left no doubt that I had the report in front of me as I wrote.

So under the splash headline 'Thatcher to be told Fortress Falklands policy is untenable' – you could get a lot in a three-deck headline in *The Times* in those days – I wrote that a committee with a majority of Conservative MPs was about to conclude that the Fortress Falklands policy, however necessary in the short term, did not offer a stable future for the islands. I said that although the committee would back the existing policy of keeping a garrison on the islands to defend them against a renewed attack, and of not embarking on any immediate negotiations, it would have to accept that in future talks on a negoti-ated settlement should not be resisted.

I noted that the committee had visited the Falklands and the United Nations headquarters in New York during its deliberations and I added what I thought was the pretty harmless bit of information that the committee would meet that following Wednesday to consider the draft report.

I suggested that rejection of the long-term efficacy of Fortress Falklands by such a powerful committee, and its willingness to countenance a transfer of sovereignty, was bound to embarrass the Thatcher Government. I said the MPs had concluded that diplomatic, financial, military and economic problems would continue for Britain and the Falklands unless or until a negotiated settlement with Argentina could be achieved.

My story stuck pretty closely to the draft which I still have – and it went on in that vein for many more paragraphs across the front and on page three of the paper. I left the paper for home happy in the knowledge, and not really worrying given the editor's full backing, that we would cause uproar in the Tory party and in Downing Street that night. I had written the story in such a straight way that it was easy for my colleagues on other papers to follow and they duly did, giving proper attribution to *The Times*.

Monday morning broke with the story getting massive prominence on the early morning radio and television bulletins. Within the Tory high command there was immediate pressure to discover the source of the leak. There was fury and it was directed not so much at *The Times* as at the person who – it appeared – had given me the report.

The matter was raised with Speaker George Thomas that afternoon as a *prima facie* breach of parliamentary privilege. After discussions with the usual channels – the network of whips and business managers from all parties – an emergency debate was set for the Commons that Thursday. Needless to say, the Wednesday meeting of the committee of which I had written did little on the draft. But I was told that MPs spent a lot of the session eyeing each other in the hope that the culprit – the guy who had given it to me – might blush. The report had also been seen by Commons officials. So, in the eyes of the committee chiefs, they could not quite be ruled out, although the overwhelming suspicion among the committee was that it must have been one of them.

I never expected to be the subject of a Commons debate. Thursday arrived and from the Press Gallery – ever so slightly embarrassed to be centre of attention among my reporter friends and the MPs below – I

watched as Sir Anthony Kershaw, chairman of the Foreign Affairs
Committee, rose gravely to his feet to move that his complaint be
referred to the Committee of Privileges. The motion, he said, arose
from a report in *The Times* on 18 April about British policy towards
the Falklands. On Thursday last, he said, the draft report was issued to
the eleven members of the committee and to six clerks and advisers.
Each copy bore the name and initials of the person to whom it was
issued. He sounded like a prosecutor opening a case at the Old
Bailey. On Monday, said Sir Anthony, an accurate summary of the draft
appeared as the lead story on the front page and another page of *The
Times*. The story was clearly based on a close reading of the draft. No
one reading both could doubt their 'consanguinity', he said, using a
word you would be hard put to get into a news story. The story
contained more than one unacknowledged but easily recognizable
quotation from the draft and followed closely the sequence of paragraphs in the draft. It looked as if Charlie and I were bang to rights.
He went on:

> Furthermore, Philip Webster, the *Times* reporter whose name is
> given in the story, was able to reveal what no other member of
> the press could have known – that the draft was to be considered
> by the committee on Wednesday.

He said it had originally been intended to consider it on Monday and
a press announcement had been made to that effect. However, because
some MPs had wanted to speak in a rival Commons debate that day,
it was delayed.

He had enclosed a slip of paper with the draft report telling
members the meeting had been postponed to Wednesday. 'No other
announcement was made and Philip Webster could have obtained his
information from no other source.' If I had really been trying to
conceal my possession of the report, that would have been a mistake
on my part. Sir Anthony went on that it often happened that well-
informed journalists, expert in their subject, could and did piece
together stories with the help of MPs, the accuracy of which surprised
those who thought they were in possession of exclusive information.
'No, or hardly any, breach of the rules is involved and we turn a blind
eye,' he said. 'In other instances, if the information improperly obtained

is not of great moment to the outside world, again sensibly we take little notice.' Now Sir Anthony lay my crime before the House:

> I submit that this case is different. There has not been an indiscreet conversation in the Lobby, or in one of the bars about a minor matter. A report of a major political controversy, both at home and abroad and inside and outside the House, has been written up from a complete document which the committee has not even considered and which some members had not, in the circumstances, had time to read before the report appeared.

My friends in the pretty well-attended gallery gave me a quiet 'Hear, hear' of support as Sir Anthony continued:

> I do not think that ignorance of our rules can be pleaded. Philip Webster is an experienced Lobby man, and his source can be presumed to know the rules. In any event on the front page of the draft appeared these words: 'The circulation of this draft report is strictly limited to members and staff of the Foreign Affairs Committee. The premature disclosure of contents of a draft report has in the past been regarded as a *prima facie* breach of privilege.'

He added finally:

> If the private deliberations of our committee are to be revealed in this way, it will destroy the confidence and trust that have been established between Hon. Members who work together on the committee and make it impossible for the committees to receive evidence, which may be considered confidential from a witness's point of view or in the area of public affairs, and generally diminish the value of the work of select committees.

I had met Sir Anthony on a few occasions and found him a very pleasant, reasonable man and I could not really argue with anything he had said. Of course, I was the messenger, and the real target, whom he would never find, was my source. MPs generally like publicity but they like it on their terms. This was not on their terms but those of

The Times. This was a classic occasion when the job of the reporter conflicted with the role of the politician.

I would by no means have been the first journalist to have been sent to the privileges committee, but that fate was beginning to look inevitable at this stage. As the debate got under way, Jeff Rooker, the independent-minded Labour MP for Birmingham Perry Barr, got up to oppose the motion. He argued that there was no case for hauling before the privileges committee journalists 'who have carried out their trade, because we never find the source of their information'. He added: 'One of the members of the committee, or one of the staff, has dishonoured the rules of the House, not the journalist who obtained a copy of the report.' *The Times* had been singled out because it put the story on the front page. Its crime was prominence. Others – like my old contact and friend Tam Dalyell, Alex Lyon, Joe Ashton and Chris Price – spoke up on my behalf but Sir Peter Emery, a Conservative committee chairman, said that if it was not referred for investigation, then every draft committee report would be fair game for publication. He asked that the privileges committee see every member of the foreign affairs committee and its staff to find the culprit.

It was a strange, amusing experience. Dennis Skinner, the so-called 'Beast of Bolsover' and someone I knew well, was gesticulating up towards me in the gallery as the debate played out and we had a laugh about it afterwards. The front-benches, in the form of John Silkin for Labour and John Biffen for the Government, backed the motion to refer me as would have been expected. Biffen said that if Sir Anthony Kershaw felt the work of his committee was impeded by what had happened and wanted it referred, his request should be sympathetically considered.

There was an interesting contribution from Ian Mikardo, the veteran Labour left-winger, who recalled that when *The Economist* published a report from a select committee on the wealth tax in 1975, it was referred to the privileges committee. Efforts to find the leaker failed but the committee recommended that the offending journalists (Andrew Knight, the editor, and Mark Schreiber, the reporter) should be barred from the House for six months. On that occasion the Commons had then rejected that punishment. Mikardo wondered whether the journalist in this case – me – was conscious of that precedent and believed he had nothing to fear.

To be honest, I had considered that possibility but felt that in this case the risk was worth it. After an hour or so, the debate ended and MPs voted by 159 to 48 that the issue be referred to the committee of privileges. The procedure of which I had warned Charlie Douglas-Home was well and truly under way.

I can do no better now than to hand this story over to the venerable Ian Aitken, the former (and at the time) political editor of *The Guardian*. He wrote in a column for *The Sunday Standard* that sometime between then and the general election (one was due at some point over the following thirteen months but was expected sooner rather than later), a comic little charade was likely to be enacted in a committee room of the Commons where a certain malefactor (by name, Mr Philip Webster) would be wheeled before a distinguished but strictly private assembly of MPs and privy councillors:

He will be there, unaided by legal representation and unprotected by recognized rules of evidence or procedure, to answer the grave job of doing his job rather well.

For Mr Webster, a slightly sinister-looking man who reminds me of the famous Holbein portrait of a pair of shifty Italian ambassadors, is a journalist on the political staff of *The Times*. Last weekend Mr Webster (whose appearance I hasten to add belies a pleasantly amiable temperament) was clever enough to obtain detailed information of a report drawn up by the Commons Select Committee on Foreign Affairs dealing with the Falkland Islands. Wasting no time he wrote the story at length and *The Times* splashed it at length across its front page on Monday morning.

Bully for Mr Webster, you might conclude ... it was a good, competent and detailed piece of reportage revealing that this august select committee, though headed by a Conservative, and counting a majority of Tories among its members, was unhappy with the Government's Fortress Falklands policy to protect it from a future invasion by Argentina.

The report was in any case going to be published by the committee in a few days, wrote Aitken, but Sir Anthony Kershaw – a splendid example of that desperately endangered species known as The Knights

from the Shires – decided that Webster's publication of the article was
a breach of the rules of gentlemanly conduct and probably a *prima facie*
breach of the privileges of the House of Commons. Under the headline 'The man who breached Parliament's no-go area', Aitken wrote:

> That is why Mr Webster will shortly have to stand before an
> assembly which will include such dignitaries as the Attorney
> General, the Leader of the Commons, the chairman of the
> Committee of Chairmen, and assorted superannuated
> back-benchers to answer the heinous crime of getting it right.

Aitken insisted he was not saying that there was never any situation
where MPs could berate a journalist for breaking its privileges. 'But I
claim that such circumstances are (or should be) very rare indeed and
they certainly do not apply in the case of a reporter doing his job with
integrity as well as success.' He said that what was now going to
happen, if the rules were followed to their logical conclusion, was that
Mr Webster would be asked to grovel apologetically for doing exactly
what the editor of *The Times* pays him to do; he would also likely be
instructed to reveal who it was who gave him the draft report or told
him of its content. Aitken went on:

> And here I must reveal a paradox. For there exists in the Palace
> of Westminster a much-maligned group of reporters known as
> the Parliamentary Lobby Journalists – the Lobby for short. Like
> me Mr Webster is a member of it. And it is because of our
> membership that we have access to the private bars, corridors
> and cafeterias of the building which are the daily hunting ground
> of political journalists. Much nonsense has been written about
> this workaday body of hacks. It is sometimes imaginatively
> invested with strange powers of its own to suppress or distort
> news, by which Mr Webster and I and the rest of our colleagues
> pay the price for our rights of access by sitting on genuine news
> which we know to be of high public interest.
>
> The reality, as in so many other fields of human activity, is
> rather less dramatic and a whole lot less sinister. We do indeed
> pay a price for being allowed to get at our informants in their
> natural habitat. It is the simple common sense one that applies to

most journalists – that we do not reveal our sources unless (as sometimes happens with politicians) they actually want to see their names in the paper.

It is on this basis and this basis alone (the rest of the so-called Lobby system is largely pretentious bunk) that we are admitted to the building. It is therefore a rule imposed on us by Parliament.

So what is to happen if the Attorney General or the Leader of the House asks Mr Webster to name the rotter who leaked the stuff to him?

He will be in honour bound – no, more, under absolute contractual obligation – to refuse to answer. And the irony of the position will be that the members of the committee will have to acknowledge in logic that they are themselves the custodians of the rule under which Mr Webster has thought fit to defy them.

He ended: 'Which should give game, set and match to Philip Webster, my honoured friend and colleague.'

As the reader will judge by the length at which I have quoted Aitken, I liked that piece a lot – not only because a senior journalist from a rival paper had been so nice about me. I forgive him the suggestion that I have sinister looks. But Ian also explained, far better than me, the need for politicians to understand that they must not hound journalists who are merely doing their job.

I was to be denied my moment in court. I was looking forward to facing up to the Attorney General, a man I knew pretty well, and refusing point-blank to name my sources, and I probably would have enjoyed the furore if the committee had decided, as before, that I should be banned from the House for a time. My editor also probably missed the opportunity to shout the case for press freedom as his reporter faced the iniquity of banishment from the Commons premises. But no, Margaret Thatcher intervened. On 9 May she visited Buckingham Palace and asked the Queen for a dissolution of Parliament, about a year earlier than she needed to. The election would be on 9 June and gave her another landslide. But it meant that all the current motions and business lying before Parliament were effectively dead. The motion to refer the *Times* report and me to the privileges committee went up in smoke with the rest. It could have been revived in the following Parliament but no one expected that to happen because it was generally accepted in everything written about the episode that it would be a waste of time. I would not reveal my sources. He would never be named. We used 'The Times Diary' to tell our readers that their political reporter was safe. Under the heading 'Uncommon luck', PHS (as 'The Times Diary' was known from its headquarters in Printing House Square) said:

> The coming of the general election denies my colleague Philip Webster the privilege of being hauled before the House of Commons privileges committee. The motion to refer Webster's full and accurate account of a select committee report on future policy over the Falklands to the privileges committee dies with the Parliament. If the matter were to be revived in the new Parliament the whole issue of whether to refer or not (carried last time by 159 votes to 48) would have to be debated again. It is highly unlikely that the new House will have the stomach for it, and even some MPs who voted for the reference on April 21 admit now that they are glad to see the matter drop.

And so it proved. But senior MPs still did not learn that our job is to disclose what we find. Three years later, my friend Richard Evans revealed in *The Times* the findings of an environment committee report that highlighted the dangers of waste from nuclear power stations. Despite the revelation clearly being in the public interest, the privileges committee recommended he be barred from the House for six months. The Commons, thankfully, and sensibly, rejected the idea when it was put to the full House.

The Foreign Secretary Who Never Was

In May 1983, two weeks before the general election, I wrote a *Times* splash suggesting that Margaret Thatcher would dismiss Francis Pym, her foreign secretary, after the election and replace him with her party chairman and close friend Cecil Parkinson, who was about to oversee an election landslide.

The story came as a result of a lunch with a senior Cabinet minister who knew Thatcher's thinking. Jim Naughtie (then of *The Guardian* and later of the *Today* programme), Margaret van Hattem (of the *Financial Times*) and I had taken the minister to the sumptuous Ma Cuisine in Walton Street, Chelsea.

Margaret, who was to die tragically young in 1989 from a brain haemorrhage, was a highly intelligent, attractive woman, with a mischievous, occasionally flirtatious, air.

The minister – tall, debonair and unbelievably smooth – who joined us that day was completely taken with Margaret, whom he had not met before. Before long, as almost always on these occasions, we got on to the subject of the post-election Cabinet reshuffle, making sure that our guest's glass of white wine was nicely topped up.

The minister was putty in Margaret's hands. Jim and I were virtual bystanders – although we were listening carefully and taking mental notes – as our friend took our guest through all the likely changes and he answered them all directly, almost as if he were privy to the Prime Minister's thoughts. He was playing to the gallery – showing off – and the gallery was Margaret. Jim and I, meanwhile, were playing gooseberry.

He was clear that Pym, by whom 'Margaret' – he was talking about Thatcher – was increasingly frustrated, was on his way out. And when our Margaret asked who would replace him, our man blushed and told her and us that he would have to leave that to our imagination. We knew what he meant and he appeared almost beside himself with excitement at the prospect of going to the Foreign Office. Thatcher, we were told, had in a way groomed him for the role by appointing him – at the time a relatively junior figure in the Cabinet hierarchy – to the War Cabinet set up for the Falklands conflict. By the time our guest had finished, we felt we had a pretty good idea of what the Cabinet would look like after the Conservatives' certain victory.

When he had left us, Jim and I congratulated Margaret on her charming interrogation techniques and talked about how we would write up the story. Ministers were never averse to such speculation, and the job of the reporter was to decide whether they were guessing or knew what they were talking about. This minister left us in little doubt that he knew what he was about. Our guest was, of course, Cecil Parkinson.

When Thatcher won her landslide and carried out her reshuffle, Pym – probably the most infuriating of the 'wets' in the eyes of his boss – was indeed sacked and refused to take any other job, retiring in dignified fashion to the back-benches. But rather than going to the Foreign Office, Parkinson became secretary of state for trade and industry. Jim, Margaret and I decided philosophically that 'you win some, you lose some' and that we had at least got the story fifty per cent right. But it was not long before we were to learn why the second half of our story had not happened.

As Margaret Thatcher was to confirm in her autobiography, she had indeed intended to appoint Parkinson as foreign secretary.

He and I agreed on economic and domestic policy. Neither of us had the slightest doubt that Britain's interests must come first in foreign policy. He had served in the Falklands war Cabinet. He had just masterminded the most technically proficient election campaign I have known. He seemed to me right for this most senior job.

She did not say this, but Parkinson was also her kind of man –
handsome and smooth, even if some found him oleaginous. She was
the daughter of a grocer, he the son of a railway man. He was the
grammar-school boy who went to Cambridge and was everything the
more privileged members of her Cabinet were not, the charmer
whom the Tory members loved.

But on election day Parkinson had visited her and told her that he
had been having an affair with Sara Keays, his personal secretary. The
following day Thatcher received a personal letter from Sara Keays's
father revealing she was pregnant with Cecil's child. She showed
Parkinson the letter when he arrived for lunch. She kept him in the
Cabinet and reluctantly sent Sir Geoffrey Howe to the Foreign Office,
a decision she was sorely to regret. The scene then shifted to the
Blackpool conference. Parkinson had publicly admitted the affair but
said he was staying with his wife. During the week I contributed to a
front-page story revealing that Parkinson would have been foreign
secretary but for the affair. Vindication!

On the Thursday of conference, the political editor Julian Haviland,
his number two Tony Bevins and I were told by the news desk that
Sara Keays had given *The Times* an interview that day and that we
should stand by to react when the paper hit the streets.

Speaking to Richard Dowden, Keays said Parkinson had first
proposed to her four years ago and again on election day. But seven
weeks later he had told her he no longer intended to marry her.
Speaking at her father's home near Bath, she said she had 'implored'
him to tell the Prime Minister but he had refused. She had decided to

speak only 'because of my duty to do so'. 'My baby was conceived in a longstanding, loving relationship which I allowed to continue because I believed in our eventual marriage,' she said. It was a sensational story and we enjoyed the rumpus as our colleagues from other papers exited the bar at the Imperial Hotel and ran around doing follow-ups.

It was a stormy night and I remember struggling to stay upright in the wind as I wandered from the Imperial back to my hotel at around 3 a.m., only to return four hours later in the hope of catching Parkinson and other ministers early in the day. Parkinson's position was untenable and he resigned quickly.

Such was the lottery of politics. But for Parkinson's affair, Thatcher would have had a foreign secretary with whom she felt happy, the tie-up between Chancellor Nigel Lawson and Foreign Secretary Geoffrey Howe that opposed her – fatally – over Europe would not have happened, and, who knows, she might have gone on and won a fourth election.

Parkinson died in January 2016 at the age of 84 after a battle with cancer. The obituaries all told of a career that had effectively been ruined by the Keays affair, and suggested that Parkinson could well have become prime minister but for it.

It is beyond doubt that back in 1983 Thatcher was already thinking of Parkinson as an heir apparent. And looking back on that lunch in Ma Cuisine, it is quite clear that even then she trusted him enough to talk about the make-up of her Government.

What was surprising, in retrospect, was that we saw no sign in Parkinson that day of the inner turmoil he must have been suffering over his relationship with Sara Keays. He must at the time have been weighing in his mind the best possible time to tell his patron about it; but he must also have felt that its revelation to Thatcher would not have stopped his elevation to the Foreign Office; otherwise why on earth allow three national newspaper journalists to think it was going to happen?

I have one further postscript to our famous lunch. I have learnt recently that in September 1983 – a few days before the Labour conference and two weeks before the fateful Conservative conference in Blackpool – Margaret van Hattem returned to her Commons office after lunch bubbling with excitement and telling her then boss, Peter

Riddell, that she needed a private word. She had picked up exclusive news of the whole Parkinson saga – the affair and the baby – that was shortly to surface. Riddell went down to the *FT* head office that afternoon and retold the story that Margaret had uncovered. The line from on high was that this was 'not an *FT* story' and it was not run, denying Margaret another scoop. We know not where she discovered the story. One possibility, of course, is that Parkinson, who clearly liked her, handed her the story in order to get it out in what he hoped would be as respectable as possible a way, but it is more likely that it came from a Government official. The story came out during the Labour conference, leaving Margaret ruing the *FT* command's lofty decision.

Parkinson stayed on the back-benches, serving his time during the 1983 parliament, and Thatcher brought him back in her 1987 victory reshuffle. But Parkinson's career had peaked early and was never to recover. When Thatcher was forced out in 1990, Parkinson was the only minister to resign with his stricken heroine, refusing to serve alongside the ministers who had helped to bring her down.

He went to the Lords but was to perform one last service to the party. In the wake of the Tory electoral defeat in 1997, he returned to his old post as party chairman for a year to help steady his party's nerves. It was during this period that the Conservatives instituted the reform of electing its future leaders by a vote of the membership rather than of MPs, a move that was to ensure the election of Iain Duncan Smith over Kenneth Clarke in 2001. Thereafter Parkinson devoted his life to business and golf. Like me, he would play occasionally for the Parliamentary Golf Society and I had several enjoyable rounds with him as he reminisced amusingly about 'Margaret and Denis'.

Dangerous Travelling
with Thatcher

The hacks were getting restless. We had been travelling all over the country with Margaret Thatcher in the press bus following her own 'Battle Bus'. We had been listening to the same speech, or variants of it, for days on end. We kept asking her press minders to let us see her and get some new material from her. We were getting fed up. A visit to a Harry Ramsden chip shop up in Yorkshire had been our highlight of the week so far.

Then they relented. Without any warning we were told on Friday, 27 May 1983 that we were heading to Newbury Racecourse in Berkshire, where the Prime Minister would be available for our questions. We had nagged them into submission.

It was worth it. The Prime Minister used the occasion to ask for an 'unusually large' majority on 9 June to give her the opportunity to play an even bigger role on the world stage. It was the eve of her departure to the United States for a summit of world leaders at Williamsburg in Virginia, and she pointed out that, apart from Pierre Trudeau of Canada, she had been in power for longer than any of the other leaders she would be meeting. 'Already one feels oneself taking a more forceful leadership role because of the combination of one's own style and one's own experience,' she said in reply to a question from *The Times* while standing on a hastily erected platform.

For the travelling pack, starved of a decent story for weeks, this was gold dust. 'She's done Britain. Now Thatcher wants to conquer the world!' shouted an excited colleague, preparing his spiel for his news desk. But we were out in the middle of a racecourse and there were no phones. What to do?

I often tell this story to my younger colleagues who cannot imagine the life of a reporter before the advent of the mobile phone, or e-mails for that matter. We took a decision. Thatcher was heading back to London. We asked our driver to take us along the M4 to Reading and drop us off so that we could find phones. He agreed but decreed that we would be given half an hour and no more. If we had not returned to the bus he would have to leave us behind.

He pulled up in the centre of Reading and twenty of us raced off the bus in different directions to look for the nearest phone box. I knew Reading and ran fast to the station, found a phone and got on to a copy-taker, pleading with him to type as fast as possible because I'd had a long week and wanted to get home. It was only after I'd finished that I asked him to put me through to the news desk so that I could tell them about the story I had filed. I raced back to the bus and was one of only a handful that made it. The rest had to get the train back to London. What days they were!

I got one of my favourite datelines the next morning. On the front page, 'Philip Webster, Newbury' recorded that the Prime Minister had asked for a big majority to give her the authority 'to play an increasingly prominent role in world affairs', adding that she saw no dangers in a landslide. 'We have to win by a large enough majority to hold the Parliament for five years. There is so much at stake internationally.' She was using the 'royal we'. 'Thatcher hopes for greater world role' was the headline. Virtually all my colleagues got similar front-page treatment and made it home, one way or another, happy.

I was with Thatcher throughout both the 1983 and 1987 elections. To the outside observer she was always heading for landslide victories in both. But she had her 'wobbly' moments. I remembered how, on the Thursday before her 1987 election victory, she and her press and policy team had been totally distracted out on the road. True, there had been a couple of polls showing Labour improving but what we did not know – until a future *Times* editor, Peter Stothard, revealed it in *The Times* after the election – was that there had been an almighty wobble when Thatcher's own internal research showed that the gap was narrowing sharply. It led to the resurfacing of angry Cabinet recriminations dating back to the Westland affair (when ministers fought over whether the Americans or Europeans should rescue an ailing helicopter company), a reworking of the campaign and her final speeches, and a victory that most would have predicted from the start. In Tory folklore it became known as 'Wobbly Thursday'.

The 1983 campaign had been largely uneventful till the end. On the last Sunday night before polling, there was a strange event at Wembley Conference Centre when sports stars and show business performers joined 2,500 young people in what I called 'an adoring display of allegiance'. This was the infamous occasion when Kenny Everett appeared on stage and suggested bombing Russia as well as 'kicking Michael Foot's sticks away'.

Just as a world summit fell conveniently for her in 1983, another did in 1987. Two days before polling, we all landed in Venice, where helpful pictures of Thatcher on the world stage again, dining with President Reagan, would have pleased the Tory image-makers. Fellow leaders even agreed to keep the agenda tight so that she could get back for her final campaigning. One of our colleagues, who had arrived before the rest of us, had discovered that the leaders were using bullet-proof gondolas – I am not jesting – for their trips along the canals, so a security story was there for the taking.

It was good sometimes to see history being made, and I was with Thatcher in Lille, northern France, on 20 January 1986, when she and President Mitterrand gave the go-ahead to the building of the Channel Tunnel. Both of them remarked that they were fulfilling an idea first suggested by Napoleon and held out the hope that one day there would be a road link as well.

I was with Thatcher again, in Washington in late 1989, when once more huge international events were mingling with her political troubles at home. She met the first President Bush at Camp David – to talk about the implications for the world of the fall of the Berlin Wall and other developments in Eastern Europe – the day after giving an interview to my boss, Robin Oakley, in which, rather than responding to concerns among Tory MPs about her leadership, she said she had no intention of giving up the party leadership in the next parliament. Indeed, she implied that she would be ready to fight a fifth election 'by popular acclaim'.

At the time, Tory back-bencher Sir Anthony Meyer had launched the first challenge to her leadership. In Washington we questioned her about that as well as her meeting with Bush, which had resulted in an agreement that the West must maintain its guard because the Cold War was not yet over. She declared that she was not 'a lame duck' leader after Sir Anthony had reacted to the *Times* interview by suggesting it was time for the party to decide whether it wanted 'a president for life'. Thatcher retorted: 'I have never regarded myself in that way. I regarded it then, as now, the biggest possible honour to be elected for my constituency and to be prime minister.'

I travelled with Mrs Thatcher again only two months before her removal from office. By then – September 1990 – her caution about the Cold War had gone and – speaking in Prague – she urged the European Community to open its doors to all the countries of Eastern Europe. She got a rapturous reception as she entered the federal assembly chamber and Alexander Dubcek, the father of the Prague Spring in 1968 and in 1990 chairman of the assembly, told her: 'For us you are not the Iron Lady. You are the Kind Lady.'

She must have wished that her MPs back home appreciated her as much.

How Thatcher Decided Our Fate: Fly On

It was the end of a productive trip as far as the travelling Lobby pack was concerned. A massive demo, one of the biggest Norway had seen, had happened in the centre of the capital the previous night and given us plenty to write home about. There had also been something of a spat between our Prime Minister and her Norwegian counterpart.

We lifted off out of Oslo's Fornebu Airport on a Friday evening in an RAF VC10, carrying Thatcher, her husband Denis, a few Downing Street officials and us. About forty in all. Only we did not get too far too quickly. Almost as soon as we had got into the air, the plane slowed noticeably and, while the take-off was not aborted, we did not seem to be going very fast. In fact, it seemed as if we were going to return to the airport as the plane laboured.

In a VC10 you sit with your backs to the cockpit and the small first-class cabin is in front of you. At this point the captain, the wonderfully named Squadron Leader Jimmy Jewell, walked urgently through the main cabin and into the first-class territory containing the Prime Minister and her husband. After a minute or so he emerged, returned to the cockpit and within seconds there was a roar of the engines and the plane was up and away and heading for Heathrow. The incident was soon put to one side as we enjoyed the RAF hospitality on the way home, with none of the crew divulging anything about the captain's visit.

As we landed at Heathrow, however, the picture changed rapidly. Fire engines and ambulances were lining both sides of the runway and as the plane touched down, they followed it along the runway to the VIP suite near Terminal 4. We were ordered to get off the plane as swiftly as possible. The Thatcher party was out within seconds. Within seconds of us leaving the plane, police went on board with sniffer dogs. The aircraft was then towed away to a more remote part of the airport.

By now it was clear something serious was afoot. As we waited in the suite for our luggage to come off the aircraft, we were told the whole story by an official. Just after the plane took off, an anonymous call to a newspaper office in Oslo said a bomb had been put on board. The message was passed on to air traffic control at the military airport and it was quickly flashed to Captain Jimmy Jewell.

We were off the ground when he received it. He decided that he should tell the Prime Minister. After listening to his explanation, and his assurance that the plane had been under watch throughout the trip, she told him: 'Fly on. We will not bow to terrorism.' I wrote in a story on the front page the next day that, although it was clear that the warning was taken highly seriously, Mrs Thatcher expressed her total confidence in the security of the plane.

Reflecting on this drama as I drove home from the airport, it occurred to me that I, and everyone else on the plane, literally had our lives in the Prime Minister's hands after that warning came through. We certainly had no vote over our destiny; indeed, we were not even told that we were under any kind of threat. I wondered whether the crew, had it been on its own and received the call, would have taken the plane down or gone on. Eventually, I decided, it was better not to have known.

The reasons for the concern were obvious because at least some of the demonstrations in Oslo the previous night were inspired by IRA sympathizers. An embarrassed Gro Harlem Brundtland, the Norwegian prime minister, ordered an inquiry into the failure of the police to prevent hundreds of demonstrators forcing their way into the grounds of the 800-year-old castle where Thatcher was to attend a banquet. Brundtland said: 'Last night was not pleasant for me as a hostess. It was embarrassing and regrettable. I apologized to our guests. A police inquiry has started.'

Asked whether she had been surprised by the strength of public opposition to her, Thatcher said: 'No. I am used to demonstrations. These looked as if they were very professionally organized.' It was one of the biggest demos Thatcher had faced since taking office and the rest of the Lobby had Gordon Greig, then political editor of the *Daily Mail*, to thank for being made aware of it.

We were left at our hotel while the Thatcher party had gone off to the dinner and we had no knowledge that trouble was brewing in what seemed an unlikely place for a big demo. We were thinking about having dinner ourselves but Gordon was tipped off by a security source and he kindly shared the news with us.

The confrontation between Mrs Thatcher and Brundtland – the Norwegian Socialist leader and the only other female prime minister in Europe at the time – had been eagerly awaited in Norway. She delivered what amounted to a public lecture in which she drew attention to the two governments' differences on acid rain and South Africa and attacked Britain's attitude to the welfare state and unemployment.

Thatcher had prepared a polite speech for a lunch, telling the people of Tromsø that they sat 'in the front line of the defence of freedom'. But she sat grim-faced as Brundtland, who had a reputation as the Iron Lady of Nordic politics, lost no time in highlighting the issues which she said marred otherwise smooth relations between the two countries. She made a thinly veiled reference to the North–South divide in Britain. She also said the Norwegian Government was determined to ensure that employment opportunities and social benefits 'are available to all of our residents'.

Thatcher did not hit back at Brundtland. It was clear that she did not want to raise the political temperature of her visit and probably accepted that the remarks were aimed at her counterpart's domestic political audience. But she was clearly shaken by the strength of the demonstrations against her.

That was on the Thursday night. But by Friday she was again in no mood for turning.

Some Stories Are
Just Too Good ...

It was just after my birthday in June 1985 when I thought I had been given a late present.

At around 6.30 p.m. the phone on the desk of my boss, Julian Haviland, in The Times Room at the Commons rang. I was finishing off a story and was alone. I picked up the call and it was my editor, Charles Douglas-Home, calling from hospital where he was being treated for cancer.

Charlie loved a story and he told me he had got a corker. He then proceeded to read out the details of a Cabinet reshuffle which, he recounted, had just been given to him by a confidant of Margaret Thatcher, who had himself been in to see the Prime Minister that day. Charlie seemed to have got every last detail. He told me he would ring the Back-bench, that part of the office where late decisions on placing of stories is made, and tell them that I would be supplying them with a splash in the next hour or so.

His final instruction was slightly worrying, He told me not to check it with Bernard Ingham, the Prime Minister's press secretary, who would, he said, be duty-bound to deny it. That went against the grain for many reasons, as there were things that Charlie had not told me, like the timing of the reshuffle, that I would have liked to run past Bernard.

I had by then learnt that the way to deal with Bernard – a gruff no-nonsense Yorkshireman – was to play it straight. As a very green Lobby man in 1981, I once rang him with half a story and, by way of an opening remark, said that I intended to run a story saying something or the other. 'Then you won't be needing me,' said Bernard tartly and the conversation ended. Had I said to him that I had heard a rumour X and would run it if it was true, and only he could tell me whether it was, it would have been different. But in Bernard's eyes I was trying to get it both ways.

The next time I had a big story to check with him, I played it very differently. Weeks later the great Peter Hennessy, then our Whitehall correspondent, rang me to say he had heard a rumour that Thatcher would announce soon that the old Civil Service Department was going to be wound up, with power transferred to the Prime Minister's Office and Cabinet Office. I called Bernard and told him what I had heard. Could he possibly stand it up? He told me that, although it would be inconvenient to see the story in *The Times* the next day, he could not deny it. We splashed on it. Thank you, Bernard. I should interject here that one of the great myths that was allowed to take root was that the era of spin came with the advent of New Labour. Rubbish. Bernard and those who followed him – and some others like Joe Haines, press man for Harold Wilson – could spin with the best of them.

Now here was my editor instructing me not to call the press secretary. When Julian returned to the office, I told him what had happened and we agreed that the editor was in the best position to know and that we should not call because, whatever else he might be able to confirm, Bernard would be unable to stand up any names I put to him, as the ministers themselves clearly had not been told. So I wrote the story predicting that Thatcher would sack two ministers, promote long-time 'wet' Peter Walker, make Norman Tebbit party chairman and promote Lord Young of Graffham. I inserted so many details into the piece that it looked as if I had the full Cabinet list in front of me.

I swiftly ran it all past an excited Charlie and we were up and running. The story, when it landed late that evening, brought the usual 'no comment on Cabinet speculation' responses from the unfortunate Downing Street press officers on late duty. But by the time of the morning Lobby briefing Bernard was ready to knock down the story and deny that a reshuffle was around the corner.

It was a couple of days later when I got a lovely handwritten note from Charlie. It said: 'Well done, Phil. Some stories are so good they repel the truth!' It was a huge relief to hear that the boss was happy, and he had provided me with an all-encompassing excuse for any story I or any other reporter was to get wrong in future. I can only say thirty years later that it was an excuse I never used again.

Whether our story had delayed the Cabinet reconstruction we never knew. But when the Prime Minister finally carried it out in September, it was not of the scale that we had predicted back in June. If I say that we were half-right in our forecasts, that would be being kind to *The Times*, but one of the two ministers I predicted for the chop was dismissed, Tebbit got the chairmanship and Lord Young was promoted. Crucially, though, Peter Walker did not get a leg-up as we had confidently foretold.

Alan Clark, the diarist, was later to claim that he had been Charlie's source. But he appears to have got his dates mixed up. In an entry for June 1984 Clark tells of a dinner with Charlie at which they had indeed discussed changes Thatcher might make to her Government. But that was a full year before Charlie had called me. They may have had another discussion but this was not noted in the diaries.

What the entry confirmed, however, was how well aware Charlie was of Thatcher's thinking. He told Clark of a dinner he had just had with Thatcher at Dorneywood, then the official residence of Willie Whitelaw, the home secretary. Clark wrote: 'She sat on a sofa with him (Charlie) and drank three Cointreaux and told him she would not bring Cecil (Parkinson, who had to resign in 1983) back into the Government.' He went on: 'Charlie says the PM is extremely worried about the succession and that is why she intends to stay on for longer than she would have preferred.'

They then had a lengthy discussion about the inner Cabinet and Clark recounts: 'I told Charlie how I had put the brakes on David Young (Lord Young of Graffham, who was being considered for promotion).'

All this proved that my editor was at the time well in tune with the thinking of the Prime Minister, who clearly did not mind telling him her thoughts on Cabinet make-up. When he spoke to me that night in June 1985, Charlie was adamant that his informant had seen Thatcher recently. The Clark diaries suggest that he (Charlie) might well have been that informant but was following the rules of the game. Charlie was old school and if his informant was Thatcher he would not have told me. I have always assumed it was.

On the day the story appeared, I spoke to Bernard following the afternoon Lobby meeting up in our eyrie at the top of the building. He was utterly charming and had clearly enjoyed pouring cold water all over my work. But I think he knew how the story had emerged, because he told me he did not think it would do me any harm. Certainly, Bernard would have known better than anyone which of the editors his boss was in the habit of talking to. That, I have since assumed, is why he was so light on me and my story.

Westland and Wapping Wars

The frail-looking table was shaking. Standing on it and addressing his staff was the editor of *The Times*, Charles Wilson. I thought it was going to collapse. 'The next edition of *The Times* will be printed in Tower Hamlets,' he told us.

It was a Friday evening in New Printing House Square, the paper's office on Gray's Inn Road, and we had been told that that night's paper would not be coming out. Monday's would, but in another office. I was on Sunday duty. I knew even then what my story would be.

The industrial war of Wapping – which was to change and probably save the newspaper industry – happened right in the middle of the political war over Britain's helicopter business. In the days leading up to News International's overnight move during its latest dispute with the print unions, Margaret Thatcher's Government was convulsed by the Westland crisis.

Westland Helicopters, our last manufacturer, was at the centre of a ferocious rescue bid row. Michael Heseltine, the defence secretary, favoured a European solution integrating Westland and British Aerospace with Italian and French companies. Thatcher and her industry secretary, Leon Brittan, wanted to see Westland merge with Sikorsky, an American company. It was a battle that led to the walkout of Heseltine and the downfall of Brittan, and at one time threatened the future of Thatcher herself.

A letter from Heseltine, stating that Westland would lose European orders if the Sikorsky option was chosen, was referred at Thatcher's orders to Solicitor General Sir Patrick Mayhew. Mayhew wrote to

Heseltine noting 'material inaccuracies' in his original claims. It was the disclosure of Mayhew's letter by an industry department official that provoked uproar because it appeared as if the Government was officially leaking against one of its Cabinet members.

As the row went on, a Cabinet meeting on 9 January 1986 provoked further disagreement over whether the policy of collective responsibility was being followed. Heseltine gathered up his papers and, declaring that he could no longer be a member of the Cabinet, walked out into the street and announced his resignation. It was fantastic theatre for the waiting reporters. It was the beginning of his period of exile that was to result in him challenging Thatcher for the leadership four years later.

The Cabinet secretary held an investigation into the leaking of Mayhew's letter, which found that Brittan had told an official to leak it. Thatcher was reported later to have asked Brittan four times why he did not tell her. Thatcher's own future looked shaky as politicians questioned whether she, or at least her press secretary, Bernard Ingham, would have known about the shenanigans over the Mayhew letter.

It was a sensational story, but suddenly something just as astonishing was to take over the lives of journalists and everyone else at *The Times*. In the edition of Friday, 24 January, I wrote – although I did not know it at the time – the last splash story to be printed from our headquarters in Gray's Inn Road, where we had been since our move from Printing House Square at Blackfriars eleven years before.

The story said that pressure on Brittan to resign had grown after Thatcher revealed in the Commons that a critical leak during the Westland affair had been personally authorized by him. At a private meeting of the back-bench 1922 Committee – the committee of all Tory back-benchers (formed after the 1922 general election) that meets weekly when Parliament is sitting – well over half of the twenty speakers called for him to go. Ministers do not survive that kind of mauling and on that Friday afternoon, Brittan went in to see Thatcher and offered his resignation because, he said later, it had become clear he no longer had the confidence of his colleagues. Before his departure was announced, I agreed with the news desk that I should get on the same train as Brittan as he headed to his constituency of Richmond in Yorkshire for the weekend. I would try to get a one-to-one interview with him.

These were the days before the mobile phone and as I waited with my ticket at King's Cross for Brittan to arrive, I thought to give the news desk one more call from a telephone kiosk to grab the latest news from Westminster. It was at this point I was instructed: 'Phil, don't go to Yorkshire; come to the office. There's no paper tomorrow.' Forgetting to cash back the ticket, I ran the short distance from the station to the office to find out what was going on.

Soon after, Wilson, who had taken over as editor after the death of Charles Douglas-Home, clambered on top of the rickety table. The upshot was that we had seen the last of hot-metal production of our newspapers. The company was in dispute with the main print unions, the Society of Graphical and Allied Trades and the National Graphical Association, and, thanks to months of secret planning, we would be moving premises immediately. Some 6,000 workers had gone on strike following the collapse of the talks and were served with notices of dismissal. Members of the Electrical, Electronic, Telecommunications and Plumbing Union would be brought in to produce the newspapers.

Wilson asked those of us who were on duty on Sunday to report to the new premises. Anticipating picket lines, he said that buses would be laid on to help journalists get into work. The next editions of News International's four papers – *The Times*, *The Sunday Times*, *The Sun* and the *News of the World* – would be produced electronically without print union labour.

It was a momentous event and produced shockwaves through the office. Friendships were to be strained and loyalties tested over the next few months and years. I had to make an immediate decision. The National Union of Journalists, of which I was a member, told *Times* journalists that they should not be crossing picket lines, and over Saturday I came under pressure from colleagues not to go in. Although many in the print unions at Gray's Inn Road were people I knew and liked – one of my duties during my years as a gallery reporter was to travel to the office each evening to oversee the composition of the parliamentary pages in the paper – I had little sympathy with the leadership of their unions, whom I felt had brought them to this crisis point. As a veteran of the 1978–9 closure, I believed that the print unions had far too much power and I was privately pleased that they were being taken on.

Many of my colleagues felt the opposite and some – dubbed the *refuseniks* – never went to Wapping, ending up a few months later on *The Independent* when it was launched. Those of us working on that Sunday felt particular pressure. I had no doubt that it was my duty to turn up and continue reporting the Westland story for the paper. I did not like the fact that friends who were not due to be on that day were ringing to tell me I should not work.

I woke on the Sunday to news that *The Sunday Times* and the *News of the World* had been published overnight despite massive protests around the Wapping plant. Sunday, in those days, was the only day we went into the head office. During the rest of the week we were based at the Commons. I decided this was not a day for the car, and took the Tube to Tower Hill. The offices, which of course I had never seen, were easy to find because of the mass of pickets and television cameras around the Pennington Street entrance. I walked in, trying and failing to avoid familiar faces in the picket lines. I got a 'Shame on you, Phil' from one of the compositors with whom I had worked for years.

That, in fact, was the easiest part of the day. Like many of my colleagues – and it seems hard to believe now – I had never used a computer in my life. Only a very select handful of *Times* staff knew in advance about the secret plans to shift locations and there was no opportunity for training. Wilson and Tony Norbury, the production editor, had been closely involved, shifting back and forth between offices without anyone knowing.

News International had flown in a team of brilliant technical experts from America and, at our desks that Sunday morning, they gave us our first lesson in computer usage. They were to stand over us all day as we learnt the mysteries of electronic production and tried to forget our beloved typewriters, never to be seen in the office again.

I could not really see how we were going to get a paper out. At that moment none of the phones were working, or even connected. Mobiles were years away. I wanted to talk to Downing Street to find out the latest on Westland, but there was no way. So I concentrated on learning computers fast. They were trying to get us connected to the Press Association and Reuters newswires, but without success at this stage.

My one hope for contact with the outside world was a solitary television set in the corner of the newsroom. I knew that Douglas Hurd, the home secretary, was due to appear for a lunchtime interview. The news desk had told me they would want me to write a splash, a page-two lead, and probably a spread inside the paper. I was watching Hurd, avidly taking down every word in the belief that it might be all that I would have at the end of the day, when I realized that I was not alone.

'Who's this? He's good.'

It was Rupert Murdoch. It was my first meeting with the chairman of News International. I told him it was Hurd. My desire to be polite towards the ultimate boss was balanced by the need not to miss a word of what Hurd was saying. After a very brief chat he moved on, with me assuring him that Hurd had already said enough to give the paper a splash for the morning.

As it happened, Thatcher herself gave an interview later to the Channel 4 programme *Face the Press*. Thatcher, looking apprehensive, had tried to unite her troops behind her by putting the blame on Heseltine. With the phones cranking into life later in the afternoon, there was now every chance we were going to get a paper out, provided nothing went wrong with the new technology. And so it came to pass that by around 7.30 p.m. I had given the news desk what it wanted.

Having written the last splash out of Gray's Inn Road, I now wrote the first out of Wapping. It told of how Thatcher would try to restore the Government's credibility after the biggest crisis since she became leader by giving the Commons answers to questions about the role of Government in the Westland leak. For me that was Day One at Wapping. *The Times* appeared the next morning with a splash headline over my story saying 'Ministers rally to Thatcher on Westland leak'. Also on the front page was a story in which Rupert Murdoch said he was delighted with the success of the operation to transfer production to Wapping. 'I'm not quite sure how we managed to keep it a secret,' he added.

For me and others who had gone into work, the day was far from over. We went on to Red Lion Square, where the *Times* chapel of the NUJ had been meeting for much of the day. There was a frosty atmosphere as we walked in. Nobody called us 'scabs' but you wondered if that was in their minds. Perhaps that was understandable. But we had got the paper out, and the newspaper business was never to be quite the same again.

It was only the start of the dispute, and our place of work justly earned the description Fortress Wapping, as police battled for months to contain demonstrations and allow people to get to work. As Jon Henley recorded in *The Guardian* on the twenty-fifth anniversary of the move:

Just over a year later, the strikers were exhausted and demoralised, and the unions were facing bankruptcy and court action. Some 1,262 people had been arrested and 410 police injured. News International had not lost one day of production, and the balance in British industrial relations had shifted.

For some, Wapping planted a decisive nail in the coffin of what Andrew Neil, a former Murdoch editor, has described as 'all that was wrong with British industry: pusillanimous management, pig-headed unions, crazy restrictive practices, endless strikes and industrial disruption, and archaic technology'. This dispute, Neil says, 'changed all that'.

Many in the newspaper business – including some who criticized Murdoch at the time – now concede that the end of Fleet Street's Spanish practices probably helped prolong the life of the British press by a good few decades. (Others, including the many 'refuseniks' who declined to move to Wapping, argue the dispute shattered journalistic self-respect for ever, subjugating journalists once and for all to the will of the bean-counters.)

For me on 26 January 1986, there was a choice to be made. I'm glad I made the one I did.

A Horse, A Horse –
My Paper for a Horse

Charles Wilson, my fourth editor at *The Times*, faced a staff crisis when *The Independent* was launched amid great fanfare in October 1986. Today *The Indy* is only with us in online format, the paper version having ended in March 2016. But back then, the appearance of a brand-new paper committed to being what it said on its masthead was a threat to *The Times* and presented serious competition for other papers as well.

It produced a dilemma for many reporters on *The Times*, who were worn down by the length and sheer unpleasantness of the Wapping dispute. *The Independent's* founders – Andreas Whittam Smith, Matthew Symonds and Stephen Glover – judged there was a market for a fresh, objective source of news, and journalists across the national titles were excited by the prospect. They also liked the name.

By then, after our shock move in January 1986, *The Times* had settled into its new premises not far from the Thames east of Tower Bridge. *The Times's* political staff, of which I was then the number three, was in some disarray. Julian Haviland, political editor and my boss since 1981, had announced his intention to leave journalism. Anthony Bevins, political correspondent and the number two, was – along with many other *Times* names – approached by *The Independent*. Tony, a dear colleague who died suddenly in 2001 from pneumonia, had never been happy since the move to Wapping and decided to take the job of the new paper's first political editor. He had famously said at a union meeting: 'I will go to Wapping with ashes in my mouth.'

He approached me and another colleague on the team, Richard Evans – who is one of my closest friends and responsible for encour-

aging me to play golf, and therefore indirectly responsible for many of
the chapters in this book. We discussed the approaches to move
together and with Tony. A couple of years earlier, I had turned down
an offer to join the *Daily Mail* when Paul Dacre, acting on behalf of
the *Mail's* then editor David English, spent the whole of a May Day
weekend (starting with an interview at a hotel by the Thames, and
then on the phone several times later) trying to coax me across with
promises of better treatment for my exclusive stories (a file of which
he brought with him) and more money. I resisted his charming and
flattering approach. Now I did not want to go through another bout
of soul-searching.

Before either of us had given our decisions to Tony, a story leaked
in *Private Eye* that the whole of the *Times* political staff was going to
move across to *The Independent*. Charles Wilson had by then received
resignation letters from several other prominent members of staff and
a mood of crisis enveloped the top of *The Times*. It was already clear
that labour editor Don Macintyre and colleagues Dave Felton and
Barrie Clement – who had declined to move to Wapping on
conscience grounds and became known among others as the *refuseniks*
– would go to *The Independent*, as did Colin Hughes, an excellent
young reporter who was to go on to be deputy editor of his new
paper.

Both Richard and I felt a personal loyalty to Charlie, of whom we
were very fond. Our shared interest with Charlie in horse racing
helped. When Charlie joined *The Times* as executive editor under
Charles Douglas-Home, he had sought me out at the Commons and
demanded to be taken to the bars. We were friends from then on.

The news that the whole Lobby team might be doing a bunk
reached Charlie when he was having a brief break on the island of
Lanzarote. I was up in Yorkshire covering the Ryedale by-election,
which resulted in a stunning loss by the Conservatives to the Lib-SDP
Alliance. Charlie phoned me and told me he was flying home and
asked whether we could meet – outside the office. I drove back that
night and agreed to meet him in the Tower Hotel on Tower Bridge, a
few hundred yards from the Wapping plant.

It was one of the most astonishing meetings of my life and the one
that put me on the path to the top reporting job in political journalism. Charlie asked for my help in saving the paper, as he dramatically

put it. I told him that Tony was beyond recall and would be going. 'What about you?' he asked. I told him I would be staying but would obviously need to be promoted. I suggested the title of chief political correspondent. Amazingly, yet it is true, I turned down his suggestion that I should take over as political editor.

I told him I needed a few more years in the Lobby before rising to that august post. He replied that if I didn't take it, I might be off in a few months. I told him that I would not. So he asked me who should be the political editor. I suggested Robin Oakley, who was then a senior political journalist at the *Mail*. Ironically, it was Robin who had earlier put me in touch with Paul Dacre over the *Mail* job. Charlie promised to see Robin and it was not long before he was appointed.

At our meeting Charlie had then asked: 'What about Richard?' I suggested that Evans was a brilliant Lobby journalist and that we could not afford to let him go. Indeed, the team would be me and him for the time being. Charlie agreed he would see Richard straightaway. I rang Richard and told him not to sign anything yet. Evans was in Scotland covering a political conference when the call from Wilson came. According to Richard, it went something like this:

'Where are you?' Wilson asked.

'In Scotland, Charlie.'

'When do you get back?'

'Tomorrow [Saturday] morning, on the sleeper.'

'Go home, clean your teeth … and come and see me – at home.'

Evans went to Charlie's Holland Park home, where he was wooed with a big increase in salary and Charlie's paeans of praise. Richard stayed. After covering Neil Kinnock's travels in the 1987 election, Evans became media editor. By now, after a visit to Paddy Mullins's stables in Ireland, he had become obsessed with horse racing. Charlie told him that he could become racing correspondent when the incumbent, Michael Seeley, retired. Charlie's promise was honoured by Simon Jenkins when he took over as editor.

Back in 1986, Charlie had at least saved the political staff, and the drift of staff to *The Independent* slowed. But he had not finished his efforts at team-building. He suggested to several of us that it was time we jointly owned a horse, and asked Evans, helped by his pay rise, to organize it. Evans took advice from experts and we formed a syndicate – headed by Wilson and including Tom Clarke (the sports editor), the

new recruit Oakley, me, Richard, John Young (agriculture correspondent), Marcel Berlins (legal correspondent) and John Jinks (news editor).

We opted to buy a horse that was in training with Simon Christian
at Lambourn. We came up with the name Sunday for Monday – a
newspaper term for a story that has been saved up for the weekend to
make a splash in Monday's paper – for this nag that was to carry the
hopes of *The Times* for the next few years. The silks were deliberately
chosen to be black and white and re(a)d – like a newspaper.

Sunday for Monday was not the greatest piece of horseflesh to
grace the tracks of Britain. In fact, it turned out to have a propensity
to burst blood vessels when travelling at speed, which is not a helpful
attribute for a horse that you want to run as fast as possible. The dear
old thing gave us a few places in races with small fields but it was clear
there was no danger of any of us getting rich on this one. After eighteen months, the horse was moved to a new trainer, Ron Hodges in
Somerset, who swiftly told us the animal was a 'bleeder' – slightly
more polite than some of the epithets we had thrown at it in the
previous months – and would never win a race. The last I heard of
Sunday for Monday was that it had become a point-to-point racer in
Norway. Thereafter it may not have had a happy end.

Hodges persuaded many of the syndicate to stick with him, and the
result was that a much more successful beast by the name of Northern
Saddler carried the *Times* colours. As is the way with these volatile
animals, it took some time to work out what the horse really preferred
in terms of length of journey and going of course. The answer was two
miles maximum and mud – once that was established, he went on to
rack up a string of wins running into double figures. He loved Newton
Abbott, with Richard Dunwoody on board.

The last syndicate horse we had was called Keshya, less successful
than the second but more than the first. I remember representing the
syndicate in its last race for us at Yarmouth in Norfolk when we had
put it in a selling race – i.e. we were getting rid of it. We had the
champion jockey Jamie Spencer on board and I had the honour of
meeting up with him in the parade ring. He sounded confident, so the
watching Webster family and friends went off to back him. He came
in second. It was the end of a happy racing career for *The Times* syndicate. None of us made any money but it was a lot of fun.

And it helped to keep *The Times* together.

The Lobby Lunch

Every weekday within a square mile or so of Westminster, small groups of highly committed individuals meet in supposed secrecy at the best restaurants of the day. Usually just before 1p.m., one, two or even three political correspondents will gather at their table and plan the tactics that will play out over the next hour or so.

A few minutes later their guest – a government minister, senior opposition figure, or a powerful political aide – will rush in. Sometimes they look around nervously, hoping no one recognizes them; others, the attention-cravers, look around rather hoping that colleagues or friends will notice that they are about to eat with the political personnel from, say, *The Times* and the *Mail*.

This is the Lobby lunch, an institution that is a central part of the discourse between press and politicians. The Lobby is the collective name given to journalists who are accredited to work in Parliament and attend Downing Street briefings, as well as visiting parts of the building such as the Members' Lobby just outside the chamber to which mere mortals are denied access. Just as in the Members' Lobby, information passed to reporters at lunch or dinner is not attributed to the source directly unless the source asks that it should be. The Lobby system, about which I write later, is the code under which politicians and press interact.

Most of the national newspaper political correspondents are in what they call their Lobby lunch groups. On becoming a member of the Lobby, your boss advises you to join a lunch group or find a colleague of similar experience to set up your own. The rule of thumb tends to be that the more senior the group, the more senior the minister they seek to take out. That is no great disadvantage to the more junior members of the Lobby; in my lengthy experience, I found it was the newcomers to the Government or Opposition front-bench who were more likely to 'sing for their supper', as we put it.

The journalists always – always – pay for the lunch. They cannot be beholden to the politician in any way. If there is more than one reporter, the cost will be shared between the papers involved. For a journalist, the main aims of the Lobby lunch are to get a story and to get to know the guest a little better. If it goes well you may be so bold at the end to ask them for their home and mobile phone numbers just in case you need to call them at a weekend or in the evening. Almost invariably they oblige. And often they become long-term contacts.

Before the guest's arrival, the team will decide broadly what they are going to ask and how to approach it. Sometimes it can feel like a military operation. For the politicians, the objective is to get to know political correspondents whom they would have little chance of meeting under other circumstances. Ministers who spend most of their time stuck in their Whitehall offices often only come to the Commons to speak or vote and have little time to fraternize.

But the way they play their lunchtime gatherings varies hugely depending on the minister. In my experience, some felt they had succeeded if they emerged into the sunlight believing they had told the journalists nothing of note. Some would say triumphantly at the end: 'Well, thank you very much. It was a lovely lunch but I don't think I've told you anything newsworthy.' To which my retort was usually: 'We will be the judge of that.' It was quite rewarding in those circumstances to see the look of alarm that would cross their faces.

Others were far cleverer, and arrived at the lunch armed with a piece of news that they could throw into the conversation – maybe a policy they would be announcing in a fortnight, or a bit of reshuffle gossip – and watch the hungry hacks devour it. In their eyes, buttering up the political correspondents would do them no harm when it came to the twice-yearly bouts of 'who's up, who's down' speculation.

Many, including the most senior, saw the Lobby lunch as the chance to float ideas that had surfaced in their own mind but had not yet reached anywhere near the Government machine. They were flying kites. The journalists would know they were being used and had to be aware that the minister's department might well have to deny that there was any such proposal if you pushed it too hard. Writing such stories in a way that would not attract a denial was an art in itself. The minister would be able to see how the idea went down with the press and his colleagues, and decide whether it was worth pursuing. Sometimes if the journalists ran it hard, the denials would come pretty quickly. Time and again during the last parliament (2010–15), we read that ministers were urging the ending of perks for pensioners such as the winter fuel allowance. Those stories came from lunches. The perks remain intact.

Generally speaking, mean lunchers – those who genuinely felt their aim was to tell you nothing – would not get another invite from the group. The talkers, the indiscreet, would get invited back. Within the Lobby, the politicians who talked were well known and well lunched. And if you saw a similar political story appearing, say, in *The Telegraph* and *The Guardian* you would know that a minister had had lunch with that particular lunch team. Late at night when the news desk called telling you that the same story had appeared in two papers, you would have your response or excuse ready. 'Ah, it must have been a lunch.'

Members of the lunch group take it in turns to send off invites to prospective lunch guests. These end up on the desks of the ministers' diary secretaries, not a senior position in Whitehall but one of far greater power than the title suggests. They would know whom their boss was lunching with and if a story relating to their department were to appear in the papers concerned a couple of days later, they would know who was responsible.

Downing Street, under governments of both colours, had its way of keeping tabs on the Lobby lunch. If something highly controversial emerged in, say, two papers on the same day, its intelligence network would soon find out who was the leaker. But often the story would have been put out with Number 10's full knowledge and encouragement.

In the days when I started as a political correspondent, the lunches were often quite bibulous affairs. The theory was that if you gave the ministers a couple of glasses before turning to the heavy political subjects of the day, you would be more likely to loosen their tongues. I remember once lunching with Alan Cochrane, then of the *Express*, and a home office minister in a restaurant near Waterloo Station. The minister sat down, told us straight off that he was going to announce an important change of Government policy the following day, and then declared: 'Right, that's done. Let's enjoy lunch.' I remember Cochrane filing the story with his paper from a phone box upstairs even before we got out of the restaurant.

But as ministers beseeched the nation to become more health-conscious, their own behaviour changed. There are not so many ministers around now who would expect their hosts to line up a bottle for them as they entered the restaurant. The arrival of the New Labour Government in 1997 saw the appearance of far more bottles of sparkling water on the lunch tables than wine. Towards the end of my spell, it was almost a relief if the guest said 'Well, I will have just a glass', meaning that you could join them for a taste of something good. Ken Clarke remains a much-sought-after lunch companion, not because he is overly indiscreet but because he still believes a good meal should be washed down with a few glasses.

At the end of the Lobby lunch there was a certain ritual. Almost before the guest had got out of the door, the team would discuss what they had got from him or her. These could become rather confused sessions when different members had different recollections of a conversation that had only taken place minutes before. We would decide what stories, if any, we had and when we would write them. Only very rarely would we produce the story that same day, it being taken for granted that we would protect the minister from identification. He might well have been seen entering the restaurant or been witnessed by other ministers there.

On becoming political editor of *The Times*, I carried on doing joint lunches with friends like Elinor Goodman, of Channel 4, and then her successor, Gary Gibbon, and Charles Reiss of the *Evening Standard*. But I would also do one-on-one lunches with senior Cabinet ministers or Opposition figures. Some would feel happier speaking frankly to one journalist rather than a group.

We were always trying to find new eating places that our colleagues had not discovered so that we could grill our political subjects without rivals knowing about it. Otherwise there was always a risk that they would guess the sources of any story that might appear in the next few days. Someone would discover a new restaurant, maybe a little further from Westminster, and the secret would last for a bit. But nearly always the guest would tell other journalists about this nice place they had been taken to the other day in South Ken, and we would be rumbled.

Over the years some of the biggest stories I and other political journalists have written emanated from Lobby lunches. Many are mentioned in this book. I remember getting a heads-up at a lunch in January 2006 that Charles Kennedy was about to resign as leader of the Liberal Democrats. We loved those ministers who were confident enough not to give a damn about being seen talking to journalists.

I remember in 1986 being in Rules, a restaurant in Maiden Lane, Covent Garden, which specializes in traditional food and does the best steak and kidney puddings in the business. Most of the tables were taken and dotted around the place were several groups of journalists, each with a senior figure from the Government or Opposition with them. Rules at this time, however, was well used by the Lobby circuit and was a favourite with some of the politicians.

Into this bustling scene on a Thursday lunchtime rushed the Attorney General, Sir Michael Havers. He was a little late and apologized because a Cabinet committee following the main Thursday Cabinet meeting had dragged on. He was looking forward to a drink, which I and my lunch partner, Charles Reiss from the *Standard*, duly ordered. I had vaguely known Sir Michael from my time as a junior reporter in Norfolk, when he held the senior legal post of Recorder of Norwich. He was a great lunch guest, utterly unpompous and quite indiscreet. In other words, ideal. On this occasion he was extremely animated about a Cabinet discussion that morning concerning the *Spycatcher* affair.

It was at this time that the Government was trying to stop publication in Australia of a book by former senior MI5 officer Peter Wright, which was to provoke uproar when it eventually appeared with its tales of attempts to unmask Soviet moles and alleged assassination plots. Sir Michael was concerned about a complicated side issue to the affair and needed to tell someone.

To our surprise – almost horror – he suddenly pulled out of his pocket a Cabinet paper and thrust it in front of us to illustrate the point he had been making. I spotted the word 'Restricted' at the top and committed as much of it to memory as I could. Charles did the same. We were well aware that our friends on other tables had almost certainly seen this extraordinary act and would be racking their brains as to the subject matter of the top-secret paper that their Lobby colleagues were looking at. For all we knew, the Official Secrets Act might have been broken.

It was already clear to us that if we wrote anything up from this encounter, we would not be able to run it for several days. For a start, our friends in the restaurant would know where it came from. More importantly, there were Cabinet colleagues of Sir Michael in the restaurant and, although he had an attractive devil-may-care attitude on many political matters, it might not have been good for them to know he was leaking Cabinet papers around the place.

I wrote up the story a few days later and, as far as I know, Sir Michael was never fingered as the source. It was a tiny issue compared with the furore later created when *Spycatcher* surfaced but I tell the story because it is a graphic example of the politician using the system and the journalist protecting their source. Detractors of the system would say that the Attorney General was using us. He obviously was, and in a rather risky way. But we were not going to complain about that and would have loved it if more ministers had seen fit to share their Cabinet secrets with us. Sadly that really was a one-off.

As a newcomer to the Lobby in the very early Eighties, I recall taking Michael Heseltine, then environment secretary, to an upmarket restaurant (again in Covent Garden) with Nick Comfort of *The Telegraph*, who was of similar vintage to me. Hezza was quite a catch even then, and we were rather pleased with ourselves to have got him. We then made a schoolboy error, one neither of us would ever repeat. We asked him to choose the wine from what we later saw was a rather top-notch list. The notably attentive waiter whispered to us that Mr Heseltine – even then he was one of the most instantly recognizable of politicians – liked the Montrachet.

It would have been a serious loss of face to have ordered anything else, although once we had sampled the delightful Montrachet, Heseltine said that, to be honest, he was not particularly fussy about wine. No wonder the waiter looked pleased with himself. Nick was distraught when the bill arrived and the cost of the wine well exceeded the sum total of the food. He told me later that he had opted to pay for some of it himself. I claimed but – very unusually – made clear on my expense form the name of the politician who had enjoyed the wine with us.

Madrid – and Dominic Lawson's Star Turn

Margaret Thatcher's fall can be traced back to any number of events. But having covered virtually every cough and spit of the ditching of a leader who had given her party three election victories, I would start the chain of circumstances at the Madrid summit in June 1989 – the gathering that paved the way, eventually, for the introduction of European monetary union and the euro.

The previous year she had gone to Bruges in Belgium and delivered an outspoken attack on the idea of a united Europe, causing deep resentment among the still-strong coterie of pro-Europeans in her Cabinet. But it was over Madrid that she first encountered utter defiance and revolt in her upper command. Madrid was one of those unsatisfactory stories for a Lobby man where you knew you had witnessed something deeply significant but you also knew that you had not really got to the bottom of what it was all about.

It took revelations in later memoirs to make us realize what had been going on. Had we known then that on the eve of the summit her chancellor and foreign secretary – Nigel Lawson and Sir Geoffrey Howe, respectively – had threatened together to resign unless she signed up to the first stages of economic and monetary union – as was to be revealed much later – all would have been clear. In the end, journalists can only write what they have been told and found out, and no one was in the mood for telling at this stage.

So on the Saturday before Madrid, *The Times* and *The Telegraph* both led on stories saying that Thatcher would soften her line at the summit, accepting stage one of the report by Jacques Delors, the European Commission president, which began the process of economic and monetary union and eventually required British membership of the exchange rate mechanism (ERM). I should explain that the ERM was a precursor to the euro. It was a broad exchange rate for what was then the European Community and has become the European Union (EU), designed to keep all countries within the same ballpark; there were upper and lower limits on either side of it that national currencies could not cross, a kind of currency straitjacket.

Further, it was reported by my *Times* colleague Nick Wood that the Prime Minister would signal a willingness to enter into talks on the second and third stages, which called for the formation of a European Central Bank and a common currency. The briefing – notably – was at the Foreign Office and it was given by Sir John Kerr, the permanent secretary.

Bernard Ingham, Thatcher's press secretary, was present but his grumpy countenance suggested he was not enamoured with what was going on. Bernard, an amiable, funny man in private, had an ability to let you know his feelings by the expression on his face. A smiling Bernard told you it was a good day for the PM. But when he scowled or delivered short, sharp retorts at Lobby briefings, you could tell that all was not well back at base.

Both papers reported that the softening of Thatcher's position would be seen as a victory for Lawson and Howe, who had been pressing her to embrace the European Monetary System (EMS). We did not know how hard they had been pressing but the PM felt, probably for the first time since the troubles with the 'wets' in 1981, that her ability to get her own way had been strongly compromised.

Back in 1988 the watchful Nick Wood, reporting from the Scottish Conservative Party conference a full year before the Howe/Lawson ambush, revealed in a splash that Howe had departed from the agreed line. He said of joining the EMS that we must do so when the time is right, before adding: 'We cannot go on forever adding that qualification [i.e. when the time is right] to the underlying commitment.' This was said in an unscripted response to a question from the conference floor. That was the first stirring of revolt.

Thatcher's position in 1989 had been weakened further by a poor Tory performance in the European elections and splits in her party. In her later autobiography, Thatcher blamed Howe for putting Lawson up to the ambush they perpetrated on her on that Sunday before

Madrid. She wrote that she knew Howe always thought one day he might become Tory leader – an ambition that became more passionate as it was slipping away from him:

> This quiet, gentle but deeply ambitious man with his insatiable appetite for compromise was now out to make trouble for me if he possibly could. Above all, I suspect he thought he had become indispensable – a dangerous illusion for a politician. There is no explanation for what he now did and put Nigel up to doing.

They had gone to see her at 8.15 on the Sunday morning for what she called a 'nasty little meeting'. Howe had urged that she speak first, setting out the conditions for joining the EMS and announcing a date for entry into the ERM. They even insisted on the precise formula, which she took down. 'If I did not agree to their terms and their formulation they would both resign.' Looking at those remarks today, the audacity of the attack by the two ministers is astonishing and does not fit with the myth of an invincible prime minister.

I was by now in Madrid. In the hours since the Friday briefing and her arrival, her position toughened and she was beginning to show that she was not going to give in to her two senior colleagues without a fight. We were told by British officials on the Sunday that she would not accept any link between stage one of the Delors report and stages two and three that would lead to the creation of the bank and the single currency.

But crucially for Howe and Lawson, she seemed reluctantly to be ready to say that she would take Britain into the ERM when inflation fell from eight per cent – yes, that was the rate then – to the average of four and a half per cent for the existing nine EMS members, and after the mechanism had proved its strength by surviving the abolition of exchange controls in 1990. The similarity between these conditions and Gordon Brown's tests for the euro in another era is striking.

She was hating every moment of it, as we learnt later, but by a combination of her usual steely determination and buttering-up of other leaders more in tune with her politics, she managed to win some concessions when the Madrid accord was put together. In *The Times* splash after the summit, I wrote that EU leaders took a historic step along the road to monetary union in the face of a defiant pledge by

Thatcher 'to fight all the way to retain British control over economic policy and to resist the imposition of a European currency'.

Despite accepting that the EU could convene an inter-governmental conference to consider changes to the Treaty of Rome, she stopped it happening as early as 1992 – when President Mitterrand of France wanted to – enabling her to claim a tactical victory. But she knew that she had been defeated, by her own ministers as much as fellow leaders, over the principle of economic union, and the federalists were delighted with the summit's conclusion that the first stage would begin on 1 July 1990. It was a decision that was to determine the future of the European Union and effectively bring down two British prime ministers: Thatcher and her successor.

The Prime Minister had been conciliatory, given her damaged position. When she informed leaders in private of her conditions for entering the monetary system, she told them that she hoped they realized she was being 'positive', which raised a few laughs around the table. But Thatcher left Madrid determined that she could never again be put into the kind of position into which Howe and Lawson forced her. She decided that they could not be allowed to work in tandem as she carried out a surprise reshuffle. Two months later, she called in Howe and told him she wanted him out of the Foreign Office. John Major became foreign secretary and Howe, after some wrangling over country houses and his title (he also took the largely meaningless mantle of deputy prime minister), became Commons leader. A dangerous man had become even more of a threat to Thatcher, but no one could have known just how.

For the first time Conservative MPs, including some whom I relied upon for sound advice about the state of the parliamentary party, could see the end of Thatcher coming, and they could see it happening before the next general election. It is rightly said that the Conservatives are far more ruthless than Labour in ditching leaders, as the survival of Michael Foot to fight 1983, Gordon Brown 2010 and Ed Miliband 2015 showed. They carried on despite fledgling plots to remove them. Only Tony Blair, after three victories, was really forced out.

But the Tories had shown throughout their post-war history that they were unsentimental when it came to winning. Now on 26 October 1989 came the biggest crisis so far. Nigel Lawson, unable any longer to accept the role of Thatcher's economic adviser, Alan Walters, suddenly quit the Cabinet after six years as chancellor. He felt undermined by Walters, who was strongly advising Thatcher against the EMS stance adopted by her chancellor. She fought to keep him but refused his demand to sack Walters. In his letter of resignation he wrote:

> The successful conduct of economic policy is possible only if there is, and is seen to be, full agreement between the prime minister and the chancellor. Recent events have confirmed this essential requirement cannot be satisfied as long as Sir Alan Walters remains your personal economic adviser.

While the knowledge of his resignation was hanging over her, Thatcher went to the Commons and made a statement about the Commonwealth summit, winning backing from Tories for her stand against sanctions for South Africa. I wrote that no one would have known that a crisis was enveloping her a few hundred yards away in Number 10.

I had reported back in March 1988 that Lawson's irritation at her interference was so strong that he would leave the Government unless she assured him she would keep out of it. Alan Walters had written several articles opposing membership of the EMS. As Lawson prepared for that year's Budget, he was frustrated that his leader had undermined his exchange-rate policy by ruling out heavy intervention or interest rate cuts to restrain the rise of the pound. I revealed, after speaking to very good sources, that Lawson wanted to present just two more budgets and to become foreign secretary in 1989.

So back in the summer of 1989, Thatcher carried out an immediate reshuffle as Lawson's resignation sent Downing Street into a tailspin. She put John Major into the Treasury, made Douglas Hurd foreign secretary and brought in David Waddington as home secretary. The pound fell and the Commons was suspended before Howe, in an unprecedented move, came in to address MPs and tell them of the Cabinet changes.

In the *Times* splash, I wrote that Howe told a packed Commons of Thatcher's efforts to dissuade Lawson from going. Thatcher had learnt of his intention to resign just before 2.30 p.m. Astonishingly, we were told, it was when Neil Kinnock had earlier asked her in the Commons whether she agreed with Walters's view that the EMS was 'half-baked' that Lawson made up his mind finally, judging her answer to be unsatisfactory. Kinnock had said there were two chancellors running the economy. That was a coup for Kinnock which failed to get the credit it deserved. Walters himself resigned in a transatlantic telephone call the same night, prompting speculation that Major might have made that a condition of accepting the job.

These were great days to be a Lobby correspondent and a Tory MP, if you happened to enjoy the whiff of conspiracy. And there was plenty of that. Michael Heseltine and his lieutenants, like Michael Mates and Keith Hampson, were regularly to be seen in the Members' Lobby chatting up potential dissidents and Lobby reporters.

Talk swiftly began of a 'stalking horse' challenger to the Prime Minister. He eventually surfaced in the form of Sir Anthony Meyer, an Eton-educated former soldier and fervent pro-European – quite the last person you would expect to run for the leadership of any party. I revealed in a *Times* splash on the eve of the contest that Sir Ian Gilmour, the former Cabinet minister dismissed in the Purge of the Wets in 1981, would have come forward as a stalking horse if Sir

Anthony had not. He desisted in the end because Sir Anthony handled himself so well and because it was felt that he would do better in detaching votes from Thatcher than other better-known contenders, including Sir Ian.

On 5 December 1989, sixty Conservative MPs withheld their support from Thatcher and either backed Sir Anthony or abstained in what was seen as a warning shot to her to change her style of leadership. She was gone within a year.

The running sore of Europe was wide open, and there was a further twist the following July when Thatcher lost one of her favourite ministers, Nicholas Ridley, over remarks he made about Germany in an interview with the editor of *The Spectator*, Dominic Lawson. He set off an almighty diplomatic row with an accusation that the Germans were trying to take over Europe. I reported that the West German Government called his remarks 'scandalous and outrageous'. Count Otto Lambsdorff, leader of West Germany's Free Democrats, said: 'Ridley had to have been either drunk when he gave the interview or he still had not got over the English being defeated by the Germans in the World Cup.'

Thatcher urgently requested that Ridley withdraw the remarks in which he said that handing over sovereignty to the European Commission was tantamount to 'giving it to Adolf Hitler'. In the Commons, Thatcher disowned the remarks which, she said, did not represent the Government's views or her own. In the interview, Ridley said of the European single currency:

This is all a German racket designed to take over the whole of Europe. It has to be thwarted. This rushed takeover by the Germans on the worst possible basis, with the French behaving like poodles to the Germans, is absolutely intolerable.

He also attacked the European commissioners, who included his former Cabinet colleague Sir Leon Brittan, calling them 'seventeen unelected reject politicians with no accountability to anybody'.

Ridley finally quit as trade secretary on a Saturday morning and Dominic Lawson, as the man who persuaded him to come out with his rather intemperate remarks, was in the limelight. I captained a cricket team called the Old Talbotians – formed from the remnants of

James Goldsmith's *Now!* magazine – and on that Saturday afternoon
we were playing at Battersea Park against a team run by Mihir Bose,
the legendary sports writer and broadcaster.

Lawson, a wonderfully enthusiastic cricketer, was one of my opening bowlers and as we arrived there were a couple of television crew
waiting to get shots of the great man in action. As it happened, we
batted first, much to the consternation of the TV guys. Looking at the
scorebook, they noticed that Lawson was down as the Number 11 and
I was approached to see whether there was any chance I could move
him up the order. I'm afraid that I had a reputation as a ruthless
captain and told the uncomprehending cameramen that Dominic was
a genuine Number 11 batsman, although a magnificent bowler, and
that if they were patient they would see our star bowler in action.

Dominic never did get into bat, because those at the top of the
order put on a big total. But he and the TV crews rushed us through
the tea interval. They were ready to catch this moment in history as
Dominic roared in to bowl. He leapt into the air to appeal for
leg-before for a ball that was missing the off stump by about a yard.
The TV boys left at speed. It was a picture that appeared in several
papers and on the news bulletins that evening.

Back in the equally exciting world of politics, Thatcher was getting
through her last summer in Number 10. The economy was in a
desperate state, with inflation high and interest rates at what seems
now an incredible fifteen per cent. After persuading Thatcher that it
was the only course open to her, John Major – chancellor for less than
a year – announced late on the Friday of the Labour conference that
Britain was going to enter the exchange rate mechanism.

I learnt the news driving south from Blackpool and spent the next
two hours in a phone box close to the motorway. It was quite a
moment. *The Times* reported on the Saturday that Britain would join
the ERM on the following Monday, when interest rates would be cut
by one point to fourteen per cent. Leading building societies immediately announced that they would reduce their mortgage rates, and
the pound and shares surged. The stock exchange remained open for
an extra hour that Friday night and dealers reported that more than
£20 billion had been added to share values.

While the decision in principle to join the ERM was taken more
than a year before, the announcement surprised the markets and poli-

ticians. There had been an assumption that entry would be delayed at least until after the party conference season. Major's announcement came on the anniversary of the day interest rates rose to fifteen per cent and almost a year after Lawson quit. A vindicated Lawson said: 'I warmly welcome this historic decision, which I have long advocated.'

At a press conference outside 10 Downing Street, Thatcher denied that she had abandoned the Madrid condition that Britain's inflation rate had to move closer to the European average before joining, or that she was seeking party political advantage immediately before the following week's Tory conference. As for Major, he said that he would have preferred not to announce his decision so close to the party conference because it would be misinterpreted as a political gesture. The previous weekend might have been a possibility but that would have been seen as an attempt to wreck the Labour conference, while the next weekend was ruled out because of practical difficulties.

The time was ripe because most of the 'Madrid conditions' had been fulfilled, he told the BBC's *Six O'Clock News*. 'The only one which has been outstanding for some time is the inflation condition, and the really important element is what inflation is going to be in future, not what it has been historically. The indications clearly are now that our inflation performance with Europe will narrow over the next twelve months.'

So Madrid was coming to fruition, but there were two more important acts in the drama of Thatcher's fall. I was standing in the Members' Lobby in the early evening of Thursday, 1 November when John Cole, the BBC's superb political editor – with whom I often happily swapped information – whispered to me that he had heard 'Geoffrey is about to quit'. 'What a story' was as always my reaction. But this truly was a belter. I checked it out with a friend, who happened to be a government whip, and his reaction, which was just a nod, told me plenty. I informed John Cole that he seemed to be right, and he then got on the phone in the Lobby to someone else. It was enough for him to go on BBC Radio 4's *PM* programme and speculate that something major was about to happen.

The resignation did not come till the evening. In his resignation letter, Howe accused Thatcher of putting her party's prospects at risk by her attitude on Europe. 'I do not believe I can serve with honour as a member of your Government,' he wrote. The final straw for Howe, or perhaps the final excuse for a course he may have planned for some time, was Thatcher's statement to the Commons that Tuesday on the Rome summit the previous weekend. Referring to what she saw as the latest federalist advances of Brussels, she shouted, 'No, no, no!' to the delight of her Eurosceptic back-benchers.

Howe told her that he was 'deeply anxious that the mood you have struck, most notably in Rome last weekend and in the House of Commons this Tuesday, will make it more difficult for Britain to hold and retain a position of influence' on Europe.

Now it was only a matter of time, as we know. Howe, who died in October 2015, had not finished with Thatcher. On 13 November he delivered a speech to the Commons that was the most dramatic I witnessed in thirty-seven consecutive years there. It was so dramatic because it was so unexpected. There had always been a hangdog look about Sir Geoffrey. On the rare occasions I had lunch with him, he was a very friendly companion but he often spoke so quietly you wondered whether he wanted to be heard. Denis Healey's jibe that being attacked by Sir Geoffrey was like being mauled by a 'dead sheep' had not seemed a mile out. But now here was Howe, letting all his frustrations at the way he had been treated by his boss come to the surface in one devastating, coruscating attack.

A few of the highlights are worth recalling for their sheer savagery. He praised the Prime Minister's economic record but suggested she might have forgotten his role:

> Not one of our many achievements would have been possible without the courage and leadership of the Prime Minister. If I may say so, they possibly derived some little benefit from the presence of a chancellor of the exchequer who was not exactly a wet himself.

He declared that the high inflation of the time could have been avoided if Thatcher had gone along with ERM membership earlier. Thatcher, he suggested, was 'leading herself and others astray in matters of substance as well as style'.

He then compared her unfavourably with Winston Churchill:

Sir Winston Churchill put it much more positively forty years ago when he said: 'Is it not possible and not less agreeable to regard this sacrifice or merger of national sovereignty as the gradual assumption by all the nations concerned of that larger sovereignty which can alone protect their diverse and distinctive customs and characteristics and their national traditions?'

I find Winston Churchill's perception a good deal more convincing and encouraging for the interests of our nation than the nightmare image sometimes conjured up by the Prime Minister, who sometimes seems to look out on a Continent that is positively teeming with ill-intentioned people scheming, in her words, to extinguish democracy, to dissolve our national identity, to lead us through the back door into a federal Europe.

Then, memorably, on the way Thatcher had thwarted the negotiations of her ministers: 'It is rather like sending your opening batsmen to the crease only for them to find the moment that the first balls are bowled that their bats have been broken before the game by the team captain.' He added:

The point is more sharply put by a British businessman trading in Brussels and elsewhere who wrote to me saying that people throughout Europe see our Prime Minister finger-wagging, hear her passionate 'no, no, no' much more clearly than the content of carefully worded formal texts. It is too easy for people to believe that we all share her attitude, for why else, he asks, has she been our prime minister for so long.

And then the coup de grace:

The tragedy is – and it is for me personally, for my party, for our whole people, for the Prime Minister herself a very real tragedy – that the Prime Minister's perceived attitude towards Europe is running increasingly serious risks for the future of our nation. It risks minimizing our influence and maximizing our chances of being once again shut out.

We have paid heavily in the past for late starts and squandered opportunities in Europe. We dare not let that happen again. If we detach ourselves completely as a party or as a nation from the middle ground of Europe, the effects will be incalculable and very hard ever to correct.

In my letter of resignation, which I tendered with the utmost sadness and dismay, I said that Cabinet government is about trying to persuade one another from within. That was my commitment to government by persuasion, persuading colleagues and the nation.

I have tried to do that as foreign secretary and since, but I realize now that the task has become futile, of trying to stretch the meaning of words beyond what was credible, of trying to pretend there was a common policy when every step forward risked being subverted by some casual comment or impulsive answer.

The conflict of loyalty is loyalty to the Prime Minister – and after more than two decades together that instinct of loyalty is still very real – and the loyalty to what I perceive to be the true interests of this nation.

That conflict of loyalty has become all too great. I no longer believe it is possible to resolve that conflict from within this Government. That is why I have resigned.

And then: 'The time has come for others to consider their response to the tragic conflict of loyalty with which I have myself wrestled for perhaps too long.'

At that last sentence there was a collective and sustained gasp in the chamber, the Press Gallery and the public gallery. Of course, it was a direct incitement to Heseltine to challenge Thatcher for the leadership. To all of us it felt like a speech she could not possibly survive – and she didn't.

Thatcher's Fall, Major's Arrival – and How the Rugby Team Might Have Saved Her

It was only 241 words but judging the story in terms of importance per word, it was as significant as anything I wrote.

On Monday, 19 November 1990, I reported under the paper's main front-page splash that John Major would be a contender in the second ballot for the Tory leadership if Margaret Thatcher failed to get through on the first and subsequently pulled out.

At that point in the fall of Thatcher – which remains the biggest, most dramatic, most sustained story I covered in my career – it looked like a straight fight between Thatcher and Michael Heseltine, with Douglas Hurd entering the race as the anti-Heseltine candidate if the Prime Minister failed to get the required votes. Under the elaborate rules – which in retrospect seemed almost to have been drawn up to stop her – she needed to have a margin of victory over the runner-up of fifteen per cent of the total electorate of the parliamentary party. This latter rule had been changed in the 1975 review, having previously required a majority equal to fifteen per cent of those voting. The overriding view around the place was that she should just see off Heseltine in the first round and that was certainly what she was being told by her lieutenants.

If she failed and stood down, Hurd would emerge and, with the help of Thatcher's supporters, win the day against Heseltine. That was the calculation of the Hurd camp and many who claimed to be backing him. That weekend Major was not seen as a likely runner, and the bookmakers' odds showed that. He was 25–1.

But after a call from a senior minister at 3.30 p.m. that Sunday – I cannot name him because the confidentiality of that conversation still applies – I began to take a different view. It was unsolicited. He knew me well and came through on my own Commons phone line. He told me there was a strong view that if Thatcher lost, the Tories would need to skip a generation and that Major, not Hurd, would be the ideal 'unity candidate'. He added that Major was tougher than Hurd on Europe and MPs were looking for a leader with an easier manner. Major, whom I had known from the first week I joined the Lobby in 1981, certainly had that.

To me it was hugely important. Major had not declared his hand in any way and was at the time at his constituency home recovering from a wisdom tooth problem. Yet here was someone, clearly acting on his behalf, telling me that I should know he was waiting in the wings. My guess is that the source was hoping that *The Times* would lead on his tip-off the next day. But as it happened, we had an interview with Thatcher, and her full-frontal attack on Heseltine's 'Labour policies' dominated the front page. My story ran underneath it. For years afterwards, friends in both the Heseltine and Hurd camps, as well as Thatcher allies, told me that they really had not considered Major as a potential runner until late in the day. The clear intention of my informant was for them to know that the man who had been chancellor since Nigel Lawson stood down a year before was indeed a man whom we should all consider to be in the running.

Among those who read my story that morning were a couple of friends who liked a political punt. I did not discourage them from a wager. It was still an outside bet because Thatcher was expected to win and none of what I had outlined would happen if she did, but money was made as things turned out.

It was not such a surprise to everyone. Tim Yeo, who was Hurd's parliamentary private secretary at the time, kept a detailed note of developments after Howe's resignation, to which I have had access. He tells of a meeting between Hurd and Heseltine two days before that resignation when it had not occurred to either of them that Major could be a candidate.

Hurd – educated at Eton and Cambridge followed by several years as a diplomat – came from a political family and wrote political thrillers in his spare time. Quietly ambitious, he was, like Major, a centre-right moderate, serving as home secretary and foreign secretary, and fancied a tilt at the top job. But on 12 November, Hurd had suggested to Yeo for the first time that Major might enter the race and even raised the prospect that Major might be the better anti-Heseltine man – a view with which Yeo disagreed.

Major and Hurd breakfasted on 14 November and it was inconclusive, recorded Yeo. Major was not yet ready to rule out standing himself. Then Yeo noted on 19 November, the day my 241-word story appeared: 'There is clearly now an anti-Hurd bandwagon which is going for John Major.' On the day of the first ballot, Yeo spoke to Chris Patten, who said he had told Hurd that he should speak to Major before making any public statement in the event of Thatcher not getting through on the first round.

The drama of the night of Tuesday, 20 November was unforgettable. The committee corridor of the Commons had never been so crowded as when it was announced that the Prime Minister had scored 204 votes against Heseltine's152, four short of the 56-vote majority needed for an outright win. I remember calling figures in all the main camps from the corridor. They had stayed in their offices to engage in immediate talks with their bosses. Hurd and Thatcher were in Paris at an EU summit. The Prime Minister swiftly, and unwisely in the view of many of those who had backed her, declared her determination to fight on but it was clear to most at Westminster that if she could not win the first round, she would never win the second. She had been denied the support of 168 MPs and that was in anyone's eyes a vote of no confidence.

My clear memory is that despite the painful twenty-four hours that followed – during which Thatcher had to be convinced that if she did not stand down Heseltine would win (the argument that in the end swayed her) – in and around Westminster that night the view was that she was finished. Senior figures certainly believed that to be the case when they gathered at the home near Buckingham Palace of Tristan Garel-Jones, the Foreign Office minister of state and one of the Tory party's ultimate fixers and power players.

I had several very good sources in that meeting in Catherine Place, including the one who had advised me the previous Sunday, and I was to write about it in the days that followed. But it started from the premise that Thatcher could not recover and that on her return from Paris she would receive a barrage of advice to retire gracefully. The meeting discussed the merits of the two most-touted unity candidates,

Hurd and Major, and it was here that the memories of the participants slightly differed. I wrote initially that the balance was marginally in favour of Hurd but it was later stressed to me that many there had ended up backing Major. Garel-Jones, who was credited with Machiavellian skills, was believed at first to have been a Hurd man but some now thought he was a Major man all along. There is no doubt that the Major campaign was by now gathering steam.

In her autobiography, Thatcher made some interesting asides on this period. She, as we know, eventually backed Major as the man to stop Heseltine but it was not long before she was having doubts about him. On the Wednesday – before ministers trailed in to see her and, one by one, expressed doubts about her prospects – Thatcher writes that she considered which of the other candidates was better placed to stop Heseltine. Neither she nor her friend Norman Tebbit believed Hurd could beat him and she doubted whether he would carry on the policies in which she believed. It was that consideration which prompted her to look favourably on Major but his prospects were at best uncertain, so she decided to stay in the fight.

'I fight on, I fight to win,' she told journalists as she left Number 10 for a Commons statement on the Paris summit. Then, Thatcher says in her account, she put John Wakeham in charge of her campaign for the second round and saw Hurd, asking him formally to nominate her for the second ballot, which he did with good grace. The chat with Major was much more strained:

> Then I telephoned John Major at home. I told him that I had decided to stand again and that Douglas was going to propose me. I asked John to second my nomination. There was a moment's silence. The hesitation was palpable. No doubt the operation on John's wisdom teeth was giving him trouble. Then he said that if that was what I wanted, yes. Later when urging my supporters to vote for John for the leadership, I made play of the fact that he did not hesitate. But both of us knew otherwise.

Ouch!

After the inconclusive result, Tim Yeo had rung Hurd and told him he should not under any circumstances be bounced into standing down for Major. The next day – Wednesday – Yeo records how Hurd, after a conversation with John Wakeham, went off and signed Thatcher's nomination form for the second ballot. In the smoking room. Malcolm Rifkind, then Scottish secretary and a Hurd supporter, had approached Yeo and told him that that he had told Thatcher that if she did not stand down, she might well be defeated by Heseltine in the second ballot. As Yeo put it: 'Malcolm thought there was a real chance she would decide not to go forward.'

Yeo ran into Heseltine in the Members' Lobby and told him there was a likelihood that Thatcher was going to quit. He was totally unaware and expressed absolute confidence that she would carry on, his notes say. It was not, of course, what Heseltine wanted to hear. His team knew that his best, probably his only, hope was if Thatcher stayed in

Yeo then went to Hurd's room where the chief and deputy chief whips were present. It was decided it was too late for soundings and that if Thatcher did quit, both Hurd and Major would have to stand and there would be a joint statement that they were acting on a friendly basis.

In a 'backgrounder' I wrote on the events of that Wednesday, I said that while Ken Baker, party chairman, was telling Thatcher that support from Conservatives in the country was strong – they did not have a vote – the message from Tim Renton, the chief whip, was so much bleaker. He knew what the MPs were thinking.

I wrote that it was the conversations with Cabinet colleagues that clinched her decision to go. She had learnt about the meeting at Catherine Place where Chris Patten, William Waldegrave, Norman Lamont, Malcolm Rifkind and Tony Newton had all agreed that she was damaged beyond recovery.

She began those chats, I wrote, by saying that it was a funny old world because she won three elections in a row, had the overwhelming support of the party in the country and had been backed in the first ballot. I noted that the official version was that everyone offered to support her if she carried on but the starkest warnings that she would lose if she did came from Kenneth Clarke, Patten, Rifkind and Lamont.

As has been recorded many times since, Thatcher gradually came to the conclusion as Wednesday drew on that she would have to go. People in the Hurd and Major camps were canvassing opinion in the Commons. I stayed down in the Members' Lobby and had never seen such frenetic activity.

By late at night the news began filtering out from the Cabinet conversations. I was rung at 7.30 a.m. on the Thursday by a friend from the whips' office to tell me that Thatcher would be resigning that morning. She did so, and Hurd and Major, who returned from his constituency, entered the race after their aides agreed their joint statement. No one who saw it will forget Thatcher's appearance that afternoon in a no-confidence debate as she declared 'I'm enjoying this' and laid into her opponents.

Within days, Major had moved from the position of outsider to favourite. The wind was in his sails and with the support of Thatcher, Tebbit and many others on the Right, he was adopted as the candidate to stop Heseltine. Tim Yeo said Hurd's campaign was 'almost innocently naïve in taking trouble to prepare a joint statement with Major at the time nominations went in, by which time the whole Major campaign team was bent entirely on crushing both Heseltine and Hurd'.

The following Tuesday, Major secured 185 votes to Heseltine's 131 and Hurd's 56. He was two votes short of a clear victory but within minutes of the result, Heseltine and Hurd withdrew in Major's favour. No third round was necessary and Major became leader. He and his allies had fought a brilliant tactical battle, coming up on the inside almost unnoticed and catching his rivals unawares. That Sunday phone call had been played out to perfection.

Thatcher's allies then and ever since have bemoaned the performance of her re-election team and of her failure to do more to win over disaffected MPs. She needed a majority of 56 votes to win outright on the first ballot and came up just four votes short.

During the course of writing this chapter I have come across former MPs who have admitted to me that while they said publicly they would vote for Thatcher, when it came to it they did not. Many others have accused Peter Morrison, her parliamentary private secretary, of utterly failing to understand the strength of opposition to her and of not setting up meetings with enough MPs to bring them round and win her a majority. I have discovered, however, that it was her treatment of one particular group of MPs that might have been a factor leading to her downfall.

These were the Conservative MPs who played in the parliamentary rugby union team and were members of the all-party rugby group. The body was formed by Humfrey Malins, the former Tory MP who was himself a former first-class rugby player with Harlequins and Richmond, shortly after his election in 1983 for Croydon North West. Also involved in the formation of the group were the Tory MPs Phillip Oppenheim and Michael Lord, a former Cambridge rugby Blue who was later to become a deputy speaker.

Rugby being a team sport, the MPs in the group (about a dozen in number) tended to stick together and, certainly on party affairs, voted largely as a block. They banded together to support Cranley Onslow against Edward Du Cann when the former became chairman of the 1922 Committee during the 1980s. When pressure on Thatcher was mounting, the Conservatives in the rugby group realized when talking together one day that they had never individually been spoken to by the Prime Minister. 'She had no interest in sport. She had no interest in us. She was astonishingly distant from many of her MPs,' one told me.

The group's alienation from their leader was compounded by the way one of their number was treated. He twice was ordered back to the Commons from foreign trips to take part in votes which were easily won by the ruling party. On the second occasion, Thatcher was steered by the whips towards him in the division lobbies and showered

praise on him for returning and helping her out. He was delighted. All
had been worthwhile. The great leader had shown her gratitude.

The next morning, however, as he passed the Prime Minister in the
Ways and Means Corridor, she greeted him with a 'Good morning,
David'. His name was not David. The incident was retold to his friends
and to them confirmed her aloofness. One figure in the group told
me that he was aware of about half a dozen colleagues in the rugby
group who had said publicly they would vote for Thatcher, but who
had not in fact done so. Had just three of them voted for her rather
than Heseltine or Hurd, she would have got through. My source told
me:

It is the great untold story. The rugby group might just possibly
have saved her. But personal treatment matters in politics. We are
all human. If someone gives you the brush-off or ignores you
completely, you remember it. She and her team did not try hard
enough with us.

How history could have been changed if the Iron Lady had been that
little bit softer.

Kinnock and the White House Stitch-Up

Ronald Reagan, as the world knew, was close to Margaret Thatcher. Neil Kinnock knew, when he planned his visit to Washington to boost his international stature in March 1987, that it would not be a cakewalk. A British general election was possibly only months away and Kinnock, though having started on his task of persuading his party to drop its unpopular policies, was still stuck with a unilateralist defence posture. That was to go in the next parliament.

So as he stepped off Concorde in New York on the Thursday before his Friday White House encounter, Kinnock was more than ready for a difficult trip. He had every reason to be. The British press pack had arrived a day early and had no trouble getting briefed by American diplomats on what they thought of the Labour leader's defence policy. There were even suggestions that he would only get ten to fifteen minutes with the president, providing some papers with a snub story even before it had occurred. It was obvious to all of us that Kinnock could not expect any help from that quarter. Not for the first time, I wondered why Kinnock had bothered with this one.

As usual, however, our preoccupation was to get a good story. So when the day arrived, expectations within the press party were high. But as they emerged from the talks, Kinnock, his shadow foreign secretary Denis Healey and chief of staff Charles Clarke (later to become a Cabinet minister under Tony Blair) were in good spirits. Kinnock told us at a press briefing not far from the White House that the meeting had gone well.

He admitted that Reagan had voiced anxiety about the impact of Labour's policies on the NATO alliance, but Kinnock said it was an argument Labour could rebut because its commitment to the alliance was absolute. He called the talks friendly and added that Reagan had given him an assurance for which he had not asked – that he had no intention or wish to interfere in the British election campaign.

We were up against a deadline, a constant problem when working in Washington (five hours behind London), and had to get writing. It looked like the story might be 'Reagan goes easy on Kinnock'. But there was an insurance policy. The excellent Stuart Trotter, political correspondent of the *Herald* in Glasgow, had a slightly later deadline than the rest and had offered to stay in the White House to hear its official briefing of the talks – from which he arrived hot-foot and red-faced. Far from it being all sweetness and light, Reagan had given Kinnock and his team a bit of a pasting, it seemed.

Stuart swiftly gave us the quotes from Marlin Fitzwater, the president's spokesman, the most damaging of which was that Reagan had told Kinnock his policy risked undercutting the American position at the current Geneva disarmament negotiations. The president had used these words: 'We must be prepared, unlike we were before World War II. We cannot let that happen again.' He had also said that Labour's policies would seriously damage the unity and cohesion of the NATO alliance. There was even a dispute over the length of the meeting. Labour said it lasted thirty minutes, the White House twenty.

Oh dear. With Kinnock and his team having moved off, we had no swift means of checking. The official version – which we assumed must necessarily be accurate, as we would with a Downing Street official statement – would have to be used alongside what we had already. It meant a lot of rewriting. I remember even Alastair Campbell, then working for the Labour-supporting *Mirror*, telling me that he would have to change his copy at least to reflect the Fitzwater version.

Stories were filed. They were what we expected more or less when we left London for Washington but we were uneasy. We were right to be. The more I thought about it over the years, the more I felt the Fitzwater intervention outrageous. Everything about the trip suggested that Kinnock was onto a loser before he left and that the Reagan support team would not see it as their job to help him. Far from it – they had gone out of the way to help the president's friend back in London.

I was anxious to put the White House version to Kinnock. Fortunately, shortly before his plane left Washington, Kinnock did an interview for *News at Ten* where politely but firmly he denied some of Fitzwater's claims. On the undercutting quote he said: 'I am certain those words were not used.' The president had been in no way antagonistic: 'That was not how it came across to me. If it had been, I would not have been able to describe the meeting as genial.'

We were pleased to have got that element of balance and I am glad, when I look at the *Times* report twenty-nine years later, that the story appeared with those strong caveats in it. But as they flew out of the American capital, the Kinnock team were more and more convinced they had been stitched up. Many of us stayed behind. But when they arrived back on the Saturday, some in the Kinnock team were ready to fight back.

Denis Healey, who died in 2015 aged ninety-eight, was always a bruiser and gladly confirmed suggestions that the president had mistaken him at Friday's meeting for the British ambassador, Sir Antony Acland. And he suggested that the president did not understand 'the rougher, never mind the finer' points of Labour's policy, appearing to think that Labour would get rid of conventional as well as nuclear weapons. Aides had earlier recalled that Reagan strode up to Healey and said: 'Nice to see you again, Mr Ambassador.' They also said that while Charles Clarke had taken sixteen pages of notes, Fitzwater had not even been present.

All in all that was an unsatisfactory trip – for Neil Kinnock and the press team with him. The truth of the encounter with Reagan lay somewhere between the two versions, but it was clear that there had been political interference. Reagan had said one thing; his spokesman had said something different. It did nothing to help the Labour leader a few weeks later when Margaret Thatcher achieved her second landslide.

As Thatcher Rules,
Labour Battles for Its Soul

A group of Lobby journalists sounded the death knell for Labour's vote-losing unilateralist defence policy when we gathered with senior party figures in front of the Lenin Mausoleum in Moscow's Red Square in February 1989.

We had spent much of the week with them as they trailed round the city, talking to Soviet military, political leaders and leading academics. The symbolism of the final press briefing taking place in front of Lenin's resting place was too good for us to miss, and some colourful intros were sent home. 'Labour's no-nukes defence policy was buried besides Lenin's tomb yesterday' was one of them.

It was a strange collection of figures sent to Moscow by Neil Kinnock to help him win backing for Labour adopting a multilateralist defence stance. It was intended to replace the unilateralist one that had helped Michael Foot go down to a resounding defeat in 1983 (on the back of a manifesto dubbed by Gerald Kaufman as 'the longest suicide note in history') and Kinnock to suffer a similar fate in 1987.

As chance would have it, Kaufman, then the shadow foreign secretary, was with us on this trip, along with Martin O'Neill (shadow defence secretary), somewhat incongruously Ron Todd (leader of the Transport Workers' Union) and a gentleman named Peter Mandelson, who was then the Labour Party's director of communications.

Labour's unilateralist and anti-Europe policies, the decisions of a special conference in January 1981 to give the unions the largest say in the election of future Labour leaders, and a belief that the party had been infiltrated beyond help by various Trotskyite groups led to the Gang of Four – Roy Jenkins, Shirley Williams, David Owen and

William Rodgers – breaking away from Labour and forming the Social Democratic Party in 1981. Kinnock had become leader in 1983.

He was of the Left but not the hard, Bennite left. He was blamed by that faction for the failure of Tony Benn to be elected deputy leader in 1981 by backing the soft-left candidate, John Silkin, and then abstaining with his supporters in the final run-off. He had made enemies for life but the mainstream party felt able to support him after the 1983 leadership election in which he heavily defeated his main challenger, Roy Hattersley, who was to become his deputy.

Now, six years on, Kinnock was at last on the point of reversing that disastrous defence policy. He had made a visit to Moscow for talks with the Soviet leader, Konstantin Chernenko, in 1984 and laid the groundwork for change, but it was only now, five years later, that he was about to pull it off.

Kaufman, using careful words because he was being watched by the strongly unilateralist Ron Todd, said enough for us to know that the mission had been a success. All the people they had spoken to wanted Britain to put its missiles into the disarmament process, and not to give them up for nothing, he suggested. It was a good week for the Labour team, and entertaining fare for the press corps who had followed them.

By then Kinnock, after the most memorable of any of the speeches I heard by a party leader during my four decades covering politics, had finally beaten off the Militant Tendency. Now, a few weeks after the Moscow trip, he staked his leadership on pushing a multilateralist policy – giving up weapons only when others did – through his party machine, and triumphed. He told his national executive: 'Unilateralism is not even comprehended by those who share our objectives in other countries. They cannot understand our policy for conceding nuclear weapons without getting anything in return.'

And so it was done. Kinnock felt with that change that he had at least given himself a serious chance of gaining power at the next election. He was, meanwhile, just about completing the organizational changes that had taken virtually as long – the rooting out of left-wing factions that infiltrated his party and made the life of its MPs a misery by watching their every word and deed in the name of so-called 'accountability'. This followed the introduction of mandatory reselection, under which every MP would have to submit to the judgment of his local management committee once in parliament. The far-left Campaign for Labour Party Democracy – which was founded by Vladimir Derer in 1973, exists still today and supported Jeremy Corbyn's successful leadership bid – had campaigned for a decade for the change, with Tony Benn in the vanguard. The battle, along with that to change the way leaders were elected, dominated the Callaghan and Foot years in the late Seventies and early Eighties.

Kinnock had galvanized his party in that speech in Bournemouth at the 1985 conference, when he accused Liverpool City Council, controlled by the revolutionary Militant Tendency, of playing politics with people's jobs. His most-quoted passage will forever be remembered: 'You end in the grotesque chaos of a Labour council – a Labour council – hiring taxis to scuttle round the city handing out redundancy notices to its own workers.'

Derek Hatton, deputy leader of Liverpool Council, leapt up and accused him of lying, and Eric Heffer, MP for Liverpool Walton, walked off the platform and out of the hall – with me and a huge posse of press people following him. There was always a tension between Kinnock and Heffer, possibly driven by the latter's envy of the former and a belief that he was a purer left-winger than the leader.

Peter Riddell, my former colleague, tells a story of how, back in 1982, he, Jim Naughtie (then working on *The Guardian*), Heffer and Kinnock were having a drink together on the terrace of the Commons. Kinnock was at his anecdotal best and Heffer was trying and failing to match his stories. They could tell Heffer felt he was being eclipsed by the rising star, which he was.

The antipathy went further when Heffer joined Tony Benn for what appeared an utterly pointless tilt for the leadership and deputy leadership in 1988. Kinnock was scathing about the costly, unnecessary contest, accusing the challengers of not caring about winning the next election and calling them daft and absurd. Union leader Bill Jordan unkindly suggested the Left had had to resort to grave-robbing to find two candidates.

The internal battle to expel Militant was well under way by 1985, of course, but Kinnock's speech gave the fight against the hard left even greater force. The two remaining Militant MPs were prevented from standing at the next election and it was not long before the group abandoned its official policy of 'entryism' (infiltrating Labour with the intention of subverting its policies and organization) – although this did not mean those who followed it had disappeared off the face of the earth. They got older, and some joined new socialist groups, ready to return when the moment came. As it did in 2015.

I tell these stories of past struggles because in 2015 and 2016 it has happened all over again as a new, younger, hard left has surfaced to take the place or stand alongside some of the gnarled veterans of yesteryear, including Jeremy Corbyn.

Neil Kinnock championed all those changes to make his party electable. He was not the beneficiary, falling short in 1992. But Tony Blair was, and it is unlikely that he would have been able to carry through his achievements, or win three elections, but for the work done during the turbulent 1980s by Kinnock and his team.

Which made it all the more amazing to me that in 2015 the Labour Party allowed it all to happen again. Indeed, it openly encouraged it. Allowing anyone to sign up for £3 (or any union member for free) to take part in the leadership poll was a recipe for the Left to return and take over. It did so spectacularly when enough Labour MPs – incredibly – agreed to put Corbyn's name on the ballot paper, allowing the Islington MP to grab a landslide victory.

Since then there has been an enormous fight. The only certainty is
that the Corbynistas, as his true followers are called, had it far easier
than the Bennites did as they tried to take over the party's levers of
power in the late Seventies and early Eighties. Indeed, it could be
argued that their decline started when Tony Benn failed by a whisker
to defeat Denis Healey for the deputy leadership in 1981.

In those days as a new Lobby man, I was assigned the Labour beat
and spent many happy hours outside the Labour headquarters in
Walworth Road waiting for interminable meetings to break up. This
was the centre of The Struggle. The make-up of the twenty-nine-
member National Executive Committee (NEC) was the key pointer
to who was winning at any given time in the fight between the
moderates and the Left.

The Left was not discriminating as it tried to take over in Labour
constituencies. In 1984 I spent a week investigating its efforts to
remove Peter Shore, a Cabinet minister in three Labour governments
and an anti-Marketeer, from his safe seat in Bethnal Green and Stepney.
He had committed the 'crime' – in the Left's eyes – of criticizing
Arthur Scargill's tactics in the miners' strike. The Left had control of
the constituency party's management committee. I wrote that its takeover had been a model of organization and discipline, its tactics legit-
imate under the party constitution, which itself had been fashioned by
left-wingers in positions of power in the years before.

Lulled by years of unchallenged power, the old Labour Party in
Stepney went to sleep, allowing the new breed of constituency activist
to enter and take over. I found that while Militant did not have a
strong influence, the hard-left Socialist Organiser pressure group
certainly did and a body called the London Labour Briefing (an
amorphous group that linked the activities of the Left in general, and
met regularly at London's County Hall) mattered a great deal.

I wrote: 'It may be a tragedy for Shore, and others under threat like
him, that the activists running local parties today make a virtue of not
being impressed by reputation and personality. To them what their MP
believes or says is more important than who he is or what he does.'
That must sound rather familiar to Labour MPs who today feel threatened by their local parties.

The following year, Shore managed to see off an attempt to deselect
him – helped by new rules introduced by Kinnock to allow threat-

ened MPs to appeal to a ballot of all members in the local party – but the Left still kept coming back for him. The following year, I went to Merseyside to look at Militant and particularly its efforts to kick out the formidable Frank Field in Birkenhead. The fact that Frank remains in the Commons today tells its own story, but there were times when Militant was running Liverpool and held sway in the area around the city that his future looked decidedly rocky.

I rang Tony Mulhearn, one of Militant's leaders in Liverpool, and arranged to meet him. I asked him if he would like lunch and he swiftly concurred, saying he would book a venue. At his request I took a taxi from Lime Street station to the printing works on the edge of the city where he worked, picked him up and at that point he took over, asking the driver if he could take us to the Adelphi, Liverpool's iconic hotel. We had lunch and Mulhearn, a personable chap who was president of the Liverpool district Labour Party, told all and sundry on adjoining tables that he was 'having lunch on Murdoch'.

At the time he was one of the names being put about as a potential challenger to Field but I got the impression, rightly, that he was not keen. Field was a redoubtable foe and his brilliant tactic of threatening, if he was deselected, to resign as an MP and fight a by-election against whoever was chosen in his place worked in his favour.

In those days – and this is a lesson for the moderates of today – it was far from one-way traffic. The Right, or moderates, were themselves well organized. The Manifesto Group, set up by Dickson Mabon to oppose the Left, had among its membership over the years the likes of John Smith, Denis Healey, Roy Hattersley, George Robertson, Jack Cunningham, Gerald Kaufman and the Gang of Four. Though not as energetic as their left-wing opponents, the Right had already begun its fightback during the latter months of Michael Foot's troubled leadership.

As ever, the success of Left or Right depended heavily on the make-up of the union leaderships at the time. At the 1982 Labour conference, the Right ended several years of Left domination by taking a narrow majority on the NEC. Foot, who was of the Left but so often on the wrong side of the argument with that faction, usually abstained, knowing that the fourteen–twelve majority for the moderates would help him along. The Right then followed up by voting its supporters on to all the key committees.

I benefited hugely from leaks from both sides of the argument in this never-ending battle. The late John Golding – a moderate Labour MP, later to become a senior union official, who despised the far left and chronicled his own part in the fight against it in a book called *Hammer of the Left: My Part in Defeating the Labour Left* – regularly briefed me on what was going on behind closed doors, and the Left were not reticent either. After one of these meetings I wrote that Eric Heffer had reacted with fury at the Right's tactics, telling them they were doing the party much harm. I thought it a pretty unexceptionable line. But in a busy Members' Lobby after business question time one Thursday, with scores of MPs and journalists looking on, Heffer approached me and started shouting at me, telling me that I had been listening too much to 'Golding and other right-wingers'.

I assumed that this outburst, which was rather embarrassing to me, was designed to show anyone listening that he was not the source of my report that morning. I left the Lobby pretty quickly after that and headed downstairs to Annie's Bar – the watering hole in the Commons that was most used by journalists and MPs who wanted to talk to each other, where you would often see the likes of Ken Clarke and Sir George Young enjoying a pint.

Unknown to me, my boss, Julian Haviland, who had seen the exchange with Heffer, gently told him that he felt he had been out of order in making a public complaint against a reporter who was only doing his job. Julian was a wonderful, emollient man who could have charmed the birds from the trees, and Eric, a gentle man behind the sometimes brusque exterior, swiftly relented. He asked where I was, and Julian told him to try Annie's. He came immediately to see me and apologized awkwardly for shouting at me. I thanked him and told him I would always be available for his counter-briefings. At that he smiled, and we never had a cross word again. I also had another contact on the Left.

For a journalist, those were happy, happy days. If you were a Labour MP or an NEC man or woman, it was often a nightmare. The Left was quick to reassert itself in the policy-making process. When it came on the eve of the 1983 election to the joint NEC-shadow Cabinet meeting to approve the manifesto, the moderates were outnumbered as they tried to eliminate items such as unilateralism and withdrawal from the European Economic Community. In the end they gave up and virtually accepted the document that had been put before them. I remember John Golding telling me: 'We have to hope no one reads it.'

But it was the suicide note that Kaufman had predicted. Margaret Thatcher was popular because of the Falklands war. Foot was gone, and it was left to Kinnock to lead the long campaign back towards power.

Was She Crying?
Oh Yes, She Was: Glenys
on the West Bank

Sometimes something unexpected comes along to turn an average news story into a very good one. Trailing around the Middle East with Neil Kinnock in February 1988 at the time of a Palestinian uprising on the West Bank and in Gaza, one such event happened.

The story up to then during the trip had been the claims made to Kinnock that the Israeli Government had used undue force in its moves to contain the protests. After talks with Palestinian leaders in Nablus on the West Bank, Kinnock and his wife, Glenys, were taken to visit protesters who had been injured in the demonstrations. I was one of the 'pool' who was allowed in with them as they went to the hundred-bed al-Ittihad Hospital, run by the Arab Women's Union. Shown around by Yousef al-Masry, the hospital director, they saw men who had recently been seriously injured in the disturbances.

The first patient, Kinnock was told, had been shot with an explosive bullet, and doctors showed the Labour leader the X-rays. He saw another who had had a leg amputated. The Kinnocks were then shown a young man whom al-Masry said had been shot in the back. Kinnock pointed to a small wound on the man's chest and asked if it was an exit wound, and was told that it was.

It was when he moved on to the next man, who was seriously ill and who was having cold compresses applied to his forehead, that Kinnock's shock turned to anger. When the doctor explained how the injuries had occurred, he asked: 'Are you telling me that this boy was shot in the back as well?' The doctor replied: 'Yes, in the kidneys and pancreas.' Kinnock was then told that the man could not move his legs.

He emerged from the hospital pale-faced and muttering to his colleagues: 'They were shot in the back.' It was when he stood on the hospital steps that something happened that turned a foreign-page lead story into a front-page contender. With Glenys standing beside him, Kinnock attacked the behaviour of the Israeli troops and said nothing could justify shooting people in the back. He was most obviously outraged and did not mind showing it. But members of the travelling press had spotted something else – Mrs Kinnock appeared to be in tears.

The first to mention it was the eagle-eyed David Kemp of *The Sun*. As we went into a huddle afterwards – and yes, the Lobby does its huddles like any other branch of journalism, as well as football teams – David suggested that Glenys might have been crying. Others, like me, had noticed her wiping her eyes. So was she in tears? Yes, she was. The Lobby was in agreement.

In the pool of reporters inside the hospital, John Williams of the *Evening Standard* had also noticed the impact on Mrs Kinnock. Looking at the injured boy, she said to her husband: 'This boy is the same age as our Stephen.' Then she started to cry. Williams wrote a 'Glenys cries' splash for his paper. Stephen Kinnock is now a Labour MP.

Five of us – including my friend and lunch partner Jim Naughtie, then of *The Guardian* but for decades afterwards of Radio 4's *Today* programme – had a taxi waiting to take us back to Jerusalem and the American Colony Hotel. I had taken down every word in shorthand and as we travelled through the Holy Land, I dictated from the front of the car to my colleagues. Without going into too much detail, this exercise made Mr Kemp from *The Sun* feel decidedly unwell, but he was not going to miss any word as I went through my notes.

The truth was – and this in some eyes will confirm the cynicism of which some accuse us journalists – the tears had made the story. This was something happening in Israel but the British Opposition leader's wife was moved to cry. That was a story for *The Sun* and everyone else. All of us got a great show the next day. The story was on the front of *The Times* with a picture.

We went to the foreign ministry the next morning where Kinnock was holding talks. A broadcast journalist who, for all we knew, had received a kicking from his news desk for not running the 'Glenys cries' line, seemed to be less than happy with the travelling Lobby and asked Mrs Kinnock directly whether she had cried the day before. Glenys, bless her, replied: 'Yes, I did, actually.'

He should not have asked, as he could no longer claim to his bosses that the Lobby had made it up. There was always a tension between the visiting pack and journalists on the ground who thought, quite rightly, that they knew the domestic story better. But we were often working for a different market – known as the front page.

Kinnock's visit had an impact. The next day, Yitzhak Shamir, the Israeli prime minister, responded to accusations of army brutality and hellish conditions in the occupied territories by insisting that Israel was doing everything it could to avoid casualties and suffering. But he did not deny Kinnock's controversial statements, repeated personally to him during the talks, that he had seen injured Palestinians on the West Bank and in the Gaza Strip who had been shot in the back.

Kinnock raised the use of so-called 'dum dum' ammunition with Yitzhak Rabin, then defence minister but later a prime minister who made several historic agreements with the Palestinians through the Oslo Accords. Rabin was assassinated in 1995 by an opponent of the peace process. Back then it was an awkward encounter for Kinnock as Rabin was a Labour minister.

For John Williams of the *Standard*, the timing meant it was a splash for his paper again. But John knew that if he stayed and filed, he would miss Kinnock's trip to Gaza that morning. I told him to stay in Jerusalem and I would fill him in. We returned from Gaza in time for me to dictate notes of our trip to Gaza, and for him – helped by the time advantage – to catch his paper with yet another splash. Which all proves that in the competitive world of political journalism, there is still time for cooperation.

Kinnock had timed his trip well. Other Western leaders visiting during this period also put pressure on Israel to soften its security policy in the so-called occupied territories. And unusually for an overseas trip, whether by an Opposition leader or a prime minister, there was no big gaffe, no downside.

Held at Gunpoint
in the African Bush

And did those feet in ancient time
Walk upon England's mountain green?
And was the holy Lamb of God
On England's pleasant pastures seen?
And did the countenance divine
Shine forth upon our clouded hills?
And was Jerusalem builded here
Among those dark satanic mills?

Bring me my bow of burning gold!
Bring me my arrows of desire!
Bring me my spear! O clouds, unfold!
Bring me my chariot of fire!
I will not cease from mental fight,
Nor shall my sword sleep in my hand,
Till we have built Jerusalem
In England's green and pleasant land.

A near word-perfect rendition of William Blake's anthem rang out through the African bush. The voice was Welsh but that made no difference to the startled listeners outside. They were bemused enough by the arrival in their midst of a strange, angry, red-haired man, wearing a rather elderly bomber jacket, who had been berating them for the last half-hour despite them pushing Kalashnikov rifles up his nose.

It was one of the weirdest, funniest – and potentially most danger-ous – episodes in all my hundreds of thousands of miles of travelling with political leaders. The singer belting out 'Jerusalem' to keep his troops happy was of course Neil Kinnock. How he, his wife Glenys, three members of his staff, and twelve journalists happened to be here, locked up in a hut on the edge of an airstrip in Mutare – a remote village in the middle of Zimbabwe – beggared belief. But it happened.

It was the last full day of Kinnock's ten-day tour of the so-called African front-line states in July 1988. South Africa was still run by an apartheid regime and Kinnock, on what had been a successful trip up to then, had spent most of his time meeting African leaders and verbally attacking Pretoria.

We had spent much of that day in neighbouring Mozambique, itself in the middle of a brutal civil war in which the RENAMO movement, funded by South Africa, was in conflict with the FRELIMO-backed Government. We had been up since 4 a.m. and had seen some truly shocking results of the long-running struggle – impoverished villages, women and children telling of how they had lost their husbands and fathers to kidnappers and guerrillas.

In mid-afternoon we were flown in a Zimbabwe Air Force transport plane from Chimoio in Mozambique across the border. The diplomatic welcoming party, including British High Commissioner Ramsay Melhuish, were waiting for Kinnock and his party to arrive – in the wrong place. Unfortunately, they were at Grand Reef Airport up in the hills, while our pilot had unaccountably received a change of instructions telling him to fly to Mutare.

Neither the young soldiers at Mutare, nor the official welcoming party, got that message and there was at least an hour's drive between the two airstrips. As we clambered off the plane it was obvious, pretty quickly, that something had gone very wrong.

Three or four soldiers raced out of a little hut to the plane and started shouting at us as we disembarked. We understood not a word, and they not a word of what we were saying. We were tired. Kinnock was absolutely furious as the guards started waving their automatic rifles at us. In the commotion, I and Simon Walters, political correspondent of *The Sun*, pulled Kinnock aside as he appeared to be directly in the line of fire of one of the waving guns.

The light was fading and the pilot, having realized the mistake, tried to obtain permission to get out fast, but the soldiers refused. In my piece that was to appear on the front page the next morning, I described how the comedy of the situation quickly disappeared when the Zimbabwean soldiers, clearly not knowing who Kinnock was, became heavy-handed.

We were told we must go into the tiny waiting room rather than stand around outside chatting. When we asked to stay outside, the soldiers became threatening. Kinnock led the protests and the lance-corporal grew aggressive. Kinnock valiantly told him he was here in Zimbabwe for talks with Robert Mugabe, the Zimbabwean president. The soldier did not understand him, or was unimpressed. He interrupted him and waved his rifle. Kinnock led everyone inside.

For the next hour, our party was under siege, fearful of even looking outside because of the hostility of the soldiers. At one point, a lieutenant entered the room and said good evening to Kinnock. He replied: 'What's good about it?' The lieutenant was carrying an unholstered revolver.

So that was how Kinnock – with the rest of us performing the role of his choir – came to be singing 'Jerusalem'. On the last days of the trip, the talented Walters, along with Hilary Coffman (Kinnock's press officer), myself and a few others had been composing tour songs to mark what had been a fun trip. We were due to spend our last night at the Troutbeck Inn in Nyanga, in the beautiful eastern highlands of Zimbabwe, a chance to let our hair down,

Now the songs made an early appearance, causing amusement in the Kinnock party as we mocked some of them and some of the people we had met along the way. But Neil trumped us all when he decided to let rip. At one point, Glenys tried to calm her husband down. 'I've got steam coming out my ears!' he exclaimed.

Soon after the incident began, the Opposition leader joked: 'Let's form an escape committee.' But by the time the welcoming party finally arrived, his temper was severely frayed. He told an apologetic Melhuish about the behaviour of the soldiers and then protested vehemently to the provincial governor. 'I can understand the sensitivity, but I don't like being abused. And I don't like being threatened by people with guns,' Kinnock told him.

Once the danger of the situation had been averted, the one preoccupation of the reporters was getting what was quite clearly a sensational story back to our offices. The reaction of our news desks, let alone Conservative politicians, to the idea that the leader of Her

Majesty's Opposition had been locked up in Zimbabwe was not hard to imagine.

No one had a mobile phone in those days, and the chance of us finding a telephone in this remote back-of-beyond place was nil, we concluded. So we decided on a pact. No one would attempt to file their stories until we reached the Troutbeck but it would then be every person for themselves. The journey to Nyanga turned out to take far longer than we expected, nearly three hours, and most of us had our stories written in our heads before we arrived.

As the mini-bus pulled up, we raced into the hotel. Walters tried the door of an empty secretary's office as we went in, I grabbed a phone on the desk at reception, and the rest had to fight over the three remaining phones in the hotel. One of our number, John Morrison of Reuters, had a Tandy laptop on which he had written his story. That dropped quickly in London, telling our offices that something startling was about to land with them.

My office was elated with the story, as was Simon's, and they kept asking him for more colour from this amazing, scarcely believable event. Simon seemed to be on the phone for hours, after his office demanded the tour songs as well.

It was an exhausting night and none of us got to eat until very late. Mixed with our excitement over having a brilliant tale to send home on the last night of the trip was the knowledge that the Kinnock party – Neil, Glenys, Sue Nye (who before joining Neil had worked for Michael Foot and was later to work for Gordon Brown), Chris Childs (a policy adviser), and Hilary Coffman – were pretty down in the dumps on what should have been a fun evening. They knew very well how the airport incident would play back home, and they were not wrong. In the early hours, after many of the others had gone to bed or even then were still filing, I had a beer with Kinnock. He worried whether it would be the only thing remembered from the whole trip.

In the Commons the next day, as we flew home, there were cries of 'Free Kinnock' during the usual points of order session and there was much mirth at his expense. The Labour leader received an apology from the Zimbabwean Government and the army over the way he had been treated. The brigadier in charge of the district went to say sorry as we arrived at another airport before flying to Harare for Kinnock's talks with President Mugabe and the flight home.

It emerged that day that the waiting party had been worried that the Kinnock plane might have been shot down by bandits or had crashed, and that the high commissioner had been on the point of raising the alarm and sending out search parties. Which only goes to show that travelling with Opposition leaders was always more hairy than with prime ministers. The support on the ground was never so strong, the aircraft never so good.

Just the previous day we had flown on two Mozambique Air Force helicopters to a godforsaken town about an hour's flying from the capital, Maputo. Kinnock was being shown the devastation wreaked by guerrilla fighters.

When the time came to leave, only one helicopter was waiting for us at the dustbowl of an airstrip on the edge of town. Whether lots were drawn I'm not sure but somehow myself, Simon Walters, John Williams (then of the *Evening Standard*) and one other were left behind with the promise that it would drop Kinnock – who waved and shouted encouragement to us through the open windows as he lifted off – and his team and the other reporters at Maputo and then come back for us.

We had our doubts and felt rather threatened in this place which had only recently been attacked by hostile forces. We were also hungry and thirsty but a walk around what posed as a market convinced us that we should wait. Nothing looking safely edible or drinkable was on offer. The afternoon drew on and the thirst worsened. We wandered round the town and found what looked like a small official building. We knocked at the door and explained our plight. A kindly man advised against the water but opened an old cupboard to find some ancient bottles of Coca-Cola, which looked as if they had been there for years. We grabbed them eagerly and left, praying that by now our helicopter might be on the way back.

We waited at the airstrip as the skies gradually darkened, and then, thank God, we heard the sound of our rescuer in the distance. However, the ordeal was not quite over. As the young pilots picked us up, no longer carrying their VIP, they decided to have a bit of fun. Surrounded by hundreds of children excited by the arrival from the skies, we took off in the opposite direction and turned round in the distance.

We realized then what was going to happen. At speed, the helicopter dive-bombed the airstrip, kicking up dust all over the kids. Because

the windows were open we were covered as well. We flew fast back to
Maputo. These flying machines had their fuel tanks strapped to the
outside and several had been shot down by guerrillas firing into the
tanks, we were gravely informed. For that reason we had to fly fast and
as high as they dared.

By the time we got to Maputo, it was dusk. The four of us were
taken to the hotel. Delighted to be alive, we ran through the hotel and
jumped into the swimming pool. We savoured a dinner of langoustines
and watched the sun finally go down over the Indian Ocean, and were
later treated to a performance on the grand piano in the corner of the
entrance hall by the man from *The Sun*. All in a day's work.

Jenkins, Owen, Steel:
Third Party Hell

Sometimes the way the Westminster Lobby worked meant that you had to grin and bear it if a story you had written on information from the best source possible was denied.

You would be told things by ministers long before their press offices had learnt of them. So when the late-night call about your story to a Whitehall press officer was made by a rival newspaper, the result was often a denial. Or a ridiculous 'this is pure speculation' comment. If called by your own news desk at this point, you would tell them to ignore the denial and stick with the story. The most annoying thing of all was when, say, the BBC midnight news led on the denial as a way of running your story even though almost certainly a few days later the story would be shown to be true.

I remember ruefully such an incident in the early 1980s, when the breakaway of the Gang of Four led to the formation of the SDP and a tie-up with the Liberal party. These were days of heady excitement when the Alliance, as it became, scored dramatic victory after victory in by-elections up and down the country.

As the newest reporter on the *Times* Lobby team, it fell to me to cover most of those contests. None was more entertaining than a by-election in July 1981, when the rather grand Roy Jenkins, former Labour home secretary and president of the European Commission, went to the northern working-class town of Warrington and almost pulled off an astounding victory. The sight of Jenkins, introducing himself as 'Woy' to bare-chested men as he knocked on the doors of council houses, has always remained with me. As has the memory of Willie Whitelaw, then home secretary, slipping up and calling the hapless Tory candidate Stan Sorrell, Stan 'Laurel' by mistake. Jenkins was soon to win at Glasgow Hillhead and Shirley Williams at Crosby, and later Simon Hughes in Labour's Bermondsey stronghold, as the prospect of serious three- or four-party politics became real.

As the Alliance soared in the polls to more than fifty per cent, there was much talk – strange as it may seem now – of a Liberal–SDP government. Remember, this was before Margaret Thatcher's famous Falklands bounce. It was in that atmosphere that I splashed *The Times* on 1 April 1982 with a story that caused massive ructions in both the Alliance parties.

After a lunch with Richard Holme (then chief adviser to Liberal leader David Steel), I wrote that Steel had told Jenkins that if he was to serve under Prime Minister Jenkins in an Alliance government, he would expect to be deputy prime minister as well as either home secretary, foreign secretary or chancellor of the exchequer. Steel had been so upbeat that at his conference the previous autumn, he had told delegates to 'go back to your constituencies and prepare for government'.

I wrote that Jenkins and Steel would present themselves to the electorate as joint leaders of the Alliance or – a word coined by Holme – as a 'duumvirate'. I also said that Steel would have a decisive voice in the appointment of the Cabinet. The story caused an outcry in the Liberal grassroots, which hated the idea of Steel deferring to Jenkins, and it upset the SDP on the rather justifiable grounds that it looked presumptuous to be talking of forming a government a full year before the election.

It also upset Dr David Owen, Jenkins's rival for the leadership of the SDP, because that vote was still three months away and his supporters were not assuming Jenkins would be elected. As things turned out, he was, defeating Owen by 26,000 votes to nearly 21,000 – a surprisingly strong showing for the younger challenger. Owen had already been foreign secretary by then, one of Britain's youngest when appointed to the post by James Callaghan in 1977. As far back as 1972, he had resigned the front-bench over Labour's opposition to what was then the European Economic Community. He was strongly principled and stubborn.

After that story appeared, I was called by Holme – an extremely genial figure who later advised Paddy Ashdown – early the next morning to say: 'Sorry Phil, but I'm going to have to deny your story – I know you will ignore the denial and you will have every right to, but the pressure on us is so great that we will have to knock some of those ideas down.'

I told him I would indeed ignore the denial and hoped that he was not getting too much grief from his party. I was annoyed but it is the sort of thing with which Lobby correspondents are familiar. We have to accept that political figures will use us – and we them – to float ideas, policies and proposals, and that sometimes the machine will not have caught up with them, or that sometimes they will just not fly.

The story was, of course, absolutely on the button and the row both over the allocation of seats between the parties and the share-out of the top jobs dogged the Alliance right up to the 1983 election. Holme died in 2008. He would have loved the machinations of the 2010–15 coalition and might have advised Nick Clegg on the pitfalls.

I caused more trouble in August 1982, when I revealed, from a different source who is still active, that Steel was being urged to insist on the return of at least twenty seats already allocated to the SDP in return for Jenkins, now SDP leader, being called the Alliance's prime minister-designate.

The row over whether Jenkins or Steel should be the main man continued almost to the 1983 election campaign. Shirley Williams declared in March that Jenkins was the obvious choice, while two Liberal MPs defied Steel to say that he was the man for the job. It was pie in the sky and three months later Margaret Thatcher won a landslide victory. Far from forming a government, the Liberals returned seventeen MPs and the SDP a paltry six, even though the Alliance secured twenty-five per cent of the vote overall. Most SDP MPs who defected from Labour lost their seats, an outcome recalled by Labour moderates who today oppose a breakaway from Labour.

The first-past-the-post system did for it. I revealed shortly after the election how Steel and Jenkins had fallen out at a summit during the campaign at Steel's Ettrickbridge home. The SDP leader was upset at the way their meeting had been portrayed in advance as a 'Steel to take over' exercise in response to obvious signs that the Alliance was not making a breakthrough.

There had been tension within the SDP from the start, with Owen strongly in favour of it maintaining a very separate identity from the

Liberals, and Jenkins backing a closer relationship leading eventually to merger. Jenkins swiftly stood down after the election, to be replaced by Owen, and the Alliance regrouped. Again it did well in by-elections, giving the Tories a scare in Whitelaw's previously safe Penrith seat, and Elizabeth Shields wiping out a massive Conservative majority in Ryedale. In September 1985 – after a successful SDP conference seen as a triumph for Owen – *The Times* reported that the Alliance had taken a nine and a half per cent poll lead over the main parties.

But again it flattered to deceive. Relations between the two parties and their leaders were not good, with the Liberals favouring an agenda well to the left of the SDP. The leaders disagreed over whom they would work with in the event of a hung parliament, and the parties split on nuclear defence. In the event they need not have worried. In the 1987 election the Liberals stayed stuck on seventeen seats and the SDP fell to five.

The parties merged in 1988 against the wishes of Owen, who re-established the SDP for a few more years. The merged party was first called the Social and Liberal Democrats and then, in, 1989 with Paddy Ashdown in charge, it became the Liberal Democrats. It was to be twenty-one more years – despite efforts by Tony Blair and Ashdown, encouraged by Jenkins, to effect a realignment on the Left – before the Lib Dems were to take part in government as Nick Clegg went into coalition with David Cameron.

Five years later, they had gone full circle. The Lib Dems emerged from the 2015 election with eight MPs, three fewer that Steel's Liberals in 1979, and fifty-four fewer than Charles Kennedy's Lib Dems in 2005. They were no longer the third party, that place having gone to the Scottish Nationalists. In the cruel world of politics they had been punished by the voters.

John Smith:
Britain's Lost PM

I remember the day John Smith was elected Labour leader for very strong personal reasons. I watched his coronation at the Royal Horticultural Hall in central London on Saturday, 18 July 1992, and then raced to Croxley Green in Hertfordshire to lead my cricket team, the Old Talbotians, against the Fleet Street Strollers. The match had just started and someone quite rightly had grabbed my opening bat berth. But I went in at number three and managed a century.

Enough private glory. Smith's election was inevitable after Neil Kinnock went down to Labour's fourth defeat in a row on 9 April. A Labour victory had looked on the cards for most of that year but a combination of factors, no doubt including Kinnock's apparently triumphalist Sheffield rally speech, turned the vote John Major's way.

I felt that Labour's late tactic – when a hung parliament seemed possible – of holding out the prospect of a deal with the Liberal Democrats on electoral reform had backfired. It reminded former Conservative voters who were flirting with the idea of going Lib Dem that by doing so they were helping Kinnock into Downing Street. I'm certain from talking to many in my own circle of friends that the idea must have sent a lot back into the Tory fold.

I sensed trouble for Kinnock when – after spending much of the election office-bound or travelling with John Major – I flew north with him on the last Monday of the campaign. We stopped first at Sandwell, near Birmingham, for a factory visit. There I ran into a great friend and contact from her Labour national executive days, Betty Boothroyd, who was to be elected speaker in the next parliament. Betty was a terrific judge of the electoral mood and told me quite bluntly: 'We are not going to make it. I'm going to be all right here [her constituency was the safe seat of West Bromwich West], but not enough people are coming across to us. It is not happening.'

I was an admirer of Kinnock as a speaker and had wanted to see him in action before the election. We flew on to Jack Straw's Blackburn seat where Kinnock spoke at a rally. He did not fire. The brilliant orator we all knew did not turn up. Watching at the back of the hall with his wife, Glenys, I asked what was wrong and she shook her head and said: 'We are worried.' It was not until after the election I learnt that, according to their private polling, Labour's vote was already on the slide just four days out.

On the Wednesday after the election, Kinnock quit with an outspoken attack on the Conservative press for helping the Tories achieve an election victory that he said they could not have managed on their own. It was a sad moment for a leader who had done so much to make his party electable, but did not convince the electorate that he was the man to take it back to Downing Street.

It was a personal tragedy for a likeable man, but it looked as if Smith would be the one to benefit. There had been a damaging clash in the latter months of the Kinnock reign after Smith, then shadow chancellor, laid out his plans for government in a detailed shadow budget that many felt was handing an armoury of ammunition to the Conservatives. Kinnock was deeply concerned about his plan to abolish the £21,000 earnings ceiling on National Insurance contributions, and there was disarray after Kinnock gave a private briefing to Lobby correspondents – including my colleague Jill Sherman – suggesting the changes would be phased in. The shadow budget, proposing an increase in the top rate of tax to 50p, was a valuable weapon for the Tories in the election.

However, when Kinnock went there was little doubt that Smith would win. Gordon Brown, at that time the senior partner in the Brown–Blair modernizing partnership, was pushed privately to stand but would not contemplate taking on a man for whom he had huge regard. Smith had been the youngest member of the Cabinet in the last Labour government, was a brilliant House of Commons performer, and highly popular. And he had made a full recovery from a heart attack in 1988.

He defeated Bryan Gould by a massive majority and the Tory Government debacle over the European exchange rate mechanism in

September gave him an easy opportunity to shine. But there were concerns among figures such as Blair, Brown and Peter Mandelson that Smith's heart was not in the kind of radical modernization they wanted. There were fears that he believed he could take Labour to power using the 'one more heave' approach and that he was not yet ready to dismantle Labour's tax-and-spend millstone.

It was against this background that Peter Riddell and I were invited to Smith's flat in London's Barbican on 7 February 1993 for his first set-piece interview with *The Times* since becoming leader. Smith rushed in after delivering a speech at a Bournemouth conference that afternoon and took head-on our questions about criticisms of his style:

> I am very anxious that we march to the beat of our own drum – not to the demands of anyone else. I am prepared to take criticism sometimes for not jumping about and producing whizz-bang policies on a daily basis. It is far more important that we consider policies carefully – that we consult about them and we get the right policies.

He told us he was ready to combine with the Tory rebels to defeat John Major over the Maastricht Treaty, which he did, and he gave notice that legislation to prevent hereditary peers sitting in the Lords would be an early priority for the next Labour government, which it was. It was a relaxed Smith who enjoyed a bottle of wine with us, even though he had changed his eating and drinking habits after that first heart attack. He was an amusing, friendly man, who nevertheless did not suffer fools gladly.

The pace of Labour reform, however, was not enough for the modernizers and they were not afraid to let that be known. Smith was not helped by the fact that his deputy, Margaret Beckett, was less than keen on Smith's 'one member, one vote' reforms to change his party's links with the unions. I remember at a dinner with Blair in English's restaurant at the Brighton conference that year that he was desperately unhappy about the speed of changes being made within the party, and he gave me the distinct impression that he would not stay on in Parliament if Smith did not do enough to take Labour to victory at the next election. Blair was really all about government, and he had had quite long enough in opposition.

I half considered a 'Blair ready to quit' story but felt it would look incredible at this stage of Parliament. Instead, I wrote a story, with which *The Times* splashed, suggesting that Smith's reforms were threatened by a rift with Beckett. She had been asked directly if she hoped Smith would win his vote on having a one member, one vote system for selecting parliamentary candidates, and replied only that she hoped they would be able to reach a decision. Thanks for nothing, Margaret!

It should not be forgotten that Beckett was once seen as a fully paid-up member of the hard left, a long way from the politician whom Blair was to make his foreign secretary in 2006 and the elder states-person of today. In 1981, she accused Neil Kinnock and others of treachery for abstaining in the vote that seemed likely to result in Tony Benn becoming deputy leader. Denis Healey won thanks to those abstentions. After the vote there was a late-night altercation in the conference hotel between Beckett and Joan Lestor, the soft-left Kinnockite. Lestor said she would not take lessons in loyalty from Beckett.

By 1993 Blair remained suspicious of Beckett, whose lukewarm backing for Smith's plan to end the union role in selections was seen as playing to the left-wing and union gallery because she feared a challenge from John Prescott for her job the following year. A senior party figure told me at the time that Beckett had appeared on the Smith leadership ticket to ensure that he won the vote of the transport workers' union. Now they were calling in the chips. And Smith, according to my informants, was exasperated by her behaviour.

As things turned out, Smith won a precious victory over the plan on the Wednesday, with Prescott delivering a barnstorming speech in his support. It was the biggest internal reform of his leadership. Beckett survived her revolt and went on to serve in government. She and her popular husband, Leo – they go on caravanning holidays together – have been permanent fixtures on the Westminster scene ever since, and Blair was to bury those reservations because Beckett showed herself to be a competent, supportive minister.

With the Tories in turmoil, Smith appeared to be heading inevitably towards Downing Street. In the local elections of 1994, the Conservatives suffered their worst reverses for thirty years and Labour's poll lead was huge. On the evening of 11 May 1994, Smith spoke at a fund-raising event at London's Park Lane Hotel and declared: 'The opportunity to serve our country – that is all we ask.'

The next morning he suffered a massive heart attack at his Barbican flat and died in hospital shortly afterwards. I wrote that, like Gaitskell and R. A. Butler, he would be numbered among the best prime ministers Britain never had. Denis Healey could be added to that list. Along with a handful of other journalists, I was invited by Smith's widow, Elizabeth, to his funeral in Edinburgh and felt privileged to be there. He was buried on the island of Iona.

After 1992, the Deluge

John Major's rise to foreign secretary, chancellor and then prime minister in no time at all should not really have caused the surprise it did among MPs and the press.

The Lobby always regarded him as one of most astute of Tory politicians, one you would go to if you wanted to know the latest on who was up and who was down in Conservative-land. I first met him within days of joining the Lobby in 1981 and always found him one of the most friendly and helpful MPs, first as a junior whip and then as he moved swiftly through the ranks of government.

He was ambitious and clever, good at collecting allies and being different things to different people. As we know, Margaret Thatcher was convinced initially that he was a worthy successor to her. It was not an opinion she held for long.

Journalists like myself and Elinor Goodman, of the *FT* and then Channel 4, rather selfishly regretted it when he rose to the Foreign Office, knowing that he would be much harder to reach for an opinion in that hallowed building. Major got where he was through being able, popular, supremely tactical and consensual. But he always seemed to be one step ahead of his colleagues and was certainly in the right place at the right time when Margaret Thatcher had to make key appointments during the crisis that ended her leadership.

Those skills were immediately on view after his shock elevation to Number 10 when he brought back Michael Heseltine to see off the poll tax. I wrote in December 1990 that an MP had called the poll tax 'the flagship that sank the admiral [Thatcher]' and Major was determined not to be a second victim. He also introduced a new style of running the Cabinet, allowing ministers to pitch in on other's territory. He was, according to the polls, the most popular PM for thirty years.

In Europe he was trying to avoid the perpetual conflict that fellow leaders associated with Thatcher's premiership. His negotiating skills were hailed the following year as he emerged from the Maastricht summit. The Maastricht Treaty, signed in February 1992, represented the biggest step since the founding Treaty of Rome towards European integration. It created the European Union and paved the way for the single currency (or euro).

But Major emerged from the intense negotiations with his aides claiming 'game, set and match' as he secured opt-outs for Britain on the single currency and the social chapter. It was a deal that held the Tory party together and helped it to go on and defeat Neil Kinnock, seemingly against the odds, in 1992. A late surge to the Tories from voters who were flirting with the Liberal Democrats saw Major, who had used an upturned soapbox as he travelled the country, achieve an outright majority. To say that was a high point would be an understatement because Maastricht and associated European issues were to dog Major throughout his 1992–7 term, leading eventually to a Blair landslide in 1997.

After the 1992 victory, it was the shortest of honeymoons and by late September I was writing about the prospect of a leadership challenge to Major. I had covered one of the most dramatic days in post-war political history when Britain was forced out of the exchange rate mechanism – the device that was supposed to keep national exchange rates close to a European norm – on Black Wednesday, as 16 September 1992 came to be known. The decision came after a tumultuous day in which interest rates were raised in two stages by five per cent as Major and Norman Lamont, his chancellor, tried and failed to save the pound's parity with the mark.

So soon after the election, it was a moment from which Major and his government never recovered because it called into question its economic competence. Major tried to defend membership of the ERM but I reported the views of senior Tories that if he even tried to go back, half his Cabinet would walk out on him and precipitate an inevitable challenge. He had indeed contemplated resignation himself. Lamont rode out the storm for a time but, seven months later, Major dropped him shortly after a disastrous defeat in the Newbury by-election and replaced him with Kenneth Clarke. Lamont, in a resignation speech reminiscent of Sir Geoffrey Howe's three years earlier, said the Government gave the impression of 'being in office but not in power'.

But Maastricht and the treaty ratification was the issue that was to sap Major's will and strength. He had implacable rebels up against him, including Iain Duncan Smith, a future leader. After a series of scrapes, he was defeated by a combination of Labour and Tory rebels on a social chapter vote and had to call a confidence vote the next day, 23 July 1993, in order to restore what was left of his battered authority.

There then came one of those moments that befall prime ministers when it's all going wrong. He did an interview with the estimable Michael Brunson of ITV. That was fine but once it had been completed, Brunson carried on his chat with Major, asking him questions that were supposed to be off the record. However, the live feed was still running, which neither party knew. When Brunson asked Major why he did not sack the conspiring ministers, he gave an explosive reply that was later picked up by other broadcasters. He replied: 'Just think it through from my perspective. You are the prime minister, with a majority of eighteen … where do you think most of the poison is coming from? From the dispossessed and the never-possessed. Do we want three more of the bastards out there?'

From then on the 'bastards', fairly or not, were identified as Peter Lilley, Michael Howard and Michael Portillo, three of the leading sceptics in his Cabinet. For me the next highlight in this seemingly never-ending saga came on the lovely Greek island of Corfu in June 1994. There Major, no longer the agreeable figure they had welcomed after the years of Thatcher lectures, told European leaders he could not accept the federalist Jean-Luc Dehaene as the next president of the commission.

The Belgian Prime Minister was the choice of France and Germany to replace Jacques Delors at the end of the year. But British officials said that Dehaene did not fit the bill, and would not command the consensus and wide support across the Community that was needed for somebody who was going to be president for the next five years.

Major had wielded the veto late on the Friday evening. Christopher Meyer, his press secretary with whom I often played squash (and who later became UK ambassador in Washington), had rung me and told me to round up the press party for a late-night briefing. Sometimes they were a waste of time; this one was not.

For us globetrotters there was no let-up and by September we were in South Africa. Major had encouraged a group of sporting icons – Bobby Charlton, Rob Andrew, Colin Cowdrey and heptathlete Judy Simpson – to come along to promote sport in the townships. Margaret Thatcher, by no means for the first time, caused trouble during the trip on which Major was trying to encourage international companies to come to South Africa. Speaking in India, she had doubted the willingness of international investors to come to South Africa because of fears of violence in words that seemed certain to undermine Major's trip.

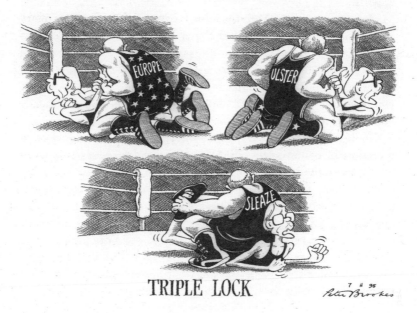

TRIPLE LOCK

The problems were smoothed over and the cricket-loving Major, a devout supporter of Surrey, appropriately went to the Alexandra Township Oval. He opened the nets, and then proceeded to show off some polished strokes and clean-bowled the South African sports minister. It was a happy relief during times of trouble.

There really was no easing up and by November Major turned a vote on increasing Britain's contribution to the EU into a confidence issue to bring his Cabinet on side. The Cabinet right-wingers, including Portillo, Lilley and John Redwood, were forced to go along with a so-called 'suicide pact' in which they all said they would go down with Major if he lost the vote, which of course he did not.

Then came the bravest moment of Major's premiership. Fed up by the constant sniping, he called the Lobby to the Downing Street rose garden on 24 June 1995 and announced that he was resigning as Conservative leader, telling his critics to 'put up or shut up'. Major – who had not lost his strategic nous – knew that a leadership challenge to him in the autumn was all but inevitable, so he tried to take his critics by surprise, believing he would attract a back-bench challenger at worst.

He was wrong. By Monday, John Redwood, the Welsh secretary and former policy adviser to Thatcher, was ready to throw his hat into the ring, resign from the Cabinet and take on Major as the right-wing champion. Major was confident of winning, and did, but it added to the sense of disarray surrounding the Government and exploded the pretence of Cabinet unity. Other Cabinet ministers tried to dissuade Redwood but he would not be moved.

On 26 June he launched his campaign. As I wrote, he came close to receiving the endorsement of Baroness Thatcher. Asked in Washington whom she supported, Lady Thatcher said the result of the leadership contest had to be that 'we must have the true Conservative policies that I pursued; policies of lower taxes, keeping our national parliamentary sovereignty and the independence of the pound sterling'. She had referred to the revival of right-wing Reaganite Republicanism in America and added: 'I suspect something similar is about to happen in my own country.' Not much doubt what she meant, and whom she supported.

Redwood accused Major of jeopardizing the party's position by quitting, leaving it in limbo when it needed firm leadership. His resignation letter said that he had put forward ideas on how Major could avoid a challenge in the autumn and that he had been devastated the next day to learn from another minister that the Prime Minister had decided to stand down.

When the result came, it was far from what the Major campaign wanted. But it was enough. I wrote that he looked certain to lead the Conservatives into the next general election after pulling off the riskiest gamble of his political life. He won a decisive, although not over-whelming, victory. The Prime Minister was backed by 218 of the 329 Conservative MPs entitled to vote, with his challenger, Redwood, receiving a highly respectable 89 votes.

I also speculated that Michael Heseltine might be made deputy prime minister, which he was. It was interesting because some MPs had been pushing Heseltine to let it be known that he would be a candidate if Major was forced out after the first round. He declined. A few weeks later Peter Riddell and I interviewed Heseltine, and he surprised us by revealing that Major had informally offered him the job of deputy prime minister three weeks before he called the leader-ship election.

Heseltine told us of a private, late-night Commons meeting in which he first learnt Major wanted him as his number two, another at which Major confided he would take on all comers in a leadership fight, and a third on the day of the election when the PM confirmed Heseltine would get the job of deputy if he won. It restored our faith in Major, the fixer. Long before the election, Major had spoken of a significant promotion with the man who at the time was considered the favourite to succeed him if he was ousted.

We asked if Major might have made the move to get him on side in advance and Heseltine, with only the hint of a smile, said he had not thought of such a 'Machiavellian interpretation'. It was clever. I had been told by several Heseltine allies that they were dismayed when he told them to vote for Major in the first round. Heseltine had given up his last chance of becoming leader, but his consolation was the number-two job.

Major had bought time, but that was all. Tony Blair was by now looking a certainty to take Labour back to power in an election that had to be held in the spring of 1997, and the Tories, also dogged by sleaze allegations, were still banging on about Europe.

In November 1996 there was yet another big revolt as pro-Euro-peans united with Eurosceptics to protest against Major's refusal to allow a Commons debate on the single currency. A private meeting of the 1922 Committee of Tory back-benchers delivered what MPs called a 'unanimous and uncompromising' message to Major that he must change his mind. Sir Marcus Fox, chairman of the committee, and two other officers were asked by the executive of the committee to seek an urgent meeting with the Prime Minister to convey the full weight of back-bench anger.

The Prime Minister was reported to be in no mood to back down. In the febrile atmosphere at Westminster, one or two Tory MPs hinted that they could be forced into resigning the whip and there was even gossip that the rift could spiral into a confidence issue which might bring the Government down. Such talk was regarded as fanciful but one senior Tory loyalist told me that a 'dangerous gulf' was opening up between the party and the Government: 'I really do not know what is going on. Who is advising the Prime Minister?'

Kenneth Clarke, the pro-European chancellor, then agreed to face his party's Eurosceptics in a gamble designed to quell the renewed Tory turmoil over the single currency and turn attention back to his Budget the day afterwards. Then Major and Heseltine joined forces to crush the hopes of the Tory Right that the Conservatives could go into the general election on a pledge to keep Britain out of the European single currency. The Prime Minister dismayed Eurosceptics by ruling out a change in the wait-and-see policy in the present Parliament and, for the first time, in the election campaign itself.

The hardening of Major's opposition to a U-turn came after two days of intense speculation that he might be about to shift and launch a backstairs campaign to persuade Clarke to go along with him. The opposite had happened. A fierce response by the chancellor to any idea of a retreat strengthened Westminster opinion that he would resign if the policy changed. The policy of keeping open options on the single currency appeared to have become set in stone.

I wrote that in the behind-the-scenes ministerial power struggle over Europe, the sceptics had been vanquished. The Right were furious with Major, alleging that he had given in to the Clarke–Heseltine axis and prevented the party adopting an electoral policy that would have set the Tories apart from Labour.

In a final victory for the pro-Europeans, Clarke won Cabinet agreement that the wait-and-see policy on the single currency could not be changed before the general election. But a group of senior ministers, led by Home Secretary Michael Howard, argued that the Government should, while leaving options open, declare before the election that the chances of Britain joining the single currency during the next Parliament were highly unlikely. It was a forerunner of the

Labour row over whether Britain should join the single currency, which was to dominate the early months and years of the incoming Blair government.

The Europe argument was settled for the time being. The election was months away and Blair was on a straight course to victory. Major had fought a courageous battle against heavy odds. Europe had cost Margaret Thatcher her job. Major had survived a turbulent parliament, often by his own cunning. But the rows over Europe presented to the electorate a party that was divided from top to bottom. Such forces do not win elections, and there was never a chance that Major would repeat 1992.

Carrying On up the Khyber

A trip by John Major to the Indian subcontinent that was to involve a stop-off at the Khyber Pass was always going to be a Carry On – and so it proved.

Major's foreign travels were always productive for the Lobby. With an election only four months away, and the Conservatives facing what looked like certain defeat against Tony Blair, this one was no exception. So we set off for India with high hopes, and they were to be realized if column inches were our guide to success – which they were.

I admired Major. He had endured four years of hell at the hands of his back-benchers, his Cabinet and the press; he knew even then that he was heading for certain defeat at the election. Yet he maintained his good nature and discipline in the face of a travelling Lobby party who were waiting for him to trip up, as he knew. The forever-toxic issue of Europe was soon to cast his party out of power for more than thirteen years. The nation had taken to Tony Blair, who had convinced voters that he had thrown aside the worst of Old Labour and replaced it with something new and fresh.

Arriving in Calcutta (now Kolkata) on 9 January 1997, we were able to write pieces saying that Major was blazing the election trail 5,000 miles from home with a speech that was a barely veiled pitch for the million-plus Asian votes in Britain. We went to a splendid diplomatic open-air party in Major's honour that night, and were looking forward to sampling the local culinary delights. However, one of our number, the excellent Henry Macrory of the *Star*, had told us he was deeply suspicious of Indian food, and had brought with him his own supply of pork pies. These he kept in his small case despite warnings from many of us that the chances of them surviving for long in the heat were not great. That evening he was seen to sneak off to the edge of the party and consume one of his pies.

Two days later I was able to write from Dhaka, the capital of Bangladesh, that Major and the people around him had given the clearest possible hint on the back of a briefing that day that the general election would be on 1 May. A by-election was imminent in Merseyside and there had been speculation that he might call the general election in March to avoid having to hold it. But Major was sticking to his preference for 1 May, which eventually became Election Day.

By this stage of his premiership, Major was cutting a pretty forlorn figure. Battered by the rows with his uncontrollable Eurosceptics, he must have been quietly looking forward to the time when he could spend more of his days at the Oval and Lord's. Yet he had to carry on with the pretence that the forthcoming election was winnable and to deal with the latest problems to emerge from Brussels. For the journalists travelling, this trip felt like his swansong, and when we got to talk to him – which was more than on some foreign trips – he maintained his geniality, patience and good humour.

Before leaving for Dhaka there was a mini-incident in Bangalore, to where we had flown from Calcutta. After filing our stories for the night, we were relaxing by the hotel pool – a rare chance for us! – waiting for the PM's convoy to arrive. The plan was for our press bus to fit into the convoy and race to the airport for the flight to Dhaka.

Sadly, our rather dozy driver lost the convoy within seconds, leaving Major heading off with the police escort and the press stranded in impossible Indian traffic. We arrived much later, severely delaying the flight, and were told in due course that Norma Major, after several years of suffering the antics of the travelling press, had suggested that the aircraft leave without us. We could understand her point, but perhaps wiser counsels prevailed.

Saturday was quiet enough for most of us to head off to a rather nice golf course in Dhaka, although I did by my bit for *The Sunday Times*. Then on Sunday we were flying to Islamabad, Pakistan, when Nick Wood, my former deputy who now worked as political editor of the *Express*, and I grabbed a quick interview with the PM. It resulted in a big story for our Monday papers.

I wrote that a compromise aimed at breaking the deadlock over Europe's direction and binding Tory party wounds was to be proposed by Major to his European Union partners. I said that the Prime Minister was tabling ideas for a multi-speed Europe that would allow Britain and other countries greater flexibility to opt out of EU activities and policies that they were happy to see the rest pursuing. All countries would retain the veto to stop small or elite groups pressing ahead with policies that they regarded as dangerous or unsuitable for the EU. Strange how the Europe debate has not changed that much over the years.

He claimed to have found a way of resolving the serious dispute over the speed at which the EU should develop and integrate. Although he declined to show his negotiating hand by giving full details, Major clearly indicated that he believed there could be agreement over a formula by which countries could choose their pace of development, I reported.

In Islamabad the press party was asked to pool and divide its forces. Most were to be driven north to Peshawar to prepare for the Khyber visit the next day, while David Hughes, of the *Mail*, and I stayed in Islamabad to cover Major's meeting with Benazir Bhutto, the former

Pakistani prime minister. The plan was for us then to be dropped by helicopter at the pass the next morning to meet up with the rest. The downside of this arrangement was that the rest would come back by helicopter but David and I would be driven back by taxi.

The Bhutto meeting gave us a decent story, which we sent to our colleagues when they got to Peshawar. I wrote that Major was drawn into the turmoil of Pakistani politics as Bhutto seized the opportunity of his visit to launch an outspoken attack on President Leghari, who had dismissed her two months previously. It was quite a moment, and one I remembered when I happened to sit on the table next to her in a London restaurant several years later. And, of course, when she was assassinated in Rawalpindi in 2007.

David Hughes and I and were taken to a military airport the next morning to be flown by helicopter to join up with the rest of our party and the Downing Street crowd. It was to be the opportunity for me to secure my favourite dateline in the hundreds of thousands of miles I flew with prime ministers.

Under the byline 'From Philip Webster, Political Editor, at the Khyber Pass', I was able to write about Major's visit, which was intended to show him how Pakistan was fighting the battle against the drug barons who use the pass and others like it to bring in their lethal stocks of opium from the Afghan poppy fields. The task faced by the anti-narcotics forces, to which Britain contributes training and other assistance including Customs and Excise officers, was massive. I indulged myself, and the paper indulged me, by allowing me to attempt the learned and the lyrical with a piece about Britain's retreat from Kabul in 1842.

There was a good story for us when Major had to call off a planned walkabout at the Khyber Pass's high point of Landi Khotal, where the Khyber Rifles are also based. The tribesmen had been asked to hand in the guns they all carry for the day. Thousands of them had come in from the hills and lined the village as Major drove through. But he was not to stop there; it was a security man's nightmare. No one could be sure who had guns. His staff were told how the tribesmen gave their sons Kalashnikov rifles as a present when they reached the age of thirteen.

It was an unforgettable experience, and not for the first or last time I reflected on how fortunate I was. The journey back to Islamabad was not so much fun. Our driver travelled at ridiculously high speeds. He was – we learnt – fasting and seemed to think that the quicker he went the quicker nightfall, and food, would come. He overtook with cars coming straight at us in the opposite direction and it was a merciful release when he stopped at a garage to stock up on oranges and other goodies.

Back in Islamabad we filed the rest of our copy and went for an evening out, a reception at the high commissioner's residence. It was nearly the end of a wonderful trip and morale was high. The drinks and the talk were flowing when the moment came to leave at around 10 p.m. The drinks table was still groaning and Messrs Macrory and Wood looked longingly at an unopened bottle of whisky, thinking that the night could not possibly end there. There was a debate as to whether it could be taken, as it was probably paid for with taxpayers' money. But Macrory considered that to be a dishonourable course. Instead he asked our man in Islamabad whether he knew of an off-licence in the area! He was told to help himself.

So it was back to the hotel, with Macrory armed with his whisky. Most of us wimpishly went to bed, thinking of the early morning flight. Sitting outside the hotel the next morning in the bus as we were about to leave for the airport with the convoy, I noticed that we were one short. Nick Wood was not with us. A call to his room by the hotel reception woke him. Within about three minutes, an utterly discombobulated Wood appeared, to be greeted in silence by irritated colleagues. He was in a smart pin-striped suit as usual, but he was wearing it over his pyjamas, a condition in which he met the Prime Minister later when we saw him on the plane.

It should be added here that on the flight out of Dhaka, there was a bang in the locker over Macrory's head. It was not enough to cause alarm but it was a definite 'phut'. His last pork pie had exploded in his case, succumbing to cabin air pressure.

A Day in the Life
of a Political Editor

A day in the life of a political editor often amounts to seventeen or eighteen hours. I did the job for *The Times* from 1993 to early 2010, and it was not unusual for the day to be that long and not impossible, as I relate in other chapters, for it to be even longer, if you include the time spent trying to sleep on an aircraft while travelling with the prime minister of the day.

But let me try and take the reader through one of those long days to give those from outside the world of political journalism an idea of what it involved.

7 a.m. Wake up, usually without an alarm, but one has been set for 7.15 just in case. Turn on the *Today* programme. The radio is within reach. Listen for a few minutes and then turn the radio up loud while showering and dressing. By now, all the day's papers have tumbled loudly through the door.

7.30 a.m. Go to the kitchen and turn another radio on. Still Humphrys, Naughtie and the rest. The *Today* programme is utterly irreplaceable. Prepare and eat breakfast while standing in the kitchen, reading the papers, praying that the others have not scooped you in the later editions. I would know by now if they had exclusives in their early editions. Start thinking about the likely best stories of the day, which ones I would do, and which I would farm out to the team.

8.30 a.m. First call of the day would come in, probably from John Wellman, if he was news editing, swiftly followed by Roland Watson, Mike Smith, Dave Taylor or Jeremy Griffin, if they were head of news for the day. Even at that stage, politics would be the obvious first choice for the main stories of the day. Only when another major non-political story was brewing would those calls not happen.

8.45 a.m. Leave home and drive from West London to Westminster, making hands-free calls to Downing Street, the Opposition party, and any other obvious sources I would need before briefing the news desk properly on what we would be doing during the day. If I was sending someone out of town, call them early and stop them coming into Westminster. I was fortunate enough to have a Commons car park pass so the drive was a good time to prepare.

9.30–9.45 a.m. Arrive at Westminster and, having collected thoughts on the way, tell the news editor all obvious lines for the day at that stage. I would not mention in this call my thoughts or hopes for any off-diary story that might give us a potential splash – the lead story – later in the day, but they would know I was thinking about it. Discuss with the team what we would be doing. For most of my time we were a team of five or six reporters, with a sketch-writer.

10.30 a.m. Take a quick look around the Members' Lobby. At this time, not too many back-bench MPs are around but the whips, whose offices are alongside the Lobby, were always busy then. Most of them liked to chat.

10.45 a.m. Head to the Treasury – it used to be Number 10 – for the first briefing of the day from the Prime Minister's spokesman. Usually a run-through of the PM's day and questions on whatever were the stories of the moment. The spokesman would have come armed with lines on everything that mattered. It lasts thirty minutes or so.

11.45 a.m. Another chat with the news desk to update them on anything I'd heard at the briefing or from anywhere else, and any stories my colleagues had told me about. They would tell me how the paper's morning conference felt about the early list, the stories the editor was keen on, any extra requests that had arisen during the meeting. The morning and afternoon conferences are the key moments in any day at *The Times*. Heads of all the paper's different departments present their list of wares for the day and take the meeting through the best of them. Home news is followed by foreign, business, sport, comment pages, features, obits, the lot. Questions follow. The various department editors have a big responsibility. Good stories can die here if they are not sold properly or they don't know the answers to searching queries.

I would then pass all of that on to the team and the day proper would be under way.

12 p.m. Return to the Lobby, and in later years Portcullis House (opened in 2001 to provide office space for over 200 MPs), to talk to ministers, MPs and other sources about the running stories, all the time trying to work up something else to surprise the office with later on. As political editor, I knew that I would have to write or pull together the main running story, but the search is always on for an exclusive line that people will not have seen on the 10 p.m. news bulletin – something that you hope will excite and interest them when they are having their breakfast. There are the open sources, such as the Number 10 briefings, speeches from ministers, committee meetings in the House, and the proceedings on the floor of the chamber, starting in the mornings on Wednesdays and Thursdays and at 2.30 p.m. on a Monday and Tuesday. And then there are the closed sources, the contacts and deep throats in all parties that you've built up over the years and call on the private Commons line in the office.

12.45 p.m. Rush to lunch at one of many favoured restaurants within walking distance or a quick taxi ride from Westminster. I was usually with a lunch partner, Elinor Goodman, and later Gary Gibbon of Channel 4, or Charles Reiss of the *Standard*. Choice of lunch partners was one of the great rituals of Westminster reporting and the tie-ups obviously changed the more senior you became. Today our guest at the Cinnamon Club is one of our favourites, and a glass or two of wine is guaranteed. Politicians and journalists have drunk less and less at these encounters over the years but the tone is usually set by the guest. If he or she fancies a drink, the journalists will eagerly go along with it. The lunch is on non-attributable Lobby terms, and that's fine because more will emerge than if it was a public encounter like a press conference.

2.30 p.m. Race back to the office, usually by going through the St Stephen's Entrance of the Commons into the Central Lobby and turning left into the Members' Lobby, which is typically beginning to bustle at this time. Phone calls or texts along the way have told me any further developments during the morning, and of any good interviews on BBC Radio 4's *World at One* or anywhere else. This is the time to grab a valuable few minutes with any politician who might be figuring in your stories later on.

3 p.m. Call the news desk which is by now frantically preparing the afternoon schedule and is still desperate for a splash. Tell them your best shots at this stage to give them their lines to go at the top. Reassure them that the top story will make a splash by the time you've made a few more calls. Don't mention anything you might have up your sleeve.

Discuss with colleagues their stories and how they are going. Has anyone got an obvious splash with which we can placate a hungry office? No, but someone has got an obvious page two lead and someone else is working on something that – if true – would be a contender for the splash.

3.40 p.m. Final pre-conference call to the news desk. Give them any new stories that have emerged and confirm best hopes for a splash. Wish them luck.

3.45 p.m. Climb the stairs to the Lobby room for the afternoon PM's spokesman briefing. Get it over with quickly. There's nothing new from there. Get down to the Lobby fast, calling a special adviser to the Cabinet minister with whom we had lunch on the way.

4.30 p.m. Call the news desk from the Lobby to see if the afternoon conference, especially the editor, is happy with what they've got so far. They are! They reckon the story at the top of the list will give them the splash. Pressure off for now, but having spoken to the 'spad', I'm thinking that the lunch story might be better because it is exclusive. By sheer chance, here's the minister we've had lunch with. Run a couple more questions by him and give him at least a hint that this might be playing big in the morning. He knows what he is doing and gives the impression that this was what he expected all along.

5.30 p.m. Now I've got two big stories to write. I tell the news desk about the new one. They are very excited because it has not been sitting on the list all day but, of course, I had not been sure about it until my call with the 'spad'. That's my story anyway, if they think I've been deliberately holding it back to achieve maximum impact later. Which is, of course, what I have been doing.

After discussions in the office, I get a call to say my new story is the splash and the other one is page-two lead. My colleague then tells me that their story had stood up well, and it, too, is a candidate for the splash. I inform a by-now-overexcited office and tell everyone else to get writing fast. Let's give 'em the stories and they can decide what they want to splash on.

6.30 p.m. Original story done and sent. Colleague asks me to look over their big one. Great stuff. Make a suggestion about tightening the intro a bit. That's sent and everyone else has filed.

I write up potential splash having told lunch partner that we are going to run it big. A flavour of it appears in said partner's two-way at the end of report on *Channel 4 News*.

7.15 p.m. File. Five minutes later, head of news calls and says it's the splash and makes a couple of suggestions about taking in lines from another story elsewhere in the office. I do that and resend.

7.30 p.m. Quick half in the Press Gallery bar. Colleagues ask if we've got anything special. We admit to having two quite good stories which will be worth them having a look at later. One or two of them reciprocate by saying they have something good as well.

8 p.m. Quick scoot down to the Lobby to catch MPs before they head to dinner.

10 p.m. Division in the Commons on fairly boring bill but should hang about just in case. Run into my minister yet again and tell him that he's responsible for the morning's splash in *The Times*. He runs off rather quickly, hoping no one has seen us talking.

10.30 p.m. Leave for home.

11.15 p.m. Call from James Burleigh, night news editor. *Guardian* have got a good Labour splash. What did I think of it? Not bad. Would he mind calling the night duty person and say I think it's worth a few paragraphs?

11.45 p.m. James calls again with a line in *Telegraph* story that could nicely be incorporated in my splash. I check it out with my 'spad' friend and it's fine. I e-mail James with three insert paragraphs, and say goodnight.

Midnight. Go to bed but listen to the late news on Radio 4. Ah, they've just read out the top of the *Times* lead story. Sleep.

Postscript: Fridays tended to be casual days at the Commons. I once went into the office in my jeans knowing that, because the House was not sitting, I would not be breaking any rules. The House demanded reasonably smart gear, and certainly a tie for men.

During the morning I got an urgent call from the office of the editor, Peter Stothard. I was told: 'Please get down here quickly. Peter's got lunch with Rupert Murdoch and wants you to be there.' 'Of course,' I said, wondering how I could possibly appear before the ultimate boss dressed as I was. At that moment, one of my great team, Arthur Leathley, entered the room. I looked him over and told him I needed his suit. We were of similar size, although I judged his waist measurement was a bit wider. We then took adjoining cubicles in the Press Gallery Gents and passed each other's clothes over the top. During the afternoon, after I had returned, we did the exercise in reverse. Such was the cooperation in the *Times* office.

PPS: Television and radio broadcasting was a regular part of life as a political correspondent. But for me, one of the happiest memories was of a live appearance on *Richard & Judy*, the daily chat show hosted by Richard Madeley and Judy Finnigan. I was no more than a supporting act. I appeared in June 2007 alongside Lee McConville, an 'at risk' youngster from a tough part of Birmingham whom I was trying to turn into a journalist. Lee had been picked to benefit from a mentoring scheme financed by the culture department and run by the Media Trust to help youngsters escape from difficult circumstances in their home areas. I agreed to be his mentor and it became one of the most fulfilling experiences of my career. I showed him how to interview Cabinet ministers and then took him to the G8 summit in Heiligendamm, Germany, when I sent him along to an early morning summit between George Bush and Tony Blair, their last official meeting.

I wrote about the whole experience in *The Times*, and so did Lee under the headline 'I thought Phil would be a boring old fart, but he wasn't like that at all'. Richard and Judy noticed and we went on together to talk all about it, Lee more than holding his own under difficult questioning. He later went on to do a full-year journalism course at Harlow in Essex, the one I had been on forty years before him, and we helped him into a new life.

1997: Granita and All That

On the evening before Labour's election victory in 1997, Alastair Campbell called me from Tony Blair's constituency home. He knew that, as always, *The Times* would be running its final opinion poll in that night's paper and, as usual, was seeking a bit of guidance for his boss.

I told him that Labour had an absolutely massive lead and was heading for a landslide. It should have been no great surprise because the polls had been saying that for some days. I did not mention that if our MORI survey was translated into seats, the majority could be more than 180.

Alastair's response surprised me. 'Talk to Tony,' he said. Blair was with him and was fighting to grab the phone off him.

'Phil, what's this about you saying it's going to be a landslide?' he said.

'You are going to get a landslide,' I said confidently.

'But if you publish that poll no one will come out and vote. You know I'm always warning against complacency,' said Blair.

'We are running that. Polls are expensive and everyone else has got one. Don't worry, they won't put people off. Everyone will want to jump on your bandwagon.'

'I doubt it,' he muttered, handing the phone back to Alastair.

'For Christ's sake, calm him down,' I said. 'He must know he's won.'

'You know what he's like,' said Alastair.

I was writing most of that conversation down as we had it, thinking it might come in useful one day. I don't think Blair seriously thought that any newspaper would suppress an opinion poll, or if he did Alastair

– a journalist on the *Mirror* and the *Today* newspaper before joining Blair in 1994 – would have told him otherwise. For me it showed the nervousness of a man who had waited so long for power. The run-up to the campaign had been cautious. Even though the Tories were in complete disarray and looking as if they needed a long period to recuperate, Blair and Gordon Brown were desperate to avoid mistakes.

A series of policy announcements in the years running up to the election – including the one committing Labour to sticking to Tory spending plans for two years – were the mark of a leadership desperate to ditch Labour's tax-and-spend image. Even now, with victory hours away, Blair was leaving nothing to chance. He went on almost to achieve the victory margin suggested by the most optimistic interpretation of our poll.

He and Brown had reached this high point in their careers after a long wait. It is easy to forget that they had both been in Parliament for fourteen years before this moment of glory arrived, and others in the New Labour world had waited even longer.

Peter Mandelson – along with Blair and Brown, the architect of New Labour – had been in Labour politics through the 1980s. He served as the party's director of communications from 1985 to 1990, when he boosted Neil Kinnock's modernization drive and assiduously promoted the cause of Brown and Blair, whom he saw as future Labour leaders. I first met Blair in 1982 when he fought the Beaconsfield by-election, the only election he lost in his political career.

The impatience created by this seemingly interminable wait for power was undoubtedly a factor in the way that the Blair–Brown relationship developed from brotherly cooperation to rivalry, and later to a bitter struggle that almost destroyed them both. As political editor of *The Times* throughout Blair's thirteen-year leadership of Labour, and Brown's time as shadow chancellor and then chancellor – and as a journalist whom I'm pleased to say both trusted – I had a ringside seat as this astonishing battle of wills took its course. I think I was trusted because I took no one's side, as no good journalist should. I have always got on with both of them, although both have told me straight over the years that they have not liked some of the things I have written about them.

As the psychodrama unfolded over the years, I on an almost daily basis had conversations with the close allies of Blair and Brown in which they would regularly talk about each other and often in the most hostile terms. But if it was material privately said, I never reported to one side what the other was saying in a telltale kind of way. For my job to work, I had to be sure that both sides – whether it be Alastair Campbell or Peter Mandelson on the Blair side or Ed Balls, Charlie Whelan or Damian McBride on the Brown side – knew that they could safely talk to me. Some of my contemporaries were character-ized as either Blairite or Brownite, and seen to be writing more from one camp than the other. But I hope and believe I managed to straddle this precarious tightrope.

I knew Blair and Brown from almost the day they entered the Commons in 1983, and Mandelson of course had spoken to me as Labour's chief spinner on a daily basis for years. As I write elsewhere, all three had become disillusioned with the progress towards modern-ization during John Smith's brief tenure, and his death was to create a fissure in their relationship that was never to heal.

Smith's death, on the morning of Thursday, 12 May 1994, shocked the nation. The newspapers the next morning all led on the mourning for a man they called 'Labour's lost leader'. I wrote the story of Smith's death and its implications for politics, but it was a second story that I persuaded the news desk to put on the front of the paper that caused intense ructions in the Blair–Brown–Mandelson team over that weekend.

My intro stated that 'Tony Blair emerged last night as favourite to succeed John Smith' and went on to say that he and Brown faced the agonizing task of deciding whether they should at last become rivals or whether one should stand aside for the other. I said that among Labour MPs 'the emerging view appeared to be that Mr Blair was the runaway favourite'. I added that leading left-wing strategists to whom I had spoken were advocating the idea of a Blair–John Prescott lead-ership ticket.

It seemed a decent second story but I could never have predicted the problems it would cause. The next day I received calls from an ally of Blair telling me that Mandelson was being blamed by Brown and his colleagues for briefing the story to me.

I had based it on chats with several MPs but mainly my own certain feeling at the time that it would be Blair, and not Brown, when the time came. As it happened, I had NOT spoken to Mandelson at all that day because my main preoccupation had been reporting the death of Smith and the reaction to it. I have learnt subsequently that my colleague, Peter Riddell, DID speak to Mandelson on the day Smith died. Mandelson asked Peter what he thought. Peter replied it had to be Blair, and Mandelson told him that 'Gordon should not be ruled out'.

During the day the story appeared, Mandelson called me and suggested I had erred too much towards Blair in my story, that it was not as simple as I thought, and that there were strong cases to be made for both men. He was taking a totally unexpected line, and it led me to wonder whether Gordon was in the room with him as he made the call. Until Gordon did make plain that he was not going to run against Blair some time later, I received several calls from Peter telling me that the race was open.

I was to learn weeks afterwards that Don Macintyre, who had written a similar story to mine on the front page of *The Independent*, was also given the third-degree that Friday for what he thought would be an uncontroversial assertion that Blair was the favourite to take over. So it was a few weeks before Brown finally reconciled himself to standing aside, doing so on 1 June. I wrote that he had kept to the friends' private understanding that they would not fight each other for the top job, and increased the likelihood of a runaway victory for Blair on 21 July, the leadership election date.

Brown and Blair had sealed each other's fate at their famous Granita restaurant meeting in Islington the previous Tuesday. Precisely what went on there, only the two of them know. The deal was that Blair would go it alone for the leadership and that Brown would have control of economic and social policy.

I'm told even now that Brown did not go into that meeting asking for a deal under which he would take over at some unspecified day in the future. It is possible that Blair mentioned that he did not intend to stay in the job forever and this was used by Brown later when the question of the succession became more urgent in the second Labour parliament. One problem for Brown, then and throughout their partnership, was that he tended to take conversations with Blair literally. That was unwise.

I do know that Ed Balls went along to Granita because Brown asked him to, but he had no intention of staying and left after Brown and Blair had perused the menu, even though Blair then awkwardly

invited him to stay. For a meeting that has been invested with so much
significance, it did not last long. I have learnt that about ninety minutes
later, Brown joined his team – including Balls, Charlie Whelan
(Brown's press secretary) and Sue Nye, who ran his office – in the
Atrium Restaurant at Millbank and ordered a steak and chips. He was
not impressed with the fare on offer elsewhere.

Brown in 1994 was in the wrong job at the wrong time. He had
been regarded, including by Mandelson, as the senior partner in the
relationship for most of the time they had been together. But Gordon
as shadow chancellor had had to make decisions that were unpopular
with activists and some MPs, while Tony was on the far more promising beat of shadow home secretary, where his 'tough on crime, tough
on the causes of crime' message had caught the mood of press and
public. So Brown settled down to be a very powerful number two, in
opposition and in government, until he finally, and in his eyes belat-
edly, grabbed the prize in 2007.

　As he swept to a convincing victory on 21 July 1994, Blair declared
that Labour must fight complacency and never expect victory to fall

into its lap – a mantra he was to repeat and repeat, and a version of which I was to hear on election eve 1997.

At his post-leadership election victory conference, Blair had a huge surprise in store. He had decided over the summer that the way to prove that he really was intent on changing Labour was to scrap Clause 4, the bedrock of its socialist past. With the backing of Brown and, crucially, John Prescott, he announced he would be bringing forward a modern constitution to bring the party up to date. He did not specifically mention Clause 4 to the conference but his briefers, notably Campbell, made sure no one was in any doubt, and he pulled it off with aplomb.

Labour still had an election to win and there was already an unexpected internal obstacle to that happening, as I was to reveal in a *Times* splash on 11 May 1996. Its appearance on the front was a bit of an accident. I had first pitched the story as a page-two analysis of Labour's internal troubles. But a night editor, Liz Gerard, saw the copy and told me it was better than anything else the paper had that night, and would I mind seeing it on the front?

I never minded seeing my stories on the front but this was to cause a storm. I revealed that Mandelson and Brown, once the closest of friends, had not spoken to each other for eighteen months, except at formal meetings where contact was unavoidable. I wrote that Blair feared the rift between two of his most important lieutenants could damage Labour's electoral effort. Brown was in charge of day-to-day campaigning and Mandelson was running the general election planning group.

I quoted a member of the shadow Cabinet as telling me: 'They owe it to the rest of us to make up.' I further ventured that Donald Dewar, the chief whip, was probably the only person who could persuade them to put aside their differences. I wrote that relations had never been repaired since Brown had suspected Mandelson of promoting Blair's chances after Smith's death.

Again the balloon went up. The Sunday papers went to town on my story and when they returned to the Commons on the Monday, all kinds of people were ringing me up and speculating who my sources had been and asking me to make clear that it was not them. As I had spoken to an awful lot of people for what I thought would be a backgrounder rather than a splash, the chances of the sources being discovered were negligible. But it was a serious problem. I was told later that my story had had the impact of Brown starting to talk to Mandelson, but it was essentially in the interests of party unity and election victory that it happened, not because they were suddenly friends again.

Labour moved inexorably towards victory, with Brown announcing first a squeeze on public spending and then delivering a pledge that Labour would not put up the basic or higher rates of income tax. Together he and Blair were assuring Middle England that it had nothing to fear from them. With Mandelson, and with quite bit of help from Neil Kinnock – who had buried Labour's unilateralist defence policy – they had remade the Labour Party. On 1 May 1997, they got their reward.

My Part in Keeping Britain Out of the Euro

The call came early on Friday, 17 October 1997: 'So, are you ready to take your place in history?'

It was Alastair Campbell, who made me his first call after his usual run from home to Downing Street. It surprised and reassured me. Up until this moment, the operation in which I was involved was solely a Treasury one. By that evening I hoped to be able to write a story that I knew would shake the political world, as well as the markets.

I hoped my story, on which I had been working for a month, would say that Britain was ruling out joining the euro for the lifetime of the 1997 Parliament. By now I was pretty certain that was to be the case. The knowledge that Alastair seemed to be aware of what was going on was a relief, as it suggested that Tony Blair was signed up to what was about to happen over the next few hours. Our chat was brief and did not go into any kind of detail. I gave him the broad line I expected to be able to take, and he sounded happy. It was the one he anticipated.

I learnt only that Gordon Brown and Blair had talked about the issue the previous evening. That again was reassuring. Blair and Brown were pro-Europeans, Brown probably more so than Blair in the Opposition years. But on the euro it was different. Blair was often portrayed as avidly pro-euro but certainly at this time his position was more nuanced. Nobody was quite sure where he was on the single currency. He had of course given a pre-election interview to *The Sun* saying that he understood people's very strong emotional tie to the pound. If he had given the go-ahead to today's exercise, all would be well. Or so I hoped.

The journey to this point of one of the biggest and most controversial stories I wrote in my career began in the China Garden, a restaurant in Preston Street, Brighton, on the last night of Labour's victory conference earlier that month. Blair and Brown were riding high as Labour celebrated its return to power after eighteen years. Brown had made the Bank of England independent and announcement followed announcement as New Labour strove to stamp itself on a country that had eagerly turned to Blair after the fourth successive Tory term was ripped apart by rows on Europe, financial incompetence and sleaze.

I was with my colleague Jill Sherman (chief political correspondent of *The Times*) and we had invited to dinner Ed Balls, Brown's chief economic adviser and a good friend of mine, and Charlie Whelan, his press spokesman. I wanted to get the conversation as quickly as possible onto the euro. I did so because the talk of the political scene at that time was a story by Robert Peston, then political editor of the *Financial Times* and now of ITV News, which had indeed moved the markets.

On 26 September, he had written a stunning tale that the Government was on the point of adopting a much more positive approach to European economic and monetary union, with a statement shortly that sterling was likely to join at an early opportunity after the 1999 launch of the single currency. Senior members of the Cabinet were openly canvassing the prospect of sterling participation around the turn of the century, possibly before the next general election. This represented a big shift from the negative tone of most Government statements only four months ago, Peston wrote.

The story was a bombshell – to me and many others. But its appearance in the *FT* gave it an added authenticity and, as a result, share prices surged to an all-time high, with the FTSE index leaping by over three per cent in a day, and the pound fell sharply. Needless to say, I and political editors on other newspapers were asked by our news desks to find out if the story was true.

Despite Robert's good reputation, and the obvious impression that the story was well sourced, I had my strong doubts because it went against everything I had heard on the grapevine since the election. But I rang Balls and Campbell. The former told me he was mystified by it; the latter said nothing that made me think it was right. Years later Robert was to write:

In my naivety I had thought I was merely doing an impartial reporter's job of describing Government thinking, based on conversations with ministers and officials in Downing Street, the Foreign Office and the Treasury.

But this was one of those occasions when a news story became a political event in its own right ... The reverberations were felt in bond markets and foreign exchanges – and caused the occupants of numbers 10 and 11 Downing Street to lose their bearings.

My own story was to have a similarly explosive impact. So when we convened in the China Garden that night, here was the chance to find out what was going on. Far from being reluctant to talk, our two guests were very keen – after a brief discussion about the relative fates of Norwich City (Ed and I are lifelong supporters, and he is now the chairman of the club) and Spurs (Charlie's team) – to get on to the single currency.

They were tired after a tough working day and looking forward to a gossip. But everything they said that night concerning the current debate about the euro going on at the top of the Government made me feel that Brown would be an obstacle to the apparent ambitions of Peter Mandelson, Europe Minister Lord David Simon, Foreign Secretary Robin Cook, apparently Blair and several others to take the plunge.

In the wake of Peston's report, Cook had said that 'if the single currency proceeds and if it succeeds, Britain would have difficulty in staying outside'. This was the night I was to hear for the first time about the famous five economic tests drawn up by Balls and Brown before the election in 1997, which they intended the Treasury to use when deciding whether Britain was ready to go in. The tests were to play a major part in the debate about the euro in the years ahead. In fact, they were to keep Britain out.

In brief, there had to be convergence between the UK and European economies, there had to be flexibility to cope with change, and the Treasury would need to be sure that impact on investment, financial services and employment would not be damaging. Our diners suggested that the tests had set a high bar.

The big question was whether economic factors would be overridden by the politics. That was the question dominating the debate among the Cabinet, and on the night of 2 October in Brighton no one had the answer to it. As our guests went out into the night, Jill and I agreed that the euro was the biggest story of the weeks ahead, and that it was hard to see how the pro-Europeans would get their wish without losing the chancellor – something quite unthinkable so early in the life of the new Government. When I got back to my room I noted: 'Ed amazed if euro tests can be met. Charlie: "Not a f***ing snowball's …"' With due respect to Charlie, it was Ed's judgment that made the deeper impression.

Over the coming two weeks I plugged away at the story, becoming more and more certain that the Government would eventually rule out membership, but reluctant to write anything firm without words from Brown or even Blair to back it up. I rang Balls and Whelan several times asking for an interview with Brown on the single currency. Interviews with the chancellor by myself and colleague Peter Riddell were already a regular feature of life at the time, and even more so in the years that followed. I was told that if anyone was to get THE interview it would be me, as much for my persistence as anything else.

During those two weeks there was growing concern within Government over the uncertainty that the euro decision was creating. One newspaper splashed on a story that Brown and Blair were split over the issue, with some Blair allies claiming – according to a splash in *The Independent* – that Brown was actually trying to bounce him into the single currency. That was off the mark but it was another reason why, in Brown's eyes, something should be done to clear up the uncertainty. It also confirms that Blair's position on the euro was never quite as clear-cut as some of his allies hoped.

So on the Thursday before my call from Alastair, the big beasts at the top of the Government – Blair, Brown, Cook, Mandelson and Jonathan Powell, Blair's chief of staff – met to consider the timing of the expected announcement that Britain would not be joining in the first wave. The strategy discussion did not apparently cover whether that announcement should go further and rule out membership for much longer.

Later in the evening, Brown spoke to Blair to tell him he wanted to do an interview with *The Times* the next day, both to show there was no split between them and to remove any suggestion that British entry was imminent. Blair agreed and Campbell was informed.

I had been tipped off that my interview might come on the Friday and I duly got the call from Charlie to stand by. Early on the day, after Alastair's call, my Treasury friends rang me to say that I would have to interview Gordon on the phone as he was on his way back to his Fife constituency. I would be sent a statement from Gordon that would form part of his words for the interview. Clearly they wanted to get those words right. But I was assured that the words would allow me to write what I believed to be the story – that when the Commons returned, membership of the euro would be ruled out for the lifetime of the parliament.

It was one of the most contorted ways of doing a story that I had ever experienced, but it all seemed to be moving the right way. At lunchtime the fax arrived. I read it eagerly and concluded that it was enough – just. Brown said in the statement that it would be folly to close down the option of entry given that it could have advantages for Britain. 'We have regard and influence in Europe following the Amsterdam summit. We would lose that influence if we followed the Tory line and ruled out joining.' He added: 'But we will only join if doing so is in Britain's national economic interest. We said in our manifesto and it remains true today that it is highly unlikely Britain can join in the first wave.'

Referring to the five tests, he stated: 'The questions we have been asking are: is our economic cycle out of line with our European part-ners; are there long-term changes we must make to ensure our econ-omy is sufficiently flexible to cope with shocks; and has British business had time to prepare?'

Then came the line on which I based my story:

I am determined that we will not fall into the trap which the Conservatives fell into over the exchange rate mechanism by saying they would join 'when the time is right' and implying in doing so that it could join the next day or the next month, allowing that possibility to dominate every waking hour and week of the Government, and then eventually being forced to make the decision for short-term political reasons – not, as it should have been, the long-term national economic interest.

If we do not join in 1999, our task will be to deliver a period of sustainable growth, tackle the long-term weaknesses of the

UK economy and to continue for reform in Europe – in other
words to make sure the British tests are being met.

My conversations with Ed Balls since the China Garden dinner and
with Alastair earlier had convinced me that Brown wanted to rule out
membership for the parliament, and those words were enough. At this
point I rang Peter Stothard, editor of *The Times*, and told him I had a
splash but that it would be some time before it landed with him.

I duly rang a nervous-sounding Gordon in his constituency,
hoping in all honesty to push him beyond the words I had been sent.
I just about managed to get him to repeat the prepared remarks to
me over the phone, but he was not for going any further. His message
to me was that I knew what the words meant and that I should write
the interview up as I saw fit. As always, the exchange had begun with
him asking me how my golf game was going. But I think both of us
were rather too tense about the matter in hand to engage in
pleasantries.

After thirty minutes or so, our chat was done and I was left to
myself – in Alastair's words – to make history. Balls was at home suffering from the flu. There is no Lobby correspondent who does not fear
that one day a story given to him by sources he or she has hitherto
regarded as impeccable collapses. There will be examples of those
elsewhere in this book. But at that moment – 4.30 on a Friday afternoon – I was alone and had to decide whether I had enough.

For days afterwards, rival papers and agencies suggested that the
story I wrote was not stood up entirely by the words I used on the
record from Brown. I would concede now, eighteen years on, that that
is true. But political correspondents are forever having to take a punt
on the strength of their sources. On this occasion I felt I had enough
to take that punt. To this day I'm not sure whether Brown and Blair
had agreed that the interview the chancellor was giving me would say
enough for it to be concluded that they were ruling out the euro for
the parliament. But everything I had been told suggested that that
would be the impact of what Brown had said.

So I wrote the following:

Gordon Brown is on the verge of ruling out British membership of a European single currency before the next general election.

The Chancellor will, as expected, announce over the next few weeks that Britain will not join the first wave of monetary union on January 1, 1999. But at the same time he will act to protect the economy from damaging speculation about the Government's long-term intentions by making plain that Britain will not join in the present parliament.

The decisions follow a five-month internal Treasury study on the tests set by Mr Brown for British entry and have been agreed with Tony Blair.

The approach runs directly counter to recent speculation that Britain would enter soon after the 1999 launch date. And it will dramatically change the political landscape: ministers' fears that the Government could get bogged down in a full-scale row over the pound will disappear.

And it went on in that vein. I was never known for holding back if I believed in a story and I suppose I gave it all barrels. At about 7 p.m., John Bryant – deputy editor of *The Times* and a man who had never, ever queried a word I had written on anything – rang me and said: 'What headline can we put on this?'

I told him: 'Brown rules out single currency for lifetime of this parliament.'

'Lovely,' said John. 'We will run it right across the top with a two-deck head.' And they did. Reporters don't often write headlines. But this time I got the one that I wanted, and started to pray.

At that moment I was pretty scared. I knew my story was right as I had written it. But I also knew that everything depended on my sources being able to get their way and that those who were not in on the operation – people as powerful as Peter Mandelson – would be outraged and fight it all the way.

I left for home in West London at around 8 p.m., knowing that I could not expect much sleep as the phone would be ringing into the night. I had not given myself any let-out, and neither did the *Times* leader writer when he read my copy. *The Thunderer* proclaimed:

Government is about hard choices, as Tony Blair recently
reminded his party. And the biggest choice of all was whether to
join the European single currency. Mr Blair and his chancellor,
Gordon Brown, have finally reached their decision. They will not
join in 1999 nor, more important, will they enter in the lifetime
of this parliament. This is the best decision the two men could
have taken, but it could not have been easy. Now, at last, they
have to come to understand that it is perfectly logical to be at the
same time pro-European and sceptical of economic and monetary union (EMU).

Charlie Whelan was by no means a policy man. It was his job to get
across Brown's message and it was a job he did zealously, occasionally
overzealously. I had not spoken to Charlie during the day, other than
to fix the logistics for the interview. We did not discuss content, but
he would have known my top line which led right back to the China
Garden.

So Charlie, as was his wont, left the Treasury on Friday evening and
stationed himself across the road in the Red Lion in Whitehall. When
the *Times* first edition dropped at around 10 p.m., it was Charlie, not
Alastair, who fielded the calls. He had prepared himself. Asked by rival
reporters what they should do about the *Times* splash, Charlie replied:
'Phil Webster is a very good journalist.'

It was an obvious code that told them that it was a story they
should follow, and most did, even though some fairly pointed out that
the headline was not quite justified by the words underneath. As luck
would have it, Whelan's shouted responses down his mobile were
heard by two Liberal Democrat press officers who swiftly notified the
Press Association, BBC *Newsnight* and the *Today* programme about the
sensational news they had just heard. It meant that their own Treasury
spokesman, Malcolm Bruce, got a slot on those programmes, but it
also meant that the story was widely circulated well before midnight.

One of the startled onlookers was Tony Blair. He tried to get
Campbell and then Brown, without success. So he rang Charlie, still
in the Red Lion. Campbell tells the story in his diaries:

TB could not get hold of GB – 10.15 p.m. – so he spoke to Charlie who professed himself 'gobsmacked' by the conversation. TB asked if we had ruled out EMU this parliament. 'Yes,' said Charlie. 'Is that that not what you want?' No, it is not, said TB. 'Oh' said Charlie.

Campbell also wrote:

It was all quiet until after 10, when TB called after he had seen the news and said what the hell is going on? 'We never agreed to this,' he said. I said I thought they (Brown and Blair) had.

It may be that Blair, who seemed able brilliantly to keep the pro- and anti-euro factions on board, felt Brown had gone too far, or that I had gone too far in my interpretation. But in the days that followed, there was no attempt from Number 10 to tell me that I had over-interpreted the interview.

Quite what Brown and Blair had agreed in their conversation on Thursday night will probably never be known. I'm not sure either of them knows precisely. Many are the politicians who have briefed a story and then been shocked to see it in print. It is quite possible that in telling Blair that he intended to clear up the uncertainty, Brown did not expect to see a headline as hard as *The Times* chose to use that Saturday morning, even though it was right. Blair at the time was the master of all. He knew that he had the pro-European lobby in all parties – particularly Kenneth Clarke and Michael Heseltine in the Tory party – relying on him to see off the Eurosceptics. Campbell admitted in his diaries that when he had spoken to me that Friday morning, he had been 'keen to push my instinctive anti-EMU feelings – the spin was applied and away we went'. When the Treasury team heard that I had spoken to Alastair that morning, they too assumed that Blair was on board.

In the years that followed, I was often told by the so-called 'friends of Blair' that privately he was not unhappy with the message plastered across the front page of *The Times*, although he was upset at what he saw as the botched manner of its appearance. Was his anger, directed at the time at Campbell and Brown, really meant to show Mandelson and the pro-Europeans – even Clarke and Heseltine – that this was the work of Brown, not him?

I went to bed reasonably happy that there had been no outright denial from Number 10, and the Treasury's comment that it was 'speculation' was confirmation to most hacks that the story was right. But I was in for one of the most testing periods of my career. My paper and my editor never doubted me, but there were times when I wondered. Peter Mandelson, a brilliant source and good friend throughout my time in the Lobby, rang me quite early on the Saturday and told me in his more-in-sorrow-than-in-anger tones: 'Philip, you have always been right, particularly when you listen to me, but this time you will be wrong.'

It was worrying because Mandelson had been totally out of this particular loop. He was utterly against ruling out euro entry for anything beyond the 1999 launch date, and was now determined to reverse *The Times*'s story. To say I was worried is an understatement. I knew Peter's power and determination, and he usually got his way.

The timing was bad for Blair, who was meeting Helmut Kohl, the German chancellor, the following Monday. The stock market, which soared on Peston's story, plummeted on mine. Brown happened to be at the Stock Exchange for an event that day and had to watch as the boards turned red.

Meetings of ministers were held daily as the Cabinet pondered how to end the uncertainty which had now been piled on the original uncertainty. I gave radio and television interviews in which I stood by my story. At moments of particular weakness, I would ring my Treasury sources and ask, half-jokingly, whether I should be ready to apply for a job elsewhere. They always assured me that I would be vindicated.

One big problem for Brown, when he spoke to me that Friday, and for Downing Street as it reacted, was that the House of Commons was not sitting. Betty Boothroyd, the speaker, had already admonished New Labour several times for making statements outside the House that should have been made first to MPs. They are very touchy about such things. In a sense, I had made the announcement on the basis of the words I had been given, which were not so categorical.

As the week drew on, my fears began to subside. I got a call from a ministerial source who told me 'don't worry, your story will be shown to be spot on'. But I endured a second uncomfortable weekend as rumours of a Brown–Blair rift continued. Over the weekend, the argument was settled and it was agreed that Brown – not Blair – should tell the Commons on Tuesday afternoon.

I knew now from contacts over the weekend that I was going to be OK. As I waited in the Members' Lobby at around lunchtime on Tuesday, Peter Mandelson approached and had the good grace to tell me that I would not be disappointed by the afternoon's statement and that Gordon had prevailed. I should interpose here that I had no real personal view on the single currency. If pushed, I would probably have voted for it!

To me and any self-respecting journalist, getting the story right is all that matters. But Peter told me that while ruling out the single currency for now, it would signal the most pro-euro stance ever to emerge from a British government. The pro-euro camp had also managed to insert into the statement a caveat that if economic circumstances changed fundamentally, entry in that parliament was still possible.

The statement was indeed couched in the most positive terms possible, given that Brown was ruling out the euro for the foreseeable future. It said:

The potential benefits for Britain of a successful single currency are obvious: in terms of trade, transparency of costs and currency stability. Of course, I stress it must be soundly based. It must succeed. But if it works economically, it is, in our view, worth doing.

So in principle, a successful single currency within a single European market would be of benefit to Europe and to Britain.

Secondly, it must be clearly recognized that to share a common monetary policy with other states does represent a major pooling of economic sovereignty.

There are those who argue that this should be a constitutional bar to British participation in a single currency, regardless of the economic benefits it could bring to the people of this country.

In other words, they would rule out a single currency in principle, even if it were in the best economic interests of the country.

That is an understandable objection and one argued from principle. But in our view it is wrong. If a single currency would be good for British jobs, business and future prosperity, it is right, in principle, to join.

However, on the here-and-now Brown's statement was utterly clear:

What we can and should do is to state a clear view about the practicability of joining monetary union during this period. Applying our economic tests, two things are clear. There is no realistic prospect of our having demonstrated, before the end of this Parliament, that we have achieved convergence which is sustainable and settled rather than transitory.

And Government has only just begun to put in place the necessary preparations which would allow us to do so. Other countries have for some years been making detailed preparations for a single currency. For all the reasons given, we have not.

Therefore, barring some fundamental and unforeseen change in economic circumstances, making a decision, during this Parliament, to join is not realistic. It is also therefore sensible for business and the country to plan on the basis that, in this Parliament, we do not propose to enter a single currency.

Phew! Story upheld in the clearest terms. I admit to being utterly relieved and delighted. The Cabinet had agreed a compromise which Brown, always more pro-euro than his chief economic adviser, had been happy to go along with. Rule it out for now but make clear that in the end, if the circumstances are right, we will join.

And as I happily wrote the splash for the paper that Tuesday night, my relief probably allowed me to be spun towards a story that implied a more positive approach than I really thought likely. So the *Times* splash on Wednesday morning declared:

Gordon Brown set Britain on course for membership of the European single currency yesterday – but he ruled out any like-lihood of it happening within five years.

With Tony Blair sitting beside him in the Commons, the Chancellor delivered the first endorsement by any British Government of the principle of European monetary union coupled with a promise to prepare for entry.

Blair insisted, on behalf of his pro-euro colleagues, on the inclusion of the 'barring unforeseen circumstances' line, just leaving a glimmer for those pushing for entry that parliament. But he also insisted on a passage saying that the economic benefits had to be seen to be 'clear and unambiguous' for Britain to join. He was clearly keeping both sides happy, and it was interesting that the pro-euro flavour of the statement, even though it was ruling entry out, led some to suggest that Brown was still trying to bounce Blair.

In a strange way that statement, although it represented a total defeat for the people who briefed Robert Peston back in September, was a high point for the pro-euro movement. In the years that followed, Blair tried constantly to get euro membership back on the agenda. At one point it was suggested he had offered to stand down for Brown to take over in the top job if Brown dropped his objections. But Brown had his five tests. My conclusion is that although he himself might have had reservations at the time about the bald way I presented my interview with him in October 1997, he did not regret it for long. The euro had a reasonable launch but was soon enduring problems. The Treasury, over which Brown had complete mastery, was institutionally opposed to handing powers – let alone the currency – to Brussels and his economic adviser was always there to harden his resolve. The Treasury had been scarred by the fiasco of ERM entry in the late Thatcher period and exit from it in the early Major years.

There is no doubt that the five tests were the brainchild of Balls, a Harvard scholar and *Financial Times* leader writer before he joined Brown as an adviser in Opposition. Balls and Brown came up with them as they visited Bonn, Paris and Brussels while in Opposition and were later worked on by a team of top Treasury officials when Labour won power. I've learnt recently that one of them, Dave Ramsden, was in the Red Lion on that fateful Friday night and watched as Whelan fielded calls from all and sundry. There is a myth that the tests were dreamt up by Balls and Brown in the back of a taxi in New York. Not so. But they were read out to an *FT* reporter from that taxi.

I think I can say without fear or favour now that Balls knew the five tests would stop entry to the euro. He could not say so at the time as it would have caused a political earthquake. But when I have put it to him in the years that followed, he has never questioned my assumption. Sue Cameron, a Whitehall expert, wrote (on the tenth anniversary of the later 2003 decision to stay out of the euro) that back in 1997 Brown had been more positive than Balls about joining the euro because he felt membership might prevent a repeat of the economic crashes experienced by previous Labour governments. He quoted a Treasury insider recalling that Brown said of the early work on the five tests, 'I hope it won't make it too difficult to join the euro.'

Balls himself, in an article published in the *FT* in August 2015 after his ejection from Parliament, wrote:

> While Gordon Brown, who became chancellor in 1997, undoubtedly had an open mind as to whether the tests could be met, I suspected from the outset that they would not be. Twelve years on, with the Eurozone locked in a costly crisis, the government's decision seems sounder by the day.

He had signposted his opposition before joining Brown. In a Fabian pamphlet in December 1992, Balls warned about the high costs of the EMU and said:

> If countries are affected differently by an economic event – such as an oil shock or German unification – then the desired policy response will not be the same. Tying countries together under these circumstances means large and persistent regional problems – slow growth and huge unemployment in different European countries, precisely what has occurred in Europe since German unification.

He then went on: 'In short, monetary union, in the manner and time-table envisaged in the 1991 Maastricht Treaty is an economically and politically misconceived project.' Brown deferred to Balls on econom-ics, and Balls to Brown on politics. It is clear who was making the running on this one.

Brown and Balls won the battle of 1997, but the war was not over. After another landslide in 2001, Blair decided it was time for a real attempt to enter the euro – quite how seriously he backed the efforts of his pro-European friends in 1997 was always a mystery – and, boosted by the support of ministers like Robin Cook, continued to press the case. But as the years went by after 1997, the five tests took on a near-biblical significance and absorbed the time of even more Treasury officials as a continuous assessment was kept.

It was widely reported, first by *The Independent* in May 2003, that Blair told Brown in 2002 that he would stand down as prime minister if Brown would give the go-ahead for a euro referendum. Some allies of Blair felt that Brown was not against the single currency but wanted to lead Britain in under his own premiership. Robin Cook said at the time that the challenge for pro-Europeans was how to 'convert Gordon Brown to the conclusion that it is in his interest to endorse the euro' and that it would be 'a triumph' for him as well as Blair.

Speculation about the alleged offer led Brown to say in a TV interview: 'I would never make some sort of private arrangement when the national economic interest is at stake.' Clare Short, the former international development secretary, revealed a year later that she was twice used by Blair as a go-between with Brown, with the PM offering to leave office in return for Brown's support on the euro. She said Brown had bluntly turned down the idea.

The truth is that whatever doubts might have been in Brown's mind in 1997 were largely gone by then. He recognized the importance of maintaining his party's pro-European credentials but he was now fully at one with his advisers over the currency. So in June 2003, as the Treasury published 1,800 pages of documents examining the impact of euro membership on the British economy – hugely expanded from the forty pages that backed up the 1997 decision – Brown again ruled out joining the euro, saying that four out of the five Treasury tests for going in had yet to be met. He warned that joining at the wrong time could see unemployment rise, cuts in public service spending and stalled economic growth.

There would be promises of future assessments but in effect the statement sounded the death knell for UK membership of the euro. The moment had passed and as the Eurozone went into crisis in the years that followed, the original proponents of British entry went quiet.

Larry Elliott, economics editor of *The Guardian*, wrote on the tenth anniversary of the 2003 assessment that the euro had proved to be exactly the job-destroying, recession-creating, undemocratic monster the doubters always warned it would be. 'This was not the received wisdom on the Left at the time,' he averred:

To suggest that the euro would be supercharged monetarism, Thatcherism with knobs-on, was deemed unseemly. People who liked the euro were civilised, supported the arts, went to Tuscany or the Dordogne for their holidays. People who didn't like the euro drove white vans decorated with the flag of St. George.

Today it is hard to find even the most fervent pro-European enthusiast in the Liberal Democrat Party arguing for UK membership of the single currency. Disillusionment with what was once called 'the project' is almost total in the face of grinding austerity, a double-dip recession that has already lasted 18 months and a jobless rate of 12.2 per cent and still rising.

But it was not like that back in 1997. With Blair at the height of his powers and popularity, he could have done what he wanted. In a book about the financial crash, Brown has said that he would have resigned if he had not got his way back then. That may be so, but Blair might have been able to withstand such a setback.

Keeping Britain out of the single currency is justifiably seen as Brown's most important achievement as chancellor. But it is impossible to overstate the role of his adviser Ed Balls in that decision. The economic tests may well have been an elaborate ruse to ensure that Britain never went in. They were provided by Balls and grasped gratefully by Brown. When the crash of 2008 came, Britain at least had its own currency and interest-rate policy to withstand it and you don't hear politicians of any colour calling for British membership now.

Nineteen years since I was the messenger who announced a barely formed government decision to the country, it remains the story of which I am most proud in my career. The cost of getting it wrong would have been massive for me and my paper. It was one where my instincts guided me, and thankfully they were right. But ask me who did more than anyone to keep Britain out of the euro, and the answer is without the slightest equivocation: Ed Balls.

Taking a Punt on the 2001 Election

It was the day of the funeral of Tony Bevins – 30 March 2001. I know Tony would have forgiven me but I spent most of that day trying to get a story, and then wondering whether the one I did write up as the *Times* splash was right or not.

Tony was a brilliant political journalist. He joined *The Times* from the *Daily Mail* as number two to political editor Julian Haviland, around the same time that Harold Evans promoted me from the gallery reporting team to the Lobby. The son of Reginald Bevins, who served in Harold Macmillan's cabinet as postmaster general, he understood the inner working of politics from an early age. He was a great story-getter, who would spend hours reading obscure reports looking for a scoop, rather than taking the easy option of doing the story of the day.

He had many friends in politics but there was no favour. No matter who you were, you had reason to fear Bevins if you had something to hide. I learnt a lot from him, particularly the lesson that you never give up on a story if you think it's there. We would often leave him in the office late at night burrowing away, and then I would find him back there, having driven in from Berkshire, when we went in the next morning. A true one-off.

Tony, who went from *The Times* to be political editor of *The Independent* and later *The Observer*, died suddenly from pneumonia at the age of only fifty-eight. The turnout at the funeral in Slough was testament to his popularity and the respect in which he was held by politicians of all parties.

I drove to Slough with my colleague Roland Watson. As I walked round the crematorium talking to friends and politicians afterwards, the gathering that most interested me was a group including Alastair Campbell, Philip Gould (Tony Blair's polling guru) and Sally Morgan (another senior aide). They spent a lot of time in earnest discussion and I sensed something was afoot.

The issue at the time was the general election. It had been expected to be on the same day as the local elections on 3 May. But the country was in the grip of a foot-and-mouth outbreak, and two weeks earlier an alliance of countryside council leaders had urged Blair to postpone voting until the epidemic was eradicated. The disease was spreading quickly and although Labour MPs and ministers wanted to go to the country in May, Blair was beginning to have doubts.

Campbell says in his diaries that he spoke to me, Don Macintyre of *The Independent* and Trevor Kavanagh of *The Sun* that day. But I don't recall speaking to him early on or at the funeral, and believe it was a later conversation that he was referring to. Campbell tells how, on the train down, John Prescott, Blair's deputy, had still been in favour of May while another MP, Rosie Winterton – who became Labour chief whip in 2015 – thought it would be 'madness'.

After the funeral I drove back into London to the House of Commons, passing my home in Osterley, West London, on the way in. I was uneasy. I felt I was missing something and needed to make some calls. I called a couple of contacts in the whips' office and other special advisers but they could not help me further. The line was that 3 May remained the likeliest date, and there was no reason to expect otherwise at the moment.

I put in calls to Alastair which were not responded to, something that always alerted me. No good press man would ever lie, or even completely steer you away from a story if it was right, but the way to avoid an awkward conversation was not to have it. By now I was getting paranoid. *The Sun* had earlier gone hard on the line that the election would be on 3 May, and I wondered if it would be the first to say that the election was off.

I left the office – dissatisfied – at 7.45 p.m. and drove my car out of the Commons car park. Halfway up Victoria Street, I pulled into a lay-by and thought I would give Campbell one more call. He answered. I asked him whether I would look silly if I wrote that the election was about to be called off and, clearly discomfited, he said that he could not speak and had to rush. That was it.

I decided I had to write the story. I called the office and told them to hold me a slot on the front if possible and I would file within twenty minutes – very late for a Friday. I then went on to the copy-taking department and dictated off the top of my head a story beginning:

> Tony Blair is ready to call off his long-standing plans to hold a general election on May 3. The Prime Minister is close to a decision to delay the election until June so that he can devote all his time to the effort to contain the foot-and-mouth outbreak.

There was an element of wriggle room in the words, but none in the headline, which declared: 'Blair to postpone election until June.' I felt that Alastair's refusal to speak – i.e. he had not told me I would look silly – was enough to go on. But I knew I was flying by the seat of my trousers.

By the time I reached home, I was feeling worried. I wondered whether I had pushed myself into writing a story without properly standing it up. I rang Trevor, a great friend, and told him what I had written. He was at first annoyed because I think he wondered if there had been a breach of security at the office. *The Sun* and *The Times* were in the same building and I think he wondered if someone had somehow seen what *The Sun* had done, given my late call. But I assured him that this was not the case, that my story was already written and in the paper, and that I had based it on instinct as much as anything. I just wanted him to put me out of my misery. At least I learnt we had done the same story, but Trevor's was better than mine and he had not held back.

In his diary note for Saturday (the next day), Campbell wrote:

> My chat with Kavanagh had been written up hard as a June election … I had been hoping to steer Trevor off May and sixty-five per cent towards a delay but he had gone with it one hundred per cent. Also Webster having chased it harder around 8 p.m. last night, it looked like a News International favouritism job and we would pay for it elsewhere.

The Sun and other papers in the News International stable had backed Labour in 1997, and rivals made accusations through the first Blair parliament that Campbell and his colleagues were unduly generous towards them when it came to placing stories.

Campbell also revealed that he had a call from Gordon Brown that day saying: 'As you know I've always been in favour of May 3.' 'Unbelievable,' Campbell noted in the diary entry. That was not too surprising. The chancellor had tailored his March Budget to a 3 May election, as *The Times* recorded with a splash entitled 'Brown woos families for May election'. The 'election postponed' story was swiftly confirmed over the weekend, and by early the next week Blair was saying that it would be on 7 June regardless of the progress made in containing foot-and-mouth.

I've told this story to show again that political reporting can be a hazardous business and that nothing is ever quite as simple as it appears. Sometimes, when it is impossible to gain confirmation of something that has not yet quite happened, you have to go with a hunch. On that occasion I did, and I hope Mr Bevins would have been pleased with me.

Tony and Gordon: Give Me the Euro, I'll Give You Britain

Whatever Tony Blair told Gordon Brown back at the Granita meeting in 1994, Brown behaved during the second Labour Parliament as if he expected his old friend to stand down for him. Political memoirs published in recent years have been full of stories of Brown marching in to see the PM and demanding his job.

Reporting the long battle for supremacy between them was a tricky business, and full of contradictions. I had the best possible contacts in both camps, even though Peter Mandelson more than once jokingly called me a 'wholly owned subsidiary of the Treasury' after I had revealed the latest grumbling to emerge from sources close to the chancellor. He WAS joking! I was indeed on good terms with senior figures in the Treasury, did countless interviews with Brown, and had many a story leaked to me from that territory. But I was on equally good terms with figures in Number 10, did countless interviews with Blair and had many a story leaked to me from there as well.

It was fascinating to watch the contest from both sides, and the terrain was constantly liable to surprise. For example, although we know that Brown was desperate for Blair's job, he more than once turned down open-goal opportunities to get it. At times it was puzzling.

In his account, in his book *The End of the Party*, of what became known in Whitehall as the TB–GBs – the feud between the two principals in the government – Andrew Rawnsley (*The Observer*'s esteemed political commentator) tells of how Cherie Blair often urged her husband to sack Brown because of his impossible behaviour, and of how Blair considered and then rejected the idea. 'There has been no more creative, destructive, talented and turbulent pairing in high British politics. Despite all the difficulties between them, no PM and chancellor were twinned together for so long since the Napoleonic Wars,' wrote Rawnsley. 'When they were working together, as in the salad days of the Government, they were unstoppable. When they were at war with each other it terrified their Cabinet, horrified their party and astounded their civil servants.'

It is clear, though, that the deal they did at Granita was deeply damaging to their relationship and to Cabinet government. Winning control of domestic policy meant that Brown walked all over his Cabinet colleagues' territory, making enemies as he went along. Perhaps the biggest mistake Blair ever made was not to insist on a contest between him and Brown in 1994, a battle which he would have won easily. Had he been defeated, the sense of grievance that dogged Brown throughout Blair's leadership would not have existed, and life would have been much different.

As I've reported elsewhere, no one was ever quite sure of where Blair stood on the euro in 1997 when a decision had to be made about whether or not Britain should enter the first wave in 1999, or whether it should be ruled out for the parliament. But by the start of the second term, there was no such doubt. Blair wanted to hold a referendum on the euro. He was under pressure from pro-Europeans on his own side, but also Conservative figures like Kenneth Clarke and Michael Heseltine, and many in the business community.

I wrote – although it was some time later – how Blair in late 2001 was so anxious to go into the euro that he used intermediaries to tell Brown he would stand down during the second term if the Chancellor would pave the way to a referendum. The idea, I was told, was first raised by an emissary from Blair at a meeting with a Brown confidant on 11 December 2001. The hope was that Brown would conclude that his famous five tests for entering the euro would be passed in time to hold a referendum in the spring of 2003. The details of the meeting were so specific that I concluded a record of it must exist, and my disclosure was never denied. Our headline to a story written in October 2004 was: 'Give me the euro, I'll give you Britain.'

I thought so at the time but I can now confirm that the emissary from Blair was Anji Hunter – a friend since they met in Scotland when Blair was sixteen, who became his political assistant when he was an

MP and director of government relations in Number 10. Anji is now married to Adam Boulton, Sky's former political editor. The Brown confidant was Sue (now Baroness) Nye, who had previously worked for Labour leaders Michael Foot and Neil Kinnock, and became Brown's director of government relations when he became PM.

When numbers 10 and 11 were at loggerheads, which was often, Jeremy Heywood (then Blair's principal private secretary and later to become Cabinet secretary) and Ed Balls would often go across from Downing Street to the snack bar on the other side of Whitehall to sort out the policy side over a coffee. But when it came to personal issues, the long-time friendship between Hunter and Nye was invaluable. Insiders say that on countless occasions, the two of them managed to keep the warring factions from falling out completely and would often sort out the mess after meetings between Blair and Brown ended in a shouting match.

By now, of course, Blair and his team realized what Balls knew all along – that the five tests were an effective veto – and he made plain through Hunter that if the tests were passed and a referendum held, he would be ready to go and not serve a third term. The message was passed on by Nye. Clare Short also disclosed in her diaries that the Prime Minister had told her that he wanted to go into the euro during that parliament, but did not want to serve a third term.

In *Brown's Britain*, Robert Peston's biography of the chancellor, it was revealed in January 2005 that at least three Cabinet ministers had gone to Brown in 2002 with the message that Blair would stand down if he helped to take Britain into the euro. The book tells that Blair persuaded John Prescott, Alistair Darling and Clare Short to be his messengers. When urged by Blair to interfere with the Treasury's assessment of whether the time was right to join the euro, the chancellor reputedly told him: 'History will never forgive us for having that conversation.'

According to one of the ministers Blair was confident that Brown would eventually buckle because his ambition to be PM would overcome his reservations about entering the single currency at the wrong moment. My own reading would suggest, however, that Blair underestimated the fact that by the second term, Brown himself was far more antagonistic towards the euro than he had been in the first term, and the Treasury attitude had hardened even further against it.

Peston recorded that the conflict reached a climax in April 2003, when Blair made a final attempt to persuade Brown to rework the five tests assessment. When Brown refused he was asked to 'consider his position'. Brown stormed out, not knowing if he had been sacked or had just resigned. As always, a rapprochement followed quickly.

That parliament was dominated by the 9/11 attacks, the war in Afghanistan and the war in Iraq. But it was Iraq that sapped Blair's will and ultimately changed the country's, and his party's, view of him. Rawnsley, in a memorable passage in his book, wrote that from the moment they won the 2001 election, Brown began to pound Blair for a leaving date. According to an unnamed Cabinet minister, all their confrontations were about Gordon saying: 'Why haven't you f***ing gone?'

But it went on because Blair declined to sack Brown, probably fearing he would be even more dangerous on the back-benches. One Blairite confided to me at the time: 'If he sacks him, Gordon would have a government in exile waiting for him to fall.'

Relations hit their direst point in the autumn of 2003 when Brown, for the first time, went for Blair publicly. In his conference speech he ridiculed Blair's 'best when we're boldest' speech from the previous year and brought the house down with his payoff line, 'Best when we're Labour'. Brown's allies knew exactly what they were doing. Blair was vulnerable because of Iraq, and now was the moment to attack. Blair hit back with a defiant speech the next day, which was seen as a riposte to his chancellor. It was an amazing spectacle: the two most powerful men in Britain arguing in public as if the Opposition parties did not exist.

John Prescott, the deputy PM, called the two men to a peace dinner at Admiralty House in London. Again, as always with this pair, it was unclear what had been agreed. Brown went away thinking he had at last got a promise that power would be handed over the following autumn; the Blairites and Prescott seemed to suggest it was conditional on his good behaviour before then.

The early months of 2004 were as bad as any Blair had endured. Iraq was bearing down on him, Lord Hutton's report on the death of Dr David Kelly was dismissed as a whitewash, and he only narrowly survived a Commons vote on tuition fees. My own next bit part in this unfolding melodrama came when I was briefed that in April 2004 Blair had met with several senior figures to tell them he intended to 'pre-announce' in May a decision to go later in the year.

Brown had been waiting for years for Blair to go but suddenly found himself telling the Prime Minister that his proposed course was unwise because it would make him a lame duck and open the way to a long leadership contest. Brown had believed Blair had given him an assurance at Admiralty House and for him, it was better to stick to it.

This really was an open goal. Prescott had hinted that a denouement was close when he told Tom Baldwin, then deputy political editor of *The Times*, that the 'tectonic plates of politics were shifting'. That was the nearest Brown came to leading Labour into the 2005 election. During the early summer, key allies like Tessa Jowell and Charles Clarke had private conversations with Blair to boost his morale. His mood lifted quickly. From suggesting privately that he was endangering his party, he started thinking more positively about standing again, and once more disappointing Brown.

The PM took the political world by storm by suddenly announcing after the end of the Labour conference that he intended to go on and serve a full third term (but not a fourth), that he was buying an expensive house in Connaught Square and that he was having an operation to correct an irregular heartbeat. Brown was left in the dark – to him it was yet another insult and broken promise.

There were briefings from people close to the Blair camp that he would have gone had not Brown reneged on a deal to support him, pointing to the opposition of Brown supporters to the tuition fees legislation and his pressure for a referendum on the European constitution. Blair had already rubbed Brown's nose in it by bringing back Alan Milburn – who had resigned as health minister soon after being defeated by Brown over foundation hospitals – as a policy supremo. But the campaign did not run well in its early stages and Blair turned to Brown to ask him to take a bigger role – which of course he did.

In the end, Blair and Brown could never quite bring themselves to split. They came close to tearing the partnership asunder many times, but it never happened. But my own view was they were lucky that they came to power at a time when the Conservatives were shot to pieces by years of rows over Europe, and that the voters were prepared to tolerate open dissent at the top of the governing party because of the quality of the alternative.

Mandelson's book, *The Third Man* – titled to show how he was always there operating in the shadows between the two – revealed better than any other the sheer intensity of the relationship. Blair compared Brown to the Mafiosi, calling him mad and bad ('mad' was a word used by Blair about Brown with more than one newspaper executive), and Brown showed his total contempt at times for his old friend.

I – like many others – have often wondered what that Labour government could have achieved if the two men at the top had found a better way of working together, or if that leadership election had indeed taken place in 1994, allowing the issue that was to poison New Labour to be settled there and then. With Brown's help, Blair went on to win in 2005 with a much-reduced majority; but the final act in the tragedy and drama of the TB–GBs was still to come.

The Naked Chancellor

Gordon Brown usually hid his famous temper when in the company of journalists, but we heard plenty about it second-hand from his staff – usually from the press advisers required to bring him news of the stories we'd written.

One shell-shocked aide told me the tale of being summoned down to the Treasury gym just after 6 a.m. by Brown, furious that the story he had briefed to the BBC was being ignored by the *Today* programme in place of some criticism he had faced from the Education Select Committee.

The chancellor was committed to do the crucial 08.10 *Today* interview slot that day and hated the idea of being ambushed. I was told that the aide entered the gym to find the chancellor stark naked in front of his open locker, fresh from the shower. Unabashed, Gordon directed an angry tirade at the aide, the Education Select Committee, and the BBC, in that order.

This was continuing when a humble official from the Revenue entered for his own morning workout. I was told that, suddenly conscious of his lack of dignity, Brown turned to fetch his towel, unaware that – in his fury – he'd moved several yards away from his own locker. He found only a locked one behind him instead, causing him to scream in anger and unleash his famous clunking fist at the closed locker. I was informed that the poor Revenue official went white and left.

Countless stories about Brown's propensity for furious outbursts have been told over the years. The one above has survived undisclosed until now. It was Tony Blair who first mentioned Brown's fist. Speaking in the Commons in late 2006, he warned David Cameron that the next election would be a flyweight versus a heavyweight and, however much Cameron might dance around the ring beforehand, at some point he would come within the reach of a big clunking fist. Brown did not hit people, but he did take it out on objects when he was annoyed.

The memoirs of many Labour politicians have told us about the two sides of Gordon Brown – the kind, funny, learned man who could light up a conversation anywhere; and the serious, driven, near-demented figure obsessed with destroying his rivals and becoming prime minister at all costs (the man who allegedly told Blair on one occasion that he had 'stolen my f***ing Budget'.)

Although Brown inspired deep loyalty among people who worked for him – people like Sue Nye, Charlie Whelan and Damian McBride (the former Customs and Excise official who became communications chief under Brown at the Treasury and later his special adviser in Number 10) – Whitehall was full of tales for years of how rough and rude Brown could be to his staff. Many were apocryphal. McBride, in his book *Power Trip*, said, for example, that in all his years working for Brown at the Treasury and in Number 10, he had never seen a mobile phone being thrown!

But there was a darker side. Andrew Rawnsley wrote in *The End of the Party* that Brown's abusive behaviour and volcanic eruptions of foul temper left Downing Street staff so frightened that he received an unprecedented reprimand from the head of the civil service. Gus O'Donnell, the former Cabinet secretary, became so alarmed by the then Prime Minister's behaviour that he launched his own investigations when he received reports of Brown's bullying of staff. O'Donnell then gave the Prime Minister a stern 'pep talk' and ordered him to change his behaviour. 'This is no way to get things done,' he told Brown, the book claims.

According to Rawnsley, O'Donnell was so disturbed by the effect on those in Downing Street that he took it upon himself to try 'to calm down frightened duty clerks, badly treated phone operators and other bruised staff by telling them, "Don't take it personally"'. The book also claims that during one rage, while in his official car, Brown clenched his fist in fury after being told some unwelcome news and then thumped the back of the passenger seat with such force that a protection officer sitting in the front flinched with shock. The aide sitting next to Brown, who had just told him the information that provoked the outburst, cowered because he feared 'that the Prime Minister was about to hit him in the face'.

A former Blair spin doctor, Lance Price, said in *The Mail on Sunday* in 2009:

> Brown has never been known for his composure under pressure. He throws things – telephones, mugs, anything to hand. He screams at people. In short, he loses it and, if your staff are never sure when they might need to duck, they are not going to give you their best advice. And Brown needs all the advice he can get.

One adviser who worked for Brown for years told me that while he was very physical, he was never violent. He would take out his frustrations on objects, like staplers, typewriters, laser printers (he shoved one off a desk on one occasion) or desks. Like McBride, this adviser had not seen a mobile phone being thrown.

The stories are legion and given the law of averages, some of them must be true. Before the Rawnsley book came out, Brown in a pre-emptive interview with *Channel 4 News* said:

> If I get angry, I get angry with myself … I throw the newspapers on the floor or something like that, but please … I was brought up – my father, I never heard him say an unkind word about anyone and I always think when you're – the heat of the moment you say things sometimes, of course you do get angry, mostly with yourself. But I'm very strong-willed, I'm very determined, I think the country wants someone that will push things forward, and not allow things to be stagnant and stale, and every morning I get up with a determination to do my best for this country.

I felt there were two sides to him in his dealings with the press. I remember shortly after he became chancellor, he invited political editors and their partners to a reception at Number 11 and it was then that I felt you saw a nicer Gordon. He had taken the trouble to learn the names of all the wives, husbands or partners and spent the whole evening concentrating on chatting to them rather than the people he knew well. They were utterly charmed and he left a lasting impression on them. I remember going to see England beat Scotland at Wembley in Euro '96 with Brown and friends, and having a great time. At summits when he was chancellor he could be the life and soul of any party.

Over the years, Peter Riddell and I did many interviews with Brown at the Treasury. They were exceedingly friendly affairs at both the start and end, but once the interview was under way the game-face came on and Gordon would deliver his clearly planned lines almost as if he was speaking in the House of Commons. There would be no frivolity, no jokes until the job was done, and then it would be back to books, sport, even a bit of gossip.

Those enjoyable encounters often made Peter and me remark upon how frustrating a colleague Brown must be when he allowed the deadly serious side of this complex character to trump the human side. Because Brown, on his good days, was very good company indeed and the sort of bloke you would happily invite to your local for a pint. McBride tells in his book of the 'hugely jolly' Christmas parties Brown and Sarah threw for close colleagues each year, usually with Eds Balls and Miliband in attendance. He invited them there because he enjoyed their company and humour so much. They'd eat Sarah's traditional lasagne, exchange presents, receive a book from Brown, followed by singing led by Balls and a political adviser called Jon Ashworth.

As McBride recalled in *Power Trip*:

But the highlight of these evenings was always Gordon's comedy routine. It was never so much the content of the jokes and anecdotes he told that was so entertaining, but his gradual inability to speak because he was laughing so much under the constant heckling from the Eds.

Anyone who remembers Brian Johnston's hysterics on Test Match Special in 1991 will know the kind of high-pitched squeal Gordon used when pleading: 'Come on, you guys, stop it.' Tears streaming down his face, he would finally make it to the punchline of a story about Donald Dewar or union leader Jimmy Reid, and would always, always botch it, the cue for everyone to fall about laughing.

So there we had it – Dr Jekyll and Mr Hyde. People who came into contact with him were never sure which one they would encounter.

That was how it was for me one late night in 1997. Around three months after Labour's election landslide, I was invited to the Treasury to be given an advance look at the International Monetary Fund (IMF)'s first verdict on the economic policies of the new Labour Government. Brown and his team were delighted that an IMF group – which had spent the last ten days in London talking to ministers, Bank of England officials and the City – was giving a glowing report on the chancellor's early stewardship, saying he had set a high standard for his economic policies and had taken decisive steps towards achieving his goals.

He was praised for his decision to make the Bank of England independent and using the Budget to make rapid strides towards sound public finances. The report, with those passages highlighted, was handed to me and I went back to the office. On reading the full report, however, I found that the IMF was also telling Brown that he might have to increase taxes on consumers, possibly through widening the VAT net, to prevent an already buoyant economy getting out of

hand. The report also cast doubt on Brown's plans for a national minimum wage, saying it would be a 'blunt instrument'.

To me this was a better news line. A good rule of thumb for me was
that the word 'tax' – whether raising it or cutting it – was always going
to make a better headline than someone or other praising the government of the day. But as chance would have it, I was talking during the
afternoon to Larry Elliott, economics editor of *The Guardian*, whom
I knew would have been given the same treatment by the Treasury.
Larry was a regular player – along with people like Ed Balls and Andy
Burnham – in what I rather grandly called my All Stars football team,
which in those days had an annual fixture against an outfit put out by
my best mate, Rob Freeman of the *Mail*, at the Arsenal training ground
north of London.

Larry, too, had spotted the 'raise taxes' line and agreed it beat that
fancied by the Treasury. My story appeared on the front of *The Times*,
and the balloon went up. My first call at around 10.30 p.m. was from
the chancellor's press man, Charlie Whelan, who complained vocifer-
ously that I had missed the real story. He ended a rather tempestuous
conversation by calling me a four-letter word not beginning with 's'.
We got on well and it was the sort of thing that happened in the heat
of the moment sometimes.

Shortly afterwards, the phone went again and it was Ed Balls.
Having been a journalist at the *FT* before becoming Brown's econom-
ics adviser, he knew better than anyone that a reporter worth his salt
would not change a story unless it was wrong or there was some other
very good reason to do so. As I had with Charlie, I told Ed I thought
my line was better; I felt he had gone through the motions, probably
to keep Brown at bay.

I went to bed and the phone went again. 'Phil, it's Gordon Brown
here.' Now the chancellor himself, perfectly politely but with a tone
of regret in his voice, was telling me that he thought I had under-
played the key point in the IMF report. I was rather flabbergasted to
have received the call but held my ground, and I think he, too, realized
it was too late to do anything about it. Years later as I prepared this
book, I checked how other papers had played the story and, to be fair
to the Treasury, most went with the line they wanted – even my old
colleague Tony Bevins in *The Independent* wrote at the top of his story
that Brown had received a 'glowing testimonial' from the IMF.

I should say here that Brown's call was highly unusual. In my long experience, ministers used their special advisers or press officers to ring up late at night and complain about the angle on a story. It was not something they did themselves, although sometimes they were not averse to having a go later if they happened to run into you.

For me, the most striking thing about the conversation was that Gordon had called himself Gordon Brown, not Gordon, when he came on the phone. We had known each other since 1983, and had always been on first-name terms. I guess he was trying to rattle me into changing my story. It did not work.

Robin Cook Interrupted
My Golf Swing

Tensions were running high on the Hebridean island of Islay. It was the inaugural Wryter Cup match between the journalists of England and Scotland. After two days of scintillating play on the world-famous Machrie links, the scores were close, and now it was the afternoon singles that were to determine the match.

Heading the field as twenty-four golfers went out on that windy afternoon of 29 March 1998, were the two captains, George Pascoe-Watson (political editor of *The Sun*) for the Scots, and Webster, of *The Times*, for the brave English. As the skippers walked up the third fairway, my phone, carried in case the news desk needed me, rang loudly. Rather embarrassed to have disturbed George, I grabbed the phone and after a second said: 'Oh, hi Robin.'

The conversation went on, with George regarding me with some curiosity. 'It's Cookie,' I said with my hand over the mouthpiece. The foreign secretary, for it was he, had things to tell me and as a political correspondent you don't put your phone down on such a dignitary. But we had eleven pairs of golfers following us, and in the twosome behind was a veritable celebrity, Lawrence Donegan – later to be golf correspondent of *The Guardian*, author of one of the finest books on golf ever written, *Four Iron in the Soul*, former bass player of Lloyd Cole and The Commotions, and self-confessed star of the Scottish side.

I will deal with the contents of the chat later but with the increasingly irate Donegan shouting at me from behind – accusing me of the golfing sin of slow play – I scribbled notes on a few old scorecards from my bag and, every now and then, put the still-talking foreign secretary down on the grass while I hit a smoking five-iron towards the green or sank the occasional putt.

Donegan was unaware of the subject of my call and was hardly placated later when he learnt. Some things are sacred, and the golf course is one of them. Eventually the call ended and the match proceeded. Scotland won the team competition and modesty prevents me from mentioning who took the individual prize.

The story of why Cook called me that Sunday afternoon began in the foreign secretary's office in Whitehall the previous Thursday. I had been given an interview to mark the halfway point of Britain's six-month presidency of the European Union. He landed me with a good story. A few months earlier – as I explain in an earlier chapter – Gordon Brown had ruled out British membership of the euro for the parliament, and the foreseeable future. The story I had written predicting the announcement had caused an almighty storm.

But now Cook, who always enjoyed winding Brown up, signalled that Britain could well be joining in the next parliament, saying it would be difficult and unwise to stay out if the single currency proved to be a success. In my story I described the remarks as the clearest hint that the foreign secretary would be pushing for a referendum early in the next parliament if Labour was re-elected.

Knowing that I was heading for Scotland, I could not have been happier. I had a potential splash in my pocket which I would send in on Sunday for Monday's paper. But as the interview ended, Robin – with whom I had always had a very good working relationship – took me aside and told me he wanted to tell me something else.

The previous August he had announced that he was leaving his wife and marrying his secretary, Gaynor Regan – after being told while at Heathrow Airport by Alastair Campbell that the *News of the World* was about to break the story of his affair. Now Robin wanted to tell me that he and Gaynor were getting married on Sunday, 19 April and that the ceremony, away from the public eye, would be at the foreign secretary's official country residence of Chevening in Kent.

Wow, I had two stories – one splash about the euro and a lovely personal sidebar about Cook's wedding plans. As I boarded the plane to Glasgow, I was content. However, on the Saturday evening one of the stories fell down. I got a call at the Machrie Hotel from Peter Bean, Cook's press man, who apologized and said that *The Mail on*

Sunday had beaten us to it. I feared for my euro story, but no, what had happened was that Margaret Cook, his former wife, had told the paper that her ex-husband had left it to their two sons to tell her about his remarriage plans. So it had the story I was planning.

This was not a huge blow and in all honesty my thoughts at the time were on deciding the pairings for Sunday to give me a chance of defeating the rather cocky Scots. I thought no more of it until the call came. Robin said he was ringing personally to apologize that my 'scoop', as he called it, had been thwarted. I did not like to tell him that the euro story had every chance of being plastered over the front anyway.

Anyway, he and Gaynor had been trying to think of any snippet that they could give me in compensation for losing the wedding story, he said. I concealed my agitation at the rumpus going on behind me and he told me that Gaynor's first official engagement as his wife would be to attend the Lord Mayor's banquet on 23 April, when he would be making the traditional foreign policy address.

He told me again about the wedding preparations and, at my urging, gave me a couple of quotes about how they were planning their life together. Job done and I got on with the golf. And his call had been worth it. Under the heading 'Banquet debut for new wife' – and with a picture of the couple together at Chevening – I wrote that Gaynor Regan had chosen a glittering City occasion to make her first official appearance as the wife of the foreign secretary. He was later to outwit the press by marrying not at Chevening but at Tunbridge Wells register office ten days earlier than planned.

Cook's call had shown me another side to this complex man, whom I had known well since the early 1980s. He clearly wanted to help Gaynor into the new role, which was why he was taking so much trouble to call me, but he also felt he owed me after the first version collapsed.

Cook often spoke to me privately about some of the big Labour stories in those years. I regarded him as a bit of a loner in the Commons. Once I ran into him on his own, armed with binoculars, at Newbury racecourse. 'What on earth are you doing here, Phil?' he asked. 'I could say the same,' I replied. He loved horse racing and had been introduced to it by his first wife. During the 1990s, he wrote a weekly tipster column for the Glasgow *Herald*. After that chance encounter, and finding out that I, too, liked the sport of kings, I always felt he treated me with a little extra respect.

Cook was a fine parliamentarian and his Commons performance in 1996 – when, after only two hours to read the 200-page Scott Report into the arms-to-Iraq affair, he lacerated 'this Government which knows no shame' with a forensic demolition of ministers – was one of the finest MPs on all sides had seen.

His early days as foreign secretary were turbulent because of the marriage breakdown and his claim to be following an ethical foreign policy, which was endlessly scrutinized. I was with Tony Blair in Tokyo in January 1998 when Margaret Cook, in *The Times*, made damaging new revelations about their marriage. It virtually hijacked Blair's trip, with the travelling press pack interested in no other story.

After the 2001 election, he was moved against his will to be leader of the Commons, probably because Blair could see an emerging new battle between him and Brown over euro entry. But he was back in the place where he felt most comfortable and set about reforming the hours and practices of the House. I often went down to the vast

Leader's room for a chat in those days and he seemed happy enough. But the Iraq war meant the end of his government career.

On 16 August 2002, I led *The Times* with a story that Cook 'would emerge next month as one of the Cabinet's leading critics of British involvement in any attempt to topple Saddam Hussein'. The former foreign secretary was said by close allies – I suppose it is safe now to admit that it was him – to have deep reservations about the prospect of military action and to be ready to make his case when Tony Blair next invited the Cabinet to discuss Iraq.

Cook, I wrote, regarded Saddam as a severe threat who had to be countered. But he feared that an attempted Western invasion would further damage the prospects of peace in the Middle East and could lead to wider conflict. I said that he would make his interventions in Cabinet and not elsewhere.

It was a strong story and, looking back, Cook was prophetic. On 17 March he resigned from the Cabinet, saying he could not accept collective responsibility over military action. He delivered a thumping, dignified resignation speech that won applause from all sides and was seen by veterans as one of the most effective ever. Cook and Brown buried their age-old animosity and some thought he would return under a Brown administration.

But it was not to be. On 6 August 2005 – just seven years after that conversation on Islay – Cook suffered a severe heart attack while walking in the Scottish Highlands, and died. He was only fifty-nine. I'm not sure many people knew him well, but those of us who had regular chats with him would miss him. And he was a great loss to politics.

Our Small Part in Winning the Olympics

When the medals were handed out to the campaign that won the 2012 Olympics for London, they rightly went to the likes of Seb Coe (who ran the whole show), Tony and Cherie Blair (for their late lobbying efforts in Singapore), Tessa Jowell (who was culture secretary and became Olympics minister) and David Beckham (whose presence in the final days undoubtedly helped). The Westminster Lobby was not mentioned in dispatches, but we played our part and, eleven years on, it is time to lift the lid on our sterling efforts.

It was 2005. We had flown with Blair to Singapore for the last few days of wheeler-dealing before the International Olympic Committee (IOC) made its decision. I sat on the plane with Jowell, a good friend, for a time on the way out. She told me she thought London would pull it off. She was very much in the minority on the aircraft.

Under our schedule, we would be in Singapore for the final lobbying meetings but before the vote we were due to fly off to Gleneagles in Scotland, where Blair was chairing the G8 summit of world leaders. The sports news correspondents were already in Singapore, so the Lobby badly needed to turn this into a political story if it was to take its rightful place on the front pages.

Two days before the final vote, I went down for breakfast in our hotel in Singapore and ran into a very bright and keen press officer for the culture, media and sport department by the name of Paddy Feeny. He pointed out to me some rather unkind remarks about British and Finnish cooking by President Chirac of France that he had spotted in *Libération*, the left-leaning French paper, while the president was in Russia the previous weekend.

Was I interested? Yes, I was very interested. We were joined by Ben Brogan, then political editor of the *Daily Mail*, and we ran through the quotes together. This was the diplomatic storm we had been seeking. Chirac was due to arrive the next day. Paris was odds-on favourite to win the bid, although there was momentum behind London. What's more, Finland had two votes in the IOC.

Not only had Chirac criticized British cuisine, he had added that you could not trust a country that turned out such bad food. As we were hours ahead of London, Ben and I decided to 'own' the story and try to have it wrapped up by the time our news desks arrived for the morning back home. We shared the news with our colleagues from other papers and got down to writing it.

My splash in the next day's *Times* spoke of a bout of international mudslinging over the Olympics and said that an astonishing diplomatic blunder by Chirac had soured relations with the UK after it emerged that he had mocked Britain's cooking and reputation for trustworthiness. I reported:

> 'The only thing that they have ever done for European agriculture is "mad cow" disease,' M. Chirac said of the British. 'You cannot trust people who have such bad cuisine. It is the country with the worst food after Finland,' he told amused colleagues during a meeting in the Russian enclave of Kaliningrad on Sunday.

It was a great story and Chirac's arrival in Singapore for what he thought would be a triumphant procession to a French victory coincided with the appearance of our stories in the first editions back home. Such news travels like lightning and as Chirac entered the famous Raffles Hotel, he was besieged with questions from reporters from all nations asking about *le rosbif*. It was quite hilarious but Chirac was not amused.

Years later, when Coe published his autobiography, we learnt that Cherie Blair had made good use of the revelations at a reception on the eve of the vote. Coe credited her with a 'banshee-like' attack on an unsuspecting president, and suggested she scared him off before he had the chance to meet any of the delegates who mattered. In *Running My Life*, which was serialized in *The Times*, Coe said she approached the president and said: 'I hear you have been making rude comments about our food.' He told her she should not believe everything she read but the confrontation ended with a 'massively discomfited' Chirac leaving.

We left for Edinburgh on a long, long flight before the final day of submissions for the 2012 bid. But we were in Gleneagles in time to watch the announcement of London's triumph, a result that had the British press contingent cheering wildly, with some joking that it was 'the Lobby wot won it'.

Blair himself could not bear to watch the ceremony in which London was declared the host. In a backgrounder, I described what happened and how Blair, who was supposed to be preparing for the summit, had his mind on events in Singapore. While his officials and advisers went into the hotel to watch the Olympics drama unfold on television, the Prime Minister took a walk in the grounds for the next tense hour with his chief of staff, Jonathan Powell. Mrs Blair, too, could not face the television and wandered round the hotel in her official blue Olympic shirt, waiting for someone to tell her the news.

Powell received a call from Number 10 and handed the phone to Blair. It was a switchboard operator in Downing Street, who then told Mr Blair: 'Prime Minister, we've won.' At that point, in Mr Blair's own words, he threw his arms into the air, did a jig and embraced his chief of staff. We were to learn later from Coe just how involved Mrs Blair had been. But there can be little doubt that Tony Blair's decision to spend two full days of his busy G8 week in Singapore helped London's case. I don't pretend for one moment that the Lobby's intervention was decisive but our move to highlight Chirac's remarks must have helped.

Coe believes the attendance of the Blairs was hugely important. Blair managed to give the IOC meeting a profile it has rarely enjoyed. Between them, he and Mrs Blair saw fifty members of the IOC. No one will know for sure whether they converted the requisite number. I wrote that by giving the Games to London, the IOC has ensured that prime ministers will ignore its future selection meetings at their peril.

Of course, London won mainly because the IOC decided it had the best case. At the time the budget for the Olympics was just over £2 billion, but a few years later it had risen to £9 billion. Nonetheless,

Blair and his wife had made a big contribution and secured at least a part of his legacy. It was a triumph – but disaster, the twin impostor, was not far behind. Early next day, as the summit was opening, we heard that bombers had struck London. It was 7 July 2005.

The Hand of History on a Snowy Good Friday

It snowed in Belfast in the early hours of the morning of Good Friday, 1998. I know because I was there and wide awake.

Sometimes journalists are lucky enough to be around when history is made, and they certainly don't want to miss it if the chance arises. I was in a cold press room set up in the Castle Buildings at Stormont, where Northern Ireland's political leaders and the prime ministers of Britain and Ireland were inching towards what became known as the Good Friday Agreement, and the hope at last of ending thirty years of bloodshed that had cost more than 3,000 lives.

On Maundy Thursday, the midnight deadline for a deal passed by. Martin Fletcher, our chief Ireland correspondent, and I kept updating our copy. In a 3 a.m. edition, we wrote that George Mitchell, the American chairman of the peace talks, was drawing up new proposals.

With final editions gone, most reporters decided to go back to their hotels or homes. But although ready for sleep, I decided against it, fearful that I would miss being there when a deal about which I had written for years was finally done. Not that I would have been able to do much if the story had broken at 6 a.m., but to me it mattered that I was there.

I hadn't so much as a tube of toothpaste with me, so I merely decided to pretend that it was still Thursday and carried on. I sat in one of the uncomfortable plastic chairs in the room and put my feet up on another. That was my bed and I didn't sleep a wink because I was freezing cold. Battle honours should also be awarded to Adam Boulton, the utterly indefatigable and legendary political editor of Sky, who broadcast through the night without looking tired at all. At another all-night European Council summit in Nice two years later, which I covered, Boulton lay flat-out in the press area and grabbed a few minutes' sleep between live broadcasts.

If the accord was one of the great achievements of Blair's term of office, the advance towards peace in Northern Ireland was also one of John Major's. He laid the groundwork with years of painstaking talks, and took the risk of allowing the covert talks with the IRA – without which peace could never have been reached.

But in April 1998, the crucial week had begun with doubts over whether enough progress had been made by Mitchell to justify Blair and Bertie Ahern, his Irish counterpart, going to Belfast to try to seal an agreement. It would need the late intervention of President Clinton to get it over the line.

Blair flew in on the Tuesday night after the Ulster Unionists flatly rejected the latest blueprint put forward by Mitchell. He arrived armed with one of his most quoted soundbites. 'I feel the hand of history upon our shoulders,' he said. But he was aware of the difficulties. 'Maybe it is impossible to find a way through, maybe even with the best faith in the world we can't do it, but it is right to try. I am here because I think it is my duty.'

By Thursday, the process set in motion by Major and Albert Reynolds five years before looked doable. Ahern, who had had to leave Stormont to attend his mother's funeral, returned ready to compromise, declaring that a deal required everyone to move a little bit.

As the day wore on, there were hints of a deal getting closer and earlier in the evening there was a surreal development when Ian Paisley, the Democratic Unionist Party leader, stormed with his supporters into the grounds of Stormont to protest at what they called a sell-out by the mainstream Unionists, led by David Trimble.

Paisley was allowed to stage a chaotic press conference. This was the man who nine years later was to become First Minister of Northern Ireland, with Martin McGuinness as his deputy, after finally agreeing that his party – by then the largest unionist grouping – should share power with Sinn Fein. Nothing would have been further from his thoughts on Maundy Thursday, 1998, as he walked angrily from what was in his eyes the scene of betrayal.

By dawn on Good Friday, sleep-starved leaders were still looking for a breakthrough. During the day it looked at one point as though the whole thing would fall apart after members of Trimble's party suggested their leader had gone too far. They resisted the idea of Unionists sitting with Sinn Fein in a new assembly if the nationalists had not renounced violence and the decommissioning of weapons had not started.

Blair's assurances that the agreement meant that the IRA would start decommissioning arms straightaway were not accepted by Trimble's party, and word went round that a deal might be off.

It was a call at around 4.15 p.m. by Blair to Bill Clinton that was critical in breaking the deadlock. After talking to Blair, the American president spoke to Ahern, Gerry Adams (the Sinn Fein president), Trimble and John Hume (leader of the Social Democratic and Labour Party). Then suddenly, after thirty-three hours of non-stop talks, a deal was announced at just after 5 p.m. The two governments and eight political parties signed up to a new future. Blair, as we wrote in *The Times* the next morning, hailed a settlement that would give everyone a chance to live in peace and raise their children free from the shadow of fear. It was indeed a piece of history worth waiting for.

But like several of the other reporters there that day, my mind went back to late 1993 when Major and Reynolds got the peace process off the ground. In late November, *The Observer* had revealed that a secret communications channel had been running for months between the IRA and the Government, with Major's approval. It was later to emerge that an informal channel had existed as far back as 1973 between the IRA and British intelligence.

It came in the run-up to an Anglo-Irish summit planned for months with the aim of forging a new Ulster peace settlement. Major defended the links and said it would have been unforgivable for the Government not to have used them. On the eve of Dublin, Major acted to assure the Unionists by saying that the British Government would never try to persuade the people of Ulster to leave the UK and join a united Ireland – dashing the Republic's hopes that Britain might be persuaded in a joint declaration to accept the 'value' of the objective of a united Ireland.

I was in the press room at Dublin Castle that Friday as we waited for the leaders to emerge after eight hours of talks. There were serious differences at the meeting and it appeared that the atmosphere had been soured by the disclosure of contacts with the IRA. But they agreed that the negotiating process should continue at the Brussels summit the next week. Work continued on the joint declaration and Reynolds offered a written promise that Ireland would hold a referendum on its territorial claim to Ulster.

I moved on to cover the Brussels summit. Under the headline 'Ulster given hope of peace before Christmas', *The Times* reported on Saturday, 11 December that the two leaders would be meeting again in London the following week in the hope of signing a pact that they hoped would bring an end to IRA violence.

And so it came to pass. The following Wednesday, Major and Reynolds stood shoulder to shoulder in front of the Christmas tree in Downing Street and challenged the men of violence to put down their weapons. Major held out the prospect of Sinn Fein joining talks on the future of the province within three months if the IRA abandoned violence. He declared: 'We cannot go on spilling blood in the name of the past.' 'Ulster holds its breath on peace accord' was the headline on my report in *The Times* the next day.

Nicholas Watt, who was then *The Times*'s Ireland correspondent and covered the Dublin summit with me, wrote many years later in *The Guardian* about the full extent of the twenty-year secret back channel between the British government and the IRA. In October 1999, Watt reported that Margaret Thatcher gave her personal approval to secret talks between government officials and the IRA leadership in 1990. Nick, a superb reporter, is now BBC *Newsnight*'s political editor.

In one of her final acts before she was deposed as prime minister, she allowed her Northern Ireland secretary, Peter Brooke, to talk to republicans through a secret 'back channel' after MI5 advised the government that the IRA was looking at ways of ending its terrorist campaign.

In his memoirs serialized in that paper, Jonathan Powell, former chief of staff to Tony Blair, told how a Derry businessman and a series of MI5 and MI6 officers had risked their lives to allow the British government and the IRA leadership to communicate in private. Powell wrote:

> It is very hard for democratic governments to admit to talking to terrorist groups while those groups are still killing innocent people. Luckily for this process, the British Government's back channel to the Provisional IRA had been in existence whenever required from 1973 onwards.

Paisley attacked Major for the secret back channel when it was revealed in 1993. But Powell revealed in his memoirs that ten years later Paisley's party established its own secret link to Sinn Fein, when the DUP won the assembly elections of 2003.

After the Downing Street agreement before Christmas 1993, there was still a long way to go until Northern Ireland could celebrate peace and its own power-sharing government. But it was a hugely important step on the way.

Why They Sack –
and Why They Regret It

Alastair Campbell executed the spin doctor's dream coup in October 1998 when he entered a Lobby meeting at 4 p.m. and told us that Ron Davies, the Welsh secretary, had resigned after a forty-five-minute conversation with the Prime Minister over an incident the previous night when he had been robbed at knifepoint after meeting a complete stranger on Clapham Common. Got that?!

None of the astonishing news had leaked out until this point and, although the questions were manifold, Campbell was able to give us a resignation, an exchange of correspondence between PM and former minister, and a new minister. I mention the smoothness of that operation because it compares starkly with the way prime ministers generally handled resignations during my time.

Tony Blair was a reluctant sacker, as was John Major. Both held on to ministers long after it was obvious to colleagues and particularly the press – which always loved a scalp – that they had to go. There were understandable reasons for this. Sacking a minister, like reshuffling generally, never guarantees a good outcome. Spurned ministers, or those who feel they have been treated badly, become enemies. Margaret Thatcher got the most dramatic come-uppance for demoting Sir Geoffrey Howe. Major had been backed for the Tory leadership by Norman Lamont but when he dismissed him as chancellor in 1993, after the fiasco of Britain's exit from the European exchange rate mechanism, he was a friend no more. Lamont accused Major in the Commons of running a government that looked to be 'in office but not in power'.

Most sackings are borderline cases. Ministers guilty of any financial impropriety or other improper conduct have no choice. They go, and go quickly. But ministers dismissed because of policy disagreements with the prime minister of the day become dangerous foes. I observed and reported on scores of sackings, and each reshuffle that condemned former ministers to the back-benches widened the internal opposition to the incumbent prime minister.

Thatcher and David Cameron were more ruthless sackers than Blair, Gordon Brown and Major. Tory MPs are certainly less sentimental about their leaders than Labour. Perhaps the same goes for the leaders. No one has ever quite matched Supermac, or Harold Macmillan. In 1962 he sacked a third of his Cabinet in what became known as the Night of the Long Knives, named after Hitler's considerably bloodier purge of the *Sturmabteilung* (SA; the Nazi storm-troopers) in 1934. Macmillan wanted to give his ageing administration new life and desired a shift away from the austere economic policy of Chancellor Selwyn Lloyd. But his plans were leaked, he rushed the changes and upset everyone involved, producing Jeremy Thorpe's memorable quote: 'Greater love hath no man than this, that he lay down his friends for his life.'

Thatcher discarded a trio of 'wets' in 1981 and continued to weed them out in later reshuffles to make way for her own supporters. But every time she did it, she left another enemy – be it Sir Ian Gilmour, Christopher Soames, Francis Pym or one of many others – brooding on the sidelines, waiting to take revenge whenever the opportunity presented itself. When one of her own faltered – Nicholas Ridley with his disparaging remarks about the Germans – they got the bullet as well.

Cameron professed a hatred of reshuffles when he took over in 2010 but he has been more Thatcherite than Blairite when it comes to the crunch. Three ministers were reported authoritatively to have blubbed when he sacked them in 2012. He showed no compunction in dismissing an angry Andrew Lansley, the former health secretary, who had been his boss in his days in the Conservative Research Department.

He showed similar hardness in 2014 when demoting Michael Gove, a friend and close political ally, from education secretary to chief whip after his relations with the teaching profession and other ministers, such as Theresa May, became difficult. He gave Gove the job of justice secretary but Gove became a key 'Outer' in the European debate after earlier promising to keep a low profile. Their relationship has not been repaired. May's reshuffle on assuming the prime ministership was brutal, as I have reported elsewhere.

In dropping Kenneth Clarke, Owen Paterson and Dominic Grieve, Cameron also knew that he was placing three potentially dangerous heavyweights on the back-benches. They were joined by Iain Duncan Smith after he resigned in a row over cuts to disability benefits after the 2016 Budget, probably anticipating his likely removal in any post-referendum shuffle.

The press gets very excited about reshuffles. They are a weapon for the prime minister of the day but so often they go wrong and leave them wondering why they bothered. The theory is that you use them to reward the up-and-coming and discard the poor performers. There is plenty of excitement during the day as beaming faces emerge from Number 10. But for every smiling visage there is a sullen one – the sacked and the never-asked.

Blair never really mastered the reshuffle art, getting his timing wrong with forced departures and sometimes missing people out because of late rows with Brown over which of their respective supporters should be included. Take Stephen Byers. The transport secretary was another whose career looked dicey from the moment his press adviser, the likeable and utterly harmless Jo Moore, was caught out sending an e-mail on 9/11 saying that today would be a 'good day to bury bad news'. It was a gruesome mistake but it reflected the climate in which Labour's army of zealous 'spin' operators worked in those days.

True, Byers had also become involved in a furious row over his decision to force the Railtrack operator into administration. Without the 'spin' problem he might have survived but after initially standing by him, Blair eventually agreed he should go. We were called to Number 10 and Byers was given the stage of the Pillared Room to announce his own resignation, another first for Campbell.

The comeback king was Peter Mandelson. He had spent his working life trying to get Labour elected – promoting in public esteem Blair and Brown, and giving his party credibility and electability after four terms in exile. Now, just eighteen months after Labour's landslide triumph, he was out as trade secretary having failed to declare a home loan of £373,000 from fellow Labour MP Geoffrey Robinson, at a time when the latter's business affairs were being investigated by Mandelson's department. This was a pretty open-and-shut case.

Despair turned to triumph when Blair brought him back just ten months later to become Northern Ireland secretary, to build on the success of the Good Friday Agreement. It was a job he loved, and in which he excelled, but before long he was out again after a row concerning a passport application from an Indian billionaire.

Despite Mandelson's insistence that he had not acted improperly, and his subsequent clearing by an independent inquiry, Blair deemed there were sufficient inconsistencies in his account of circumstances surrounding an application for a passport from Indian-born business magnate Srichand Hinduja. The story centred on whether Mandelson had or had not had contact with Mike O'Brien, the former immigration minister, over the case.

24 January 2001 was another extraordinary day. Alastair Campbell had arrived late for the morning Lobby briefing because he had been sitting in on an inconclusive meeting between Blair and Mandelson. Blair wanted to lead Mandelson to the conclusion that he should go, but was not finding it easy. As I was to reveal later, Campbell at one point drummed his fingers on the table to indicate his impatience.

He came to the Lobby and told us that the two principals were meeting, and added that it would be wise if he could get back to us later to give us the conclusion. That was it. He was effectively telling us what would happen. Mandelson was doomed – again – and broadcasters raced from the room to tell that to the world.

The Times felt there was enough doubt about the circumstances to warrant an investigation and I wrote a big two-page spread in the *Times 2* supplement asking the question: was Blair panicked into sacking Mandelson? After hearing all sides, I concluded that Mandelson was probably at fault in failing to give a clear account of what had happened, leading the Government into making conflicting statements. But there appeared to be no hard proof at all that he had done anything wrong and I questioned how an affair that had done Blair much damage and deprived him of his key ally should have been allowed to get out of hand. The rest is history. Mandelson resigned his seat, went to Brussels, and his third coming was in 2008, when Gordon Brown asked him to return.

David Blunkett, too, had a second bite at a Cabinet career after resigning over the claim that he had used his position as home secretary to push through a visa application for his former lover's nanny. His troubles started when it was revealed that he had had an affair with Kimberly Quinn, the American publisher of *The Spectator*. But Blair was swift to give him a second chance, bringing him back as work and pensions secretary in the reshuffle after his third election victory in 2005.

However, support in the Labour back-benches for Blunkett collapsed just five months later when it was revealed that he took a two-week directorship at a company while he was out of the Cabinet. He broke ministerial rules by doing so without consulting an independent committee that advises former ministers on whether they should take up jobs. It was a tragedy for Blunkett, one of the most remarkable men to adorn British politics in recent times. And it was another blow for Blair, whose majority had been cut in half at the election and who seemed to be paying the price yet again for his kindness to a friend and ally. Our headline, 'Decline and Fall' was not only about Blunkett.

The local election results in May 2006 were dreadful for Labour. Blair was moving into the final straight of his premiership, as Gordon Brown's allies again pressed him to move on. The Prime Minister used his reshuffle that month to suggest that that was not his intention. 'Blair turns butcher after polls carnage' was the excellent headline on my splash.

While he sacked an ally, Charles Clarke, as home secretary because of the row over foreign prisoner deportations, he threw down the gauntlet to Brown by promoting supporters such as John Reid and Alan Johnson – who could have been seen as leadership alternatives to the chancellor – while demoting ministers who had appeared sympathetic to Brown.

Blair angered the chancellor and his backers by appointing, without any consultation with Brown, two avowed Blairites, Hazel Blears and Jacqui Smith, to the posts of Labour Party chairman and chief whip. Brown's supporters said that Blair had shown he had lost interest in the transfer of power and one said the reshuffle was an 'act of war'.

Clarke went despite Blair offering him two alternative jobs, including defence secretary and trade and industry secretary. The PM wanted a new face at the home office to restore public confidence but, in a bitter exit, Clarke stood his ground and insisted he was the man to put things right. Blair was to miss Clarke when the pressure on him from the Brownites became intolerable just three months later.

In retrospect he regretted sacking Clarke and in the eyes of many, Blair's biggest mistake was in NOT sacking Brown. Had he done so, he might have gone on to win a fourth term without Brown snapping at his heels and he might have got further with his reform agenda without the brake of his chancellor. We can only surmise.

As for poor old Ron Davies, his 'moment of madness' on Clapham Common, as he was to call it himself, destroyed his career. I knew Ron and played a few games of squash with him. Once he flew into a blind fury when I walked into a squash court where he was playing another Labour MP without knocking on the door, a dangerous thing to do. And two days after he entered the Cabinet, I met him as he walked into the Commons and said: 'Congratulations, Ron.' 'Secretary of State to you, Phil,' he retorted. He was joking.

But Davies's resignation and its announcement, carried out with the ruthless efficiency for which Campbell and his team were renowned, was a graphic example of how fragile Cabinet ministers' careers can be. In that case, both Campbell and Blair knew that Davies could not survive the 'lapse of judgment' that led to him going to a stranger's flat and being robbed. It was better to end it there and then.

In his diary for 27 October 1998, Campbell tells of how Jack Straw (then home secretary), having being told by the police about the incident, called Downing Street to warn the PM and then how an 'absolutely shattered' Davies had come in to tell his story. Campbell writes:

> I could tell looking at TB's face that he had pretty much decided this was a no-hope situation for Ron, and that the only way for him to salvage anything from this was to get ahead of the curve, resign before anyone knew the first thing about it, and maybe get some sympathy and understanding.

I and the rest of us at the briefing were dumbstruck when Campbell told us some of the news. He admits in the diary:

> It was not easy. As I knew they would they got straight to the point – what had he done wrong? – and I didn't want particularly to dump all over him, so I was avoiding a lot of questions.

Blair got that one right. But he and other leaders got so many wrong.

Blair and Gaddafi

If Iraq was the foreign policy engagement Tony Blair had most cause to regret, ruining his legacy and cutting short his career as prime minister, Libya was another that has left abiding question marks over the course he charted.

It was Blair who famously brought Muammar Gaddafi in from the cold. I travelled with him when he shook hands with Gaddafi in his tent a few miles outside Tripoli on 25 March 2004. And I interviewed Blair in Jerusalem seven years later, hours after he had appealed to Gaddafi to stand down and leave as revolution and bloodshed gripped his country. It was a futile gesture. Weeks later, Gaddafi was murdered and his mutilated body paraded before the people he had brutally ruled. Today that country remains in chaos, with the so-called Islamic State taking advantage of the turmoil to set up a new stronghold closer to Europe. Whatever the good intentions of the original mission – and Blair would claim that Gaddafi's decision to give up weapons of mass destruction in return for acceptance in the West was the prize – it has not ended well.

None of us could have foreseen that when, on that March day in 2004, an ancient bus raced us from Tripoli airport to Gaddafi's Bedouin tent which, like his female bodyguards, he took with him on his travels. Indeed, we felt we were at a significant moment in history. Blair was still riding high as a world statesman, the full scale of the disastrous aftermath of the Iraq war having yet to emerge.

It was 7,282 days since a female police constable, Yvonne Fletcher, had been killed by a shot fired from within the Libyan embassy in London. It was 5,573 days since Pan Am Flight 103 exploded 31,000

THE BLIND LEADING THE BLIND IN IRAQ, AFGHANISTAN, LIBYA, SYRIA... *Peter Brookes* AFTER BRUEGEL

feet above Lockerbie. And by becoming the first British prime minister to visit Tripoli since Churchill, Blair was conferring an international respectability on Gaddafi that seemed impossible during his decades as a pariah.

Blair arrived to a relatively low-key red-carpet welcome. Symbolically, many of the country's leading politicians, rather than the military, were there to meet him as he walked along a guard of honour made up of about sixty of Colonel Gaddafi's Revolutionary Guard. The first we the reporters saw of Gaddafi was his head. He was waiting in his khaki tent in the desert countryside south of the capital. Few people were allowed there; even the bus driver taking the press missed his turning. About fifty camels were wandering round the simple complex, which was surrounded by eucalyptus trees, dandelions and cornflowers. It was quite surreal.

Reporters, given the kind of access of which they could only dream in Europe, were gawping outside when 'the Leader of the Revolution' peeked from behind a fold of the tent to see whether Blair had arrived. We watched the brief handshake, a broad smile from Blair and pleasantries that could have been scripted for any encounter between world leaders. They engaged in some jokes about the ageing process and how their jobs accelerated it. All very friendly.

Gifts were exchanged: Blair was given a signed copy of the *Green Book*, the Libyan leader's personal credo. Colonel Gaddafi was given a leather-bound book about the Palace of Westminster and an Armada silver dish engraved with 'Number 10 Downing Street'. The fripperies over, they got down to serious talking, with only an interpreter and one official from either side with them. For a good hour they talked in the tent decorated with a mural of pineapple and palm trees. On some things they disagreed but on the need to cooperate against al-Qaeda they were in harmony.

According to aides, the conversation was easy and the two men got on perfectly well. Gaddafi told the Prime Minister that 'the past is the past but many things have changed'. He added that Libya's commitment to giving up its deadly weapons was 'irrevocable'.

Gaddafi – wearing a flowing black robe, white shirt, maroon and brown tunic, a black fez-style hat and shiny black Western shoes – walked with the suited Blair to a tent next door. A lunch of olives, salad and fish couscous had been prepared, and they carried on talking with their officials for another fifty minutes or so. I wrote that Blair had been to Gaddafi's tent, but he could hardly have believed that his own Big Tent – New Labour's original philosophy of trying to attract support from all parties – would have been stretched so far.

There was one piece of 'colour' from which I spared readers then, but can provide now. Gaddafi committed many sins against the world. Flatulence has not been mentioned as one of them. But one of the aides, who had got close to the room in the tent where the leaders met, told us of the awful odour which Blair managed to appear not to be aware of. Gaddafi unfortunately had a habit of breaking wind as he made his points, and he made a lot of points. John Simpson, the BBC's long-time foreign editor, also suffered this experience one day. John said in an interview about his oddest interviews: 'He also broke wind very heavily. I noticed he seemed to be smiling a certain amount and moving around in his seat. And the cameraman said to me, "Did you hear Gaddafi farting?" I said no but when I listened to the tape, well, let's face it, we all know what it sounds like.'

Blair received a good press, mainly because the two leaders expressed desire to unite in the battle against al-Qaeda. The two countries agreed to exchange intelligence information about terrorism as Blair forged a highly improbable alliance with a man who had been, until recently, a world pariah because of Libya's sponsorship of terrorism.

At the time, al-Qaeda considered Gaddafi an enemy because of his more liberal approach to Islam and the role of women, and the perception that he was more interested in Africa than Arab nationalism. Blair announced that the British Council would open an office in Tripoli to build trade and educational links. Back in 2004 this seemed to have been a step worth taking. But any hopes that Gaddafi had suddenly become a reformed character were to be cruelly dashed.

Fast-forward seven years. It was Friday afternoon in late February 2011 and I was asked if I could pop in to see the editor. With James Harding was Richard Beeston, our brilliant foreign editor who sadly died in 2013, and Anoushka Healy, the managing editor. By now James had made me editor of *The Times* digital editions after my thirty-seven-year spell at Westminster.

Britain was close to taking part in United Nations-backed action to prevent Gaddafi killing more of his own people. Word had reached *The Times* that Blair was prepared to talk. He was in the Middle East that weekend. He was special envoy for the Quartet – the group made up of the United Nations, United States, European Union and Russia involved in trying to further the Israeli–Palestinian peace process.

Blair had a gap in his diary. I had known him since 1982. We got on well. I was the obvious man to go, said James. I had friends visiting London for the weekend, but of course I would go. The office booked the overnight Saturday flight to Tel Aviv for me, I met the photographer Matt Lloyd at Heathrow that Saturday evening, and in the early hours I was landing in Israel.

Blair's office was at the delightful American Colony Hotel, which I had visited before on a trip with Neil Kinnock, and I had been booked in there as well. I was told that Blair, who was in Kuwait, would not be arriving before 4 p.m. and as I sat around the hotel all day, I wondered how he would handle my inevitable questions over whether he regretted ever having offered the hand of friendship to this brutal man.

As the day wore on it was obvious that 4 p.m. was wildly optimistic. I knew the office was counting on me – as usual – for a splash and maybe a spread, and time was tight. We wanted to video the interview as well, so spent the time setting up equipment in the courtyard of the hotel. When Blair rushed in with his team it was after six and he told me, very apologetically, that he had about ten to fifteen minutes before he had to race off to the West Bank for meetings with Palestinian leaders, but he would talk to me when he got back if I was still in need.

Given what the office wanted, I would be severely lacking. But I determined not to let him go until I had at least got my splash. As it happened, he had plenty to tell me. Gaddafi was in denial, said Blair, and had refused his personal plea to stand down. That previous Friday he had spoken twice to the dictator and urged him to go. Blair had spoken to Hillary Clinton, the US secretary of state, before making those calls.

I asked about the 2004 meeting. 'We thought it right if they were willing to change their policies at a time when Libya was at the top of everyone's concerns,' he said. 'It was the right thing to respond.' He had deliberately maintained his contacts with Gaddafi after leaving Downing Street and becoming a Middle East peace envoy. Although the Gaddafi family has claimed that Blair was a friend, he said no when I asked if he had profited personally from the relationship. He added that the message he gave the dictator in their latest conversation was that it was time to go, and he pressed for a transitional government.

Blair was on his feet after about twelve minutes and I kept talking to him as he walked through the hotel to head off. I was short of words for the inside pages, but I would survive. I wrote about the irony of Blair, the man who paved the way for Gaddafi's return to respectability, now revealing to me that he had told the bloodstained colonel that it was time for him to go and open the way for a transitional government and then democracy.

I reported that Blair seemed affected by the criticism that had come his way and by the fact that the man to whom he gave status had been ordering the killing of his own citizens. I suggested that his efforts to intercede were clearly the act of someone who felt that he had to use the relationship he built with Colonel Gaddafi to influence him as the end-game approached. He was appalled by what had happened and admitted openly that his stomach churned at the thought of what a man with whom he was on first-name terms should have done to his own people.

Blair had been deeply involved in the Libyan crisis since it became apparent that the people were going to follow others in the region and try to ditch their dictatorial leader. I said Blair was cagey about the next steps, although he admitted that the international community faced difficult decisions over the next few days. Asked about his calls to Colonel Gaddafi, he said: 'I am not going to say any more than this – that what I asked him to do is consistent with the message from the international community and his message was the message he has given publicly. He was in denial that these things are going on.'

He added: 'There is now one major strategic objective and the rest is a question of tactical decisions. The strategic objective is that there is a change in leadership in Libya with the minimum further bloodshed.'

Only a few minutes after leaving the hotel, Blair called me mobile-to-mobile and apologized for his haste, and I was able to enlarge on his quotes. As I pressed him on Gaddafi, he declined to speculate on whether he should be allowed to go to a safe haven. 'The single most important thing is that this ends as quickly as possible with him standing aside and a new leadership taking over.'

By 2011, Blair's political reputation had taken a battering because of Iraq and he had got used to it. He defended his 2004 venture:

Is it a good thing that Libya went from being a state sponsoring terrorism to a state cooperating in the fight against it? Surely the answer must be yes. Is it a good thing it went from being a state developing a nuclear and chemical capability to a benign state that gave it up? The answer must be yes.

I am as appalled as anyone else about what has been happening. It is awful to think that people should die in this way. But the reason we brought Libya from a position of being ostracized by the international community into the community of nations was precisely because they changed their policy externally in a way that was extremely important for our own security and that of the rest of the world.

He understood why people whose families had been the victims of the terrorism that Libya used to support should wonder what on earth he was doing with a person like Gaddafi. He faced a similar situation when people in Northern Ireland asked him why he was talking to Martin McGuinness and Gerry Adams. 'But my answer was always the same – to stop this happening to others. What has happened in Libya is utterly unacceptable but it is worth saying that some of the help they gave in the fight against terrorism was extremely important for us.'

Looking back, Blair was hardly unrepentant about his links with Gaddafi but he felt he could justify them. For me at the time, as usual, all that mattered was that the trip had delivered. I produced an exclusive splash for *The Times* about his recent contacts with the dictator and other pieces about Blair's caution over where the Arab Spring – the flowering of barely formed democratic movements in countries like Egypt and Tunisia – was going.

Soon, with David Cameron and Nicolas Sarkozy in the vanguard, NATO launched bombing raids in support of the Libyan rebels. Gaddafi, once brought in from the cold, was now feeling the heat, and his days were numbered. But Cameron's decision to take action in Libya was controversial and fraught with difficulty, as I explain in a later chapter.

In January 2016, Blair revealed the full transcript of his 2011 conversations with Gaddafi, the ones he told me about when I saw him in Jerusalem. It was handed to members of the Commons foreign affairs committee as part of their inquiry into UK policy in Libya. In the conversation he urges Gaddafi to get to a 'safe place' in order to promote a peace process in the country. The former prime minister had told the committee that the phone calls were his idea and that he had contacted Gaddafi as 'a concerned private citizen' after clearing the phone calls with the US state department and Cameron.

Both men speak of Gaddafi in the third person. 'The position of the leader is crucial. If he indicates that he wants this to occur now, and that he will stand aside and go somewhere safe, I think this will resolve this peacefully,' Blair tells him. He continued:

> If he wishes this to happen I can take this message back to the people I have been talking to. There is a process of change that is going to take place – that has been made clear by the leader

himself. He needs to signal acceptance of that change and he needs to stand aside to let that happen peacefully.

But the transcript confirms Gaddafi was in denial. He repeatedly denies there is any fighting going on in Libya and tells Blair to come to the country's capital to see the support for him.

Blair told MPs that his ultimate concern was for the situation of the country rather than Gaddafi's own health. 'It's been presented as if I was trying to save Gaddafi. I wasn't trying to "save Gaddafi",' he said. 'My concern was not for his safety; it was to get him out of this situation.' Blair again defended his 'deal in the desert' with Gaddafi, suggesting it may have prevented chemical weapons falling into the hands of Islamic State. Blair said:

> Otherwise, we would have had a situation where Libya was continuing to sponsor terrorism, was continuing to develop chemical and nuclear weapons and would have remained isolated in the international community.
>
> I think it is important that we brought them in from the cold, as it were, and important also in today's context because I think – particularly if we had still had the residue of that chemical weapons programme in Libya today, given the state of Libya today and given the presence of Isis there – it would have constituted a real risk, even.

Ironically Cameron faces criticism over the lack of post-intervention planning in Libya similar to that levelled at Blair and George W. Bush over Iraq. The failed state it has left behind, with Islamic State seizing the opportunity to dig in, has been cited as evidence of the dangers of removing Middle Eastern leaders.

The Commons foreign affairs committee in March 2016 warned that Libya's collapse since the overthrow of Gaddafi had turned it into a security threat to the UK, with illegal migration from Libya helping it stage attacks in Europe. The committee said there was a 'particular responsibility' on the UK to help Libya 'repair itself' and restore a stable government.

Although he was in denial when he spoke to Blair back in 2011, Gaddafi was right on one thing. The transcript reveals that he warned him that jihadists would attack Europe if his regime was allowed to collapse. He said: 'They [jihadists] want to control the Mediterranean and then they will attack Europe.'

As with Iraq, Blair awaits history's judgment on Libya and Gaddafi.

Blair and Iraq: A Legacy Damaged Beyond Repair

For years his critics had predicted a whitewash that would let Tony Blair off the hook. But when Sir John Chilcot delivered his report into the Iraq war on 6 July 2016, more than seven years after Gordon Brown set it up, there was no escape for the former prime minister, who emerged from a torrid few days with his reputation and legacy damaged beyond repair.

In a withering verdict, Blair was found to have taken Britain to war unnecessarily and to have overstated the case for it because of his personal commitment to George W. Bush. He presented the case for war in 2003 with 'a certainty which was not justified' based on 'flawed' intelligence about Iraq's supposed weapons of mass destruction (WMD) that was not challenged as it should have been, Sir John concluded.

His voice breaking and looking deeply troubled, Blair expressed his 'sorrow, regret and apology' for the 'failures' over Iraq, but insisted he stood by his actions – and would make the same decision again.

I was surprised neither by the findings of the report nor his reaction to it. I was with Blair at every point along the way as he made the journey from his first encounter with Bush to the fateful decision to go to war with Iraq in 2003.

It was in February 2001 at Camp David (the presidential retreat) that he made his new friend at what became known as the 'Colgate summit' – they found at their meeting that they used the same toothpaste. It was an alliance that was to dominate politics for years, and one which many around Blair – and probably the man himself, though he would never admit it – came to regret. Even more so since Chilcot.

On that first encounter the Blairs and the Bushes bonded by watching *Meet the Parents* in the retreat's family cinema, and appeared together at a press conference – Bush wearing a brown leather flight jacket and Blair in pullover and cords. I travelled with Blair a few days after 9/11 to New York, when we flew over the ruins of the Twin Towers and went to the memorial service for the Britons killed in the outrage. We then made our way down to Washington to watch Bush and Blair at Congress, preparing the ground for war on the Taleban.

I was with him when he flew under cover of darkness into Afghanistan to see British troops at Bagram Airfield during the war, and I was with Blair when he visited Bush in 2002 at his ranch in Crawford, Texas, and moved a few steps closer to conflict. And I was with them both on the Azores when Bush flew in from Washington, and Blair from London, and they agreed to send their troops into action.

I was also with Blair when, in the weeks after 9/11, he travelled at least 40,000 miles around the world, building up support for military action against the Taleban and the attempt to find Osama bin Laden (seen as the organizer of the attacks on America). And I was with him at any number of Anglo-American summits in the years between 9/11 and the fall of Saddam.

The travelling press pack is well looked after on its trips with prime ministers. In those days, we usually flew in a British Airways 777. There were plenty of seats to sleep on during the almost obligatory overnight flights, the food was always good, and a glass of champagne was usually waiting when we got back to the plane – sometimes after hours trekking round capitals with the PM. When we flew into war zones like Afghanistan, and later Iraq, we were always in the secure hands of the RAF and their *Hercules* transport planes. There were hairy moments, with everyone worried about our safety when we dropped into Pakistan just after the start of the Taleban offensive, and again as missiles flashed in the sky during our midnight visit to Afghanistan.

On these trips, the access to the PM and his officials was good. He would come back and talk to us – sometimes on the record, sometimes off – but the trips produced stories, often delivered by Alastair Campbell or his colleagues. Blair and his wife, Cherie, were deeply moved, as was everyone on the aircraft, as we flew into New York days after the 9/11 attacks to attend the memorial service in a church not far from the scene of the carnage.

New York was in a state of lockdown and we felt guilty being there, fearing that the security surrounding Blair's trip would interfere with the rescue efforts still going on at the remains of the World Trade Center. After a struggle to get through the traffic, we were off again to Washington, where Bush rallied his nation for a lengthy campaign against terrorism and where, turning to Blair standing beside him, he said, 'Thank you for coming, friend.'

Blair was a man on a mission, moving from country to country to build up the largest possible coalition for Bush and the imminent military action. In Moscow on 4 October, he lavished praise on President Putin for backing Britain, America and Europe in the efforts to track down the perpetrators of 9/11. It was then on to Pakistan and India.

But it was shortly after this that those of us covering Blair's marathon began to notice something that was to take on massive significance in the months ahead. It is something about which I have thought very often in the years since the war as Blair's actions over Iraq have been condemned, including by many who supported him at the time. I was told by Blair aides of concern in his camp about hawkish members of the American administration wanting to extend the battle to Iraq. There were fears that they could damage the fragile support for the coalition in the Arab and Muslim worlds.

We went with Blair to visit British troops preparing in Oman for the Afghanistan campaign. Escaping the blazing heat in a tent at the army headquarters, Alastair Campbell handed us a document entitled *Defeating Terrorism: Campaign Objectives*, which was effectively Blair's blueprint for his campaign against terrorism.

Campbell's aim was to show us that the West's aims were currently limited to the conflict in Afghanistan and that the overall objectives were to bring bin Laden to justice and rebuild a post-Taleban Afghanistan. I believed strongly that this was the first real show of concern in the UK Government about the way some of Bush's team were now eyeing Iraq. In his diaries, Campbell refers to his action in releasing the secret document:

> We were running into a problem with the sense being commu-
> nicated by the US they were constantly trying to link Iraq into
> the equation. TB was keen to pull it back and through a mix of
> my briefing and his interviews at the army base we just about
> did that, but it was difficult to do while simultaneously avoiding
> UK–US split stories.

In the years since, as Chilcot has deliberated over the war, it has often been forgotten how cautious Blair and his aides like Campbell were initially about extending action to Iraq. How they must wish they had maintained that caution.

Blair travelled to the Middle East, trying to shore up faltering support for the bombing campaign in Afghanistan. In Damascus we witnessed an extraordinary scene as President Bashar Assad (yes, he was there even then) – who had invited Blair to his country – then stood alongside him at a press conference and attacked the war, called Palestinian terrorist groups freedom fighters and said Israel was a terrorist state. It was a straightforward ambush that embarrassed Blair and gave us a story we had not expected.

Then it was off to Washington again for another meeting with Bush. By the time he got home on 8 November, Blair would have completed thirty-one flights, covering over 40,000 miles, in the weeks since 9/11, and I had been on nearly all of them. The military assault brought early success and by 17 November the Taleban surrendered control of Kandahar, marking the end of its control in the country.

The mission continued early in the new year as Blair set off for India and Pakistan, where I caused a mini-stir by allowing my mobile phone to go off in the middle of Blair's press briefing with President Musharraf, who had agreed fresh action against terrorist groups on Pakistan's soil. Blair informed the president that *The Times* was the culprit.

Then at just around midnight on 7 January, we clambered aboard a Hercules plane at Islamabad and flew for a scary hour to Bagram, enduring a stomach-churning landing at the darkened airfield. Blair was the first foreign leader in since the fall of the Taleban government but the battle was far from over and the plane was an obvious target. He was greeted by Hamid Karzai, leader of the interim government. Mobiles did not work there but I somehow passed the story to London by lying on my back on the freezing tarmac and getting through on a satellite phone.

By early in the new year, any doubts Blair had about Iraq seemed to have been dispelled. A memo leaked in 2015 showed that Colin Powell, former US secretary of state, was telling Bush on 28 March 2002: 'On Iraq Blair will be with us should military operations be necessary. He is convinced on two points: the threat is real; and success against Saddam will yield more regional success.'

Something inconvenient then happened to me. I survived the midnight flit to Afghanistan. But I did not do so well in the Austrian Tyrol. Shortly after getting back, I was skiing with friends in Lech when, taking my skis off at the bottom of a lengthy run down to the village, I slipped on rock-hard ice and broke my femur. The thigh bone is the largest in the body and I refused to believe my misfortune for a time, struggling to a bar and then being driven back to St Anton, where we were staying. But broken it was. There followed an ambulance ride to the University Hospital at Innsbruck, a 3 a.m. operation, and a flight home to London five days later. I was truly crocked but I

kept busy and my dear colleague Tom Baldwin visited me with goodies and gossip from the office before I limped back to work.

I was well and truly recovered by the time Blair set off again, this
time given the honour of a visit to Bush's ranch at Crawford in Texas.
On 29 January, Bush had identified Iraq as part of an 'axis of evil' in
his State of the Union address. We stayed in a town miles from the
venue and were only allowed nearer when they were ready to talk to
us. By now, Blair's closeness to Bush and his apparent readiness to
expand the 'war on terror' was causing consternation in the
Parliamentary Labour Party. He said after Crawford: 'If necessary the
action should be military and again, if necessary and justified, it should
involve regime change.'

On the way home he told us he understood the anxieties of Labour
MPs and he promised that any action would be taken 'for the right
reasons in the right way.' I wrote: 'Mr Blair is believed to have told Mr
Bush that when the time comes Britain will back action against Iraq.'
When Chilcot was published, much was made of a letter dated 28 July
2002, in which Blair began: 'I will be with you, whatever.' But to those
of us who covered the summit, that was obvious, and we wrote as
much.

Much of the rest of the year was absorbed by the efforts of Blair to
convince his party and the public that war to remove Saddam's alleged
armoury of weapons of mass destruction (WMDs) was justified. In
September, a dossier claiming that Saddam's WMDs could be used
within forty-five minutes of him giving an order was published. It was
to cause massive controversy in the months ahead.

Iraq allowed the weapons inspectors back in and in January 2003,
Hans Blix said they had not yet found 'any smoking guns'. But Saddam
was accused of failing to cooperate and on 29 January Bush announced
he was ready to attack Iraq even without a UN mandate. We were
travelling again – to Washington via Madrid – and from Madrid I
wrote that at their summit the next day, Blair would urge Bush to stick
by the UN route and secure a second resolution authorizing force to
disarm Saddam.

In Washington, bad weather prevented us from flying to Camp
David, and at their White House meeting Bush and Blair mapped out
a timetable for war that pointed to conflict beginning in mid-March.
Blair persuaded Bush to keep open the option of UN backing, but

Roland Watson, then our Washington correspondent, and I wrote that he showed little enthusiasm for the idea.

On the way back, Blair told us that the second resolution would be a trigger for war if Saddam did not comply, and within a day he was in France trying to persuade Jacques Chirac to go along with the plan. In a frank admission to the Commons, Blair accepted that his support for Bush had left him out of line with public and Labour opinion.

Efforts to get a new UN resolution continued but France and Russia stood in the way, arguing against an ultimatum to Iraq while the weapons inspectors had still not completed their work. On Sunday, 16 March, we flew with Blair to a mid-Atlantic summit with Bush and the Spanish prime minister, José María Aznar, at Terceira on the Azores. It was the 'moment of truth for the world,' said Bush. A grim and strained Blair said: 'We have reached the point of decision.' They set a 24-hour deadline for the UN to authorize force. The next day the diplomatic process ended without success. I had written of Blair:

> Within days he may have to decide whether Britain is with the US in a war to disarm Saddam or with the United Nations and Europe in opposing it. He is caught up in a crisis unlike any of the others that have hit him during his premiership.

A crisis it was, and some 139 Labour MPs withheld support from Blair when the Commons approved military action on 18 March. A third of his parliamentary party was against and it was the biggest anti-government rebellion in parliamentary history. *The Times* was to reveal on 26 April that Jack Straw, foreign secretary, and Blair would have resigned if many more Labour MPs had denied them support. Straw told me in an interview of the 'very dark moments' in the build-up to war, and that if the revolt had been much bigger, the two of them would have gone.

They believed until fairly late in the day that there was real risk that a majority of Labour MPs might have voted against. Had the PM resigned at that point, John Prescott would have taken over as acting PM pending a swift Labour leadership election, in which Gordon Brown would have been the overwhelming favourite.

On 20 March, the invasion of Iraq began. On 9 April, Baghdad fell. On 2 May, Bush declared victory. Peter Stothard, former editor of *The*

Times, was given access to Downing Street in the run-up to war and during it. His account, *30 Days: A Month at the Heart of Blair's War*, had Blair casting aside his usual caution about talking about his strong religious beliefs. He told Stothard he was ready to meet his Maker and answer before God 'for those who have died or who have been horribly maimed as a result of my decisions'. He also accepted that many who believed 'in the same God' may assess that the final judgment will be against him. Blair and the political world waited an awful long time for the Chilcot Report.

My own adventures in Iraq and Afghanistan were far from over, as I was to return later with Blair and Gordon Brown. I was again with the former as he flew secretly into Baghdad just before Christmas in 2004. It was a highly dangerous visit at a time when the US-led coalition was under attack from insurgents across the country.

We flew in an RAF Hercules from Jordan. Then arriving at the international airport in Baghdad, we were told to run to a group of American Black Hawk helicopters. US airmen literally threw us on board and we flew low over the washing lines to the green zone. Blair called on the Iraqi people to defy the bombers and hailed as heroes the organizers of the forthcoming elections.

I have always believed that Iraq shortened Blair's prime ministerial career and that he could well have won four elections but for the unpopularity it brought him, particularly in his own party. Even so, he managed to bring off an, in retrospect, comfortable third victory in 2005, but his authority had been so weakened within Labour that he could not see off the final assault from the Brownites in 2006.

Along with our foreign editor, Richard Beeston (who died in 2013), I interviewed Blair in September 2011 to mark the tenth anniversary of 9/11. Meeting him at his London office in Grosvenor Square, I asked him whether he suffered great personal cost because of Iraq. He replied:

> Yes, but I don't think the cost to me personally matters one way or another. Look, when we are debating 9/11 just go back to that day and understand – just refix our minds on that day, and we know those people would have killed 30,000 people or 300,000 people if they could. That is what motivated people like me to take the view that I did: that the world had changed, that

we had to take an emphatically different view of this threat than we had before.

Blair once told Labour MPs that he pursued the actions he had in Iraq and elsewhere not because the Americans were telling him to do so, but because he believed in it. He believed that he could combine a policy of liberal intervention to save lives – he also went to war in Kosovo – with a strong alliance under any circumstances with the US, and a commitment to put Britain at the heart of Europe. But it was beyond him. He could never be the bridge between Europe and the US that he had aspired to be. His support for the Iraq war eventually placed him on the opposite side to France and Germany, who stood out against it.

But for Iraq it is hard to see how Gordon Brown could ever have become prime minister. Many Labour MPs believe Blair could have gone on for as long as he liked, winning in 2005 more comfortably than he did and possibly going on to thwart David Cameron in 2010.

Iraq, however, was the biggest mistake of his career, one that has blighted it and one that – after Chilcot – has left many British families wondering whether their loved ones gave their lives in vain.

The Death of David Kelly

I was playing golf against the Cabinet secretary. As you do! It was the annual Whitehall v. Press match on 18 July 2003, and we were on the Old Course at the RAC Club in Epsom, Surrey, close to the Epsom Downs Racecourse. On the green of the twelfth hole, Andrew Turnbull's phone rang. Aware that such devices were banned, he grabbed it from his golf bag and disappeared into a bunker. As he emerged, the genial and ultra-calm Turnbull looked shocked. 'David Kelly is dead,' he told me.

Kelly, the man at the centre of a ferocious row between Downing Street and the BBC, had gone missing from his home in Oxfordshire the previous day and had been found dead early that morning in an area of woodlands about a mile away. Tony Blair was travelling in the Far East and I, for once, was not with him, possibly because I did not want to miss the golf. As the senior civil servant in the Government, Turnbull was one of the handful first to be told.

That was the end of the golf. As we returned to the clubhouse, other matches were finishing early as the news spread. It was back to Westminster and Whitehall for reporters and opposition. Kelly's death was the tragic outcome to a story that began on 29 May, when Andrew Gilligan, the BBC journalist, accused the Government of sexing-up the Iraq war dossier by inserting the claim that WMDs could be fired within forty-five minutes, even though it knew it to be dubious. Later he claimed Alastair Campbell was responsible.

I have to enter an apology here to readers because I seem to be giving the impression that whatever was happening, I was there. Of course I was not everywhere but let me add now, to get it out of the way, that I was with Campbell and Blair in Basra, Iraq, when they learnt of the Gilligan broadcast, and I had spent the day at Wimbledon with Campbell, by chance, when on 27 June he – in the classic words of one of his distinguished predecessors – 'flipped his lid'. He had raced from the Centre Court to the Channel 4 studios in central London, and unleashed a fierce live attack on the BBC in front of an astonished Jon Snow.

Kelly, a ministry of defence expert on Iraqi weapons, had proofread the war dossier and been unhappy with parts of it, including the forty-five-minute claim. In May he met Gilligan and they spoke on a non-attributable basis. He told of his concerns about that claim. Gilligan presented his report on *Today* at the end of the month. Blair, his team, and the press were walking around what had until recently been Saddam Hussein's opulent summer palace on the banks of the Shatt al-Arab waterway in the southern Iraqi city of Basra.

The Prime Minister was visiting the 7th Armoured Brigade – the Desert Rats – who had made it their headquarters, and he used it as his platform to thank the British troops who had helped depose Saddam. We were several hours ahead of the UK, and Campbell and his colleagues were getting frantic calls from London telling them about the Gilligan broadcast. By now Campbell had moved away from front-line briefing and his PM's spokesman duties were shared between Tom Kelly and Godric Smith.

Gilligan had set off a huge storm and the next day the papers were full of demands that Blair and Bush publish evidence of the weapons of mass destruction that they had used to justify going to war, and on the row over the forty-five-minute claim. No one knew at this stage who had been a source, or THE source, for Gilligan's report.

A military war was succeeded by a war of words as Campbell accused the BBC of lying with the assertion that Downing Street had swept aside the concerns of the intelligence community to insert the forty-five-minute claim into the dossier. Number 10 demanded an apology but the BBC went on the attack and responded to Campbell's request for answers to twelve questions about the Gilligan report by accusing him of pursuing a personal vendetta against the reporter. The corporation launched a point-by-point rejection of Campbell's criticism and stood by its story. The response from Richard Sambrook, the BBC's director of news, reached Campbell at Wimbledon.

I had been invited there by Gavin Partington, the former GMTV political correspondent, who was now communications chief for the Lawn Tennis Association. I was surprised as we gathered for lunch before the tennis that Alastair, his son Calum and his best mate Charlie were there, as well as several others from the world of politics, including Julie Kirkbride, the Tory MP.

I sat to the right of Alastair in the Centre Court, with Calum to his left. We watched wins by Andy Roddick and Venus Williams but Alastair was not with us in spirit. He spent almost the entire afternoon furiously tapping on his phone, and occasionally disappearing to make calls. His son's entreaties to concentrate on the tennis went unheeded.

At around 5.45 p.m. it began to rain and further play looked doubtful. Alastair and Calum left smartly. I thought no more of it until, when I was returning to Wapping for an evening function, the news desk called me and asked if I knew that 'Campbell had just flayed the BBC' on Channel 4. I had to admit that I had been with him an hour before.

I learnt that on his way back to town, Campbell decided he had to respond after listening to the way the BBC had presented the story. He went back to Number 10 and, after a discussion with colleagues including Blair, headed straight to Channel 4. The office had been divided on whether he should do it. Blair told him not to go over the top.

His appearance was a surprise to Snow, who thought Campbell had turned down the chance of an interview – as he had, twice. 'The first I knew about it was when I was told through my earpiece "Alastair Campbell is in the building",' said Snow. Within seconds he was on the set, railing at the state of BBC journalism and attacking its refusal to respond to his call for an apology:

> This is an attempt by the Government to get the BBC to admit that a fundamental attack on the integrity of the Government and the Prime Minister and the intelligence agencies, let alone people – the evil spin-doctors in the dark who do their dirty work in the minds of a lot of journalists – let them accept for once that they have got it wrong.

It all spilled out, Campbell's frustration left him less fluent than usual. 'I have never met Andrew Gilligan. I don't have a vendetta against him,' he insisted. It was an outspoken performance, and the spin doctor had truly emerged from the shadows.

The next day, Sir Bernard Ingham, Margaret Thatcher's press secretary, opined: 'There are only one or two explanations for his behaviour. One is he has flipped his lid, or he is demob happy. And if he is not demob happy someone should give him cause to be.' Campbell himself admitted in his diaries that he got too angry, although the clips used in later bulletins were good, he thought. Blair felt he was too angry and Fiona Millar, Campbell's partner, was livid he had done it at all. 'But we kept going and I was sure we were going to win,' noted Campbell in his diaries.

In July, David Kelly was rebuked by the ministry of defence for an unauthorized meeting with a journalist. His name emerged into the public domain after reporters rang the MoD press office with different names and kept going until they got the right one. It would probably have come out anyway but Downing Street and the ministry wanted the name out there, mainly to show that Kelly was not an intelligence official but a weapons expert. On 15 and 16 July, he gave evidence to the Commons foreign affairs committee and the intelligence and security committee. At the former he was given a tough time, being dismissed as 'chaff' by one MP. The next day he went for his afternoon walk, never to be seen alive again.

Blair set up the Hutton Inquiry into the circumstances leading to Kelly's death. A journalist friend, Tom Mangold, said: 'I guess he could not cope with the firestorm that developed after he gave what he regarded as a routine briefing to Gilligan.' Alastair Campbell, by his outspoken appearance on live television, had become part of the story, something that spin doctors before and since knew they could not afford to allow to happen.

Midway through the Hutton Inquiry in August, Campbell announced that he and Fiona Millar were leaving Downing Street, a move he had contemplated a year before. By now, Blair was ready for him to go, as he had not been earlier. His nine years at Blair's side came to an end. For people like me, who had known him as a friend since his days at the *Mirror*, his departure was sad but probably inevitable. The death of David Kelly was one of the blackest moments in Blair's and Campbell's careers.

It was inevitable, given the vehemence of their denials of Gilligan's report and their pursuit of the BBC thereafter, that one way or another Kelly's name would come out. A good man who until then had pursued an anonymous, middle-ranking career was suddenly across the front pages and in front of a senior Commons committee, something for which he was clearly ill-equipped. The threat of disciplinary action by the ministry of defence for talking to a journalist weighed heavily. He became the tragic victim of a fight in which he was not a contestant; and his death left Campbell, Blair, the intelligence community and the defence ministry shattered.

In a splash on 16 January, I wrote that Blair was facing a tumultuous twenty-four hours that would decide whether he was prime minister at the time of the next election. It was not hyperbole, although I've been guilty of that many a time, I'm sure. The Hutton report was due the day after the second reading vote on tuition fees, the most important in his years in power. Again it showed the burdens on any prime minister; often they are fighting two, three, four critical battles at the same time, and you wonder how they can possibly concentrate on all of them.

At the end of January 2004, Lord Hutton reported, clearing Blair of any 'dishonourable, underhand or duplicitous' conduct in the lead-up to the death of Kelly. He also concluded that the Government had not 'sexed up' intelligence on Iraq in the run-up to war. He said the allegation that the Government knew that the forty-five-minute claim was false was 'unfounded'. He also found that no one could have anticipated that Kelly would take his own life.

The report was slammed in many quarters as a whitewash but Blair had come through the most perilous period of his premiership. However, he no longer had his closest aide and friend by his side. And the death of David Kelly and the repercussions of the war would stay with him forever.

My Part in the
Fall of Tony Blair

It was the last day of a holiday in my native Norfolk in August 2006. I was on the fourteenth green at Sheringham golf course when the phone in my bag began ringing. It was David Hill, director of communications at Number 10.

David was a true veteran of the Westminster scene. I first knew him in the early 1980s when he worked for the deputy leader, Roy Hattersley, whom he had also served in the 1970s Labour government. He had taken over from Alastair Campbell. The appointment of the straight-talking, no-nonsense Hill was meant to be a signal that the era of spin was coming to an end. And Hill, who had also been the party's head of communications, was not a spin doctor in the modern sense.

That afternoon he was straight and to the point, once we had got the latest news about our respective teams – Aston Villa (his) and Norwich (mine) – out of the way. It was a Tuesday. Would I care to come to Chequers (the Prime Minister's official country residence) on Thursday, for an end-of-holiday, pre-conference interview with the boss? I asked David if there was a particular purpose for the interview, given the papers were again full of stories about Labour MPs and Gordon Brown pushing Blair for a leaving date. He told me there would, as usual, be plenty in it, clearly saying nothing or an awful lot.

I jumped to the immediate conclusion that I – and my colleague Peter Riddell, whom I would be asking to join me for the interview – had been chosen as the vehicle for an announcement that the upcoming party conference would be Blair's last as leader. The pressure from the Brownites on Blair at this stage was near intolerable. They had convinced themselves that the Prime Minister, having seen off their man so many times in the past, had to go now because of his growing unpopularity with MPs who had once backed him. Internal opposition had grown over his stance on the Lebanon war, when he resisted pressure to call for a ceasefire in the battle between the Israeli defence forces and Hezbollah, which was costing hundreds of lives.

I was a relaxed golfer as I finished my round and then headed south to my house near Norwich in the village next to the one in which I was born, before heading off the next day for London. I called the picture desk and arranged for Chris Harris, Blair's favourite photographer at *The Times*, to meet me at Chequers the next day. A big story awaited. I did not know it then but it was to be the story that brought down Blair.

I rang Peter that evening and we speculated on how Blair would phrase the timing of his departure. In our minds there was no doubt that that was why *The Times* had been summoned. On the way there with Peter in a taxi organized by the office, we wondered how what we expected to be Blair's departure announcement would play. The news desk was aware of the interview but I did not fully share with them my high expectations. They were, in any case, used to me holding material back from them until I considered they really needed it. My theory was that a story handed to them just before they went in to address the paper's afternoon news conference in front of a hungry editor would always make more impact than one they had put on the schedule hours earlier.

While we waited for the PM, Nicky Blair, the second son, walked in, had a look at us and walked out. We were given a warm welcome by a tense-looking Prime Minister, who had been talking earlier to some key allies, including Sally Morgan, Peter Mandelson and Jonathan Powell, his chief of staff. Powell was still at Chequers. David Hill sat in on the interview.

Sitting on armchairs in a drawing room near the side entrance door, we engaged in the usual preliminaries about holidays and the books he had read. Then, assuming he had something prepared, I asked him straight whether he had anything to say about his departure date. The answer was no, and our surprise was palpable. I asked him again, and again, and again whether he intended to tackle the issue at the party conference and once more he said no.

He had no intention of saying any more either, before or during the conference. But he then went on to tackle the issue with a formula which – we were to learn much later – had been discussed endlessly by his aides in the run-up to the interview, and probably in the Chequers garden a little earlier. He told his party to 'stop obsessing' about the leadership and get on with the business of government. If it kept talking about the leadership, people would think the Government was paralysed or had run out of steam.

MPs who carried on and on about his leadership were doing so because they wanted a change of direction. But in words that had been agreed as part of his riposte, he insisted that he would not go 'on and on and on' and promised to give 'ample time' for his successor to bed in. The last was clearly directed at the followers of Gordon Brown, and I knew immediately that it would not be enough for a faction that felt it had been kept waiting for too long.

He added for good measure that by announcing in advance that he would not fight the next election – he had done so shortly before the 2005 poll, his third victory in a row – and guaranteeing time for his successor, he had done more than any other prime minister in such a situation. 'Now at some point I think people have to accept that as a reasonable proposition and let me get on with the job.' I knew instinctively that this was a fantastic story, but it was the precise opposite to the one I had expected.

Being greedy in such situations, I decided not to let it go and asked similar questions for several more minutes, noting down as I went how many times he had declined the chance to give any semblance of a leaving date. I went on probably too long, sensing the ever-patient Blair's growing impatience with my persistence. Peter smiled, knowing exactly what I was playing at. The eager Harris, whose news sense was as sharp as that of any reporter I have known, was loving it, snapping off pictures every few seconds, and as usual from every angle. They included a genius picture of Blair holding a mug with the name Anthony in capital letters and listing the characteristics of that name, including a 'man who is in charge, and who others follow'.

Blair touched on other issues and, as so often, attacked the unions who had presented a wish-list of demands before the conference. I know that one of his big regrets was that he did not go even further in diminishing the influence of the unions. As the interview ended, Peter asked whether we would be meeting for the same end-of-summer interview in a year's time. The Prime Minister laughed and brushed it aside.

Blair had kindly invited the three of us to stay for lunch. Harris declined to be fed and raced off to another room, where he started getting his pictures across to the office. As I sat on Blair's right in the small dining room, with Peter, Powell and Hill opposite, he turned to me and said, 'OK Phil, what's the story?'

Sometimes a reporter would take care about being too blunt, worrying that the subject might feel he or she had gone too far and might seek to soften their words. But it was obvious that everything Blair said had been planned. So I told him: 'It will be: "Blair defies party over leaving".' The headline chosen later that evening by the splash subeditor at *The Times* was pretty similar.

Blair looked straight across at Jonathan, and got a smile and a nod. David was inscrutable. Blair seemed reasonably relaxed and we got on with a wholesome Chequers meal, washed down with a glass or two of wine. Peter gave him a copy of the paperback version of his book,

The Unfulfilled Prime Minister, with a picture of glum-looking Blair on the front.

They had got across what they intended to get across. I felt straight-away that it would not work and said to Peter as we made our way back to the car that we would be setting off a firestorm that night. It was a full seven years later when we realized just how much had gone into the planning of that interview and how vital it was regarded by the Blair team. Downing Street e-mails describing the battle by the Prime Minister's allies to stop him giving way to Brown were released to *The Guardian* by Benjamin Wegg-Prosser, a former Peter Mandelson aide, who was working for Blair in 2006. At the time, he was director of the strategic communications unit in Number 10. In 2013 he said he was releasing the e-mails partly given the intrinsic interest in one of most dramatic weeks in recent British political history, but also to remind the party of the dangers of factionalism.

The e-mails reveal Number 10 aides disagreeing with one another at the end of August 2006 over how to calm back-bench opinion about Blair's leadership intentions, and suggest that Blair was prepared to go even harder than he did in our interview. He had contemplated saying 'all bets are off' if the internal wrangling did not stop. His even-tual formulation to us was that he would give his successor 'ample time'. Here are some of the entries, as reported by *The Guardian*:

Wednesday, 30 August 2006 [the day before we went to Chequers]

Patrick Wintour (PW; *Guardian* political editor) writes: The Blair team are preparing for a set-piece interview in *The Times* for that Friday designed to lay to rest further speculation about whether he will name a date for his departure, and are debating how hard a line the prime minister should take. Back-benchers have been agitating through the summer for him to quit.

8.43 a.m. from Liz Lloyd (deputy chief of staff in No 10) to Wegg-Prosser:
Did you spk to him? He is mulling a tougher line than this.

8.43 a.m. from Wegg-Prosser to Lloyd:
I did. I know he wants to go much further.

Blair wanted to say: 'This is the debate. These are the choices.
We need to get on with this. I have given more clarity on timing
than my predecessors. If this nonsense does not come to an end
all bets are off.'

Wegg-Prosser's view: While this is all fine the danger is that
he seems a) wildly out of touch b) it precipitates a more formal
challenge. I think also internally we need a line and need to
discuss further, without him, to clarify what we think.

PW: Recognizing their political weakness, the Blair team sense
they may need to convince Blair that he has to offer something
specific about his departure date. They start to map out some
new lines to take.

2.57 p.m. from Wegg-Prosser to others in Blair's office:
I have had another idea. A potential concession which
strengthens.

3.33 p.m. from Wegg-Prosser:

Phase 1
Times interview. Make argument that by giving a date under-
mines position of PM. 'If I thought that speculation would come
to an end if I name a date, then I would consider that. I will be
taking soundings and listening to the people in the run up to
conference.'

Phase 2
Letter from cross section of MPs saying PM has made clear to be
happy to indicate when he intends to leave office if the speculation came to an end.

Phase 3
At conference or maybe before (but conference better because
it keeps GB guessing).
  'People have made clear that the instability will come to an
end if I gave an indication of when the next leadership elections
will take place. In politics you can never be certain of anything,

but I have informed the national executive that they should be making plans to hold an election early next autumn.'

If this was seen as to be reasonable and sensible there is a chance that things might die down.

3.46 p.m. from Lloyd:
I thought of a different formulation. 'GB knows perfectly well when I am stepping down as I have discussed it with him.' I don't really like your formulation because it does not look as if he is in control of his destiny – but maybe this is a small price to pay for peace and another 9 months.

4.01 p.m. from Wegg-Prosser:
I know but if things don't take a turn for the better by mid-September then it might not be a bad option.

PW: Sensing the political danger is growing, the Blair team discuss a group of ex-ministers writing a letter to defend Blair.

9.06 p.m. from Wegg-Prosser:
I am now the benefactor of hourly phone calls from [former health secretary Alan] Milburn and [former transport minister Stephen] Byers. They have been in touch with the ex-ministers group and they have suggested a letter to *The Guardian*. The obvious danger is that we get into willy waving with the other MPs saying TB should go.

Thursday, 31 August 2006
PW: The SCU (strategic communications unit) prepares the lines to take in the wake of Blair's set-piece interview for the next morning's *Times*, in which he will set out his plans to stay in office.

4.11 p.m. from Wegg-Prosser:
The PM has made clear he will not be setting out a timetable for when he leaves office. He has given more clarity on the issue than any other previous prime minister in office he will not be going on and on like Mrs Thatcher.

He will not be serving a full third term. He will be giving his successor ample time.

There are three groups of people who are demanding the PM goes further than this. Those who are concerned by the polls … Those who are concerned he will be going on and on – he has dealt with those in his interview.

The biggest concern amongst those wanting him to leave is that they want a change of direction and that is why we need a genuine debate about the future direction of the party – there are big issues which the party needs to face up to, anything from immigration security and the future of our public services. These are the issues that the PM intends to address in the coming period.

Friday, 1 September 2006
PW: The *Times* interview with Blair is published, in which he tells his party to 'stop obsessing' about the leadership and get on with business of government, stressing he will give his successor 'ample time' and not go 'on and on' like Margaret Thatcher.

No 10 anxiously watches how the Press Association (PA) is reporting the response inside the party.

Members of the SCU note that the PA report reads:

The PM came under fire yesterday after declaring he would not bow to pressures to name a date for his departure at this month's party conference. He used an interview in *The Times* to urge colleagues to stop obsessing about his leadership and instead concentrate on getting on with governing the country.

That all came years later, but it was gratifying even then to see the evidence of how much Blair had prepared for that interview. It also showed they were just not ready for the scale of rebellion that immediately ensued.

So back to 2006, as Peter and I were being driven fast to London we concluded that, if anything, our interview would make things worse for Blair, not better. There was a minor hiccup at this stage. John Wellman, our news editor, rang, as usual impatient to hear what his splash would be. We were listening to the tape at the time and Peter pressed the wrong button to pause it while I spoke to John. We lost a precious few minutes of the tape.

For the thousandth time in my career, I thanked the Lord a) that I had very good shorthand and b) that I never really trusted tape-recorders and took notes during interviews as I went along. As did Peter. So we quickly pieced the interview together. I always felt that taking notes persuaded the subjects you were interested in what they were saying: allowing a recorder to do the job meant they had no way of knowing whether you were getting bored.

We returned to The Times Room at the Commons, with me, in the usual way, taking the lead on the front-page splash and Peter writing up the detailed interview inside after we had transcribed what we needed from the tapes and notes.

In the inside spread, we wrote that – talking in the calm of Chequers – Blair had brushed aside the queue of Labour MPs and commentators angrily calling for his resignation. He had done what no previous prime minister has done in saying that he would not fight another election, while giving 'ample time' for his successor. We commented: 'However, his words will not end demands for him to set out a firm timetable for this departure, a question that we posed in eight or nine different ways during the fifty-minute interview.'

The story on the front appeared in much the way I had described to Blair. During the afternoon I received a call from David Hill to ask if we were still on the same course as discussed, and I said yes. But I sensed in that call a certain amount of concern and was to learn much later that calls had been made to some other papers trying to soften the impact of what they knew was about to appear in *The Times*. The Brownites were well aware that the interview was taking place, and were expecting what I had expected, not what we got. It was going to be quite a night.

Calls from the Brown camp were made in the early evening but I refused, as always, to let on about what we had got. One word out of place at this stage and the story would very quickly be a Brownite outrage story eclipsing our 'Blair hangs on' one. In his book *Power Trip*, Damian McBride says that I have a voice that gives away the nature of the story, and that he sensed it was bad news for them. I told him it would be of great interest.

It was only after the first edition dropped, and was therefore avail-able in newsrooms around the country, that I spoke to Damian and others in the Brown camp, to insert some reaction in the story which, by now, had caused an explosion in Westminster and other parts of the country. The biggest explosion, which had nothing to do with the food, came at a curry house in Wolverhampton.

In what became known as the Balti House Conspiracy, Tom Watson – now Labour's deputy leader but then an ardent Brownite – met with Sion Simon, formerly a Blairite, and six other friends to discuss the future of the Prime Minister. News of the *Times* interview had reached the Midlands fast and the diners, enjoying their biryani, were in uproar.

Watson, a junior defence minister, and six parliamentary private secretaries signed a letter from a group of MPs calling on Blair to quit. Over several days of near-anarchy, more and more groups called for the same. McBride confirmed in his book a leaked story at the time which said that Brown, watching the mayhem on television, had said: 'We've got to stop this.' Ed Balls, his leading ally and by then an MP, retorted: 'We can't stop it.' McBride said the words did not impute complicity; Ed was clear with Gordon: 'We're not in charge of this; it is not ours to stop.'

Blair, having pre-announced his departure before the 2005 election, was not strong enough to survive this time. Brown went in to see him on the Wednesday after the *Times* interview and a compromise emerged. Blair allies briefed that Brown had demanded Blair step down by the following spring, or he would inevitably be forced out by the surge of demands on him, and that he should silence the New Labour figures such as Alan Milburn and Stephen Byers who had questioned the chancellor's belief in New Labour principles.

McBride reports that Brownite supporters were livid at the idea of a compromise because Blair was on the 'edge of a cliff' and should be forced out immediately. The spin doctor's conclusion was this:

It's not a popular view but Gordon saved Tony that day; he got him his final year in power. And he was right to do so; the unceremonious, immediate ousting of Labour's most successful leader would have been a terrible scar for the party to bear, in the same way that Margaret Thatcher's removal affected the Tories for decades afterwards.

It was nonetheless a humiliating end for Blair, and the manner of it did no favours to Brown. It left scars that would never be removed, as other chapters in this book will show.

In his book *The Third Man*, Peter Mandelson said that at this time Brown had lost all patience. Placated, strung along and then disappointed time and again, he was at the end of his tether. The final trigger was the *Times* interview, said Mandelson, adding that when Blair had asked him about it beforehand, he had questioned the wisdom of doing it, fearing it was likely to make the situation with Brown worse. He was right.

I wonder what the plotters against Blair think today, having seen what has happened to Labour since that day. In their worst nightmares, they could not have imagined a future in which a hefty defeat for Brown was followed by a worse mauling for Ed Miliband, and finally Jeremy Corbyn – yes, Jeremy Corbyn.

But back in 2006, Blair lost the will to fight any more. Even that Wednesday – 6 September – Watson and seven government aides resigned over his apparent determination to cling on. Blair called him 'disloyal, discourteous and wrong' and said he would have dismissed him had he not gone first. My splash headline the next morning said 'Labour paralysed as the poison spreads'.

And on that Thursday, exactly a week after we went to Chequers expecting him to pre-announce his departure, Blair did so. On a pre-arranged visit to a school in London, the Prime Minister apologized to the country for his party's behaviour and said: 'I am happy to confirm in public what I have already told senior colleagues in private: that Manchester will be my last conference as party leader.' He had finally given in to the inevitable: Gordon would at last take over, but not quite yet.

It was not a specific timetable, but it was an end date. The interview he had given to *The Times* to shore up his position had had the opposite effect. In the years since then I have at least twice discussed that interview with Blair and wondered whether he regarded it as misconceived. He defended the stance he took, saying there was no alternative at the time. But he was angry with himself over what he regarded as a slip-up on his behalf earlier that year, which he said allowed speculation to run riot. Again I have to admit my part in this episode.

In late March 2006 the Lobby travelled with Blair to Melbourne, where he was to attend the final days of the Commonwealth Games. It was a non-stop seventeen-hour flight from Brussels, where he had attended an EU summit. We were used to long trips with the PM but this was a non-stop record. After meals, sleep and more food, David Hill told us that Blair would be coming down for a chat – customary on such travels – as soon as we were ready for him.

He told us the terms. It would be off the record AND not for use, a formula designed to help the PM be a bit more open than he might have been, but one of little use to reporters who wanted to get a story from the exchange. Still it would be good see the PM and, as we flew over Perth with a few hours to go, the great man appeared. We covered all manner of subjects, including the prospects for British success at the events we were about to attend.

But inevitably the conversation turned to his leadership. I thought I would try something different and asked him whether, in his own mind, he had got a date in mind for his departure. 'Yes, I have actually, Phil,' he replied. I was stunned. Was it the altitude? Tiredness? He clearly had not been drinking, and rarely did on these trips. He should have said 'No'. Handed a gift, I said rather weakly: 'I suppose you don't want to tell us when!?' 'No, I won't and I've probably said too much anyway,' Blair laughed as a look of concern crossed David Hill's face.

The chat ended, Blair wished us a happy trip, and the usual post-match huddle began. I have to admit that in these circumstances, the Lobby is a rather excitable, uncontrollable, occasionally unreasonable beast. The conversation was off the record and not for use. Surely that should have been the end of the story. Go back to sleep. But no. The PM of the UK had just told us he had a leaving date in mind. Surely that was a bit of a story? You bet. But we could not write it without breaching the terms under which Blair had come back to see us. This had to be handled carefully.

Fortunately, we were landing late on Saturday Australian time, early Saturday at home. There were no Sunday reporters on board so our next deadline was Monday morning in Britain, providing the broadcasters played ball. At Sunday lunchtime, still just after midnight back home, we met up in a restaurant after a good long sleep. The story did not seem quite as good as it did at 40,000 feet, but it was the best we had. Some bright spark, and I honestly don't remember whom, came up with a way to bypass David Hill's not-for-use condition. We knew Blair was doing an interview with the Australian Broadcasting Corporation. Surely we could brief the interviewer to ask questions 'on the record' rather similar to those we had asked confidentially. This happened, and it came up trumps – in fact, even better than that.

Yes, he accepted that he had a leaving date in mind, but he went further still. The interviewer, primed by hardened Westminster hacks, got the PM to cast doubts on whether it had been right for him to have told the world that he would not fight the next election, expected in 2009 or 2010. George Pascoe-Watson, political editor of *The Sun*, told his readers that Blair 'sensationally admitted last night he was WRONG to tell the world he would not fight the next election. The PM confessed it was a boob that had dogged his leadership with questions for 18 months.'

I wrote that Blair accepted that his announcement before the last election had backfired because it had failed to dispel speculation about his future. I was also happy to reveal – legitimately under the terms under which he worked – that he had a leaving date in his mind. The whole episode threw the normally imperturbable David Hill into a tailspin. He announced that all of us had gone collectively 'f★★★ing bonkers', which may well have been fair comment. His line was that Blair had not said he regretted ruling out fighting a fourth term, but that he had had got it wrong in suggesting that he could end speculation in his third term.

When I saw him in Jerusalem in 2011, four years after he had stood down and serving then as the Middle East envoy for the previously mentioned Quartet of powers, he smiled about that trip and said: 'I should never have answered your question.' I took no pride in playing the tiniest part in the downfall of a prime minister who, helped by his predecessor Neil Kinnock, had made Labour electable again and who, but for Iraq, would almost certainly have gone on and on.

Blair was an extraordinary political phenomenon, one whom people in all parties, including the likes of David Cameron and George Osborne, secretly admired. We will never again witness a scene such as that in the Commons on 27 June 2007, when Conservatives led the ovation at the end of his final Question Time. He had admitted never pretending to be a great House of Commons man and in his final words, which provoked unprecedented applause, said: 'I wish everyone, friend or foe, well and that is that, the end.'

For Blair it was not really the end. Other careers and controversies lay ahead and he would forever provoke anguished debate and argument. But no one can question the unforgettable impact he made on British politics.

Gordon's Three
Missed Chances to Win

Gordon Brown became Labour leader on 24 June 2007, in an uncontested election after his only challenger, John McDonnell, shadow chancellor since the 2015 election, failed to get enough nominations to stand. Tony Blair – given a reasonably quiet last few months after bowing to Brownite pressure to name his departure date – departed the stage as prime minister with a flourish three days later.

The tale of the 2007 general election that never was has been told many times and in different ways. History has shown it to be the biggest missed opportunity in Brown's career. It was called off in the end not because Brown thought there was a big chance of him losing, but because the doves in his team thought – on the basis of one new poll – that the majority bequeathed him by Tony Blair might be reduced. The fears of Labour MPs who believed they might be casualties in a quick rush to the polls played an exaggerated part in the discussions whose final conclusion left the likes of Spencer Livermore and Ed Balls – who had been pushing for an early election to build on Brown's fledgling popularity – dismayed and fearing for the future.

I can reveal that it was not just one missed opportunity, but at least three. What has never been reported is that Brown had earlier gone much closer to laying down a timetable for an election that, in retrospect, he could easily have brought forward and which probably would have seen him become prime minister in his own right. Nothing is certain in politics but an attempt to win early would have been better than the fate eventually to befall him in 2010.

I have learnt that, on the morning of Brown's speech on 24 June 2007, when he was crowned in Manchester as Tony Blair's successor, there was serious discussion of using it to give strong hints that he was planning an election for about nine months' time. The idea went so far that I and George Pascoe-Watson of *The Sun* got the strangest of calls from Damian McBride, Brown's communications chief. He told us 'off the record, not for use, and "don't tell the news desk yet"' that there might be a very good story emanating from the coronation speech.

Nothing had been finally decided, and it might well not happen, and if it didn't we were never to say a word. But it was possible that Brown would set out a very firm, short-term programme for government that would lead people to conclude the election would come next spring, possibly in March. If so, the story would be that Brown was already preparing to call an election within nine months.

Our discussions with McBride were the sort that could only take place if there was complete trust between briefer and reporter. He was giving us a heads-up to be ready for something quite exceptional, which would give us time quietly to prepare election timetable pieces, but if it didn't happen he was relying on us not to mention what we had been told. With this kind of deal, if either side broke their part of the bargain, there would be no further bargains.

Brown and his confidants discussed how far to go. And eventually they decided on an upbeat speech giving the impression that an election might not be far away – he announced the appointment of an election coordinator, Douglas Alexander – but leaving out any specific clues as to timing. Brown did not want to be boxed in by dates, not knowing how long any honeymoon he might get would last, and not wanting to be in a position the next spring where he was committed to an election but behind in the polls.

McBride made no reference to the discussions about Brown's speech in his book *Power Trip*, but with his knowledge I publish them here. Knowing what we knew, George and I still wrote election stories. I said that Brown put Britain and the Labour Party on the alert for an election in 2008. George wrote the election would come within a year, with the most likely date the following June. But our stories lacked the specific commitment that could have been there if the hawks had won out in the pre-speech discussions.

What the plan showed for sure was that if the conditions were right, Brown certainly did want to go for an election in 2008. Deprived of the one he had warned us about, McBride needed to get another story out there quite quickly. To the surprise of the Brown camp, Harriet Harman took the deputy leadership just ahead of Alan Johnson, whom they had expected to win. We were briefed that Brown would be making her party chairman but not deputy prime minister despite earlier indications that he would give that job to his elected deputy. I wrote that Brown had shown his ruthless streak.

But what happened then took everyone by surprise, including the Prime Minister. His honeymoon was fast and furious. He then missed his second opportunity. As early as July, Spencer Livermore, who had been Brown's chief strategy adviser when he was chancellor and took the same job in Number 10, was the lone voice calling for an early election in the autumn. After Brown had summoned the Cabinet to Chequers late in July for a discussion on the new political landscape, and ministers were given a poll presentation comparing Brown favourably with David Cameron, Livermore told him he should go to the country soon because the omens looked good.

Brown, it appears, was still thinking – as he had done on the day of his election, although he declined to say it then – about the prospect of going in April or May of 2008 and he brushed aside Livermore's idea, presumably as too bold. But Livermore had his own reasons for pushing for the early poll. While at the Treasury he had opposed Brown's decision in his last Budget to abolish the 10p rate of tax, and feared it would come back to haunt him when the measure came into effect the following spring. He was to be proved right. As it happened he had also pressed for Brown to cut inheritance tax and was dismayed by later events on that front.

So early in August Livermore presented a memo to Brown again putting the case strongly for an early election. He wanted it to be announced the next month. Brown's handling of the foot-and-mouth outbreak, bomb attempts in London and Glasgow, flooding and even the crisis at Northern Rock contributed to a strong surge in popularity for the Government that had led to a wave of speculation about a snap poll. Livermore's memo was shown to aides and, according to Andrew Rawnsley in *The End of the Party*, Douglas Alexander told Brown he must look at it seriously.

But Brown, distracted by Northern Rock, did not properly discuss it in August and only dug it out again in September. After rereading it he told figures like Alexander, Balls and Ed Miliband to keep the story running even though he was far from persuaded. According to Rawnsley, Brown later told his circle that one of his great regrets was 'those lost weeks' when he could have acted on the Livermore plan.

Brown again discussed the possible election with his Cabinet before the party conference in September and found it to be split, and some of the older members, including Jack Straw, opposed. But Livermore, still trying very hard to persuade his boss, and Bob Shrum, the American pollster whom Brown liked, suggested that he should call the election in his conference speech.

Brown was far from convinced but asked the team to prepare the ground in case that was what he decided as the conference approached. The polls continued to bode well and on the eve of the conference Douglas Alexander, the campaign chief, gave an interview which appeared to be putting the party on a war footing.

On the Sunday of conference, Ed Balls, interviewed on BBC Radio 4's *The World This Weekend*, spoke of 'the coming weeks and months' when asked about election timing, a formula that others around Brown considered too careful. McBride was sent out to brief that Balls was not damping things down.

As the week progressed the momentum increased, the party prepared further, and by the Thursday, Balls was on the radio saying that the bigger gamble might be to wait rather than go now. As the conference wound up, the party was indeed on a war footing, and serious money was spent on the usual preparations such as advertising and poster sites. But Brown had missed another chance. Calling the election in his speech would have thrown the Conservatives into a tailspin. Their own conference would have been curtailed.

Even so, by the end of that conference week most ministers thought the election was on, and Brown ordered several events, including the Pre-Budget Report (PBR), to be brought forward in readiness for a snap poll. Things started to go wrong when the Tories began meeting in Blackpool. Brown had clearly hoped to spook them. But the speculation had the opposite effect and produced a united front.

It was George Osborne's dramatic pledge to cut inheritance tax that gave the Tory conference a massive morale boost. More people had been sucked into the inheritance tax net in recent years because of the rise in property prices, and here was Osborne promising to free all but millionaires from the threat. The numbers affected would be small but the message to the middle classes was clear, which was why Livermore and others had pressed for action the previous spring. Alistair Darling, the chancellor, was asked to match Osborne's scheme in the PBR.

But it was Brown's long-planned trip to Basra – with pictures coming back of him glad-handing British troops on the Tuesday of the conference – that really got the Tories going, allowing them to accuse him of an election stunt and puncturing the patriotic image he had built up over three months. Even so, on the Thursday after the Tory conference, Pascoe-Watson, Andy Porter of *The Telegraph* and I invited McBride for lunch in Westminster. He took calls throughout, as was usual, and many were from within Number 10, but as he left us we were still in little doubt that Brown would go for it. McBride certainly wanted him to.

Back in Number 10 the Brown team were shattered by the Osborne gambit, and for some like Livermore it confirmed why going early would have been right. It would have denied the shadow chancellor his conference platform. On the Friday, the whole election team, apart from Balls, who was in his constituency, met with Brown again at Number 10. At 6.30 that morning Brown called Balls and told him the election was on. As Balls reports in his book, published in 2016, he told him: 'I've thought hard about it, and we're going to go for it.' The public polls had shown a narrowing in the Labour lead and here Stan Greenberg, another American pollster, presented an analysis of fieldwork from marginal seats which suggested that, although Labour would win, its majority could be cut by thirty to forty seats. The internal poll really worried Brown, who asked what he would say to the thirty MPs who lost their seats through him going early.

I had a pretty good read-out of that meeting and I wrote later that Greenberg had drawled in his deep American accent that if Brown went for it, he would win but he might not win well. It is obvious today that far too much attention was paid to that one poll, and nobody seemed to be thinking about how the Government would almost certainly be able to improve its position during the campaign. Livermore, refusing to give up, said they had gone too far down the road to pull back now, but he had little support.

McBride wrote in his book that some of the MPs and advisers who had Gordon's ear were clearly thinking about their own futures, shifting their positions and giving him a lot of subjective advice:

> Inappropriate as it would have been he should have asked the likes of Michael Ellam (his official spokesman) what they thought, or listened more to long-serving advisers and friends like Bob Shrum and Sue Nye (his office chief), who he knew only had his interests at heart. He could have listened to me tell him that every journalist I spoke to was convinced we should go for it. And he certainly should have listened more to Ed Balls.

McBride wrote of Brown:

> You'd have forgiven him for lashing out at those who'd urged him along at every stage and were now counselling caution, but he just seemed stoical. Finally he said: 'Right, does anyone else have anything they want to say?' like the lawyer of a condemned man hoping someone in the courtroom will produce an alibi. Everyone looked at the floor.

Brown's mind was made up overnight and the next day, Saturday, Ed Balls called me in my Norfolk village, ostensibly to talk about Norwich City's fixture that day. But he was despondent and told me that the election was off and that the news would be put out that night via a pre-recorded interview with Andrew Marr of the BBC. He regretted not being at the meeting but doubted whether he would have been able to turn the tide. He predicted that the Sunday papers would be awful for the Government, and he was not wrong.

The leadership then descended into recriminations, with McBride being blamed for the presentational cock-up which meant that the contents of a pre-recorded interview were splashed over the Sundays. In the Rawnsley book, McBride was also accused of trying to distance Brown and Balls from the 'election off' fiasco by pinning the blame on Alexander, Livermore and Ed Miliband, and he was said to have been caught in the act by Livermore, with whom he had a furious row.

In *The Brown Years*, a Radio 4 series, by Steve Richards of *The Independent*, Livermore said that McBride had told him he had been instructed to blame certain individuals, and that McBride had told him the order came from Balls. Livermore claimed that McBride worked for Balls as well as Brown. Balls denied ordering the briefing, saying he had never told McBride to brief against any colleague, elected or unelected: 'So it's not true.'

No one denies, however, that by now the atmosphere in the previously tight-knit group around Brown had become poisonous, which would not help him in the months and years ahead. The caution shown by Brown on the day of his coronation was perhaps understandable. But if he had listened to Livermore in July, and Balls, Shrum, Livermore and Alexander later, he could still have called his election without giving the Tories any chance to fight back. Livermore left Brown's side in 2008.

Brown's strategic brain would have told him that he should go for an election as early as he could. That is why he did not stop his inner circle presenting it as a live prospect. But when it came to the decision on that Friday in October, he allowed short-term tactical considerations – such as the loss possibly of a few Labour seats, which would have been quickly forgotten in the elation of a victory – to stand in the way. Tactics beat strategy.

After he had made the decision, and following the subsequent deterioration in his position, Brown did not react in his customary way by getting angry. Someone who watched him throughout told me:

Contrary to his normal behaviour, Gordon didn't shout at anyone or seek to blame anyone. He was actually very introspective about it, as if he knew he'd made a very significant mistake, and that he knew the gravity of that mistake – that he'd probably blown his only chance of winning an election. It was certainly the only time I saw him react to a bad situation in that way.

The honeymoon had ended and the remaining thirty months of his premiership were riven by internal strife, plots against his leadership, a financial crisis and a general mood of despair as his party came to the end of its long spell in power, and made a return to the wilderness.

Mandelson Returns as the Wolves Gather

After the election that never was, Gordon Brown's standing with his party never recovered. Although he listened, probably too much, to his advisers before calling the whole thing off, it quickly became seen as a spectacular political bottle job – something which some of his closest friends believed he could never get over. He was to win genuine international acclaim later for his handling, as chairman of the G20 group of nations, of the financial crash, but from now on, internally it was a struggle to survive.

One of the joys of being a political editor is that you get the chance to travel with the prime minister of the day, and as can be deduced from the stories in this book so far, I was clocking up the air miles by the hundreds of thousands by this stage of my career. For a prime minister, these trips often looked like an opportunity to get away from domestic trouble – but they rarely were because the travelling Lobby (something of a beast at home but even more ferocious when away) never let them forget.

One example of a trip that combined some genuine excitement about events normally outside our ambit with the political news that we always hungrily sought, was Brown's trip to the Beijing Olympics in August 2008. Of all the trips I was offered during my years in charge, this was the one I was never going to hand over to a colleague. (My one-time deputy, Tom Baldwin, reckoned I only ever sent him to northern, cold capitals in Europe while grabbing all those in warmer climes for myself.)

In typical Brown fashion, however, we were made to earn the pleasure of being in the Chinese capital for the last couple of days of the

Games and to see its closing ceremony, as well as Boris Johnson's hilarious speech – 'whiff-whaff is coming home' – preparing the way for the London Olympics in four years.

Brown took us there via Afghanistan. We flew to Muscat in Oman in our usual style. But then we transferred to the less comfortable RAF Hercules transport plane, with its very hard seats, flew for four hours to Camp Bastion, visited British troops, flew north to Kabul for talks between Brown and President Karzai, and then flew all the way back to Muscat. There, after the briefest stop at the airport, we boarded our waiting plane to fly for another ten hours to Beijing. No beds were involved in any of this; we just kept going.

The trip happened in the middle of a turbulent summer for Brown. From being ahead in the polls in the autumn, Labour's position had plummeted by the spring, and in Brown's first electoral test in the May local elections, Labour lost a quarter of its councillors while Boris Johnson ended the reign of Ken Livingstone as London mayor.

The month before, Brown had virtually been forced into reversing the last big decision of his ten years as chancellor – scrapping the 10p rate of tax. He blinked first in a trial of strength with his back-benchers and was forced to come forward with a package of help costing hundreds of millions to compensate the losers.

The summer got worse. In July, Labour lost the Glasgow East by-election and the following week, just after Brown had left for a pre-Beijing summer break, David Miliband, the foreign secretary, wrote a notorious article for *The Guardian* outlining his vision for the Labour Party without giving Brown a mention. It was perceived as an outright attack on Brown's leadership, and Brownite MPs called for Miliband's resignation. I and other Lobby colleagues were told by friends of Miliband – as we had to call them – that it was indeed intended as an assault and that we should consider him to be a candidate in any contest that arose.

Miliband was the leading hope of the Blairites to replace Brown at the time. Some, including probably Blair, had hoped that he would stand against Brown in 2007. He had entered Parliament in 2001 after being Blair's head of policy in opposition and then chief of his Number 10 policy unit for the first term. I have always regarded his politics to be to the left of Blair's but he was the best chance that wing of the party had.

So it was against that background that Brown set off for the Olympics. This is a huge irony given what was to happen later, but I can reveal from conversations with impeccable sources that around this time there was a suggestion that Brown might make David Miliband his first secretary of state – effectively his number two – as he tried to broaden the appeal of his embattled government. But Miliband's behaviour rendered that out of the question.

Britain was doing well at the Olympics but any hope Brown may have had of a 'Beijing bounce' on the back of medal successes was dashed by the latest monthly Ipsos/MORI poll, which gave the Conservatives forty-eight per cent of the vote and Labour twenty-four per cent. Brown had stayed silent since the Miliband article but on the way out to Beijing, he came down the plane to see us as usual and we got him to talk. Damian McBride, his press man, rightly had persuaded him it was an issue that would not go away and he might as well deal with it rather than have it hanging over him for the full trip.

He dismissed suggestions he was about to be challenged and insisted the public was interested in what the Government was doing to help them, rather than in internal politics. He said:

We are getting on with the job. You will find that, as we get into September, what the people of Britain are concerned about is what is happening to their mortgages, their gas and electricity bills and oil prices and petrol prices at the pumps.

They are the issues they want us to look at and address; that is what we have got to deal with. You will see us dealing with some of these issues as we come back in September.

Unconvincingly he told us that the foreign secretary's controversial article which sparked a summer of turmoil could have been written by any member of the Cabinet – including himself. Labour would 'go on and win the next election'. Brown said his relations with Miliband were fine and I wrote that three times he referred to him as 'David' during an on-the-record press briefing. To be fair, what else could he have done? Privately, friends on the plane told us they had no idea whether Brown would be challenged in the run-up to party conference.

In Afghanistan, the questions still followed him. At Camp Bastion he addressed 300 soldiers in the 39°C (102°F) heat, telling them that the whole country owed them a debt of gratitude. He said that the reputation of the British Forces for professionalism had been enhanced by their mission. Their achievements surpassed even those of the country's Olympic stars in China. He told them they were heroes every day of the week and showed the same dedication, professionalism and courage as the triumphant Olympic competitors. Brown seemed to come alive during these meetings with the troops and his tribute was well taken by the men.

But at a press conference in Kabul with President Karzai, the questioning from British reporters was dominated by Brown's relations with the Cabinet, particularly Miliband. Karzai looked on as Brown, clearly irritated that the questions were not about the British mission in Afghanistan, maintained his insistence that the British people were looking to him to get on with the job and deal with their fuel, food and mortgage problems. At one point Karzai, trying to be helpful, joked: 'Cabinet ministers plotting is nothing new. We have them here too.'

On to Beijing and at last Brown, a great lover of sport, could enjoy himself. He watched several of the events and we were able to wangle tickets for ourselves to some through our friends and contacts on the ground. I had a brilliant time at the Olympic football final between Nigeria and Argentina, watching in the searing heat as twenty-year-old Angel Di Maria – many years later to join Manchester United – scored the only goal at the impressive Bird's Nest Stadium. It was so hot that players were given formal breaks to rehydrate themselves.

In a press briefing, Brown called for an end to the medals-for-all culture in schools and announced plans to give all children five hours of sport a week by 2012. All too soon the trip was over. We had a great last night at London House in Beijing, an open-air bar for British competitors and visitors, set up to promote the 2012 Games. Boris stormed in late on and produced gales of laughter, from Brown as much as anyone, by insisting that table tennis, in which the Chinese had again excelled, was really a British sport invented on the dining tables of England and known as whiff-whaff. 'Whiff-whaff is coming home!' he shouted, and sent everyone home happy.

McBride was at Brown's side throughout the trip, clearly the adviser then on whom he most relied. Spotted as a rising star as an official in revenue and customs, McBride had been made director of communications at the Treasury in 2003. Soon he became a special adviser, allowing him to behave in a political manner as Brown moved towards Number 10. In 2008 he was moved from the briefing job to be head of strategic planning, but he fell from grace in 2009 when his e-mails to a former Labour official, Derek Draper, suggesting ways of smearing leading Conservatives – including George Osborne – were leaked. He was sacked, went off to work for a charity and wrote his book before, in an unlikely return, he was appointed as an adviser to Emily Thornberry, shadow defence secretary, in 2016.

The summer wobble had hardened Brown's resolve to fight and he decided to take on the doubters. I was leaked the Prime Minister's personal foreword to a report from the Cabinet on the upcoming party conference, in which he warned his colleagues that he would confront his current problems in the way he had his personal ones in the past. In a rare show of emotion, he referred to the death of his daughter just a few days after she was born and the loss of an eye because of a rugby injury at school. I wrote that they were a warning to critics, including Charles Clarke, who had called for him to stand down the previous week, that he had no intention of going quietly.

That was soon to become obvious. Unknown to all but a few, Brown had been talking for months to his one-time close friend – and more recently enemy – Peter Mandelson. Mandelson was by now the trade commissioner in Brussels. Having been sacked twice in Blair's first term, he had won re-election at Hartlepool in 2001, with his emotional 'I am a fighter, not a quitter' acceptance speech one of the more memorable episodes of the election. However, Blair would not bring him back a third time, and I wish I had gone to the bookmakers when I told my colleague Rosie Bennett that the only way he could ever return was under Brown. I would have got good odds as they were not talking at the time.

Mandelson stood down as an MP and went to Brussels in October 2004. As Brown's first year fell apart over the non-election, the Prime Minister officially met Mandelson when they spoke about the world trade talks during a meeting at the European Commission headquarters in Brussels. They got on far better than could have been expected and it was not long before Brown was regularly calling Mandelson, as he had done twenty years before when they could only dream of returning Labour to power. The bond that held Blair, Brown and

Mandelson together in the early days had, to all their surprise, still not broken – despite everything.

David Muir, Brown's director of strategy, sounded out Mandelson about a return on a visit to Brussels and before long Mandelson was back in Number 10, settling the details of his reincarnation, for the third time, in government. Blair had advised him to take the role; others had been less encouraging. He was made a life peer, immediately taking his seat in the Lords as Baron Mandelson of Foy in the County of Herefordshire and of Hartlepool in the County of Durham, and becoming business secretary. The 'comeback kid' had returned. Brown at the hour of his greatest need had turned to him to rescue him.

Mandelson joked it was 'third time lucky'. The PM said he needed 'serious people for serious times'. He added: 'Whatever the ups and downs have been in the past, everybody has got to come together and make sure that as a nation we come through this successfully.' At one stroke Brown had neutralized – for now – any suggestion of a mass walkout in the autumn to force his departure. Labour politics had come full circle. Blair was gone and Mandelson was back with Brown. Who would have believed it?

How James Purnell
Took His Leave

At 9.45 p.m. on Thursday, 4 June 2009, James Purnell, Labour's fast-rising work and pensions secretary, rang 10 Downing Street and asked to be put through to the Prime Minister. Told that the PM was not available, Purnell insisted it was critical that he spoke to him, and waited, hearing a few clicks on the line as the operator tracked down Gordon Brown. Soon Brown came on the line and greeted Purnell. The minister said: 'Hello Gordon, I have rung to tell you that I am resigning from your Government.'

'What?!' said a stunned Prime Minister. Then another voice came on the line, which may have explained the earlier clicks. 'No, James, you cannot do this,' said Peter Mandelson, the recently installed business secretary. He had been listening in. Purnell told him: 'I'm afraid it's too late, Peter. It's in *The Times* and *The Sun*.' And it was, as Adam Boulton, then political editor of Sky, told the nation a few minutes later as he displayed a copy of the *Times* front page just before the 10 p.m. news.

This story, like quite a few in this book, began on the golf course. For many years Purnell, his best friend Tim Allan (former number two press spokesman to Alastair Campbell in the early years of Blair), George Pascoe-Watson (then political editor of *The Sun*) and I had had a summer golf holiday together, usually in Scotland.

Hugely competitive affairs, in which the politicos always took on the journalists in what they styled as a contest between the forces of light and darkness, these trips became a highlight of every summer. Occasionally others, like Peter Morgan – a fine golfer as well as being screenwriter of *The Deal, The Last King of Scotland, Frost and Nixon* and many more – joined us but the battle was usually so ferocious that they felt they were intruding on private territory and politely stayed away.

During those weeks after every last hole was diagnosed in the evenings, there was time for politics. We became and remain very close friends. So when Purnell, increasingly disillusioned with the way Brown was running his government and fearing that his continuation in office would hand the 2010 election to the Tories, decided to quit, he tipped us off. He'd considered and decided upon the drastic step the previous week during a short parliamentary recess.

He told George and me of his intention to go on that day. He did not consult his old boss, Tony Blair – who happened to be in the country – knowing that he would try to talk him out of it. Neither did he tell Mandelson, another good friend, for the same reason. Mandelson, acting for Brown, had consulted Purnell the night before on what jobs he would consider in the imminent reshuffle, and when asked whether he would like to be education secretary, he told him that he would. But even at that point, his mind really was made up.

Purnell informed George and me that he wanted, out of courtesy, to talk to Brown before he learnt the news from our newspapers. So our timing was crucial. One of the other handful of people to know what was going on was Phil Collins, then *The Times*'s chief leader writer and former Blair speechwriter, another close friend of Purnell. It is assumed that David Miliband, foreign secretary, also knew but he was not expected to join Purnell in resigning, having failed to instigate a revolt against Brown's leadership almost exactly a year before with his celebrated piece in *The Guardian* outlining his vision for the Labour Party. Purnell wanted to avoid any suggestions of plotting against Brown, so kept his news from other leading Blairite politicians like Alan Johnson.

To maintain confidentiality George and I had arranged for our front pages not go to the broadcasters, who often show them on the late evening news and current affairs programmes, until later than usual. But someone in my office did not get that message and Sky got theirs before ten. Hence Adam's excitement. George had tipped off Nick Robinson at the BBC and Tom Bradby at ITV News, so that they could lead with the breaking news.

Under the headline 'Dear Gordon, I quit', I reported Purnell had informed Brown of his decision minutes before polling ended in the

European and local elections, and that he had told the Prime Minister to stand down to save the Labour Party. In his letter to Brown he wrote: 'We both love the Labour Party. I have worked for it for twenty years and you for far longer. We know we owe it everything and it owes us nothing. I owe it to our party to say what I believe no matter how hard that may be.' Prophetically, he added: 'I now believe your continued leadership makes a Conservative victory more not less likely.' He continued: 'We need to show that we are prepared to fight to be a credible government and have the courage to offer an alternative future. I am therefore calling on you to stand aside to give our party a fighting chance of winning.'

By resigning in the way he had, Purnell had ensured both that he could not be talked out of it, and that Brown aides could not turn the story round and say he had been fired. Purnell knew from his conversation with Mandelson earlier that he was killing off the chance of Cabinet promotion. Education would have been a job he would have liked to do. He knew that if others did not follow him and force Brown's resignation, or if Brown himself did not face up to the stark message contained in his letter, then his political career was probably over. And it was. He stood down as an MP and during the 2010–15 Parliament he was to return to the BBC as director of strategy.

Purnell had been one of Blair's great hopes for carrying forward the New Labour torch. Bright and personable, he went to school for several years in France, emerged from Oxford with a first, and worked for a policy group and then the BBC before joining Blair as a special adviser in Number 10 in 1997. He became an MP in 2001.

Suggestions that he resigned merely to protect the position of Alistair Darling, whom Brown wanted to replace as chancellor with Ed Balls, were wrong. He hoped that his resignation might somehow force Brown out, and in any case Balls had been making clear that he had no wish to leave the post of education secretary. Balls had said as much to Brown. Whether he would have been able to resist if Brown had insisted is hard to tell. But it did not arise after the Purnell bombshell. Mandelson was feverishly trying to stabilize the shaken world of the Prime Minister, and would not have allowed him to drop his chancellor as well.

But the episode described at the top of this chapter also tells us something about the never-ending capacity of politics to surprise.

Mandelson was now Brown's right-hand man, the man who would have stopped the Purnell resignation if he could, and worked overtime in the hours that followed it to stop others going down the same route. Sources in Number 10 at the time believe this was the moment when Brown was at his most vulnerable and would almost certainly have fallen if there had been more planning by his opponents or if Mandelson had not been by his side.

One former aide recalls walking into Downing Street at around 10 p.m. that night and encountering a scene reminiscent of *The Godfather*:

> It was if they had all assembled after the latest hit. Although rather than hitmen with their tommy guns, we had the special advisers with their mobiles calling round their ministers and asking them if they were prepared to make statements of support for the PM.

One adviser told them that his boss was asleep but still put out a statement backing Brown in his name.

As described elsewhere in this book there were times during the Blair reign when Mandelson and Brown were not on a speaking terms, the former never having been forgiven by the latter over the 1994 leadership election. Now, the betrayer had become the saviour. In what turned out to be an inspired move to save his premiership, Brown had brought Mandelson out of the cold, made him a peer, and put him in the Cabinet as business secretary. In the two years that followed, Mandelson became Brown's most important ally. He saw off the 2008 threat and in 2009 helped Brown organize the reshuffle that kept the Government going for another year. In those changes, he became first secretary of state and effectively the Prime Minister's deputy.

In an interview with *The Times* at that time, Mandelson called Blair, Brown and himself the 'two and a half musketeers. I am the half.' He continued: 'We built up New Labour and we're not going to throw it away just because we have hit economic turbulence or we're in a political crisis.' Asked about his original alleged preference of Blair over Brown, he said: 'We were a triangular friendship. At that time the hand of history was placed on Tony's shoulder, not Gordon's. I did not place that hand. It was what people wanted.'

Purnell's resignation was probably Labour's last chance to stop a terrible spiral of decline that led to Brown's defeat in 2010, Ed Miliband's in 2015, and the virtual invitation to the hard left to take over the party after the 2015 election. Had his departure triggered a Cabinet insurrection, Brown would have fallen and virtually any other leader would probably have given Labour those few extra seats it needed to be the party that the Lib Dems opted to work with in a coalition rather than the Tories. But after the summer of 2009 it was too late. The election loomed. New Labour was no more.

The Final Coup

Gordon Brown should have learnt from the traumas of the previous decade-and-a-half that a good relationship between prime minister and chancellor is essential to the smooth running of government. His preoccupation with getting Tony Blair's job held back the Government and could have destroyed the whole New Labour project. So much more could have been achieved if he had not seen everything through the prism of how it would affect his eventual leadership prospects.

So it was pretty astonishing that, having finally secured the leadership of his party and the keys to Number 10, he allowed his relationship with the man he appointed chancellor – his old friend Alistair Darling (the two were regular visitors to each other's homes for years) – to deteriorate to a point where it almost certainly damaged his own prospects of winning in 2010. I have learnt that his behaviour left Darling so upset that when the last internal attempt to remove Brown came in January 2010, he did not move to help him. Neither did Tony Blair, who told Peter Mandelson, then at the Prime Minister's right hand, to stay neutral when Geoff Hoon and Patricia Hewitt launched a last attempt to oust Brown.

Brown survived that threat, as he had before, but it was a closer call than anyone realized at the time. Many ministers believe that Brown had become so reliant personally on Ed Balls during his years at the Treasury that he had always been his first choice as chancellor. But Balls got the job he wanted, schools secretary, when Brown took over from Blair.

Darling believed that Labour's credibility on the economy could only be maintained if it showed it was serious about tackling the deficit. Brown, obsessed with his strategy of marking out dividing lines with the Tories, wanted to offer the country an alternative based on growth and not cuts.

The episode that set back their partnership more than any other came at the end of August 2008, when Darling gave an interview to a *Guardian* feature writer warning that economic conditions 'were arguably the worst they've been in sixty years'. He also raised eyebrows by warning that the voters were 'pissed off' with Labour. It all contrasted with the more positive message Brown was trying to put out about the resilience of the UK economy. Some in Downing Street accused Darling of taking his eye off the ball. In fact his 'sixty years' remark was deliberate and he had said the same thing to *The Times* a couple of weeks earlier.

The interview appeared on a Saturday. I was officially off-duty on the Sunday but the calls started coming in early that morning, so I rang the news desk and told them that I would be handling the Darling row. In a story that caused fury in the Darling camp – not with me, I trust – I wrote that Darling's future was in question after Whitehall insiders said that he could be involved in an imminent reshuffle and that the interview might well have harmed his position. And, very unusually, I was told that Darling's assertions in clarifying interviews over the weekend that Government personnel changes were unlikely were 'wrong'. There was to be a reshuffle the next month, as it turned out. Darling could hardly have said anything different; to suggest otherwise would have put questions over his own position and sent the markets spinning.

The Treasury – my old friend Catherine Macleod, a journalist, was working as a special adviser for Darling at the time, and I spoke to her several times then and in coming days – was convinced that my story had come direct from Brown or someone very close to him. As ever I stayed mum about my sources, although the story had referred to 'Whitehall insiders' and unnamed Cabinet ministers, so they had something to go on, but not much, as they speculated. Catherine's Whitehall intelligence network was formidable, so it would not surprise me if she managed to work it all out.

Darling survived the October reshuffle, but by the following summer, Brown again wanted to shift him out of the Treasury, a move that was ultimately made impossible by the instability caused by the unexpected resignation of James Purnell. Brown had wanted to put Ed Balls into the job.

In the late autumn of 2008, the world and UK economic crises ironically gave Brown a breather from his domestic political problems. The collapse of Lehman Brothers in September 2008 almost brought down the world's financial system. The US Government allowed it to go bankrupt, killing the notion that international banks were too big to fail. The previous year the UK Government had nationalized the ailing Northern Rock bank after failing to find a buyer.

When Lehman went down, it meant that no bank was safe and Western governments were forced to inject vast sums of capital into their financial institutions to prevent them from collapsing. Whitehall was in permanent crisis mode and Darling and Brown agreed billions should be pumped into Royal Bank of Scotland, Lloyds TSB and HBOS in one of the country's biggest ever nationalizations.

The G20 summit of the world's top twenty economic powers was due to meet in London in the spring of 2009 and Brown and his team devoted most of their time to preparing the ground for it. In a sense, it was Brown back in the environment where he was most happy, persuading leaders to go along with financial deals, on the details of which he had made himself an expert. Barack Obama arrived for his first big international occasion at the summit in the London Docklands, and Brown was in his element as he and fellow leaders put together what was hailed as a $1.1trn boost to the world economy.

All leaders – particularly Brown, Obama and Nicolas Sarkozy, the French President – heralded a successful outcome. The boost was completed by a $6 billion sale of IMF gold reserves to help the poorest countries. The measures were announced alongside a far-reaching clean-up of the banking system, including what Brown described as the 'start of the end' of tax havens, an issue that threatened at one stage to hold up an agreement.

The next day, Brown won plaudits for the massive amount of personal effort he had invested in the efforts to reach a deal. But that and his early success after becoming prime minister in 2007 were the high points of his premiership, and from now on, as Mandelson was to describe in his memoirs *The Third Man*, it was all downhill towards the end.

No one knew more about the Blair–Brown relationship than Mandelson because he was very much part of it, and his book, published shortly after the 2010 election and the establishment of the coalition, was full of new material. Because *The Times* was serializing it, we were much involved in the promotion of the book. At a packed *Times+* meeting at the Royal Northern College of Music in Manchester, I interviewed him and took questions from the audience about its contents. I had known him for twenty-five years or more, but I was struck by his professionalism in preparing for the event and by his surprising touch of nerves before going on stage.

The book's contents were explosive. On the second day of our serialization, I wrote a front-page story based on Mandelson's quotes from a string of ministers, including himself, acknowledging at various times that victory was impossible under Brown. I said that, despite a series of failed plots, he had painted a picture of a Cabinet that was unwilling or afraid to strike. Harriet Harman had proposed basing the 2010 election campaign around 'three Fs' at a meeting before Christmas – future, family and fairness. In response, Douglas Alexander, Mandelson himself and Darling had suggested three Fs of their own: Futile, Finished, F★★★★d.

Mandelson revealed that Brown was so desperate at one stage that he had proposed saying before the election that he would only stay for one more year to secure the recovery. But Brown and the Treasury were in constant conflict. He refused efforts to force him to use the word 'cuts', apart from when he employed it once, reluctantly, in a TUC speech. He vetoed a proposal from Darling to put up VAT to help attack the deficit. And then Darling opposed a proposal from Brown to rule out VAT rises during the next parliament. Darling told Mandelson before Christmas: 'We're going to lose.'

In an interview with *The Times*, Mandelson said ministers never acted against Brown because he had been involved in taking momentous decisions on the financial crisis and it would have been wrong for Labour to put electoral calculation before the country and the economy.

Mandelson threw a protective shield around Brown after he was brought back and was a key factor in stabilizing him after Purnell's resignation. As I explained, Purnell knew that David Miliband would not follow him out of the Government, but Mandelson telephoned others because, as he said in his book, a Blairite putsch was not the way to go.

I have learnt, however, that neither he nor Tony Blair was minded to act so quickly when the last move against Brown happened in January 2010, when the Blairites Hoon and Hewitt suddenly urged a secret leadership ballot. It was a desperate move just five months before the general election and it followed a series of anguished Christmas discussions among Cabinet ministers, at which several agreed Brown was leading Labour to certain defeat.

Hoon and Hewitt wrote to Labour MPs saying the party was 'deeply divided' and the issue must be sorted out 'once and for all'. They said the continued 'uncertainty' was 'damaging our ability to set out our strong case to the electorate' and only a secret ballot of all Labour MPs would resolve the issue. They wrote: 'There is a risk otherwise that the persistent background briefing and grumbling could continue up to and possibly through the election campaign.'

While Darling was not involved in the Christmas discussions, he had been aware of what was going on behind the scenes. The chancellor was not in a good mood, angry at some of the briefing between the Pre-Budget Report in December and the Commons recess, and had hardly spoken to Brown. Regarding the PBR, he was convinced that he had to show that Labour was serious about the debt because, as things were, the markets, the press and the country did not believe it was. While he and the Treasury had tried to present the PBR as the first step in a concerted attempt to get to grips with the deficit, some ministers – presumably with Brown's backing – boasted about increases in their budgets, distorting the political and economic message Darling was trying to sell. I understand that he and Brown barely saw each other between the PBR and the Christmas recess. Had he been getting on better with a man who had been his friend for decades, Darling would probably have tipped him off about the trouble brewing.

I can reveal that Michael Dugher, who was then Brown's political press spokesman but had been Hoon's special adviser, had warned the Prime Minister's closest confidants that he should expect trouble from Hoon, who was deeply disillusioned with Brown. The two had not got on well when Hoon served as Brown's chief whip when he became prime minister in 2007. Hoon stood down in the 2009 reshuffle but believed he had a promise from Brown that he would back him to be the EU's first high representative for foreign affairs when that post was decided later in the year.

In the event, Brown was felt neither to have pushed hard for Hoon nor for Mandelson, who would also have liked the job. Brown got a British figure in the post but went along at a Brussels summit in November with the choice of other European leaders of Cathy (Baroness) Ashton. It was an outcome that left neither Hoon nor Mandelson happy.

Brown did nothing to act on the warnings about Hoon. When Hoon and Hewitt made their move, they felt they had reason to believe others would follow. Tony Blair knew of the plot, but Hoon and Hewitt had hoped colleagues would take this very last chance to oust Brown and put in a last-minute substitute – and again Alan Johnson was the favoured choice – to fight the election.

It never got that far. No one else had the stomach for the fight. Hoon later told friends he had 'gone over the top into the hail of gunfire' only to look back over his shoulder and see everyone else was sitting in the trenches. Meanwhile, Mandelson's relations with Brown had deteriorated because – among other things – of the Prime Minister's refusal to face up to the need for a tougher austerity line.

Mandelson found out about the Hoon–Hewitt move on the day in a conversation with Blair, who had picked up on rumours that something was about to happen.

I understand that, given the critical situation the party was in, Blair suggested to Mandelson that unlike in May 2009 he should stay neutral. Mandelson has told me: 'I did stay my hand for a few hours.' Various ministers went in to see Brown. As Mandelson recorded in his book, Alistair Darling was in no mood to hand him a revolver, and neither Harriet Harman nor Jack Straw, who also went in, raised the leadership issue. I have been told that Darling told Brown in their meeting that he felt he should have warned him that trouble was afoot because of the unhappiness within the Cabinet. However, the latest and potentially most serious coup was over.

Had Darling, Straw and Harman joined Hoon and Hewitt, Brown would probably have fallen. But the prevailing view was that the election was just too close and the spectacle of Labour holding a leadership election in the weeks before polling day would have meant a deserved pasting from the electorate. Others believe that even then, Labour would have gained from dropping Brown, who had become toxic with the voters. But it was all over. Labour had again shown its sentimentality – compared to the ruthlessness of the Tories – about its leaders. Only one had ever been forced out against his will – and he, Blair, was the most successful of all.

What all that shows, of course, is that Blair never really could bring himself to try to finish Brown off, until it was way too late. It backs up Mandelson's view that Blair was always far too obsessed with buying Brown off than building up a potential successor who could beat him when the time came. Blair hoped that Charles Clarke, the former home secretary, would stand against Brown in 2007, but only as a way of bringing David Miliband into the fight. As Mandelson explained, Miliband was wary of being seen as the Blairite candidate in a tribal showdown with Brown, and after some consideration over Easter that year ditched the idea and backed Brown.

Mandelson provided a first-hand account of what happened after the 2010 election resulted in a hung parliament and Nick Clegg, leader of the Liberal Democrats, negotiated with Labour and the Conservatives. He told how Clegg ended Brown's lingering hopes of clinging on by telling him to his face that he had to go as the price of a coalition deal, and that Blair had also told him it would be seen as an outrage if he tried to stay on.

After some delay Brown finally accepted that, told Clegg that a new leader would be in place by October, and then announced as much in a dramatic statement in front of Number 10. It was Brown's last stab at keeping Labour in power, admittedly under someone else. But talks between Clegg and Labour fell apart. After saying the deal was 'knack-ered', Clegg rang Brown again to try to keep Labour in the race to get more out of the Tories.

But Brown had had enough and, in any case, Mandelson – pres-entation man to the last – did not want him to leave Number 10 in the dark. 'That was not the image I wanted for his leave-taking,' he said. As Clegg protested, Brown told him: 'The public have run out of patience and so have I. You have to make a decision. I have made mine. It is final. I am going to the Palace. Goodbye.'

One of the most astonishing political careers of modern times had ended – as Enoch Powell said they all do – in failure.

Leveson and the Lobby

I made my appearance at the Leveson Inquiry into the culture, ethics and practices of the British press on 25 June 2012, when I did my bit in arguing against the statutory regulation of newspapers. I found that the main interest of my questioners, however, was in the relationship between press and politicians and the operation of the Lobby system, of which I had been a part for thirty years.

It was a strange experience giving evidence in the Royal Courts of Justice, with two of my oldest friends and colleagues, Elinor Goodman (former political editor of Channel 4 News and someone with whom I had lunched politicians for years) and George Jones, former political editor of *The Daily Telegraph*, watching intently from the back of the court. They were on the panel appointed by Lord Justice Leveson to assist him in the inquiry set up in the wake of the phone-hacking scandal.

Even though I was in it for so long, I was not always an unqualified supporter of the Lobby but I have yet to be convinced there is a more effective means of reporting the doings of Westminster and Whitehall. Under the system, reporters chosen by their editors are accredited by the Commons authorities to work in the Palace of Westminster and have access to certain parts of the premises not open to normal mortals apart from MPs and peers. In practice, in the decades I roamed the corridors of Westminster, that meant I could go to the Members' Lobby – just outside the Commons chamber – after which our institution is named.

If I added up the hours I spent standing in the Lobby – there is only one seat where a reporter is allowed to sit down with an MP – it would come to months, probably years, in total. I loitered there waiting for the right people to come along, or engaging in conversations with ministers and MPs in the hope that something would turn up. We could also stand in the Ways and Means Corridor, which leads into the Lobby, and catch people as they raced through to vote. When the division bell rang we had to hotfoot it out of the Lobby to avoid being trampled by MPs hurrying to join the queue to have their names ticked off.

Being in the Lobby also gave us access to the twice-daily Number 10 briefings by the prime minister's spokesman. Since the early years of New Labour, those briefings have been taken by civil servants based in Number 10 rather than by political appointees of the government of the day. The morning briefing used to be at Number 10 but is now in the Treasury, and the afternoon one is still in the Lobby room, a place specially designated for us decades ago at the top of a long staircase near the roof of the building.

It was there that the likes of Bernard Ingham, Alastair Campbell, Christopher Meyer and Gus O'Donnell – the latter two under John Major – would arrive at 4 p.m. and tell us what the PM had been up to during the day, and then face generally pretty tough questioning on the stories of the moment. But in those days their responses were not attributable to Downing Street.

As previously mentioned, the rules of the Members' Lobby were always that conversations you had there with the politicians were, unless they stipulated otherwise, on Lobby terms. That meant you could use the information they had given you but not directly attribute it to them. The same rules applied when you met the politicians in other places, such as lunches, receptions, in the street, or wherever.

It is here that I should explode one myth. Critics of the Lobby have always suggested there is something unusual about that way of doing things. That is, in the favourite word of Bernard Ingham, bunkum. Every branch of journalism – education, crime, business, sport, whatever – has a similar way of operating. Reporters in all specialisms have people they talk to on an off-the-record basis who give them information, which can lead to stories without their fingerprints on them.

But there were quaint additional rules applying to us that those in other areas of journalism would not have had to worry about. I mentioned the seating rule, but there was also a weird one that we were not supposed to take notes while talking to politicians, presumably to prove to them that Lobby terms were fully operational. There was also a good rule that you did not interrupt another journalist talking to another politician unless invited to do so. There is nothing worse than to be following an exclusive line with an MP and to find a colleague barging in and possibly overhearing what you had been talking about.

I loved the Members' Lobby. I would often go there from the Press Gallery at around 11.30 a.m. and stay for several hours until I really felt I must go back to the office and start writing. MPs who regularly passed through would smile and ask whether I had not got anything better to do, but there was no better place to meet people from all parties. Sometimes they would line up to speak to you if there was good story running.

Today, for many reporters Portcullis House – the new parliamentary building opened in 2001, with its coffee bar, restaurant and cafeteria – has taken over from the Members' Lobby as the place where they are most likely to run into MPs, as well as their advisers, although for the old-timers it will never be quite the same as the Lobby. That seat I mentioned was apparently where one of my predecessors as political editor, the great David Wood, would sit and be joined by Cabinet ministers, including Prime Minister Harold Macmillan, as they passed through. Legend had it that he picked up the first signals of Macmillan's impending 'Night of the Long Knives', when he sacked a batch of dissident Cabinet ministers, while perched there.

You never quite knew what might come along if you had the patience to wait. Jack Warden, political editor of the *Daily Express*, and I were standing together in the Lobby on the night of 9 July 1982. Apart from us it was deserted. At about eight in the evening we were approached by a very excited Alan Clark, of diaries fame. He had just come from the back-bench Tory home affairs committee, after which the home secretary, then William Whitelaw, always briefed the officers. 'Willie', as Clark called him, had just told them that early that morning a man – whom we were later to discover was called Michael Fagan – had broken into Buckingham Palace and spent ten minutes talking to the Queen in her bedroom.

Fagan had scaled the walls round the palace and somehow got up a drainpipe to the Queen's private apartments. The Queen, showing amazing sangfroid – a word used by Clark to us – quietly pushed an alarm button when Fagan had asked for a cigarette. There were many more details but Jack and I needed to get to our offices. We ran back along the committee corridor and told our near-disbelieving offices about the story. Sadly I did not make the first edition, which had gone by the time I got back, but Jack was able to catch his. It was yet another reminder to me of how important it was for reporters those days to be in that Lobby. You never quite knew what you were going to hear next. But so many of the big stories of our times started there.

In my evidence to Leveson, however, I said that I had observed the virtual disintegration of the old-style Lobby system that had been in operation when I first went to Westminster in 1973. In those days, the briefings from Number 10 were completely non-attributable, and there were all manner of mysterious briefings. Long before I became a Lobby reporter I used to take a sly look at the Lobby noticeboard. On Thursdays, the leader of the Commons would give a briefing after the Number 10 gathering at 4.15 p.m., and the leader of the Opposition at 5.15 p.m., in their office behind the speaker's chair. But they were supposed to be secret. So during a Tory government, the message would go up on the board 'Blue Mantle, 4.15' and 'Red Mantle, 5.15'.

The Lobby itself was happy to maintain this mystique. It suited journalists who had a ready-made source of news and a set of confidentiality rules that allowed them to hide the fact that stories could occasionally drop into their laps. But it also played into the hands of the government of the day, making it far easier for it to control the flow of news. It was at one these afternoon briefings where Bernard Ingham famously referred to John Biffen, a veteran Cabinet minister who was in dispute with Margaret Thatcher at the time, as 'semi-detached'. For a Number 10 spokesman to be using a Lobby meeting to attack a member of the Government was a very good story but the Lobby had to go through all sorts of contortions to avoid saying who did it.

My qualified support for the Lobby was because I did not enjoy the institutionalized secrecy surrounding it. As I told Leveson, I shed no tears at all when the system became more and more transparent from the end of the 1980s – thanks in big part to the likes of Tony Bevins (who took *The Independent* out of the system for a time with *The*

Guardian following) and Alastair Campbell (who as a former journalist vowed to change the system when Labour returned to power in 1997). The arrival of the 24-hour news cycle and digital round-the-clock journalism, as well as the increasing use of social media outlets like Twitter – which I would say has become my fastest source of news in recent years – has helped to break down the old barriers.

Boycotting those Lobby meetings was a brave, even foolhardy, move because it denied *The Independent* and *The Guardian* an important source of information: the Downing Street view. Those of us who attended soon found ourselves being asked by those who had chosen not to what had gone on. We filled them in because it was in our interests that they succeeded. They soon returned.

So in 2002 the old-style morning briefing was replaced by a press conference at which the prime minister's press spokesman gave the daily line on issues. There was no longer any doubt where the story was coming from. The Masonic-style barriers were gone. (Talking of freemasonry, there were persistent rumours that one of the Commons lodges used to meet in the Lobby room when the Commons was not sitting.)

That does not mean that politicians have suddenly stopped talking non-attributably to journalists. This book is full of stories that could not have come to me in any other way, and it is the same for journalists in every other sphere. As I said under questioning at Leveson: 'You will get more out of a politician off the record than you will on, and that is always going to be the case.' I recorded that I had often said to young reporters who came back to the office and reported a conversation with an MP: 'Yes, but what did he tell you off the record?' That would invariably be more interesting.

I did have qualms sometimes about allowing an MP to attack another in their own party under the cloak of anonymity. For example, an MP might say: 'Jack Smith is useless – we all know that.' I used to treat each case on its merits, but most of the time I would use the information with the rationale that if an MP was prepared to say that about a member of their own party and see it in print, that in itself said something about the state of relations and added value to the story.

The other brickbat thrown at the Lobby by those who have never worked there is that somehow it is a club where we all stuck together and wrote the same story. I have acknowledged all through this book that there were times when we would indeed consult together and decide upon the best line on a story. If the story was around generally, there was no problem with that.

And there were times when the Lobby, working collectively, was an active life force. It was always amusing to see the bewilderment and annoyance of foreign correspondents on some papers – but not, I hasten to say, *The Times*, where there was greater maturity about these matters – when the Lobby landed with the prime minister of the day on their patch, and proceeded to run amok. They didn't really understand that for our few hours on their territory, we were seeing whatever the story was in their neck of the woods through the domestic prism. They hated it when these ignorant so-and-sos from London breezed in, grabbed the story, and got the front-page articles they had been struggling to get in the paper for months.

That was the Lobby collective. But there is no more competitive branch of journalism than politics. The fact that we all worked in the same place in offices next door to each other obviously meant that you became close friends with people on rival papers. But your aim was to beat them, and your editor demanded that you beat them. Yes, there was cooperation on running stories but the aim was always to get the one that no one else had got. We lived for exclusives and those who did not get them died for the lack of them. That was how you were judged back in the office.

You always knew when someone had got a cracker of a story. They disappeared, usually from the Commons back to head office. The routine was that the person on late duty would always do a trawl of the Press Gallery offices in early evening to try to get some idea of what the rivals were up to. It was to make sure that we did not miss something that everybody else had got. But if they had an exclusive, they would tell us – as we would tell them – that it would be worth not going to bed too early. And you always knew who had done the exclusive because he or she would not be there. There was sometimes a herd instinct, a temptation to divine what line the rivals were taking on a story in order to avoid awkward late calls from the news desk as the first editions dropped.

I told Leveson that after my forty or so years, I felt the relationship between press and politicians was one of mutual dependence, mistrust and occasional bitterness. I welcomed the disappearance of the deference shown by some journalists to politicians that I had seen in my early days but added that the relationship between press and politicians had grown steadily more confrontational over the years, with politicians complaining that we were far more interested in any shortcomings they had than the good things they had done. They cited the end of straight gallery reporting, which I have described elsewhere, for lowering the esteem in which they and Parliament were held.

There was undoubtedly a sense among the political class generally that we were out to get them, a view that was strengthened by *The Telegraph*'s brilliant exposure of the expenses scandal. And yet we had to work together – the politicians needed us to spread the word about what they were doing, and we needed them to tell our readers about the issues of the day. I have given a feeling elsewhere in the book about a day in the life of a political editor, but for all political reporters it was a matter of getting to know politicians well enough to get their home phone numbers and feel comfortable about ringing them at weekends or in the evening. So apart from contact in the lobbies, there would be lunches, dinners, drinks parties, interviews.

Inevitably, you would come to know them – and they you – on first-name terms. But that was not cosiness, more politeness. As I told the inquiry, most politicians understand that the journalists with whom they had once lunched convivially might well be predicting or writing about their demise sometime soon.

Politicians carefully chose whom they would lunch with, and journalists were the same. We liked the indiscreet for obvious reasons but the best were the informed. In the lunch partnerships with which I was involved over the decades, we set a high bar. If they came to lunch without a story, or told us nothing of use during the meal, they would not be getting another invitation.

Lunches were fun and it was amazing how the ambitious politician trusted us. They would do down their own colleagues when it came to talking about reshuffles. They would give us a list of the jobs they would like when the moment came. And they relied on us never to let on. We helped to make careers, of that there is no doubt. It was a common practice for the whips to let out the names of MPs they thought were doing well. We would write them up as tips for the top in reshuffle stories and, as if by magic, they would appear in the Government list on reshuffle day.

The Leveson Inquiry was interested in my observation that civil servants also had a big impact on who was promoted and demoted. The mandarins, who were far more indiscreet than people realized, would let slip the names of ministers they thought were performing well or badly. Soon the word was out that X was really not up to it. Sometimes the PM of the day would take note; on others they would ignore.

Another myth to dismantle is the idea that because you were friendly with politicians, that would somehow help them when they were in trouble. I can think of no instance involving myself or anyone else where that was the case. I have friends in all of what were the main three parties before the Lib Dems collapsed, nearly all of them developed through sporting links – playing in the Parliamentary Golf Society, skippering the press football and cricket teams for some thirty years in matches against the parties, and through playing squash at courts close to Parliament. But the idea that any MP, through getting to know journalists, would somehow be protected at a time of trouble is ludicrous beyond words because of the very nature of Westminster.

As I told the Leveson Inquiry, there are a handful whom I have got to know so well that I would consider them friends first, and politicians second. But it is precisely because they are friends, and understand the world as it operates, that they knew that if misfortune befell them – as it did in some cases – I would have had to treat them as if they were somebody I did not even know. At Westminster, friendships are known about and it would very quickly become a matter of some comment if a reporter or paper eased up on someone because they were a friend.

So I would conclude today that the Lobby, more transparent than the one I started in but still with its curiosities and mysteries, is a force for good in our democracy. It must be in the public interest that senior politicians and the media talk to each other, formally and informally. It can only help public understanding of what the Government and its opponents are doing.

The Lobby keeps ministers and their shadows on their toes. If a minister fails, the Lobby is merciless. There have been plenty of scalps over the years. If a policy is flawed the media will be out there killing it. If there was a better way of covering politics, someone would have introduced it by now.

The Mystery of
Michael Portillo

The Conservatives had five leaders while Tony Blair ran Labour –
John Major, William Hague, Iain Duncan Smith, Michael Howard and
David Cameron. No wonder they clapped Blair out of the Commons
when he finally departed.

There were Conservative leadership elections in 1997, 2001 and
2005, and an uncontested handover in 2003. In the years of Labour
dominance, the most exciting part of covering the Conservatives was
their elections. Conservative contests are invariably more vicious than
Labour ones; and Conservative MPs will always be more ruthless than
their Labour rivals, as their treatment of Margaret Thatcher showed.

The biggest mystery of all those battles was not that Kenneth
Clarke, who tried three times, did not win. His stance on Europe was
always likely to be a block. It was that Michael Portillo didn't. Portillo,
the former Thatcherite who became a modernizer, seemed to be
ideally placed several times in his career, only for fate or his own
refusal to compromise to intervene.

It is the strong view of the people who worked for him when he
was the hot favourite to win in 2001 that by the end of the contest he
did not really want to win it. But of that, more later. There was no
doubting Portillo's desire for the top job in the years following
Thatcher's overthrow. When John Major launched his 'back me or
sack me' challenge in 1995 and John Redwood took up the cudgels,
Portillo's allies set up a campaign HQ, along with banks of telephone
lines, in case the contest went to a second ballot.

It was a tactical blunder and his equivocal backing for Major
became obvious. It was something he regretted later, and it was used

against him by his enemies. His 'Who dares wins' speech at the party conference restored his reputation with activists but left the centre wondering. But the Tory Right wanted him to stand then. David Martin, former MP for Portsmouth South, has told me that he urged him to do so and believes that his failure of nerve on that occasion cost him the leadership and the premiership.

Even so, he would almost certainly have been the frontrunner in the 1997 Tory contest when John Major stood down after the Labour landslide. Unfortunately for Portillo, however, the tsunami that swept away scores of Tory MPs caught him as well at Enfield Southgate, providing the famous 'Portillo moment' which seemed to watchers to encapsulate the demise of the Conservatives after eighteen years in power.

After the election Portillo accepted broadcasting work before taking the biggest gamble of his career. In an interview with Ginny Dougary published in *The Times* on 9 September 1999, he admitted to having homosexual experiences as a young man in a move to tackle persistent rumours about his sexuality.

I reported that on the front page of *The Times* but I combined with it the exclusive line that he had decided to put himself forward as the Conservative candidate in the forthcoming Kensington and Chelsea by-election. He said nothing in public because the holder of the seat, Alan Clark had just died and it would have seemed inappropriate. But I had no doubt that he would stand, and wrote that I had been told authoritatively that he would. That meant he had told me, in case the reader wonders about these things.

Dougary had been working on her piece for some time and had sensed that Portillo might be ready to open up. The interview actually happened several weeks earlier, at the end of July – long before he knew that he would soon have to make a decision about Kensington. When she asked him if he had homosexual flings at Cambridge in the early 1970s, he replied, after some hesitation: 'I will say what I want to say. I had some homosexual experiences as a young person.'

By now Portillo was on a political journey, having rethought his approach after his shock defeat. In a speech at a fringe meeting at the 1997 conference, he called for a new era of sexual tolerance and urged the Tories to 'deal with the world as it is now'. His chance to put the reinvented Portillo to the Tory party came after the 2001 election and, having served the previous two years as Hague's shadow chancellor, he looked to be in pole position. Hague had succumbed to another Blair landslide and decided to go immediately after the election, despite the efforts of friends like Andrew MacKay, Lord Strathclyde and, ironically, Iain Duncan Smith, to persuade him to stay on.

On the night of that election, the three of them, and Ann Widdecombe, waited at Smith Square for Hague to return from his constituency to try to convince him to carry on. But a call to Seb Coe, Hague's chief of staff, told them that it would be a waste of time to try. MacKay and IDS hung on for him nonetheless but a relaxed Hague finally arrived and told them that he wanted to go straightaway, leaving MacKay thinking that Portillo was the obvious candidate. Even though IDS had hinted to him that night that he might be interested in running too, MacKay got hold of Portillo – at Casablanca airport as it happens – and told him he wanted to work for him in the campaign.

At that stage Portillo looked the odds–on favourite but it was almost certain that Clarke would run again, and Duncan Smith, who was being pushed by some to go for it, quickly announced that he would as well. The rules for the election had changed, with the final say going to party members. But MPs chose the two candidates – just two – who would go through to the ballot. If either Portillo or Clarke had done a deal with the other, it would almost certainly have ensured that one of them won.

As it was, the Portillo campaign got off to an altogether dangerous start, with suggestions that he had got the support of two-thirds of the shadow Cabinet and at least seventy-five MPs. For several days, the story ran that Portillo was heading for victory. Mackay, who had been deputy chief whip in government and shadow Northern Ireland secretary during the previous parliament, was by this time on the campaign and realized the figures were wildly optimistic. He therefore called me at *The Times* with the express intention of playing down suggestions that Portillo was the runaway leader. Whoever was responsible for inflating the original expectations was not clear, but the fears of his camp was that if the ultimate tally turned out to be less than that being touted, he would lose momentum in later rounds. Mackay insisted there were a lot fewer than fifty MPs 'in the bag', an estimate that would turn out to be accurate.

Stephen Dorrell, a former health secretary, used an interview with me in *The Times* to announce that, having backed Clarke last time, he would go for Portillo in this election in the interests of rebuilding the party. Portillo supporters talked up Clarke as their main fear, but in truth they were worried about the right-wing candidate, Duncan Smith. After the first ballot Portillo led with fifty votes, Duncan Smith was second with forty-two and Clarke had thirty-nine. David Davis and Michael Ancram, fourth and fifth, withdrew.

Several Davis supporters switched to Clarke rather than Portillo and the general assumption was that the race between the remaining three candidates vying for the two winning places could not be tighter. And then strange things began to happen as Portillo's team – Francis Maude was in charge – strove for the last few votes to get him over the line at least into second place. They fancied he would beat Clarke in the run-off because of Europe.

But he did nothing to help himself. MacKay, speaking to me recently about this, takes up the story:

As we reached the most critical stage of this struggle it rapidly became clear that he did not want it. To use a phrase that was not around at that time, he lost his mojo. He behaved in a strange way. He was semi-detached, disinterested, just not up for the fight. Normally you would have to calm down an election candidate; Michael just was not motivated anymore.

Cheryl Gillan was the team's 'gatekeeper', organizing meetings between wavering MPs and Portillo in the hope of bringing them on side. But it appeared that he was going out of his way to alienate them, rather than attract them. A classic case, says MacKay, involved Graham Brady, who is now the chairman of the 1922 Committee of Tory back-benchers. Then, as now, Brady was a strong believer in grammar schools and hoped to persuade Portillo particularly about the merits of a constituency case. 'The opposite happened,' MacKay says. 'Instead of sympathy, Graham got the next potential leader telling him he did not believe in them. That kind of thing was happening a lot. He would not meet people halfway. Francis Maude was furious. "What the hell is he playing at?", he would storm.'

MacKay says that as things turned out Brady still voted for Portillo, believing he was the only candidate who would change the party, but his treatment at the candidate's hands did not endear Portillo to him. Tim Yeo, another key member of the Portillo team, also told me recently of his doubts about Portillo's desire:

From the moment Hague stood down, Portillo acted strangely. The first thing he did was to go to ground abroad for a couple of days where he remained virtually incommunicado apart from a tiny handful of people.

When he got back to the country he remained hidden from view by going to stay with his eccentric friend David Hart, whose weekend home was in my constituency and whom I knew quite well. It wasn't until about Tuesday or Wednesday that he emerged into public view, an odd way to act if your goal was to win the support of enough colleagues to become leader.

Yeo says it was clear to him and Maude that Portillo would not bend his views in the way that David Cameron was later to do in 2005:

The Eurosceptics were out for red meat on both occasions and to entice people like Bernard Jenkin, Cameron pledged withdrawal of Conservative MEPs from the more pro-European European People's Party, something which Portillo refused to do in 2001.

Yeo thinks *The Telegraph*'s support for Duncan Smith was crucial to his victory over Clarke in the final run-off. Of Portillo, he says:

I believe he would have given Blair a much tougher run for his money in 2005 than poor old Michael Howard, who inherited a difficult legacy from IDS and was a competent but excessively cautious and conventional right-winger. If Portillo had become leader in 2001 he might even have forced Blair to delay the election till 2006. Even if Labour had won, the majority would have been much smaller and Portillo would have survived as leader.

But Yeo says the key factor in Portillo's failure was the man himself. He recalls: 'Several of us were so frustrated that we joked about it and wondered whether he even voted for himself.'

Despite his indifference on the eve of the final ballot, Portillo's camp reckoned they had got second place by a whisker until they saw one of their own supporters emerging slyly from the IDS HQ. That MP, who became a marked man, may well have turned the political future of Britain because when the votes were announced, Clarke was leading comfortably, IDS had fifty-four votes and Portillo was down and out with fifty-three. That one MP had done in Portillo.

It was a triumph for Clarke but Portillo's hopes of ever leading his party were in tatters. Despite Clarke's success there was, in retrospect, no doubt how things would turn out. The party membership had the final say and Clarke had never tempered his euro-enthusiasm. Clarke was popular with the general public but the predominantly elderly membership was deeply suspicious of Europe and still hankered after Margaret. IDS got 156,000 votes to Clarke's 101,000.

The notoriously right-wing Tory membership would have had an interesting choice if Portillo rather than IDS had got through – an avowed Europhile in Clarke, and a candidate who had admitted to having homosexual experiences. I'm as sure as I can be they would have gone for Portillo. This is mainly because the Tory party was still not over the Europe wars that had afflicted Thatcher and Major. Today, Cameron knows how they felt. And although Clarke was one of the biggest politicians of his generation, he was rebuffed yet again, even though he prepared for victory, asking key figures if they would serve under him. Yeo, a Portillo supporter, was invited to be shadow foreign secretary. It was not to be.

William Hague had beaten him as well. Hague entered Parliament in the Richmond, Yorkshire, by-election in 1989 that followed Leon Brittan's appointment as a European commissioner. My lunch partner Elinor Goodman, political editor of Channel 4, and I took some pride in our ability to spot winners on the back-benches. We had cultivated John Major as a back-bencher, which was a good spot, and we decided Hague was heading for the top too. We regularly invited him to lunches at Westminster and dinners at party conference, and watched with pleasure as he rose swiftly into the Cabinet.

But when he opted to run in 1997, after strong pressure from close friends, I wondered whether he had gone for the big job a parliament too soon. I believe he originally intended to back Michael Howard, the former home secretary, but was talked out of it. It was again a strange election. In the first ballot Clarke led, Hague was second and John Redwood third, with Peter Lilley and Michael Howard fourth and fifth. The Right vote, which together was dominant, had been split. Howard and Lilley withdrew and announced they were giving their support to Hague. At the second ballot Clarke was still ahead, but only by two votes, Hague second and Redwood third.

We then had one of the greatest miscalculations in modern-day politics as Redwood, a hard-right Eurosceptic, switched his support to Clarke, an out-and-out Europhile. It looked cynical as Redwood had been promised the job of shadow chancellor if Clarke won. So distraught was Margaret Thatcher at the prospect of Clarke winning that she rode back into battle and supported Hague. He won by ninety votes to seventy-two; the novice – albeit a hugely able one – had beaten the professional street-fighter whom many believed would have given Blair a run for his money. Europe, then and now, does strange things to the otherwise sound judgment of Tory MPs and members.

Hague was only thirty-six and the task in front of him was gargantuan. The Tories looked irrelevant for years and Hague managed to get the headlines with politically trivial stories only, like when he went to a theme park with his chief of staff, Seb Coe, sporting a baseball cap emblazoned 'Hague', or when he claimed to have drunk fourteen pints a night as a student. There were tensions when he appointed Portillo as shadow chancellor. Portillo had swiftly embraced Labour's policies of the national minimum wage and independence for the Bank of England.

Hague's biggest political storm came when he delivered his famous 'foreign land' speech to the Conservative spring conference in Harrogate in March 2001, attacked by Labour and the left of his own party for its nationalistic flavour. He had said: 'Just imagine four more years of Labour. Try to picture what our country would look like. Let me take you on a journey to a foreign land – to Britain after a second term of Tony Blair.'

The 2001 election campaign was always going to be another struggle for the Tories, and they duly lost. The bad blood between the Hague and Portillo camps erupted afterwards when Amanda Platell, Hague's press chief, accused the dreaded 'friends of Portillo' of briefing against Hague and his campaign tactics.

So into this vipers' nest known as the Conservative parliamentary party came Iain Duncan Smith, the next in line to take on Blair as he entered the most critical period of his premiership after the 9/11 attacks. And it was an unhappy two years. Duncan Smith started with many disadvantages. The mainstream parliamentary party remembered him as one of the leading rebels of the Maastricht saga and were in no mood to show him the loyalty he denied John Major then. The friends of Ken Clarke and Michael Portillo, who both led at different stages of the recent leadership contest, declined to show him respect and the word was out from the start that he had only won because the vote had gone to the membership, not to the people who were better judged to decide – the MPs.

But his backing for military action against Iraq as early as November 2001 was important to Blair when the Commons made its decision in February 2003. Duncan Smith was not making a mark with the general public, though, and he led a sullen party. He told the 2002 party conference not to underestimate 'the determination of a quiet man' but in truth they, and the public, did. My sources in the leader's camp were good. Nick Wood, my deputy when I became political editor, headed up the press operation and I could sense the deep frustration within that office that the leader was not getting the support he deserved.

On 6 November 2002, I wrote a story that, looking back now, looks bold. I wrote that Clarke and Portillo were being accused of being at the head of a plot to undermine Duncan Smith. I said that friends of the leader had identified the two heavyweights, and some of their supporters, as the 'enemy within' engaged on a conscious effort to oust him. I further wrote that the pair were seen as using the crisis of confidence in Duncan Smith's leadership to pursue their own ambitions, Clarke to be leader and Portillo – who now knew he could not be leader – his deputy.

Duncan Smith had ordered his MPs to vote against a Commons move to allow unmarried couples to adopt children. Portillo and Clarke were among the Tories who had voted with Labour in support of the plan. A furious leader the next day called on the party to 'unite or die' and then, in an extraordinary speech, accused a small group of his parliamentary colleagues of deciding 'consciously to undermine my leadership'. He suggested that for a few – and everyone knew whom he was referring to – the vote had not been about adoption but 'an attempt to challenge my mandate to lead this party'.

It was a stunning attack and, if nothing else, bought the embattled Duncan Smith some time over Christmas. But the new year brought more misery for him and soon it was being said that MPs were trying to get enough signatures together to force a vote of confidence in his leadership. This went on all summer, with Sir Michael Spicer, the 1922 Committee chairman, forever facing questions as to whether he had received the requisite twenty-five names needed to trigger a vote.

The party conference was clearly going to be crucial and Duncan Smith's agony increased as he had to fight new allegations of making improper payments to his wife. On the eve of his conference speech, I wrote that the leader would tell his critics that he would not go quietly and that blood would be split if they tried to take his job. As I've said, Tory civil wars were so much more savage than Labour ones.

The quiet man was here to stay and he was 'turning up the volume', said Duncan Smith hopefully to rapturous applause from the faithful. Again he bought himself a little time, but not much, and by the time we got back from Blackpool the doubts were being reinforced yet again. The following week he was lashing out at the 'cowards in the shadows' as he accused anonymous opponents of trying to take him on through his wife. Referring to a newspaper article in which he warned that a new leadership contest would push the Tories into third place at the next election, I wrote that Duncan Smith had chosen the anniversary of the Battle of Balaclava to make his last charge.

As the speculation heightened over whether the twenty-five names had yet been collected, he made his final, desperate gamble, telling his critics they had a 48-hour deadline to challenge him or to stop the plotting. They took him at his word, the names were indeed in Sir Michael Spicer's hands, and a confidence vote was set for the night of 29 October. That morning in *The Times*, he appealed to be allowed longer in his job, saying that he was 'halfway to Downing Street – now is not the time to turn back'.

It was not to be. They voted him out by the surprisingly small margin of ninety to seventy-five. Many decent MPs convinced that Duncan Smith would easily lose voted for him to ensure he was not humiliated, with Duncan Smith's bravery while under fire in recent weeks seen as having encouraged some of his doubtful supporters to carry on backing him.

At that moment, the Tory party's yearning for unity after six torrid years at last asserted itself. Michael Howard had emerged as the favourite to take over from Duncan Smith and one by one the other likely candidates, including David Davis, melted away. The former home secretary – crucially a strong admirer of David Cameron and George Osborne, whose careers he was to advance – became leader on 6 November, and the next stage in the party's slow rehabilitation was under way.

Clarke and Portillo were their party's lost leaders. But it mattered far less to Portillo than it did to Clarke. Andrew MacKay, who remains a close friend of Portillo, reflects:

> His behaviour was frustrating at the time. But I fear he was a man in turmoil, deeply uncertain about his future in politics. Now I am pleased to say he is happy and fulfilled in his new ventures. We were trying our hardest to get him a job he did not want, and never regrets not getting.

How Michael Howard
Handed It to David Cameron

David Davis, and not David Cameron, would have become leader of the Conservative Party but for Michael Howard.

When Howard announced he was resigning as Tory leader after losing to Tony Blair in 2005, he said he was staying on till the autumn to give the party plenty of time to choose his successor. Had the election been held quickly, Davis, overwhelming favourite at the time, would have won. But time was what Cameron needed, and Howard gave it to him, as I will explain later. But back to earlier days.

Cameron was a regular figure on the political scene at Westminster long before any of us thought of him becoming an MP, let alone party leader. He worked for the Conservative research department for five years after graduating from Oxford, during which time he worked in Number 10 briefing John Major in advance of Prime Minister's Questions and, later, before his press conferences in the 1992 election.

It was after he was appointed a special adviser to the chancellor, Norman Lamont, and later the home secretary, Howard, that he became a frequent visitor to the Press Gallery, and a name and number in all our contact books. He would breeze into The Times Room – we had moved by now from our office near Hansard to what looked like a Portakabin along from the Press Gallery bar – and offer us the latest press release from his boss, or background briefings on what they were doing. Cameron always came in with a smile on his face, and really did look as if he was enjoying himself. He was jaunty without being cocky.

Cameron appeared in several pictures with a beleaguered chancellor on Black Wednesday, the day Major and Lamont decided to quit the exchange rate mechanism, but he survived Lamont's sacking and was soon appointed by Howard. His visits to the gallery, along with another adviser called Patrick Rock, became even more frequent until he went off in 1994 to become corporate affairs director at Carlton.

If you had asked anyone in the Lobby in those days if they regarded Cameron as a likely future candidate for the top, I doubt whether any would have thought it at all credible. He somehow lacked the earnestness and deep interest in policy that went with politicians destined for the Cabinet, a criticism ironically directed at him by his opponents as he effortlessly rose after entering Parliament in 2001. Cameron prospered under Howard's leadership, helping him prepare for the Hutton Inquiry into the death of Dr David Kelly, overseeing a policy review and writing the 2005 manifesto.

His ability to be and look relaxed was an undoubted asset. In the updated version of their biography of Cameron in 2012, *Cameron: Practically a Conservative*, Francis Elliott and James Hanning quoted an ally as saying: 'If there was an Olympic gold medal for "chillaxing" he would win it.' I co-wrote a newspiece on the book, saying the secrets of how Cameron switched off from the pressures of work had been revealed: karaoke, snooker, tennis against a machine nicknamed 'The Clegger' (after Nick Clegg) and three or four glasses of wine at Sunday lunch.

The Lobby rekindled its interest in Cameron in 2005, when we suddenly picked up that David Davis was not going to have the clear run through to an expected victory that had been anticipated.

Looking back, it is obvious that Howard, the outgoing leader, killed the chances of Davis. But it was interesting that Howard's first choice was George Osborne, whom he made shadow chancellor in a swift reshuffle after announcing on losing the general election that he was standing down, but not until after an elongated election process ending in November.

As the Elliott–Hanning book says, Howard had initially thought of giving the shadow chancellor job to Cameron, but Cameron had fought to ward off the job, preferring instead education. The authors speculate he was anxious to avoid a confrontation with Gordon Brown, who had seen off six shadow chancellors in eight years.

Howard – quietly spoken, tough, ambitious, one of the Eurosceptic Cabinet ministers whom John Major was thought to have in mind when he lashed out at 'the bastards' – had taken over from Iain Duncan Smith without a contest. Elliott and Hanning say of him:

> By the end of the campaign he was having serious doubts about whether Cameron was the right candidate to stop Davis. He told senior aides that he believed Osborne would be a better successor than Cameron. He had been angered by his former special adviser's criticism of the campaign's focus on immigration and further irritated to be told … that he didn't want the shadow chancellorship.

Howard urged Osborne to run. Osborne considered it and discussed it with friends, and a fortnight later announced that he would not. Michael Gove is quoted in the book as saying: 'I think there was always an understanding that if one of them stood the other one wouldn't. And I think that George thought about it and then quickly realised that, for a variety of reasons, Dave would be better.'

It may be that Howard regarded Osborne as the stronger of the two in having a firm vision of where he wanted to take the party. But when Osborne rejected Howard's suggestion, it is clear he switched to his former adviser, Cameron. Cameron was now to become the modernizing candidate, even though the debate over whether he really was a modernizer had still to be settled after five years as Opposition leader and five years in coalition government.

By spinning out the election till the late autumn, Howard ensured that Cameron – after Osborne said no – had time to develop his campaign and prove himself to the ultimate electorate – the party membership. Again, the top two candidates among the MPs were to go through to the membership run-off.

Howard made Cameron shadow education secretary for the few months before the party election, giving him a higher profile. The Davis camp has always believed that Howard wanted to stop him by this tactic. Tim Montgomerie, in a piece for *ConservativeHome* after the contest, said that a few days before the 5 May general election, Howard picked up that supporters of Davis were collecting signatures to trigger a confidence vote that he would face if he had not resigned by the weekend after poll day.

So Howard's announcement came very quickly, but with a process that fatally damaged Davis's hopes. At the time he was the preferred candidate of the grassroots, was believed to have some sixty MPs in the bag and would almost certainly have won an immediate election. Although the Davis camp believed it had been outfoxed by the old fox, as the party conference approached he remained the strong favourite. All was to change suddenly. I remember a pleasant evening when News International invited the candidates to a dinner at the conference with the group's editors and political editors. It was jolly having them round the same table, but no one made a stunning impression. Andy Coulson, then editor of the *News of the World* and later to become Cameron's communications director, was there, as was Rebekah Brooks.

But on the same day Ken Clarke, the veteran candidate running for the third time, roused the Tory faithful with a vintage attack on Labour. Then Cameron took the place by storm when – speaking without notes and wandering around the platform – he gave an inspirational speech about attracting a new generation of Tories. At that moment the Tory party, which knew little about him, fell in love with David Cameron. He was new, he was fresh, he was smiling, and he was young. My splash in *The Times* next morning said that the race for the leadership had been thrown wide open and that Davis was now under pressure to produce the speech of his life if he was to stay out in front.

It failed to materialize. I remember thinking that if the vote had been down to the people at conference, Cameron would already have walked it. And when Davis delivered a competent but less-than-inspiring address, and Liam Fox, another candidate, got a much better reception, the skids were under the long-time favourite. I can vividly recall the sheer brutality of the assessment by Tom Bradby, ITN's political editor, that Davis 'had bombed, and bombed badly'. If one speech ever made a leader, and another unmade one, it was those two performances at Blackpool. Cameron was to go on to win the MPs' ballot and the membership vote by miles.

Cameron had been nervous about facing Blair – who had seen off four Tory leaders – and Osborne about facing Brown – who had seen off even more shadow chancellors – but they held their own in that first year before Blair finally succumbed to Brown's pressure to go. Apart from the first few months of his premiership, Brown presented an easy target for Cameron as one mishap followed another and one putative plot after another failed to be followed through.

Even so, the Tory leader had his friend Osborne to thank for bursting Brown's early bubble when the polls looked so good for Labour that there was very serious consideration of a snap election. Osborne's promise to cut inheritance tax provoked strong public and press approval and the wind went out of Brown's sails.

Cameron maintained his easy-going approach to high politics that we had become accustomed to. George Pascoe-Watson, of *The Sun*, and I were invited to go on one of the first overseas trips – to the Middle East – with Cameron and his team in early 2007. It was a very friendly jaunt which allowed us to get to know better some of his staff.

Cameron went sightseeing in Jerusalem in brown cords and fashionably untucked blue shirt, looking every bit the tourist, but as soon as the local press turned up, he swiftly reverted to politician mode, using an informal press conference to criticize Blair's close relationship with President Bush. His own ties with Washington would be 'solid not slavish'.

George and I travelled in Cameron's car to Tel Aviv, where he raised the question of Israeli settlements on the West Bank with the Israeli foreign minister in what was clearly a heated exchange. In the car, my phone rang and, in front of Cameron and his chief of staff, Ed Llewellyn, I told the foreign editor what I was intending to write for that night's paper. Cameron smiled as I told him I had just been talking to Roland Watson, who was at Eton with him, and much banter ensued.

I have often thought that coalition was the ideal government arrangement for Cameron. In the early years of his leadership, Steve Hilton, his policy guru, and Michael Gove pushed Cameron to be the great modernizer, trying to do for the Tories what Blair had done for Labour. But concepts like the Big Society came and went, the 'hug a hoodie' era departed, and the pledge to be the greenest government ever descended into farce when he was alleged to have told civil servants to get rid of all the 'green crap'.

Becoming prime minister was the goal Cameron set himself. Having Nick Clegg looking over his shoulder, and being in a minority, meant that some of the more radical plans that a strong right-wing Conservative government would have pursued could be put on the shelf. Elliott and Hanning captured this superbly in their updated book when they said that Cameron 'can appear suspiciously at ease managing the day-to-day demands of power'.

They revealed that Hilton believed Cameron had become too focused on power rather than forcing through radical change. Cameron had charged Hilton with acting as his 'conscience' after he became prime minister, as a guard against a tendency to coast. But, the authors said, Cameron in 2012 was finding the demands of his 'conscience' wearisome and preferred to listen to the cold calculation of Osborne. Gove said of the Prime Minister: 'He is a model of how to have a clear divide between the world of work and then relaxation so that you can clear your mind. There are few people who have such a finely developed capacity to do that.'

Cameron was like several leaders who went before him, constantly having to look to his right flank. Today, as he considers what to do with the rest of his career, he must regret promising them a European referendum at a time of weakness. It finished him. But just as his predecessors were unlucky that their main foe was Blair, who had shown he could conquer Middle England, Cameron was a lucky general in having as his three leaders of the Opposition Brown, Ed Miliband and, incredibly, Jeremy Corbyn. He was also lucky that when he entered the leadership fray, most of his main rivals like Clarke and Davis had been around for a long time and had stood before. He had the advantage of freshness, and no known ideological stance on anything much, and played both to considerable advantage.

Even then he failed to beat Brown outright in 2010. Britain's voters went for Margaret Thatcher and Tony Blair in a big way because they believed they knew what they stood for. With Cameron they were not so sure what they were voting for – but neither were Tory MPs and members. His lack of a guiding ideology or set of principles may have communicated itself to voters and resulted in his less-than-enthusiastic endorsement in 2010 and 2015 (when fear of a Labour–Scottish National Party link-up was a key electoral factor rather than wide-spread enthusiasm for the Conservatives).

Cameron's disclosure during the 2015 election campaign to James Landale, deputy political editor of the BBC and former member of my Westminster team, that he would go before the next election was stunning and without doubt the story of the campaign. It fitted, though, with the image of a man who clearly enjoyed being prime minister, but would not at all mind, having achieved his life's ambition, if he was doing something else.

However, that moment arrived far earlier that he wanted. As we now know, the lucky general's luck ran out when his gamble on a referendum on Britain's membership of the European Union spectac-ularly blew up in his face. One of the prominent figures in the campaign that defeated him was … David Davis. What goes around comes around.

David Miliband Blows It and Balls Falls Out with Brown

David Miliband spurned at least four opportunities to run against Gordon Brown. But the leadership of the Labour Party was his for the taking if he had made the right moves in 2010.

Gordon Brown's decision to favour Ed Miliband over his long-time adviser, Ed Balls, undoubtedly helped the younger brother to a victory from which David and the rest of the Miliband family – let alone the Labour Party – have not recovered.

But David Miliband, who served as foreign secretary under Brown, had only himself to blame for a tactical failure that led to his defeat, sources close to Brown, Ed Miliband, David Miliband and Balls have told me as I have retraced one of the most significant and traumatic periods in Labour's history. We have no way of knowing, but most Labour figures believe that the history of the 2010–15 Parliament would have been different as well, and that Labour would not (as of the summer of 2016) be under the stewardship of a hard-left MP who had never been anywhere near his party's front-bench.

The move that would have ensured David Miliband's victory would have been to indicate that Ed Balls, one of the other four candidates, was set to be his shadow chancellor, key figures from the different factions agree. It would have brought together the Blairite and Brownite wings of the party and undoubtedly taken votes away from Ed Miliband. Both James Purnell, one of David's best friends, and Peter Mandelson urged him to bury his reservations about Balls and do it for the Labour Party but he refused.

It was, after all, because he believed that a David Miliband–Balls deal would have led to victory for the older Miliband brother that

Gordon Brown desperately tried to stop such a deal being reached. And Peter Mandelson remains very disappointed that David Miliband did not make the move that would have ensured his victory.

'We don't know for sure but I think it is most likely that a Miliband-led Labour Party would have got into power in one form or another in 2015, perhaps in a hung parliament deal with the Liberal Democrats,' Mandelson told me. He continued:

> If he had won the leadership, none of this nonsense that has happened since would have occurred. We would not have had the five wasted years and we would not have been in the madcap situation we are at the moment.
>
> But David was either too proud or too complacent to do what he was urged, which was to form an alliance with Ed Balls. You know that at the time I was talking a lot to Ed Balls. I knew his mind. But David would not do it. The trouble was he never believed he would lose. But in these situations you have to talk to anyone who will listen to you. That's what Tony did in 1994. Of all the tragedies to strike Labour, this was the biggest in recent years.

Stewart Wood, an adviser to Brown and later Ed Miliband, believes that David Miliband did not countenance an arrangement with Balls because he was going to take a different economic line to Balls if he won:

> Ed was proposing reducing the deficit at a slower pace and in his Bloomberg lecture of August 2010 was effectively saying there was an alternative to the kind of austerity Osborne was proposing. David obviously did not want that, and so he did not take the obvious avenue open to him.

As *The Guardian* revealed in June 2011 – when it got hold of the final draft of a speech David Miliband would have delivered had he won – he planned to warn that the great danger to his party lay in underestimating the challenge of the deficit. He had been planning to announce that Alistair Darling, the former chancellor, would head a commission to draw up rules on deficits and public spending designed to restore lost trust in Labour's fiscal discipline.

As Damian McBride reveals in his book, *Power Trip*, Brown called him out of the blue during the election – McBride had stopped working for him in 2009 in the row over his leaked e-mails containing his suggestions for smearing top Tories – and told him that if he was speaking to Ed Balls, he should tell him not to do a deal with David Miliband but to do one with Ed Miliband instead. McBride wrote: 'Gordon and others close to him urged me that – if I had any influence over Ed Balls or his team – I should tell him he had to reject any deal offered by David, and instead pursue the same deal with Ed Miliband.'

The call surprised McBride, but it showed the former leader's determination to stop David at any price. By that stage Balls was not talking very much to Brown. One of the most successful political relationships of the Labour years was, if not in deep freeze, frostier than anyone realized at the time.

Brown's stance – while it may well have helped Ed Miliband in the ultimately decisive union section of the electoral college – would not have stopped David if he had intimated he was ready to embrace Balls. Balls was eliminated at the third stage of the contest, Diane Abbott and Andy Burnham having dropped out previously. At that point, Balls had 43 votes from MPs, Ed Miliband 96 and David 125.

However, after Balls dropped out, 26 of his votes went to Ed Miliband and only 15 to David. Although David won the MPs' section by 140 to 122, just three more switching to him from Ed Balls would have been enough to win the leadership. Everyone I have spoken to says that the hint of a deal with Balls would have easily done the trick. According to friends, however, David Miliband was determined to win on his own terms, and believed that he was going to do so. One close friend said: 'In his own mind he could never quite accept that Ed Miliband would beat him. When it comes to hard politics David is a bit of an innocent.'

The key to winning the election was lining up the second preferences of MPs known to be voting for someone else. So Ed Miliband spent hours talking to MPs, asking them politely if he could be their second choice and that he totally understood why he was not the first. David Miliband, according to one of his close aides, lined up those MPs who were known to be backing Ed Balls and 'treated them like a group of naughty children'. Several gave Ed Miliband their second preferences – which in the end, of course, decided the race for him – because he had been so understanding and David had not.

One story that has done the rounds ever since was of a newly elected Labour MP who let it be known that she was keen to vote for David Miliband. She sought a meeting with him to tell him, only to be told by his office that one of his team would be talking to her. When she ran into Miliband in the corridor, he acknowledged her and said: 'Ah yes, I must organize for one of the team to talk to you.' That was not the kind of attitude to win friends and influence them.

The other huge problem was that David Miliband, according to another friend, was trying to run before he could walk. He was thinking more about how he would take on David Cameron than what he needed to do to beat his brother. The great obstacle to a deal with Ed Balls in his own mind was that the man whom others were telling him to make shadow chancellor wanted to reduce the deficit at a slower pace than currently suggested by the Government at the time.

Under the putative deal, David Miliband would have made positive remarks about Ed Balls, which would have been an obvious hint that he would be shadow chancellor and a clear signal to the supporters of

Balls to make David Miliband their second preference choice. The Tory Government was accelerating its cuts plan, but David Miliband did not want a dividing line at this stage because he believed it was his task to rebuild Labour's shattered economic credibility. To him Balls, someone who was so closely associated with Brown, was an obstacle. But he was not thinking enough about the job in hand.

'He was already worrying about how he would face up to David Cameron in the House of Commons if he was being seen to relax a bit on austerity. It was crazy,' a close friend said. Phil Collins, former speechwriter for Tony Blair and then working at *The Times* as a leader writer, also urged Miliband to work with Balls, and said as much in an article at the time.

Similarly, Miliband had balked during one of the election hustings when asked whether he would line up with TUC protests against the cuts. Other contenders had said they would; he prevaricated. A colleague said: 'David was not really a politician. He did not get the whole business of alliances. He was far too obsessed with what was to come after and how he would look up against Cameron rather than with winning against Ed.'

Another friend said: 'He should have gone to Ed Balls. Ed [Balls] could hardly go to him because he was the underdog. But David was being told by lots of his friends this was the way to win and he was stubborn.' And still another former Brown aide told me: 'In the end Gordon backed Ed Miliband because he thought that was the way to stop David Miliband. History would have been different if David had done a deal with Ed Balls. He would have won.'

There had been one other opportunity for David Miliband, back in 2007 when Gordon Brown took over. Many of the Blairites wanted him to have a go at that time. He also, I've since discovered, got unsolicited advice from a former Tory MP. David Martin, who represented Portsmouth South for ten years, wrote to him quoting Brutus in Julius Caesar: 'There is a tide in the affairs of men … Which, taken at the flood, leads on to fortune.' Miliband wrote a polite letter back to his correspondent telling him he had decided against standing. Martin had given the same advice to Michael Portillo in 1995 when he stepped back from challenging John Major.

Gordon Brown believed that Ed Miliband should offer Ed Balls the shadow chancellorship as a way of uniting the two men who had served him for so long. Stewart Wood, Ed Miliband's adviser and formerly Brown's too, backed the suggestion. But Miliband told him it would be a bad idea. 'Ed said that while David, his brother, would be seen as the Blairite candidate, Balls would be seen as a Brownite candidate, allowing him [Ed Miliband] to be seen as the change candidate,' Wood told me.

As it happened, of course, Miliband did it without having to offer a deal to Ed Balls. The majority view appears to be that David would have won if he had offered some kind of deal to Balls, however informal. But everyone around Ed Miliband at the time talks of his strong confidence in his chances. Wood's disclosure shows how confident Ed Miliband was that he could do it on his own, and how his strategic brain was working at the time. It also shows why he first appointed Alan Johnson as his shadow chancellor, only for Johnson to stand down for personal reasons in his first year. It was only then that he appointed Ed Balls to the job for which his talents seemed well suited.

The Brown–Balls partnership had survived most of the Labour years but during the Brown premiership it came under strain. McBride tells of how, rather than back the man who was his more senior adviser, and the one on whom he had relied for so long, Brown decided to give both Balls and Ed Miliband a chance to succeed him.

Both Eds became secretaries of state when Brown became leader. McBride reports that at the 2007 party conference, Brown had instructed him to:

> … build up the young guys. Turn it into a beauty contest about who'll take over from me. Don't for God's sake say I won't serve a full term but say 'Brown doesn't want to go on forever. Brown will start putting the next generation into all the senior posts and one of them will become leader.'

McBride asked him which names he should put out there and was told James Purnell, Ruth Kelly, Andy Burnham, Yvette Cooper and Balls. He also mentioned Miliband and Miliband and when McBride queried this he said: 'Both of them … You need to watch Ed Miliband. He's the one to watch.' Brown also told McBride that one day he would have to choose between the two Eds. McBride believes that to have said this to him, and presumably others, was a mistake because from then on people who had seen them as an indivisible double act began to treat them as separate entities and inevitably took sides.

Deep down Brown knew that probably one day he would have to choose too, and if a Blairite contender like David Miliband or Purnell became the frontrunner he would have to back the one he felt most capable of setting out an alternative Brownite vision. Brown's conversation with McBride was a revelation to his former aide. It showed him that when decision time eventually arrived Ed Miliband had a serious chance of getting the backing of Brown. Brown's appreciation of Ed Miliband was limited, though. He once told Mandelson: 'He's more a preacher than a politician. He's never had to make a difficult decision in his life.'

The alliance between Balls and Brown had become strained long before the leadership contest. Balls was frustrated that in the run-up up to the 2009 reshuffle, Brown had allowed the suggestion to gain credence that he wanted him in the Treasury to replace Alistair Darling. In fact, as already mentioned elsewhere, Balls wanted longer in the post of schools secretary to enhance his reputation as a politician who could handle an important government department.

The James Purnell resignation on the eve of the reshuffle put paid to any suggestion of moving Darling, but it was still presented as a defeat for Balls – something his friends knew was far from the case. I was called by Ed Balls on the Tuesday of what would have been reshuffle week – and I gathered that other journalists had been as well – to be told that stories about Brown wanting him to go to the Treasury were wrong. But that did not stop some papers being briefed after the Purnell shock that it had stopped Darling being replaced by Balls. Balls was exasperated. So as they entered the last months of the parliament, the two men who had worked together on so many of the key decisions of the Labour Government were no longer as close as they once were.

For Balls, the last straw came at the start of 2010, when the PM faced the last attempted coup on his leadership. As detailed previously, Geoff Hoon and Patricia Hewitt, the former Cabinet ministers, had suddenly called for a secret leadership ballot in a last-ditch attempt to remove Brown, just months before the election. It was no more successful than any that had gone before, but several ministers – who delayed for hours before giving their support to the beleaguered

Prime Minister – extracted concessions from him about the coming campaign and his attitude towards the cuts in public spending needed to tackle the deficit, about which they felt he was in denial.

Ironically, Balls was one of the few to go out publicly and support Brown from the start. But to pacify some of the dissident ministers, Brown apparently told them he would restrain the influence of Balls, who was still seen still to have a big say in policy and strategy. At Brown's request, Balls had been making occasional visits to Number 10 for strategy chats.

Balls was furious when Brown allowed his team, using the evidence of those occasional chats, to brief the press that he – the most senior figure in Brown's inner circle – was to be 'reined in'. The episode damaged their relationship for good.

Together Brown and Balls had shaped the early years of the New Labour Government, making the Bank of England independent and keeping Britain out of the euro. But eventually even their close bond was broken by the strains that politics will always impose.

Cameron 'Ate Us Up and Spat Us Out'

David Cameron wanted to stay on as prime minister until 2019. I was told that by one of his closest friends. But it was not to be, and on 24 June 2016, just hours after we learnt that Britain had voted herself out of the European Union, he announced he was quitting. The issue of Europe, the one he said he wanted his party to stop banging on about, finished him as it had finished Margaret Thatcher.

We had learnt not to underestimate Cameron. Until June 2016 he had been a successful and fortunate leader, taking charge of his party in 2005, becoming prime minister in 2010 and running a coalition with the Liberal Democrats for the full five-year term, stunning most people by winning the 2015 election outright, and triumphing in referendums on the voting system and Scotland. He was fortunate until it came to his most important decision of all, the EU referendum. It was then that he lost the biggest wager of his life – and to his ill fortune it will be the decision that defines his premiership.

If friends and foes of Cameron agreed about one of his characteristics, it was that he could be extremely ruthless if the conditions warranted it. Whether it be axing a recalcitrant minister or requiring a minister to change an already agreed policy, Cameron would do it if his own or his party's position was threatened.

Cameron's handling of the coalition, which allowed him to govern for a full parliament between 2010 and 2015, summed up his tough streak. In the words of Norman Lamb, one of the Lib Dem ministers who served in government and survived the 2015 election (along with only seven of his colleagues): 'He hugged us for five years and then he strangled us.'

Cameron enticed Nick Clegg into the Number 10 rose garden in 2010, and then proceeded to watch as his partners took the flak on behalf of the Government for most of the unpopular policies adopted by the two parties during the Parliament. He then ordered party chiefs to spend tens of thousands killing off the Lib Dems in the territories over which they had fought at recent elections, especially the southwest.

Looking back on the 2015 election, Lamb, who held on to his North Norfolk seat, told me the Coalition was for the Lib Dems an experiment which would determine whether a minor party could, under the first-past-the-post system, take part in government and live to tell the story. 'The conclusion obviously is no,' he said.

Lamb said that early on in the coalition, the Lib Dems had been warned by sister parties in Europe that the golden rule in coalitions was that the minor party got the blame for unpopular moves. He said the only way for third parties like the Lib Dems to win seats was to build up a coalition of support of former voters from the two main parties to add to a core of Lib Dem voters:

But then if you go into coalition with one of the main parties, your vote fractures and also those who voted for you because they hate the Tories accuse you of betrayal. In the end it destroys you. The same would happen if you went into a coalition with Labour and you upset the people who supported you to keep them out.

Lamb told me: 'You can justifiably say that we contributed to five years of stable and successful government but we got absolutely no credit for it.' The party's contribution included steering Cameron away from right-wing policies favoured by much of his party, but again earned little credit. What the Lib Dems are remembered for is putting up tuition fees after promising not to, giving the wealthy a tax cut, and keeping the Tories afloat.

Veteran Westminster observers felt there was a naivety about the Lib Dem leadership as it had its first taste of power in decades – a desire to please its coalition senior partners without any obvious reciprocation. The coalition agreement gave Clegg the option of abstaining over the rise in tuition fees, but he asked his party to support it in by far the biggest single mistake of the Parliament and one from which he, personally, never recovered. In his book *In it Together*, Matthew d'Ancona reveals even that George Osborne advised Clegg not to sign up to a tripling of tuition fees. But as Vince Cable, business secretary, had drawn up the policy and Clegg had come to believe in it, he made a disastrous decision.

Meanwhile, the Tories gave the Lib Dems a referendum on the alternative vote system for Westminster elections and then went out of their way, Cameron included, to kill it. In their book *Cameron: Practically a Conservative*, Francis Elliott and James Hanning recorded that Cameron had always told Clegg he would play no part in the 'No' campaign, but that he went back on that when the polls suggested the two sides were running neck-and-neck. An ally quoted him as saying: 'Right, we are going for this and we are not going to take our foot off the gas.'

This was Cameron the ruthless. Clegg's other big coalition demand was turning the House of Lords into a much smaller and mainly elected chamber. But when ninety-one Conservative MPs voted against the legislation it quickly fell, and there was a feeling on the

Liberal Democrat side that Cameron had done little to help it through by pressurizing his party. As a result Clegg withdrew support from the measure that would have shaken up parliamentary boundaries and cut the size of the Commons by fifty MPs. His own party would have been hit by the boundaries change, but his action produced no obvious benefit when the election came. And on reform of party funding, Clegg's other pet issue, there was no sign of the Tories giving anything. 'We were Cameron's shield protecting him from his right wing. But he gave us nowt,' said Lamb. Another veteran Lib Dem told me: 'They ate us up and spat us out.'

Cameron's luck held up to and during the 2015 general election. Quite apart from his Labour opposite numbers, he was fortunate that the leader of the Lib Dems was Nick Clegg, someone who was not inherently averse to a deal with the Conservatives and a person with whom he got on reasonably well. And he was fortunate, ironically and counter-intuitively, that the Scottish National Party performed so strongly in the 2014 referendum despite losing in the end. It meant that Nicola Sturgeon, the SNP leader, entered the 2015 contest on a roll and it was obvious, after years of Labour decline north of the border, that the SNP would be the massive beneficiaries.

As May approached, the polls suggested that the SNP could wipe out Labour in Scotland and suddenly it seemed that the only way Labour could become the main governing party was through a deal with the SNP. Cameron and the Tories had their weapon and they exploited it to the full. Tory posters showing Ed Miliband in the pocket of Alex Salmond, the former SNP leader who was trying to return to Westminster, had a devastating impact. The lucky general had been handed a late campaigning gift.

Norman Lamb had been in the southwest, trying to help the mass of threatened Liberal Democrats there. He returned to Norfolk on the Monday night of election week, having concluded that his party might sink to under twenty seats from fifty-six. Travelling round his constituency the next day, it suddenly seemed even worse:

Everything had changed. I had always put my estimate of 'definites' and 'probables' as I went round at between fifty and sixty-five per cent. Suddenly it was down over ten per cent. I was so freaked out that I bought cigarettes for the first time in ages to calm my nerves. I went to a house in North Walsham where I had always had a good welcome. They said: 'Norman, we love having you as our MP but we are really worried about the SNP.' As I walked out of their drive I knew in my heart they were going to vote Tory.

Cameron's outright victory in 2015 was a bigger surprise to him than his failure to win outright in 2010, against an unpopular leader at the end of a thirteen-year Labour spell that had finished in recession. But according to many around him, it was the failure that made Cameron. The decision to make a coalition offer to Nick Clegg the day after the election was very much his own and surprised even George Osborne. It was the move of a man who was desperate not to throw it all away after coming so close. The clinching offer of a referendum on the alternative vote was again very much Cameron's, even though he made it on the premise – which turned out to be wrong – that Labour were touting something similar. Not long afterwards, Cameron had the bonus of Labour electing a left-leaning leader, which would enable his new Government, certain to last for five years provided the Coalition held, to make a grab for the centre ground of British politics.

Before he was leader, he laid claim to being the heir to Tony Blair at a dinner with *Daily Telegraph* executives during his triumphant week at the Tory conference in Blackpool in 2005. And the longer his leadership lasted, the more that comparison felt apt. Like Blair, he looked as if he belonged as prime minister. While aides sometimes despaired of his lack of attention to detail on the finer points of policy and his tendency sometimes to speak before he thought, Cameron was a consummate handler of the big occasion and looked right in the job.

Like Blair, too, he showed himself to be a foreign policy interventionist, committing British troops to military action on three separate occasions and failing on a fourth. As with Blair there have been questions in the aftermath over what seemed like successful operations at the time. Cameron boldly authorized air strikes along with the French against Muammar Gaddafi's brutal repression of his own citizens, probably succeeding in preventing a massacre at Benghazi. But he did so despite the initial opposition of President Obama and some of his own ministers, and the early months of the offensive did not go well. But Tripoli fell in August and Gaddafi was murdered two months later.

Some claimed that Cameron had got lucky over Libya, but Elliott and Hanning quote Oliver Letwin, one of the ministers closest to Cameron, as saying that the response was the product of five years of thinking on how to make liberal interventions.

It was not until 2015 that we learnt from Anthony Seldon and Peter Snowdon, in their book *Cameron at 10*, of how concerned the military had been about both the Libyan action and the failure to take tougher military action when the Syrian crisis erupted in 2012, which in turn assisted the rise of Islamic State. General Sir David Richards, former head of the armed forces, accused Cameron of being more interested in a 'Notting Hill liberal agenda' than showing 'serious statecraft'.

On Syria, where the military had proposed an assault including ground troops and air power, he said: 'If they had the balls they would have gone through with it … if they'd done what I argued they wouldn't be where they are with ISIS. And the authors tell of a show-down over Libya between Cameron, Richards and John Sawers, head of MI6, at a National Security Council meeting. Told bluntly by Cameron that the action to depose Gaddafi was in the British national interest, Sawers told him it had nothing to do with the national interest and insisted that Cameron was acting for 'humanitarian reasons'.

Another book, *Call me Dave* by Lord Ashcroft and Isabel Oakeshott, carried more criticism, from Richards and others, about Cameron's military operations. Richards says he had to tell Cameron that 'being in the Combined Cadet Force at Eton' did not qualify him to decide the tactics of complex military operations. At times, the PM was at war with the chief of the defence staff, who disagreed with him strongly on strategy. Former Tory chairman Michael Ancram said Libya is Cameron's 'Iraq' – with the country now more dangerous than when the PM decided to topple Colonel Gaddafi.

In August 2013, Cameron suffered his most wounding parliamentary defeat after recalling the Commons during the recess to approve UK military action against Syrian President Bashar al-Assad's Government to deter the use of chemical weapons. This followed a suspected chemical weapons attack on the outskirts of the capital, Damascus, in which hundreds of people are reported to have died. Thirty Conservative MPs and nine Lib Dems voted against Cameron as he sustained a 285–272 reverse in a move that was to bring a new caution to the Prime Minister's attitude to foreign ventures. According to the *Daily Mail*, which serialized the Ashcroft book, there was astonishment inside the White House at the Government's 'incompetence' over the vote in 2013. Cameron had wrongly assumed he had Labour's support. During repeated clashes over foreign policy, Richards had to point out that military interventions were more complicated than supporting the 'good guys' versus the 'bad guys'. A former member of the National Security Council backs that assessment, saying of the PM: 'His instinct is to support the underdog, without analysing what that really means.' On Libya, Ancram told Ashcroft and Oakeshott that the intervention played into the hands of terrorists.

In 2014 Cameron won all-party agreement to join the US in air raids against Islamic State in Iraq. But wary of another defeat, he declined to ask MPs for similar attacks in Syria, although he believed they were necessary. After his election victory and the horrific Islamic State attacks on Paris, Cameron went back to the Commons and asked for approval to extend the strikes to Syria, but only after assuring himself that he had backing of enough Labour MPs to get it through.

In a slip that was not untypical of him, he undermined his consensual public approach to winning support with a private attack – swiftly leaked – in which he told his MPs not to vote alongside 'Jeremy Corbyn and a bunch of terrorist sympathizers'. Labour called it a slur and it gave MPs looking for a way of avoiding backing strikes a route out of any commitments they had made.

I was among many Westminster observers who believed that the Coalition would not last the five years. I felt that the Lib Dems were being utterly blotted out by the Tories, while taking all the blame for disliked policies, and would need to reassert their identity before the end of the parliament.

But the men at the top – Cameron, Osborne, Clegg and Danny Alexander (the Treasury chief secretary and fourth member of the Quad, which ran the coalition show) – got on well and there was little thought on the Lib Dem side of breaking it all off. The first three had similar upbringings, leading Boris Johnson, in D'Ancona's book, to call the coalition a 'triumph for the public school system'.

Cameron had the hurdle of the Scottish referendum to clear in September 2014. *The Times* launched the 'Red Box' political bulletin, with me as its editor, in the summer of 2014 in order to be ready for the general election the following year, but before that came the

Scottish campaign. On Sunday, 7 September, less than two weeks before the vote, a YouGov poll for *The Sunday Times* put the 'Yes' vote just ahead for the first time and sent the unionist 'Better Together' campaign – including Cameron – into panic. He cancelled PM's Questions so that he could race north to save the Union and came up with lots of last-minute concessions. He had left it late to become fully engaged, in keeping with the Cameron his friends knew, but again he helped to pull it off. The lucky general? Maybe, maybe not.

While Cameron prospered, so – for most of the time – did his friend and right-hand man, Osborne. But he hit trouble in 2012 with what became known as the Omnishambles Budget, when what seemed like a decent package on the day turned into a nightmare, with a string of Tory revolts on a range of issues from a tax on pasties to a charities tax. It was a warning shot to the all-powerful chancellor, who vowed never to make the same mistake again. In an early 'Red Box' bulletin, I revealed that he no longer wanted to move to the Foreign Office – as had been suggested by a series of briefings – in the event of a Tory victory but wished to remain chancellor. A leadership bid is better launched from there. He never got the chance to launch that campaign. Theresa May, on becoming prime minister, told him he was no longer wanted, and the man who had been favourite to be the next PM just twelve months earlier returned to the back-benches.

James Landale, the BBC's deputy political editor who cut his teeth on my Westminster team, managed to get Cameron to admit during the 2015 election that he would not fight a third, prompting a years-long contest to replace him – with Osborne, Boris Johnson and Theresa May in the box seats.

Cameron began the 2015 Parliament knowing that his biggest task in the years ahead would be to implement the promise he made early in 2013 – under pressure from the Right in his party and the resurgent United Kingdom Independence Party (UKIP) – to hold an 'in/out' referendum on British membership of the EU by the end of 2017. The momentous decision, which followed months of Tory unrest, meant that Cameron had set the terms of his legacy – he would be the Prime Minister who kept Britain in the EU or took her out – without really knowing how Europe would respond to his demand for a new deal. He now knows to his cost that Brussels did not give him enough to satisfy the British people.

As the previous Parliament wore on, the Eurosceptics continued to doubt whether Cameron was serious about a root-and-branch reform of Britain's relationship, and certainly about his ability to deliver it, and

he suffered two defections to UKIP (Douglas Carswell and Mark Reckless). But just as the first-past-the-post system helped to obliterate the Lib Dems, UKIP also desperately failed to meet expectations, returning just Carswell to the Commons with even Nigel Farage defeated in May 2015. Farage was to gain massive consolation. He more than anyone else forced Cameron to concede a referendum that the PM was eventually to lose.

Cameron carried on for just one year before resigning. He became the fourth-longest-serving Tory leader in modern times. His self-confessed pragmatism, untrammelled by ideology, had served him well, even though it had left some wondering why he ever sought to lead his party and the country. He was called with justification the 'essay-crisis PM', only tackling the big problems at the last minute when he was forced to do so, and often rushing and fluffing them as a result. Many are the Tory Cabinet ministers and MPs who wonder privately how they came to be utterly consumed for the first year of a non-coalition Tory government with an internal row about Europe. The answer is that Cameron saw it during the previous parliament as a way to see off the Right and Farage's party. It was the 'essay-crisis PM' par excellence. And for good or ill, his legacy is the unwanted one of taking Britain out of Europe. No wonder he was close to tears when he announced – wife Samantha by his side – that he was going.

How the Grandees Tried
to Enlist Alan Johnson

There was a hint of regret in Alan Johnson's voice when he appeared on the *Today* programme on 17 November 2015, in the middle of a prolonged period of turmoil in the Parliamentary Labour Party.

Labour MPs had shown no sign of coming to terms with the accidental leadership of Jeremy Corbyn – accidental because he would not have won without the votes of MPs who did not even support him – and some who had said they were prepared at least to try to work with him had given up hope.

Corbyn and his allies seemed ready to accept the PLP's opposition as the natural and almost expected backdrop as they tried to seize control of the policy-making machinery and turn Labour into an old-fashioned socialist party of the type they had tried to establish in their heyday in the 1980s. Johnson told the BBC: 'Jeremy Corbyn will perhaps be the servant of the party that I never was, that perhaps I should have been. Many people criticized me for that.'

I have been told by Johnson's closest confidants that he would have run if Gordon Brown's troubles from the winter of 2007 on had led to him being forced out. 'At that point he would have been the obvious caretaker leader and I think he would have gone for it,' Mario Dunn, his long-time adviser, said. But there were several other opportunities in his career for Johnson to go for the top job.

The chance that many Labour MPs hoped he would take came in the autumn of 2014 when, after a bad summer and dreadful conference for Miliband, Johnson was seen as the only hope of the party recovering before the general election in May 2015. Miliband had made a mess of his conference speech by forgetting to mention the deficit, enhancing the charge that controlling it was not his top priority. The decision to show the press what Miliband had intended to say in the speech he had prepared but did not read gave the story rocket fuel and infuriated Bob Roberts, Miliband's press secretary.

His aides felt he was spending too much time in Scotland on the referendum when his unpopularity meant his presence was counter-productive. There was a sense of disillusionment in the team around him, according to some sources. Over a frantic two-week period, names were collected and opinions sought, as MPs waited for word on whether Johnson was willing to stand. Some believed they had received indications from MPs who knew him well that he was up for it. Others did not know, but the fact that Johnson did not come out immediately and squash the idea gave them hope.

I talked to many Labour MPs at the time, and have done so again since then, and I have found few who do not believe that the party would have swung behind Johnson had he stood. That may well have been in his mind when he said what he did to the BBC. He probably knows that his refusal has left many of them upset, given the problems the party has hit since. I have learnt that Johnson's closest aides wanted him to stand and had hoped that the pressure from fellow ministers on him would have been heavier.

The doubts were sufficient for two of the party's grandees – Alastair Campbell and Peter Mandelson – to be asked to find out from Johnson whether he would stand. The *Financial Times* revealed their approaches in a story on 6 February 2015, but with the election so close at that time, the two grandees and the party firmly denied that they had urged him to strike against Miliband, and insisted that they had merely been sounding him out on the rumours. My inquiries suggest that Campbell and Mandelson went further than that and did indeed tell him that the party would welcome it if he came forward.

Around ten MPs asked Mandelson if he could find out what was going on. When he spoke to the former home secretary and health secretary, the conversation went like this:

Mandelson: Alan, a lot of people want to know if you are prepared to become leader in the event of Ed losing a vote of confidence.

Johnson: The public would never wear a change of leadership so close to a general election.

Mandelson: Alan, you would be blown away by the sigh of relief coming from voters who don't like Cameron and the Tories but are also worried about Ed. The party would follow you.

Johnson: I can't do it, Peter. At this stage of my life I'm not sure it's right for me.

The conversation continued but Johnson showed no sign of wanting to change his position and left his interlocutor with the impression that he was enjoying his new life as an author. He had by then written two successful volumes of memoirs, recounting his upbringing in the slums of Notting Hill in the 1950s and his time as a postman.

Campbell spoke to Johnson twice during this tumultuous period. He asked him to take seriously the prospect that a change of leadership might be the only way Labour could win, and that he was clearly the figure that people felt gave Labour the best chance. It was only after Campbell accepted that Johnson was not up for it that he told him, in that case, it should be knocked on the head as hard as possible. The danger otherwise was the worst of all worlds – no viable candidate but continued doubts swirling around.

Others believed that Johnson suffered a loss of nerve at the crucial moment; or that he may have lacked the self-confidence to go for it. Some felt there was a lethargy about him. Some felt he owed it to his party to try. Labour MPs have told me that Johnson delayed long enough in ruling himself out as a late successor to Miliband to give them hope that he might be persuaded. The services of Mandelson and Campbell would not have been required if his position had appeared unequivocal.

Stewart Wood, Miliband's chief adviser, told me that the Miliband office wondered about the Alan Johnson rumours for a few days:

But we really did not think he would do it. Alan is a very loyal man and I knew that he was enjoying his new life. I remember thinking after he gave up the shadow chancellorship for personal reasons that he would not be coming back to the front line.

Others who were in the office seriously believed a challenge was on the cards. But Bob Roberts, Miliband's press chief and a former political editor of the *Daily Mirror*, knew Johnson from his days working on the *Hull Daily Mail* in Johnson's constituency city. He also knew Johnson's intentions better than most and was a calming influence in the office.

Mandelson himself believes the PLP would have gone over 'almost en bloc' to Johnson had he said yes. Hilary Armstrong – chief whip in the Labour Government and, later, in 2010 to become Baroness Armstrong of Hill Top – was among the many senior Labour figures who wanted Johnson to be drafted in as emergency replacement for Miliband. She told me that for a short time in the autumn of 2014 there was a 'groundswell' of support for Johnson, with whom she had served in government. She said:

> The Labour Party has been traditionally loyal to its leaders but it became pretty obvious to all of us that we were not going to do well. Alan was the only credible candidate and for a few days it seemed possible that he might emerge. It was left to Peter [Mandelson] and Alastair [Campbell] to find out whether there was any chance, and of course we got the answer we did.
>
> I don't think Alan would have been a long-time leader, but he would have given us a much better chance of winning the election, and it would have opened up the way to David Miliband coming back.
>
> Perhaps at times Labour is too loyal. Looking back now, and seeing what has happened since, it makes you wish that more people had spoken out because if you think you are going to lose, it is your duty to do something. But in the end Alan did not want it. It was his, I think, if he had made himself available. But by then life had moved on for him and he really did not want to go through with it.

John Woodcock, former chairman of the Blairite Progress group, recalls that suddenly everyone was having conversations with each other about a late change of leadership:

The mood of the PLP was dire. There was a recognition that we were in deep trouble and that the public had made up its mind about Ed.

That translated into a view that rather than walk into defeat and let the Tories have a second term, we have a responsibility to see if there is an alternative. And the conversations kept coming back to this – if Ed cannot deliver the Labour government we want, who can? And virtually all those conversations ended with the conclusion that the best person to beat Cameron was Alan Johnson.

The Alan option was out there. And I do know that for the best part of a week, Alan did not close it down. What I don't know is whether that was Alan being clumsy and not knowing quite how to put the lid on it or whether he was genuinely thinking it over.

Woodcock told me: 'If Alan had said yes, it remains my view that he would have become leader very quickly. The level of despair reached way beyond people who had always had doubts about Ed's ability to win. It included some of those who had backed him for the leadership.'

Ian Austin, Labour MP, said that if Johnson had agreed to run there would have been a stampede of support for him. He commented:

People who said they were in a position to know said that Alan might be up for it. That was why his name came into it and that was why the story continued to run till that *Guardian* article which completely ruled it out. There was nothing dishonourable in having these discussions. Ed was twenty per cent behind on leadership and it was desperate. We were right. Look where we are now.

Party sources also told me that MPs were told that if sufficient numbers came forward, Dave Watts, chairman of the PLP, would go to Miliband and confront him. But they also said that within minutes of the confidential discussions, names were made known to the leadership. Anna Yearley, Miliband's political secretary, had a good intelligence operation in the Commons and the dissidents were swiftly flushed out.

After a week of turmoil early in November, Johnson gave a Saturday interview to *The Times* in which he told anyone plotting against Miliband to 'get a grip' and said he had no intention of going back to frontline politics. He went on: 'I'm a candidate at the next general election, so I've got an interest in it and I think it's eminently winnable. Even if I was completely despondent – as I'm not – the law of political gravity is that you do not spend two or three months of a precious six-month period up to the general election having an internal fight about who the leader should be.'

But even that was not enough to kill it all off. *The Observer* that Sunday reported that Johnson's comments did not rule out a coronation, an uncontested election. It recorded a plotter as saying: 'Were Alan's comments categorical? I am genuinely not sure.' A second Labour MP confirmed:

There is a significant number of front-benchers who are very concerned by Ed's leadership, or lack of it, and would be ready to support someone who is a viable candidate. And Alan Johnson is that candidate. If he was to indicate an interest there would be a massive move. It would put a smile on the face of the front-bench. And the back-benchers. It is up to Alan now.

The *FT* reported an MP as saying: 'If Alan Johnson gave any indication he would be prepared to do it, Ed Miliband would be finished by the weekend. But I don't think that will happen.'

It was then that Johnson paid heed to Campbell's warning that if he was not up for it, he should kill it fast. The result was an article by Johnson in Monday's *Guardian* which did the job. He had never stood for the leadership and 'regardless of the circumstances never will', he wrote. He continued:

> At the beginning of this Parliament the Labour Party lost precious months conducting an overlong leadership campaign that allowed the coalition to develop their big fat lie about the global recession while we examined our collective navel. The question of the leadership was settled then. It must not be reopened.

Regretful though they were, the MPs who had been pushing for Johnson accepted that as the final word. I spoke to several of them that week and they were agreed, in the words of one: 'It's Miliband or bust.'

The people who know Johnson's mind best, though, still wonder. He is a naturally diffident, modest man and would need to be convinced that he was good enough to do the top job. It is possible that his surprise failure to win the deputy leadership when Brown became leader – he was narrowly beaten by Harriet Harman – increased his reticence, his fear that he was not quite up to it.

Mario Dunn says that he wishes Mandelson and Campbell had been more forceful in pressing Johnson to go for it:

> They felt they had to be careful because the election was so close but I do so wish they – and people in the shadow Cabinet who mattered – had pushed him harder. I honestly don't know if it would have worked, but it might have done and I wonder where we would be now if they had badgered him harder and he had agreed. We would not be where we are now.

Dunn has fewer doubts about 2009 after James Purnell walked out of Brown's Cabinet:

> John Hutton and Hazel Blears went as well but if David Miliband had followed James Purnell out I am convinced Brown would have fallen. He could not have survived that. And Alan would have been ready to go forward in those circumstances.

When it came to 2010, Johnson again declined calls to stand and instead threw his weight behind David Miliband. Many believe that he would have beaten Ed Miliband. Call him the Nearly Man or the Lost Leader, Johnson remains a great enigma. Like the rest of his colleagues, he must often wonder 'what if?'

Could Miliband Have Stopped Corbyn?

On election night 2015, shortly after Ed Miliband and his team had learnt the terrible truth that their hopes had been shattered, Tom Baldwin – his communications chief – prepared a memo for his embattled boss urging him to stay on as leader while the party chose his successor.

It said that holding on to the levers of power would be good for him, reducing the likelihood of his record being trashed as soon as he was out of the way, good for the party because demoralized parties – including Labour – rarely make good decisions in the wake of thumping election defeats, and good for the country because otherwise the new government would have a clear run against a disorganized Opposition and be able to get away with just about anything.

As he wrote it, Ed and his wife Justine Thornton, together with aides including Greg Beales (director of strategy), Anna Yearley (the political secretary), Bob Roberts (press secretary) and adviser Stewart Wood, were on their way back to London from Miliband's Doncaster constituency. A helicopter had been laid on for what they had hoped would be a journey reinforcing the sense of him being the next prime minister. The three scenarios for which Labour had prepared were all about another hung parliament. No one foresaw an outright Tory victory. Sensibly, in the downbeat circumstances in which they found themselves, it was decided that the helicopter should not be used and they returned by car.

Baldwin, a former *Times* journalist, was advised by colleagues who already knew Miliband's mind that he should by all means make his argument, but that he should not push it too hard, as he was sometimes inclined to do. As Tom's boss myself for several years, I know what they meant.

Beales had argued that it would look more dignified for Miliband to go immediately and that the country would expect a clean break. When they got back at around 8.30 a.m. on the Friday, Miliband was cheered by exhausted, tearful but defiant party staff. He immediately convened a meeting in his office which one said resembled 'breakfast at a morgue'. Miliband had used the journey down from Doncaster to write a resignation speech and he was in no mood to be dissuaded.

He began by distributing copies of his speech and asked for comments. Baldwin said they should discuss whether Miliband should stay on before they got to the speech. He then went round the table. Baldwin made his case, supported by Lord Charlie Falconer (whom Miliband had brought in to help with transition planning for a Labour-led government), Spencer Livermore (the campaign director), Torsten Bell (head of policy) and Harriet Harman (the deputy who had been caretaker leader before in 2010 and knew the dangers better than anyone). Spencer (now Lord) Livermore, who worked on the 1997, 2001 and 2005 elections as well as 2015, argued that Miliband

could give the party a little more time to understand why it had lost
if he stayed on. He told me later:

> I wanted to separate the inquest from the contest. Instead there
> was no inquest and we stepped straight into a contest when
> everyone was exhausted. I understood Ed's point of view given
> what had happened to him. But we were repeating the same
> mistakes as in 2010 when we never properly considered why we
> lost. We did not have an inquest in 2010 and that was part of the
> reason why we lost in 2015. We did not have an inquest in 2015
> and if we lose in 2020 that will be one of the reasons why.

On the other side were mainly those who had travelled back with
Miliband – Bob Roberts, Beales and Wood. They knew his mind
better than the others at this stage. Marc Stears, the Miliband speechwriter, was strongly in the 'Ed should be allowed to go' camp.

Ed's wife, Justine, listened to the political discussion and then gave
her own view, which the participants say held sway, not least because
it was so human. She said her husband could not be expected to carry
on and face the jeering, braying massed ranks of triumphant Tory MPs
at Prime Minister's Questions. She said he had worked as hard as
anyone could for five years and now it was time to leave and spend
time with his two young boys. A participant said: 'It was moving and
she was right. Ed had done enough. Ed had done his bit.'

Miliband made his decision and said he would continue with his
speech, which he delivered in Westminster two hours later. Both
Falconer and Baldwin had made explicit reference to what happened
when Michael Howard stayed on as Tory leader after his defeat in the
2005 election. As I explain elsewhere in this book, had he not done so
David Davis would almost certainly have become leader and David
Cameron would never have had the chance to make the stunning
conference speech that propelled him into the limelight and then to
the leadership.

Miliband must have been in a state of shock at the time. Right up
until the last, he had hoped and believed that the result would come
out in a way that would ensure he got to Downing Street. Throughout
his five years, he had always regarded the internal threat from Labour
opponents as his greatest obstacle. 'His motto was "If I can survive the

Labour Party for five years I will get into Number 10",' says Stewart Wood. Even before the election, Miliband had been urged to stay on if he lost. Neal Lawson, chairman of the influential Compass pressure group, speaking on behalf of a group of like-minded colleagues and MPs, including Jon Cruddas, told him he should not go quickly, to give the party time to regroup and recover. But Miliband was not thinking of that. He told them he hoped and expected to win.

While the Tories believed the rise of the SNP was the biggest factor in their victory, Miliband had been careful to leave open the door to a deal, although using extremely cautious language. Alastair Campbell, who was helping the campaign, believed the best way to counter the Tory propaganda was to embrace the idea of an SNP deal and make a virtue of it. As they waited in Miliband's Doncaster home on election night, Stewart Wood admits he was apprehensive. In the room were Ed, Justine, Tim Livsey (chief of staff), Rachel Kinnock (daughter of the former leader and Miliband's gatekeeper), Bob Roberts and Wood.

But at about 9.55 p.m., five minutes before the fateful poll dropped, Wood saw Beales reading a text message and his face 'went as white as a sheet'. 'He said nothing but my guess is it was a tip-off and the news was clearly not good,' said Wood. 'When it came, there was a terrible feeling. When Nuneaton was held by the Tories, we like everyone else knew the game was up.'

One of those who was in Doncaster told me that the clincher was when it became obvious that the Tories would get a majority: 'If they had been in a minority, there was a case for arguing that he should stay on in a caretaker role.' Ed told them at that stage: 'I have put my prospectus to the British people. They have rejected it.'

Politics is full of 'ifs' but it is at least arguable that Labour would not have got itself into the position of electing a leader who was out of sympathy with the vast majority of his MPs if Miliband had indeed stayed on. He felt the full fury of Labour MPs for quitting so quickly because – tired and disconsolate – they and the leadership candidates were swiftly thrown into an election that dominated the summer.

Some of Miliband's team believe that the criticism of him by the mainstream candidates made the soft-left territory he had occupied in the party wide open for Jeremy Corbyn to colonize. Two of the participants at that Friday morning meeting have told me they believe Corbyn would not have been elected if the party had had more time to consider where it was going. 'What we needed was time. Ed gave us none at all. We left the front door open for Jeremy,' said one.

Looking back on Corbyn's election in 2015, it is all too easy to blame the changes to the constitution in March the previous year for opening the floodgates to hundreds of thousands of new activist members, who delighted in cocking a snook at the establishment and putting the unlikely veteran of the hard-left battle of the 1980s into power. It should be remembered that those changes were backed and worked on by New Labour figures in the leadership including Ray Collins, the former general secretary, and Baldwin, who was close – both personally and politically – to the Blairites.

The reforms – which included a straight move over to a one-member one-vote system (replacing the old three-way electoral college of unions, MPs and members) and a requirement on union members to opt in to their affiliation with Labour, rather than let their leadership do it for them – had been backed by such luminaries as Tony Blair and most of his closest advisers, as well as Lord (David) Owen (the former Labour foreign secretary who defected to the SDP) and the widow of the former leader, John Smith. Some Blairites, including Pat

McFadden and Jim Murphy, had warned of the dangers of entryism by the hard left through the trade unions. But it is worth pointing out that their fears on this issue did not materialize – the number of ballot papers issued to affiliated supporters from the unions was less than a quarter of the total and significantly fewer than in 2010.

Where the party missed out was not then going out to the country and selling those reforms, encouraging people to sign up to a mass membership party in the months between then and the general election. Little if anything was done. The party machine did not want to upset the unions still further at a time when they saw the reforms as a Blairite plot to water down their influence. But if Labour had embraced the spirit of these reforms in the fifteen months before the general election – maybe even using some of its 'five million doorstep conversations' in the campaign to sign up supporters – the electorate would have been larger and more broadly based than that which eventually chose Corbyn.

Once the general election was lost, it was not the new rules that were most responsible for giving the party Corbyn. The safeguards on which MPs had insisted when they lost their thirty-three per cent vote after the demise of the electoral college were not used. They required that any candidate must have the backing of fifteen per cent of the parliamentary party before going through to the one member one vote election.

Corbyn was nowhere near to getting that figure, and a number of MPs, like Margaret Beckett and Jon Cruddas, 'lent' their votes to Corbyn, enabling him to get on the ballot paper. They were labelled 'morons' by the former Blair adviser John McTernan, and Beckett later openly admitted that she had indeed to accept she was a moron.

Having got on to the ballot paper, there was no stopping the Islington MP. Tens of thousands of people paid £3 to become registered supporters, and similarly union members clambered to affiliate. Corbyn may have looked uncomfortable at times but that helped. He caught the anti-establishment mood of the time and stormed to a massive victory over Yvette Cooper, Andy Burnham and Liz Kendall.

Looking back, Wood believes it would have been very hard for Miliband to stay:

His view was how could he possibly stand at the despatch box with lots of MPs behind him who would be blaming him for what happened. People say it would have stopped him being criticized, but it was important that MPs had free rein to criticize him as part of the examination of why we lost.

Another confidant said: 'It is highly unlikely that Ed staying on would have stopped the catastrophic decision of the PLP to abandon their role as the gatekeeper and allow Corbyn into the contest. Ed cannot be blamed for that.' Wood says Miliband was almost serene in the hours after his defeat became obvious: 'It felt like a bereavement and that is the way some people react.' Wood was struck by Miliband's parting words that day: 'They can't get me anymore.' He meant the press.

In the eyes of Labour MPs, Corbyn had a disastrous start to his leadership, encountering one policy clash after another, while hard-left activists beavered away on the sidelines, targeting vulnerable MPs and preparing to stand en masse after the planned review of parliamentary boundaries. A win in the safe seat of Oldham West and Royton after the death of Michael Meacher brought some relief, but a botched reshuffle early in 2016 prompted renewed dismay.

Labour's decline began during Tony Blair's third term and accelerated through the leaderships of Brown and Miliband, reaching its nadir under Corbyn. Front-benchers and MPs who went close to trying to oust both Brown and Miliband were left to lick their wounds. Corbyn proved just as hard to eject. Labour had become a different party than the one that carried all before it for thirteen years. It will take another revolution at the least to make it electable again.

Uncle Jeremy, the Sea-Green Incorruptible

I first became aware of Jeremy Corbyn as a peripheral figure in Tony Benn's campaign to become deputy leader of the Labour Party in 1981, the nearest the far left came before 2015 to taking its citadels of power.

In the years that followed, I got to know scores of Labour MPs very well but I have to admit that Corbyn was not one of them. He was a perfectly friendly and approachable chap, although possessing the Left's inbuilt suspicion and distaste for the capitalist press. But I just did not think it was worth trying to build a relationship with an MP whose politics seemed irrelevant and grounded in a bygone age.

In addition to that, he and his friends, like John McDonnell, were utterly predictable. In just about every Commons division that mattered, you would see their names in the list of those who had opposed the Labour leader, whoever it was. You did not have to ask what they were doing, you knew. To me they seemed to be playing to a strange, virtually invisible extra-parliamentary audience that had had its day in the first half of the Eighties.

But for Corbyn and his allies, the Struggle – Marx's conflict between the right-wing capitalist bourgeoisie and purist far left representing the proletariat – was never ending. It had scored notable successes, engineering the left-wing takeover of London that put Ken Livingstone into County Hall, the shake-up of Labour rules to give massive power to the unions and constituency activists, the rise of Militant and the near-election of Benn.

Although defeated by Neil Kinnock and Tony Blair, the forces that controlled the hard left in the last century never went away. Corbyn and co. were their parliamentary figureheads, and they let their friends in the country know what they were doing. Whenever there was a contentious division, someone representing the hard-left Campaign Group of MPs – at its high point never more than forty MPs – would be up in the Press Gallery, telling us how they had voted. And it went on year after year, vote after vote. Nearly always the same MPs between elections; the names sometimes changed after elections when Old Left MPs stood down or lost and new ones got in. Neither I nor any of my colleagues in the Lobby regarded Corbyn as having leadership qualities. I could not see him leading the Campaign Group, let alone the party.

As Philip Cowley, the leading authority on the history of parliamentary rebellions, says on his Revolts blog, Corbyn was the sixth most rebellious MP in his first Parliament from 1983. Over the thirteen years of Labour government, he defied the whip 428 times and was the most rebellious. During the five years of opposition – 2010 to 2015 – he dropped down to second place, just one vote behind McDonnell. Cowley says that he once asked Corbyn what issues he rebelled on and he was clear he did not do it willy-nilly, only on issues of war and peace, liberty and socio-economic policy. Cowley pointed out to him that this covered everything the Government could possibly do.

But what it shows is that this group led by Corbyn never gave up. Maybe they hoped that one day in the dim and distant future, they or their successors could succeed in their primary aim of changing Labour. They could not have envisaged that their chance would emerge without warning in the aftermath of Labour's dreadful defeat in 2015, when a number of Labour MPs decided misguidedly that the Left should have a chance to put its case in the leadership election and helped Corbyn – who had no thought of being able to get the required number of backers – on to the ballot paper. At least fourteen MPs – including Margaret Beckett, Jon Cruddas, Frank Field and Jo Cox, who was killed during the referendum campaign – were identified as helping him get his nomination figure up to the magic thirty-five without any intention of voting for him in the actual poll. Well, we know what happened thereafter.

After a disastrous ten months as leader, as Labour failed to make headway in the country and Corbyn was regularly embarrassed by poor Commons performances, the Europe referendum was the last straw for most of his MPs. The pain of defeat was made worse by their perception that their leader had not fought a whole-hearted campaign – he had never in the past been a supporter of the European Union – and the overwhelming majority of them supported a vote of no confidence in him. But as leading figures dithered over who should challenge him, Corbyn stood firm, declaring that he had a mandate from party members to stay on.

As David Cameron said farewell to the Commons he praised Corbyn for his tenacity. That was a fair point. After the referendum, Corbyn's MPs pleaded with him to go. He would not budge. Then 172 of them – eighty per cent – passed a vote of no confidence in him. He refused to go. Then they tried changing the rules to get him out. It did not work. Tenacious? Certainly he appeared to have the skin of a rhino.

To find out what drove Corbyn for all those years in a self-imposed wilderness, I turned to someone who knew him when he first emerged as a figure that counted on the London hard left. Back at the start of the 1980s, one of my best contacts on the Left was Nigel

Williamson, who was then close to Tony Benn and was a key member
in his team for the 1981 deputy race which was won by a whisker by
Denis Healey. Williamson later became editor of *Tribune*, then worked
for the Labour Party at Walworth Road – including as a press officer
to Neil Kinnock in the 1987 election – before joining *The Times* as a
Commons reporter, later to become diary editor, Whitehall correspondent and news editor.

Williamson first met Corbyn in 1980 at County Hall, at meetings
of the London Labour Briefing collective which was plotting the
takeover of the Greater London Council, and was the key body in
getting left-wing candidates elected and organizing Ken Livingstone's
elevation to leader of the Labour group. Corbyn was a Labour coun-
cillor in Haringey and a National Union of Public Employees official.
Williamson told me:

> He had a definite aura about him as a proto-revolutionary leader.
> He was five years older than me and I suppose at the time he was
> everything I aspired to be – committed, principled and the first
> man you'd want at your side in a lifeboat because you knew he'd
> never flag and never stop rowing in what he believed to be the
> right direction.

But then, as until very recently, Corbyn was not interested in personal
aggrandizement. Williamson says:

> You could see how personally ambitious and calculating people
> like Ken Livingstone were. Even with Diane Abbott, another
> prominent member of the Briefing collective, you could tell she
> was positioning herself to get a safe Labour seat as the first black
> woman in Parliament.
>
> But Jeremy seemed different; he appeared to be unconcerned
> with office and position and his commitment was purely to 'the
> struggle' as we called it. In retrospect, I can see that he was ambi-
> tious. But even today, I don't think it was *personal* ambition;
> whatever ambition he had was all about furthering the left-wing
> ideals which drove him. And there seemed to be no left-wing
> cause he didn't support with unbridled commitment.

Livingstone in 2016 has become something of an unofficial spokesman for Corbyn and has seen his own lengthy career revived by the election of his one-time helper. But Williamson recalls how once Livingstone got his hands on the levers of power at the GLC, he found himself accused by the Left of selling out. Says Williamson:

> Once Livingstone became leader of the GLC, the far-left criticisms that he was 'trimming' soon followed and Jeremy took as hard a line as anyone. I don't recall him ever directly accusing Ken of 'selling out'; but he was certainly among those who felt the GLC should have been even more radical and provocative than it was.

Williamson describes the Corbyn of those days as a Stakhanovite, an obsessive hard-worker who attended every meeting and every demo and seemed to have almost no life outside 'the cause'. He recalls: 'But he was also good fun, personable and excellent company. He seldom came to the pub after meetings; but he was outgoing, had a dry sense of humour and was very human.'

Williamson was treasurer of the Benn campaign, and during the TUC week in 1981, he rented a large six- or seven-bedroomed house in Blackpool as the campaign headquarters: 'Jeremy was one of those who stayed in the house with his dog, Mango. I took my two children, aged three and four, along for a seaside holiday, and they loved "Uncle Jeremy" and were thrilled to take Mango for a walk with him.'

When Williamson went to the softer-left *Tribune* paper, Corbyn was critical that he had gone off-message, but that was nothing compared with his attitude when he joined *The Times*:

> He told me in no uncertain terms that he was disappointed in me and that I had sold out. It was not said with any rancour, rather with sadness. And in his terms, he was right. I felt slightly guilty and I never lost my admiration for him as the ultimate of Robespierre's sea-green incorruptibles.

Williamson says that what both Corbyn and McDonnell had in common was an ostensible lack of personal ambition, which made them quite different from others on the London Left at the time, such as Livingstone. Did they have a long-term plan to take over the Labour Party?

100 DAYS – AND COUNTING...

SEASON'S GREETINGS

Never in a thousand years. But what I see now that I didn't necessarily comprehend at the time was that Corbyn and McDonnell were both as tough as it comes. They couldn't be bought, they couldn't be bullied and they wouldn't compromise their views one jot for something as sordid as courting power or influence. If it happened, it was always going to be on their own uncompromising terms.

They weren't for sale. Looking back, that made them highly unusual, if not unique, while almost everyone else around them – even others who were ostensibly on the hard left – was busily trying to climb the greasy pole.

Williamson's account of those early days is for me the best explanation I have seen of the convulsions that have occurred in the Labour Party since the 2015 election. It was indeed the authenticity of Corbyn, his refusal to trim to the established political and economic nostrums at the time, his apparent lack of interest in power, that made him so attractive not only to the socialist Left that had waited for decades for this opportunity, but to the uncommitted and those who felt disenfranchised by the old party system. And it was his toughness – and that of McDonnell – that meant they would not trim once they got their hands on the party, leading to a continuous battle over policy and personalities.

For them the Struggle will never cease. Having got their hands on the levers of power in 2015 they were never going to give them up easily. We heard little from them about winning the next general election. For them, the objective was always to change the political landscape and the party they represent first of all.

Our Power-Driven Politicians

In his student days, Michael Heseltine, according to his biographer, mapped out his future on the back of an envelope and concluded that he would become prime minister in the 1990s. He went awfully close. He and Sir Geoffrey Howe were regarded as Margaret Thatcher's assassins, he was duly punished by Tory MPs and John Major got the job instead.

But Heseltine should be commended for his honesty. His ambition was not unusual. It is shared by many who enter politics. Tony Blair, Gordon Brown, David Cameron, Margaret Thatcher, Yvette Cooper, Boris Johnson, David Davis, Andy Burnham, David Miliband, his brother Ed, anyone who has stood to be leader of one of the main parties, did so in the knowledge and hope that one day he or she might walk into Downing Street. Otherwise why do it? Whether it was a lifetime objective of Jeremy Corbyn is highly questionable, but that's a different story.

The desire for power to influence events is what drives most politicians to give up the prospect of a quiet life and put themselves into the firing line of public opinion. By no means all want to be prime minister, but most would probably like a taste of government office if it came along. All have a view of the world that they would like to see implemented, and stand for office in the hope that, whether at government or constituency level, they can help to achieve it. They certainly don't do it for money. Many back-bench MPs could earn more in virtually any other job they could have chosen, although ministerial jobs are now better remunerated. So power drives them. No mystery. The power to run their own party, and then the power achieved from defeating the Opposition and running the country.

Most politicians are public-spirited. Most are perfectly amiable but are they all good people? Most certainly not. Some, maybe most, will behave badly at some time along the way. Politicians are ruthless, they will back-stab, they will speak ill of their rivals. Do they all think highly of each other if they are from the same party? Certainly not. The most vicious insults hurled around at Westminster are those from within the same party. I have heard ministers verbally knife their rivals – 'he's not really up to it', 'she's not in the real world', 'frankly he just does not get it' – in the competitive climb up the greasy pole.

The venom directed at Iain Duncan Smith from the rest of the Cabinet, and from his friends at George Osborne when he resigned after the Budget in March 2016, had to be heard to be believed.

From the moment he walked out of the Cabinet in 1986, Heseltine's aim in life was to replace Thatcher. A man who was little seen in the Westminster lobbies and bars during his early days as a minister was suddenly available to all of us. I never got the impression he regarded it as important to get to know journalists or back-bench MPs. He was altogether too dashing and busy. But once the leadership became a realistic prospect the change was massive. This Heseltine was ultra-available, patrolling the corridors, talking to whoever he ran into, building up his team. It was so shamelessly, so nakedly deliberate.

Many politicians will be happy to help those of greater ability take the big jobs while they remain the foot soldiers. But it is all about power. In Labour since the 2015 election it has all been about a different power struggle – as MPs have tried to resist the power grab of the hundreds of thousands of members who signed up to back Corbyn.

The relationship between press and politician is naturally tense. The business of government is often at odds with the practice of scrutiny and exposure. They may not like us but most politicians believe they have to woo the press to get ahead. Thatcher was not in that category. I travelled thousands of miles with her on trips abroad and in election campaigns but, without being aloof, you felt that she just did not regard it as part of her world to get to know reporters.

She had Bernard Ingham for that and nobody had a better understanding of what was going on in the minds of the political press than he did. She was not a person for small-talk, so on the rare occasions

when you were able to catch her in a relaxed situation, a lecture on
the issue of the day was far more likely than a bit of old-fashioned
gossip.

In other ways she was a reporter's dream. In her day, she was the
best-known woman in the world and knew it. She understood the
power of language and rarely disappointed at press conferences in any
part of the world. And Denis was wonderfully sociable. On trips
abroad, when the Iron Lady and her team were working at the front
of the plane, he would pop back for a G-and-T and a gossip.

And, of course, she had achieved her aim – power – by the time we
started travelling with her. Cameron and Boris Johnson appeared to
have been competing against each other for power and influence since
their Oxford days. Cameron was in the lead until he fatefully called
the 2016 referendum and Johnson promptly took a leading, ultimately
triumphant, role in the opposing camp. It all went wrong after that.

Before 2010, Johnson – as mayor of London – was the only
Conservative running anything substantial in Britain. The tension
between them was best summed up by a mutual friend of both who
said: 'They have never been able to understand each other's success.'

Johnson, of course, hails from our world. Lobby veterans got to know Boris when he was European correspondent of *The Telegraph* in Brussels. Thatcher liked his pieces highlighting the latest madcap scheme to emerge from the European Commission. There was never any doubting his political ambitions. He has an uncanny knack of making the public like him at the same time as ignoring his faults and flaws.

His articles upset the pro-European journalists around the place but, for us, the real entertainment was to watch Boris and George Jones, the excellent long-time political editor of *The Telegraph*, working on a story together, with Jones trying to curb the natural overenthusiasm of his colleague. Once, when Boris was working on a Saturday at a European summit in Edinburgh, George and I – not having to be there on the Saturday as our papers were daily – went to the press centre in the evening to see how Boris and the other Sunday writers were getting on. Boris showed George his first edition story which boiled down to a 'disaster for John Major'. Jones quietly made some queries around the place and told Boris, ever so politely, that he might just have got the emphasis wrong. Boris swiftly agreed and wrote for the next edition, with just as much panache and certainty, that the meeting had become a triumph for Major.

Part of Johnson's bumbling persona is genuine and endearing but it fails to hide one of the acutest political minds of his generation. Few if any of his interventions that were awkward for Cameron or Osborne were accidental. He is funny, but he is tough, and exploits weakness in others. And given his background, he is masterful at handling the press. But does he have convictions? Judging by how he played the Europe referendum, they are skin-deep and driven more by what the Conservative Party members think. They were the people, after all, who would decide whether *he* was to have power. Or were they? In the end he was struck down by friendly fire.

Michael Gove falls into the category of the politician who is more highly rated by his peers than the public. I worked with him for several years at *The Times*. He was a good colleague, unfailingly courteous and friendly, and frighteningly well informed. I never doubted his Euroscepticism but I and many others were surprised that he left Cameron's side to take the effective leadership of the 'Leave' campaign. We were totally shocked when, just days after winning the referendum with him and Johnson at the helm, and having agreed to be Johnson's campaign manager in the leadership election, he suddenly announced that his friend was not up to the job and said he was standing himself. In a party where betrayal is sometimes seen as a way of life, this appeared to be an act of utter treachery.

One of the most ambitious politicians to have emerged in recent years is Theresa May. When she launched her leadership campaign in June 2016, May made much of her image as the unclubbable minister who does not gossip, tour the Westminster bars, or lunch with journalists all the time. It was a deliberate attempt to portray herself as the serious, even dull, candidate who could help Britain through the post-Brexit crisis.

It was fairly disingenuous. True, it was a waste of time taking May to lunch or dinner because she would tell you nothing about what was going on – she is the ultimate soul of discretion. I recall *The Times*, including the then editor Robert Thomson, inviting May and her husband, Philip, out to dinner at the Tory conference in Bournemouth. We looked at each other in frustration as one question after another was batted away. Getting blood from a stone would have been easier.

But May knows better than most how to play the system. When as party chairman in 2002 she told the party conference that some people regarded the Conservatives as the 'Nasty Party', she knew that it would raise her profile, and it did. Her habit of wearing striking clothes, including exotic heels, always guaranteed broadcast coverage as she strode into Cabinet meetings.

And although she did not leak directly, no one was better at ensuring that her case was put across in the media. She had a series of utterly loyal and able special advisers, such as Fiona Cunningham (now Hill) and Nick Timothy, who ensured her interests were well protected. Her record as the longest-serving home secretary of modern times – always one of the most difficult posts for a Conservative minister – shows beyond doubt that she has always known how to look after herself.

One of her notable scalps was Gove, who was demoted from education secretary to chief whip after a row between them over the alleged infiltration of Birmingham schools by Islamist fundamentalists. Friends of Gove accused the Home Office of failing to 'drain the swamp' of extremism in Britain. The Home Office retaliated by publishing confidential Cabinet correspondence attacking Gove for failing to act on warnings about Birmingham schools. Cunningham was forced to resign for briefing against Gove and, on the advice of Lynton Crosby, his chief strategist, David Cameron exiled Gove.

Other ministers admit privately that they have found May a tough opponent in Cabinet and have smiled ruefully after stories about how she stood up to colleagues, including the Prime Minister, found their way into the newspapers. She has as many enemies at the top as admirers and is regarded as a deadly opponent. Nobody ever really doubted that her mind was always on getting the top job eventually.

While many see Number 10 as their ultimate goal, others would prefer to be the power behind the throne. Step forward Peter Mandelson. Mandelson features in many chapters in this book, which is not surprising as at times he seemed omnipresent. He was a party researcher, then a press officer, in Labour's unelectable days in the Eighties. An extraordinarily driven man whose whole life's work, when I first knew him and since, has been devoted to getting Labour back to power and then keeping it there.

He shamelessly promoted Brown and Blair in the media while both Neil Kinnock and John Smith were leading their party. While Brown and Blair are seen as the leaders of New Labour, Mandelson was its architect, identifying the two of them as Labour's route back and helping create the conditions for it to happen. He seemed to most of us to be doing it in memory of his grandfather, Herbert Morrison, a Labour foreign secretary in the late Fifties, but there was more to it than that. Mandelson wanted to be part of Labour's return to government and was, as he survived two sackings under Blair to return, like a Phoenix, under Gordon Brown.

A sinister image of Mandelson as the Prince of Darkness, or High Priest of Spin, had dominated the political press for years and his Machiavellian and roguish qualities are legendary. He is acutely mischievous and is quick to spot mischief in others. But power drove him, like the rest. John Major did it differently, but the aim was the same and the outcome successful. He made his way by being popular with his fellow MPs and the press.

In the early years of the Thatcher Government, Major, as a whip who therefore regularly found himself crossing the Members' Lobby where journalists loitered, was the go-to man who seemed to known better than most what was happening within the parliamentary party, and outside.

I always expected politicians to be clever and manipulative, so to me Major was a reassuringly calculating figure who seemed to know, well before the subject in question did, whose fortunes were up and whose down. He was expert at cultivating good Lobby contacts such as Peter Riddell, first of the *FT* and then of *The Times*, and Robin Oakley, first of the *Mail* and then of *The Times*. For those of us who spoke to him a lot, including my Channel 4 friend Elinor Goodman, it was a significant loss when he moved into the great offices of state, and away from our easy reach.

John Major was generally liked by voters because they saw him as homespun. In fact, there was no better user of the political system. No one more understood the strengths and weaknesses of his colleagues. While his elevation to the Tory leadership might have shocked the political world, it did not surprise him. But for a man who had cultivated such good relations with the press as he rose up the ladder, he did not have a happy time as the newspapers turned on him shortly after he won the 1992 election. For a man who had been so good with the press, the shift was marked as he became prickly and edgy with journalists.

Blair was a politician utterly dedicated to power, and it was no surprise when he quit Parliament altogether after standing down as prime minister. He had no interest in being a back-bencher. He hated the long toil of Opposition after his election in 1983 and, as I report elsewhere, I had the distinct impression that he would have quit politics if he had not become leader.

Always friendly and courteous in his public dealings with the press, he could be scathing about others in private with journalists he trusted. Probably more ruthless than any recent prime minister, Blair's reputation has suffered badly from his political afterlife, with his accumulation of wealth and properties contributing heavily to his fall from public favour. Greed is now the charge most often heard from voters who have turned against him. *The Times* reported in April 2016 that Blair now spends at least one in three days abroad and his travels include meetings and consulting work for some of the world's most controversial regimes, including Kazakhstan, Rwanda, Albania and Burma.

From being the leader whom the country, including Conservative voters, and his party admired in 1997, Blair – despite winning three elections – has never escaped the shadow of Iraq. The long delay over the publication of the Chilcot Report made that even harder. Brown, as we know, was thinking about succeeding Blair almost from the moment he agreed not to stand against him for the leadership in 1994. He, too, knew how important it was to have the press on his side if he was going to make it.

Back in 1997, Brown was seen as the unsmiling sidekick to the triumphant Blair but I remember a party he threw for political editors and their partners at 11 Downing Street and he utterly confounded that reputation. The men and women who met Brown for the first time that night left the gathering shaking their heads. The Labour chancellor worked the room magically. He and his staff had done their homework on the partners and it was upon them he concentrated, oozing charm and apparently genuine interest in what they did. Over the years I heard many similar stories of how Brown, who has a prodigious memory for personal details, would meet people again and pick up on conversations they had had long before.

He also inspired extraordinary loyalty among the people who were closest to him and saw at first hand his occasional temper tantrums.

He was utterly demanding, calling his aides before dawn as he stomped round Downing Street, and he could be utterly insecure and suspicious, even in private. But, like Mandelson, he could be funny, particularly as he told anecdotes, and often messed them up. A true workaholic, Brown could be seen at his best when he relaxed, turned on the TV to watch a game of football, or discussed one of the books he had voraciously read. In the end he got what he wanted – Downing Street – but was it really all worth it?

George Osborne, whom Cameron wanted to succeed him, is another who belies his public image. Osborne can be the most relaxed and charming person in private. He has had voice-coaching over the years but has never quite escaped that slight whine to his voice when he is delivering a speech or doing an interview. But when not in public, he even sounds different.

He has always prided himself on being a political strategist and, even in a private conversation with him, you get the feeling he is weaving his way towards a master plan. He may have fooled us all but most journalists feel that Osborne enjoys talking to them, probably because we are all part of the political game he so enjoys playing. He is also liked by some of his political opponents. He will take them on in the Commons, and they him, but afterwards they often josh together. He is a consummate player of the political game but his chances of taking the crown disappeared during the referendum campaign when he was accused of scaremongering and overstating the economic pitfalls of leaving.

Is he nice? Ask Iain Duncan Smith, characterized by Osborne as 'just not clever enough', according to Matthew D'Ancona in his book, *In It Together*.

And the pursuit of power overrides family loyalties if the Miliband story is anything to go by. Far from being geeky and hesitant, as the public saw him, Ed Miliband was demanding and focused, and ruthless enough to deny his brother, David, the leadership of the Labour Party.

David was always seen as the senior of the two Milibands but he proved not to be as tough as his brother when the time came. I used to come up against the older Miliband regularly on opposite cricket sides long before he became an MP. He was a strong batsman and highly competitive, and appeared destined for the very top when he worked as Blair's policy chief. He seemed totally sure of himself intellectually – and that was his undoing when he came to take on his brother. He overestimated his own standing and underestimated his brother's. Labour MPs saw him as arrogant and that did him in eventually.

Cameron was derided as the 'essay-crisis' prime minister, the leader who only faced up to serious problems when he really had to and then muddled through. Elsewhere I deal with his apparent lack of serious political convictions. But Cameron's generally relaxed approach should not be mistaken for lack of ambition. He was a pragmatist, as shown by his bold and enthusiastic grasp of the Lib Dems when they gave him the route to a full term. As I explain in an earlier chapter, he was ruthless with them when the moment came to ditch them.

His promise of a Europe referendum worried some close to him because they knew it was possible to lose control. It was done to get the Right and UKIP off his back and from the early negotiations, he did not appear to have a clear idea of what he could get from Brussels, instead believing in his ability to convince the country that what he had got was enough. Cameron's lack of ideology was a positive advantage to a man who clearly believed leading the country, and not changing it drastically, was enough. In private he was shrewd and personable, liked a joke and a gossip, and appeared rather bored by suggestions that he should have more of a vision with which to excite the electorate.

Other ambitious politicians have been thwarted by events outside their control. Norman Tebbit, the man whom Michael Foot called 'a semi-house-trained polecat' – an insult that did no harm to its target's career – was once in line for the leadership of the Tory party. The complete antithesis to the rather grand Heseltine, with whom he never really got on, he had similar base political skills that enabled him to rise swiftly under Thatcher. The Brighton bomb of 1984, which severely injured his wife, Margaret, meant that Tebbit never got to take on Heseltine for the leadership, as had looked very likely. From that moment, Tebbit's priority was looking after his wife.

So what is it that makes the public image of many politicians so at odds with the private person? Most of our legislators are intelligent, perfectly friendly people who because of ambition, a desire to serve, or both, go into politics. That changes them, at least while they are in the public eye, because they are the property of the voters and their party. In front of a TV microphone or at the dispatch box, they are talking to a prescribed line. In debate they have to conform to the way their tribe expects them to behave. As they climb the career ladder, sometimes they – metaphorically at least – take out their opponents.

The politician we see in the Commons or on *Newsnight* is at work. How many of us are completely different characters in the office from the ones our families see at home? And what about those politicos who appear far nicer in public than their colleagues know them to be in the privacy of their homes or the Commons smoking room? Perhaps they've got the message that looking friendly and empathetic will get them re-elected. They are politicians, after all. They want the power to rule and change things.

The Men Who
Followed Delane

I worked under nine editors at *The Times*. None went close in terms of youth when they took over and longevity in the job to John Thadeus Delane, who became editor at the age of twenty-three in 1841 and did it for thirty-six years.

Delane, a confidant of Cabinet ministers and others high in government, was born into the Establishment as the son of a prominent barrister and author, and was responsible for creating the national and international prestige of *The Times* and the importance and influence of the role he held.

All who have followed him have regarded it as their duty to maintain that authority, a quality that to this day means that the view of *The Times* on the matter in hand is important to all its readers, including those in power everywhere. *The London Times*, as it is known abroad, remains the paper that rulers and people in foreign lands still look at to ascertain the current state of Britain. It was to *The Times* that eight former US Treasury secretaries wrote in April 2016, warning of the dangers of the UK leaving the European Union.

I'm often asked what the editor does and how he does it. He is responsible for every word that appears in his paper. Because he cannot possibly read every word or headline in every edition – although they have been known to try – he needs people in charge of every department that he can trust to do things in a way with which he can be comfortable. So top appointments are a priority.

At *The Times*, the editor will preside over the two daily internal news conferences when department chiefs from home news, foreign, sport, business, features, obits and others set out their wares, and broad decisions can be taken about where they will appear in the paper. He will by then have a good idea of the size of tomorrow's paper, after receiving an early indication of how much advertising space has been sold. That is what dictates the number of pages in each edition.

At 11.30 each morning, the paper's leader writers will convene in the editor's office where the subjects to be covered, and lines to be taken, are discussed and agreed. He will then lunch, sometimes in the office but often outside with a key politician, business figure or colleague. In the afternoon, he will keep tabs on the news stories and the progress of the leaders, asking to be told at all times of anything new and breaking. He will want to be briefed on the paper's latest digital developments and will often convene meetings to discuss coverage of upcoming big events. He will still be there in the evening, probably making the final decision – if it is not quite obvious – on what should be the lead story of the day and what should be the picture on the front.

In other words, the paper would come out quite happily if he was not there. And does. Editors have days off like everyone else, and a reader would not be able to tell whether he was in or not. But that is because the editor has set the tone of the paper. He has deputies, reporters, subeditors, night editors and picture editors – and all of them know what he wants, the paper design he likes, the stories he likes. So long as he is in the editor's chair, that's the way it goes. When he is replaced, a successor will lay down how he wants the paper to look and feel. Each will in the end be judged by how well it does.

With *The Times*, in particular, editors will have in mind the paper's history, its position at the top of the quality market, and the need to maintain the authority and prestige that Delane, his predecessors and successors, gave it so long ago after it was launched as *The Daily Universal Register* in 1785, before swiftly becoming *The Times*.

Those successors have gone about it in their different ways and with varying degrees of success. In my time, the editors could roughly be divided into those whose preoccupation was the voice of *The Times* through its leading articles and comment pieces, and those for whom the priority was the news, and giving readers the most authoritative, comprehensive and exclusive stories and features that could be found.

Into that first category would come William Rees-Mogg, who was editor from 1967 to 1981 and in place when I joined the paper in

1973. A scholarly, serious man who happily left the production of the paper to his team, he was always capable of surprises, such as his famous 'Who breaks a butterfly on a wheel?' 1967 leader criticizing the severity of a custodial sentence for Mick Jagger on a drugs offence.

Like most of the young journalists on the paper, I was rather in awe of this learned chap who looked like a professor, but found he was a gentle, kind man very early on when, again surprisingly, he decided that in 1973 the Liberal Party was the one to watch. He heavily staffed its party conference that year at Southport, which was my first of scores of such gatherings in the service of *The Times*. I sat next to him at the dinner he threw for the party and did my best to match his piercing questions to the Liberal politicians about the issues of the day.

Rees-Mogg would leave the office usually in the early evening, long before final decisions about front-page content had been made, and he would see the first edition much later on when it was delivered to him at his home. But he would have written or overseen the leaders before he left. He was in the Delane mould.

So, probably, was Charles Douglas-Home, next but one editor after Rees-Mogg. The nephew of the former Conservative prime minister, Charlie's contacts in the political, diplomatic and defence worlds were immense. He spoke to Margaret Thatcher regularly. Those conversations were not too unusual. All *Times* editors have access to the prime minister of the day if they want it, but in Charlie's case he spoke to her as a friend. He came to *The Times* via the *Daily Express* and worked his way up through various executive jobs to become deputy to Harry Evans, and then took over, editing till 1985 and his death at only forty-eight from cancer. Charlie was a buccaneer who did not mind his team pushing stories to the limit. A hugely brave man, he continued editing the paper from his hospital bed during his illness.

In the category of editors driven by the news, I would immediately place Harry Evans. He came to *The Times* from *The Sunday Times*, where he won a huge reputation as a campaigning editor. He was appointed by Rupert Murdoch when he acquired Times Newspapers in 1981, and his hands-on style contrasted sharply with his predecessor.

It left some of the senior staff uncomfortable. Accustomed to the quiet, unobtrusive style of Rees-Mogg, they had become used to looking after their own territory and did not like interference. He left after only a year after senior figures wrote a letter complaining he had lowered standards. He himself later claimed it was because he had frequently criticized Margaret Thatcher's monetarist policies. I was far too junior at the time to know much of these machinations but I owed Harry much as he promoted me to the Lobby from *The Times* gallery team. I used to put the parliamentary pages 'to bed' in the composing room at New Printing House Square, and came to Harry's notice because – being able to read the type upside down – I spotted a mistake on the front page just before it was due to go to print. Harry was there when I noticed it, and I like to think he remembered that when I applied for the Lobby job.

Charles Wilson, who succeeded Douglas-Home, was the reporter's editor. He loved news, understood news, demanded news. He did what was required on the leader front but he judged the paper, and himself, by the strength of its news, sports, business and feature coverage.

He was the ultimate journalist hard-man, who was feared and respected at one and the same time, never averse to bawling out a sub or news desk chief in front of the rest. Utterly direct and unpretentious, you were never in any doubt where you stood. A newsman to his boots, Charlie had a way of letting you know that you might not be delivering. After successive mornings on which Wilson entered the office and hailed a news editor as 'fingertips', the poor man asked why he was being called that. 'That's what you're hanging by, son,' said the editor.

Most editors have little chance, or even inclination, to write once in the job. But Simon Jenkins, who followed Wilson, was a writer then and, after his brief spell in charge, continued to write columns for *The Times* and, later, *The Guardian*. The newsroom found him rather distant and aloof but I enjoyed Simon's short spell in charge because of his deep interest in policy. At the time, John Major and Michael Heseltine were finding a replacement to Margaret Thatcher's unloved community charge (poll tax), a story that Simon and I were equally obsessed with. His regular tips to me on the latest developments that he had picked up as the Government finally devised the council tax were gratefully received. He used to unnerve his staff with quirky ideas for leaders. He perplexed sports editor Tom Clarke twice, once suggesting that the golf hole should be enlarged to make putting easier, and on another occasion suggesting that the goal in football should be widened to avoid boring scoreless draws.

Peter Stothard, who took over from Jenkins and edited for ten years, and Robert Thomson, who followed him, were genuine all-rounders, both interested in hard news stories and comment. Stothard, who had written for *The Sunday Times*, appointed me political editor in 1993. He presided over a big rise in the circulation of *The Times* during a newspaper price war, and he was another editor whose own contacts in Westminster and Whitehall gave him an abiding interest in politics and policy – extremely helpful if you happen to be writing about politics for the paper.

Thomson, an Australian who edited *The Times* from 2002 to 2007 after joining from the *FT*, has since gone on to become chief executive of News Corp. Having spent most of his career outside the UK, Robert took a deep interest in UK politics during his time in charge, particularly in the machinations in New Labour that saw Gordon Brown eventually succeed Tony Blair. A man with a sharp sense of humour, Thomson saw the funny side of Brown's regularly thwarted efforts to reach the top, and he clearly enjoyed the lunches and dinners we arranged with the top politicos at party conferences. After taking over, he asked me to fix up a series of dinner dates so that he could get to know British politicians. After meeting one senior figure Thomson pronounced him to be a 'tosser' when he had barely got out of the door of the restaurant. I was frightened that he might have heard.

Another *FT* man, James Harding became one of the youngest editors of *The Times* in late 2007, after a spell as business editor, during which time we did several joint interviews of politicians (including then chancellor Alistair Darling and, later, Gordon Brown when he became PM). After I had been the election editor in 2010, Harding persuaded me to become editor of the *Times* website and the other digital editions (including the iPad and phone) after we adopted a 'paywall' for digital products. James was a popular editor with the newsroom but he was removed in late 2012, with some speculating that it was because of his strong criticism of the way News International had handled the phone-hacking dispute, while others cited falling circulation and rising costs.

One story that emerged during his time was the MP expenses scandal, a story that *The Times* and other papers could have had –

rather than *The Daily Telegraph* – if it had bought a disk being hawked around newspapers containing all the details. A member of my team was contacted and at a meeting with an intermediary, reporters were asked for a large sum of money for the disk. The contact did not know what was on it but the very real impression gained was that it had been stolen. So we were being asked to pay upfront for a disk of whose contents we were unaware. *The Times*'s legal department advised that taking the disk could be seen as handling stolen goods and that we could not be sure of any public interest defence for doing so. That was the position Harding took and others, including *The Sun*, also turned it down. It was, however, the one that got away.

The disk containing information on the widespread abuse of MPs' allowances was eventually bought by *The Telegraph*. They handled it and presented the stories contained in it brilliantly. Asked why the paper turned down the story when he appeared at the Leveson Inquiry, Harding said *The Times* had a general policy of not paying for stories and that 'on this occasion we took the view that we shouldn't be in the business of paying for stolen goods'. There were also concerns that there 'might not be necessarily' a public interest defence for buying the information. Harding said that 'hindsight is a wonderful thing' and that he now felt there would have been such a defence.

Another from the Wilson school of hard news is John Witherow, my ninth and last editor. He came back to *The Times* as editor in 2013, having first joined the paper as a reporter in 1980 and covered the Falklands war while on board HMS *Invincible*. He was editor of *The Sunday Times* for eighteen years and during his spell at *The Times*, it has picked up the 'newspaper of the year' gong in the annual Press Awards, now run by the Society of Editors. Like others who have been reporters on their way to the top, Witherow has the reporter's enthusiasm for a good, hard story and the paper, which has managed to make a profit under him, has reflected that. It was his idea to go for the 'Red Box' morning e-mail which had me working from 5 a.m. every day for eighteen months at the end of my *Times* career.

I asked *Times* veterans recently to name their favourite editors and there was no unanimity. Some, like Stothard and Wilson, were regular patrollers of the newsroom and reporters got to know them better than others. Wilson came out well in my straw poll because of his appreciation of the art of story-getting. Harding – always charming and friendly – was liked by most. Some found Jenkins and Thomson occasionally remote but in private the latter has a marvellous sense of humour. Many appreciated Witherow's moves to ensure more space was devoted to news. As with politicians, I made it my business to get on with them all – and I did.

For five decades, these were the men charged with maintaining the traditions of *The Times* and preserving the legacy of Delane and other giants of the past.

Goodbye to All That

The Prince of Wales gave me my first front-page story for *The Times*. When, on 13 June 1974, he delivered his maiden speech to the House of Lords, I was deemed to have the shorthand necessary to handle the occasion.

It was a debate about leisure and I wrote that he had called for better coordination of facilities 'to remove the dead hand of boredom and frustration from mankind'. Not the most exciting intro to grace the front page, but the paper was altogether more formal in those days. Sitting alongside my story, as I look at an original copy of the paper, is a political story that begins: 'Mr Heath last night announced a reshuffle of his front-bench spokesmen after the appointment of Mr Whitelaw as Conservative party chairman.' Note no 'Edward' or 'William' in front of Heath and Whitelaw.

This book has been about my career at *The Times* but I will just mention one big byline that came before I joined the paper. At the end of my full-year journalism course at Harlow in Essex, for which I had been sponsored by my first paper the *Eastern Daily Press*, I had the thrill of writing the splash below in *The Harlow Sentinel*, our course paper produced at the end of the year.

The chap with whom I share the byline is indeed the same Mark Knopfler who went on to become one of the most successful guitarists in the world, the founder and frontman of Dire Straits, and who is now still touring the world and writing his songs as he enjoys a wonderful solo career. Mark joined the *Yorkshire Evening Post* after college but went on to become a world star in another sphere and remains a great friend. We often have breakfast together to put the world to rights.

The style of that 1974 paper is yet another reminder of how much newspapers – and *The Times* in particular – have altered in the last five decades. My job changed beyond all recognition. On that momentous day when we moved to Wapping in 1986, I used a computer for the first time. But I never used a typewriter after that. Our method of sending stories while out of the office moved from the copy-taker, to the Tandy machine which had to be linked up to a landline, to the occasional story texted on a mobile phone, and then to the simple e-mail by phone or any other device. We started using e-mails in 1996 and invited readers to send in letters via e-mail the following year. Transmitting stories to the office today is so much easier than when you had to run around looking for public phones or knocking on people's doors and asking if you could borrow theirs.

The Times, the paper that ran classified adverts on the front page until 1966, has modernized time and time again. But its ethos – informative, straight, accurate reporting and sharp, innovative, incisive comment – has remained the same through the generations. And working for it has been utterly rewarding.

I could never have dreamt when I joined in February 1973 as a junior reporter in the Commons Press Gallery that I would still be at the paper forty-three years later, having written many thousands of stories and served as chief political correspondent and political editor through an amazing period in British politics. Or that I would finish my *Times* days as an assistant editor of the paper, still writing about politics in a groundbreaking daily e-mail to tens of thousands of subscribers, including anyone who moved and shook in Westminster and Whitehall.

Through most of my four decades and more, print has been king. But with the demise in early 2016 of the print editions of *The Independent* and its Sunday sister, both becoming digital-only productions, the future of print journalism has again come under scrutiny. Circulations have fallen, advertising revenue has dropped, journalists have been laid off all over the world as the internet and social media have become the preferred method of receiving breaking news for millions of people (as well as siphoning off the advertising cash that would otherwise have gone to the papers).

Online newspapers can supplement their storytelling and comment with audios and videos, as well as directing readers to their archives for historical stories at a handful of keystrokes. For many young people, the BBC and newspaper websites or social media are the way of getting news that they have grown up with. Many have never bought a paper. For me, in recent years Twitter was easily the fastest source of incoming news as I ran the *Times* website.

For people whose lives have been immersed in print journalism, this has all happened with worrying speed. It is quite obvious that papers can only survive long-term if they embrace the digital model as well. But the death of newspapers is greatly exaggerated. *The Times* may be an exception but its print circulation today is massively greater than it was when I joined it. True, that circulation has come down since the heady days of the price war in the 1990s when we virtually gave it away.

The Times was also the first truly to acknowledge the digital era by introducing a paywall for its website and being among the first to launch an iPad version. Fully realizing I was taking the short straw, I accepted James Harding's invitation – still gasping from the 2010 election and my thirty-seven straight years at Westminster – to become the first editor of the paywalled site and see the number of reader hits drop by millions virtually overnight as they were suddenly asked to cough up. But *The Times* is *The Times* and its readers are the most loyal in the business. It was not long before our digital-only subscribers passed the 100,000 mark and, with a newly designed website based on editions at different times of the day launched in early 2016, both the print and digital sides of the paper continue to do well. The word 'profit', not traditionally associated with *The Times*, has been whispered quietly in recent years.

I believed that when we erected the paywall, others would swiftly follow, meaning a more level playing-field between the papers. It did not really happen but it may be the only route to survive for some in the future, although so long as the BBC website remains free – and therefore highly unfair competition – it will be an uphill struggle.

The Independent went digital in the end because it was not selling enough papers. But most papers still get the majority of their revenue from print advertising. Online ad sales would never at this stage be enough to support big newspaper companies. Reading habits are cyclical and just as reading books has become fashionable again for young people, papers – particularly the 'qualities' – must find ways of attracting them if they are to keep the print as well as the digital circulations steady.

Readers devoted to the print versions cite the pleasure they enjoy in just holding the paper before them and turning over the pages, knowing where to find the pieces in which they are interested. Readers who are often bamboozled by the 24-hour news cycle, needing to make sense of what is going on in the world, turn to the long-form stories in print to tell them. And stories still make more of an impact in print than those that appear only online. They last longer than their online counterparts, which disappear swiftly within hours when another story comes along. Communications companies are always happier if the stories and lines they are pushing appear in print rather than online.

Let's be honest about this – newspapers have dumbed down over the years as the availability of instant tweets telling you what has happened at the Commons or in court, and 24-hour news television, have shortened the attention span of readers. But because there will always be a need for in-depth reporting and comment to flesh out the

140-character news flashes, I am more optimistic about the future of journalism and newspapers than some of my friends and former colleagues. But all will have to change to survive.

Politics, too, has changed beyond recognition. It has always been a 'rough old trade', as Alan Watkins used to tell us in virtually all his columns in *The Observer*. And if you recall that in 1948 Aneurin Bevan called the Conservatives 'lower than vermin', or the reputed exchange between Winston Churchill and Bessie Braddock – 'Mr Churchill, you are drunk.' Reply: 'And you, madam, are ugly, but in the morning I will be sober.' – you might think little is different, but it is. Politicians have watched helpless as power has drained away from them and the House of Commons – some of it to Europe, some to Whitehall, some to the multinational companies.

I've written of how newspapers like *The Times* used to have many more reporters covering the proceedings of Parliament – i.e. what was said – than what went on in the corridors outside. Little today gets reported after Question Time and government statements. The Commons can still make or break a minister, or indeed a government, if they fail to get the votes needed in a particular division, but speeches made after showpiece events of the day tend to be aimed purely at the local papers and broadcasters of the MP in question. Most MPs would happily spurn the chance to speak in the chamber if they had been invited by a broadcaster to appear on the green outside the Houses of Parliament.

And it was interesting that after his dramatic resignation in March 2016, the political world waited excitedly for Iain Duncan Smith's grilling on *The Andrew Marr Show* rather than any appearance he might make in the House. An interview on the *Today* programme or *Newsnight* is now held to have more influence on events than anything the politician might say in the Commons. Politicians believe the relationship with the press has swung against them, with the media now almost taking on the role of elected politicians. But their answer has been to court the owners and editors in a way that has somehow looked demeaning.

MPs, too, have lost power over their own parties. When I started and for some time after, it was the MPs who elected their leaders and prime ministers. But both the main parties have now handed over that task to the party memberships, meaning again that the performance of the politicians on the television or the *Today* programme – not in the House of Commons – is what will be judged by the members when they come to cast their vote for a new leader

And the make-up of the Commons is very different from when I started. A former *Guardian* political correspondent, Julia Langdon, reported in a BBC programme in 2015 that the background from which today's MPs are elected is almost exclusively that of the comfortable middle classes. While this might have been expected given the rise in living standards and the growth of university education, it is still remarkable that forty years ago there were more than thirty miners, twenty engineering workers, many other manual workers and a total of over 150 teachers sitting in the Commons.

Many MPs in the 1970s, notably the lawyers – of whom there were more than 150 – had other jobs, paid employment which enabled them to afford a relatively affluent lifestyle. That was one reason why Parliament did not sit until the afternoons – to enable those who wished to do so to earn their money in the mornings. Some had family money, others had business interests. But the majority had to live on a pretty meagre parliamentary salary. Today's would not be regarded as generous by people who have the means to earn more. Most head teachers and GPs today earn more than our MPs.

But there are few who are not university educated and few who have much experience of working in industry. As Langdon related, David Cameron was canny enough to get a job working in public relations for a TV company, when he had already worked as a Conservative adviser for six years and had perhaps spotted that his lack of outside experience could have been a career handicap. Now the miners and the plumbers and the telephone engineers are almost all long gone and at the last count there were just twenty-four teachers.

MPs have become more diverse in terms of gender and ethnic background. But they have become less varied in terms of their educational background, and the extent to which they represent the changing world outside Westminster. The first female MP was elected in 1918 and, according to a Commons paper, 143 women MPs were elected in the 2010 general election, twenty-two per cent of the total. The first contemporary black and minority ethnic MPs were elected in 1987 and the number has grown since then. Following the 2010 general election, there were twenty-seven minority ethnic MPs – eleven Conservative and sixteen Labour.

Over seventy-five per cent of current MPs are graduates; in the period 1918 to 1945, around forty per cent were. As the numbers of MPs with manual and legal backgrounds has fallen, so the number with a professional political background has increased. In 2010, fourteen per cent of MPs from the three main parties had previously been politicians or political organizers, compared to around three per cent up to 1979. Somehow – and these changes in make-up explain it – politics is more workaday than it was.

Occasionally politics throws up big characters, such as Boris Johnson. But in general, Parliament lacks the giants of yesteryear – the names, the brilliant speakers who could hold the chamber in the palm of their hands, who would send MPs and reporters scurrying back to their seats in the House and the Press Gallery.

Just look, whatever your political leanings, at the big figures in the troubled Labour Government of 1974–79 – Wilson, Callaghan, Jenkins, Crosland, Foot, Williams, Castle, Healey, Benn. Look at the first Thatcher Government – Whitelaw, Carrington, Hailsham, Howe, Joseph, Pym, Walker, Heseltine, Prior. Look at the former Liberal leaders – Grimond, Ashdown, Kennedy. Compare them with the politicians on today's front-benches. This is not one veteran reporter complaining about the end of a political golden age but I don't think I'm being unduly sentimental in suggesting there is little comparison on the personnel front.

For the political journalist so much has changed, but so much remains the same – particularly the joy of breaking a big story or the satisfaction of following a story all day and then presenting it well in a way that the reader can easily understand. Politics remains in my view – along with sport – the most exciting area of journalism to be involved in. It is dominated by personalities and it is the area that on a consistent, day-by-day basis provides more good stories than any other.

I can't say that every single day at *The Times* was great. But ninety-nine per cent of them were. Thanks for reading.

Acknowledgements

I suppose I should start with a big thank you to all my sources, including the scores I went back to as I wrote the book years after the original stories appeared. You know who you are and those of you who look through the book to see if you have been exposed will be either disappointed or relieved. Except where express permission was sought and given to name my living informers, their secret remains safe.

Thanks to all at HarperCollins who made this possible, most of all to Arabella Pike, publishing director and editor, whose enthusiasm and brilliant guidance from the start were invaluable; Laura Brooke, who handled the publicity; and to the copyediting and proof correction team, Silvia Crompton, Dan Smith and Jamie Ambrose.

Thanks to the legendary Peter Brookes for allowing me the privilege of using his marvellous interpretations of some of the big stories of my career.

Thanks to all the wonderful people I worked with at *The Times*, and particularly to the many long-suffering correspondents who were in my team at Westminster. Apologies to any I've forgotten but I must mention these superb reporters: Nick Wood, Jill Sherman, Richard Ford, Martin Fletcher, Andrew Pierce, James Landale, Nick Watt, Tom Baldwin, Arthur Leathley, Helen Rumbelow, Roland Watson, Rosie Bennett, David Charter, Jonathan Prynn, Alice Thomson, Polly Newton, Siobhan Kennedy, Mark Inglefield, Suzy Jagger, Sam Coates, Greg Hurst, Anthony Browne and Francis Elliott, now political editor. And these superb sketch-writers: Matthew Parris, Ann Treneman, Giles Coren and Ben Macintyre. There was a lot of talent in that Commons office.

Huge thanks to Peter Riddell, chief political commentator of *The Times* during all my years in the hot seat, for being a marvellous fount of knowledge, wisdom and good sense, and for his advice on this book.

Everlasting gratitude to Steve Baker, picture and information services manager at *The Times*, who went beyond the call of duty to help me find ancient cuttings and pictures, and Rose Wild, the archive editor, who was equally supportive.

Thanks to my family for the backing they have always given me, even when I have disappeared at crucial moments, including Christmas morning every year, to file long-planned stories for the Boxing Day edition of the paper.

Thanks to Eastern Counties Newspapers for giving me a great start in journalism. And thanks to *The Times*, still the greatest paper of all, for giving me the chance and sticking with me.

Index